re

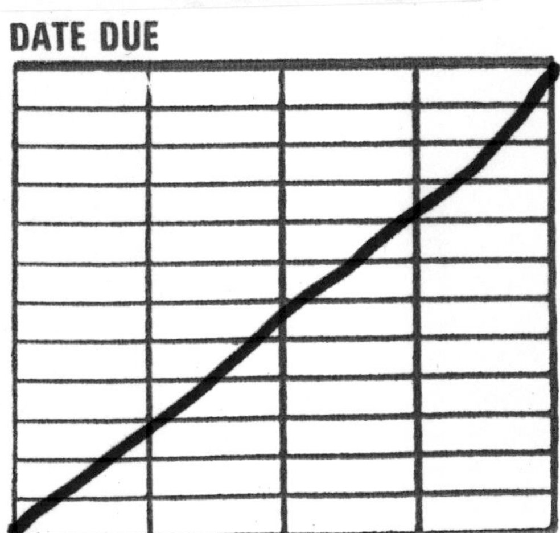

ACADEMIC FREEDOM AND TENURE

A Handbook of
The American Association of University Professors

Edited by Louis Joughin

1969 Edition

The University of Wisconsin Press
Madison, Milwaukee, and London

Published by
The University of Wisconsin Press
Box 1379, Madison, Wisconsin 53701
The University of Wisconsin Press, Ltd.
27–29 Whitfield Street, London, W. 1

1969 Edition

Printed in the United States of America
SBN 299–05450–X cloth, 299–05454–3 paper; LC 67–25947

Foreword

The American Association of University Professors has long needed an orderly compilation of information and basic documents relating to its concerns in the area of academic freedom and tenure. Policy in this vital field has evolved gradually but continuously ever since the Association was founded in 1915. Many different individuals and groups have had a hand in the development of this body of practices and doctrines, including successive General Secretaries, officers, Councils, Annual Meetings, and *ad hoc* and standing committees. The chief agency has of course been Committee A, the Association's standing committee on academic freedom and tenure. Many principles have been stated in formal reports, while others are merely part of our common law way of doing things. Thus our principles have come to us from different points in time, from various sources, in many forms, and with varying degrees of explicitness and clarity. The great, overriding purpose of this handbook is to pull together this large body of doctrine and practice into a manageable and orderly compilation which will be readily available to all who deal with these central concerns of the academic profession.

I am certain that this compilation will prove valuable to future officers of the Association, to future Council members, to the staff in the Washington Office, to chapters and conferences, and to individual members. In addition, one may anticipate that college and university officials and governing boards, and others who are vitally concerned with higher education, will look to this book for guidance and information. Thus we may hope that this handbook will help in the ongoing process of education in acceptable principles which is the central purpose and the most important activity of the Association.

In addition, one may hope that the publication of this handbook will contribute in a substantial way to the Association's historic efforts to spell out basic minimum standards for the whole community of higher education in America. For one of the most significant and also most obvious characteristics of the American system of higher education is that it is not a system at all. We have over 2,000 colleges and universities in this country, but they conform to no common pattern from the point of view of structure, organization, and government, or indeed, from any other point of view. The American scene in higher education is a vast chaos, a sort of administrative anarchy. Since there is no central law-defining authority which has the power to state and administer uniform national standards, it has been the historic mission of the Association to contribute to filling this void in the educational scene. This first effort at an orderly arrangement of the principles we regard as essential to academic freedom and tenure for college teachers should contribute to the considerable efforts which have been made during the past half century to define and enforce minimum standards of academic propriety. Furthermore, this handbook should serve the additional purpose of encouraging members of the teaching profession in higher education to take stock of where we stand, so that we can better understand where the points of further growth are to be found. For it is difficult to move forward, as we must surely do if we are to avoid losing ground already gained, unless we have a clear picture of our present position. I believe this handbook supplies a vital link in the chain between the past and the emerging future.

This body of practices and principles is the product of many minds and of the devoted efforts of many professors who have concerned themselves with the larger problems of the teaching profession. To all of them we are deeply indebted; this compilation is, in fact, a small token of our awareness of the magnitude of the debt. At the same time, I should like to express a special word of appreciation for the devoted efforts of the editor, Dr. Louis Joughin, the senior Associate Secretary in the Washington Office of the Association, who is largely responsible for the original analysis contained in this book, and for the selection and editing of the relevant documents. Dr. Joughin brought to this work a thorough knowledge of the problems of academic freedom and tenure and great familiarity with the Association's policy development and case action in these areas. And, in an office which is both overworked and understaffed, it has been no simple matter for a fully-engaged member of the staff to find the time and energy to handle a task of such magnitude and importance. In addition, I should add that Professor Clark Byse of the Harvard Law School, and Professor Ralph Fuchs of the Indiana University Law School, have given invaluable advice regarding the substance and form of the handbook. Of course, the General Secretaries, Dr. William P. Fidler and Dr. Bertram H. Davis, have kept a benign eye on the project from its inception to its completion.

I hope, at the very least, that members of the Association will read this handbook. I also hope that the Association will hear from them, for all work, including the work of Committee A, requires sustained and intelligent criticism. There will be, some day, a revised edition of this book, and if enough criticism is forthcoming, it will be even better than this first one.

DAVID FELLMAN

University of Wisconsin

Preface

The first policy formulated by the American Association of University Professors dealt mainly with the protection of academic freedom; in fact it can be said that the Association came into being because of the need for such policy. The first application of Association policy was in cases involving tenure, which was recognized at the outset as the chief support of academic freedom. Policy statement and case action date from 1915; the Association and its standing Committee A on Academic Freedom and Tenure began life together.

Fifty years later, in 1965, the Association deemed it proper to scrutinize its work through the agency of a Self-Survey Committee. At the same time a Special Committee on Procedures for the Disposition of Complaints under the Principles of Academic Freedom and Tenure was appointed to survey the work of Committee A and connected staff service. The reports of these Committees, published in the May, 1965, *AAUP Bulletin,* furnished necessary and invaluable comment on countless points covered by this handbook, and should be read by all who wish to have a comprehensive view of these matters.

The editor acknowledges with pleasure his indebtedness to Professors Glenn R. Morrow, James M. Darlington, and York Willbern (the members of the Self-Survey Committee), Sanford H. Kadish, Ralph S. Brown, Jr., and Walter P. Metzger (the members of the Special Committee) whose labors in large measure coincided with the work of analysis, exposition, and compilation here presented. Professors Clark Byse and Ralph F. Fuchs furnished most helpful guidance; a colleague and friend, Bertram H. Davis, contributed important editorial insight. A further personal indebtedness of the editor becomes enlarged and merges in the indebtedness of the Association and its members to Professor David Fellman, Chairman of Committee A from 1959–64 and President of the AAUP from 1964 to 1966. Having decided that the handbook needed to be,

Professor Fellman brought to bear upon his fellow officers, the Council, Committee A, and the Washington Office staff the force of strong conviction, an inexorable but friendly pressure, and the stimulating example of his own productivity. That this handbook is now published is a tribute to Professor Fellman's leadership.

The policy statements and other official material here presented had their first printings under a variety of editorial and typographical styles. This variety has been maintained wherever it is necessary to preserve an original substantive emphasis. But in other situations, where differences are only matters of form, some normalization has taken place in the interest of the current reader's right to orderly and logical presentation.

Ellipsis marks are used to indicate excisions within the body of a paragraph but not at its beginning or end.

Questions regarding the handbook should be addressed to the editor, or in general terms to the American Association of University Professors, 1785 Massachusetts Avenue, N.W., Washington, D.C., 20036. Information, suggestions, or criticism which will lead to improvement of the handbook will be most welcome.

LOUIS JOUGHIN
EDITOR

Washington, D.C.
April 24, 1967

Editor's Note on the 1969 Edition

A Supplement, beginning on page 341, brings in as new material the 1968 *Standards for Committee T Investigations in the Area of College and University Government,* the 1968 *Statement on the Role of the Faculty in the Accrediting of Colleges and Universities,* the 1968 *Statement of Policy on Representation of Economic Interests,* and some additional Advisory Letters. Selected passages from the *Constitution* of the Association (pages 73–74 of the 1967 edition) are now to be found in the Supplement. The 1967 *Joint Statement on Rights and Freedoms of Students* (pages 66–74) replaces the tentative statement used in the 1967 edition. Chapter VII, *Lists* (of censured administration reports and actions, and other reports) has been updated through August 31, 1968.

L. J.

September 1, 1968

Table of Contents

Foreword v
Preface ix
Editor's Note on the 1969 Edition xi

PART ONE. INTRODUCTION

Chapter I. The Nature of the Association's Concern 3

Chapter II. Model Case Procedure 11

A. The Complaint; Possible Mediation 11
1. Formulation of a complaint 11
2. Receipt of a complaint 12
3. Acknowledgment of a complaint 12
4. Communication with the local chapter of the Association 13
5. Decisions regarding the possibility of a violation and the usefulness of mediation or investigation 13
6. Attempted mediation 13

B. Case Status; Investigation 14
7. Case status; letter from the General Secretary to the chief administrator of the institution 14
8. Decision to appoint an *ad hoc* investigating committee 15
9. Special and emergency investigations 15
10. Appointment of the *ad hoc* committee 16
11. Briefing of the *ad hoc* committee 16
12. The investigation 18
13. Avoidance of publicity 19

C. The Report and Action Thereon 19
14. The received report 19
15. Committee A consideration of the report 20
16. The submission of the report to the parties 21
17. Publication of the report 21
18. Recommendations of Committee A before the Council and the Annual Meeting 22
19. Publication of Annual Meeting action 23
20. Withdrawal of censure 23

D. Chapter Action in Academic Freedom and Tenure Cases 24
21. Before case status 25

22. During case status 26
23. Following publication of an *ad hoc* committee report 27
24. During censure status 28
25. The general responsibility of the chapter 28

E. Conference Action 29

PART TWO. PRINCIPLES AND PROCEDURES

Chapter III. Academic Freedom and Tenure: Basic Statements 33

1940 *Statement of Principles on Academic Freedom and Tenure* 33
Academic freedom 35
Academic tenure 36
Interpretations 38

1958 *Statement on Procedural Standards in Faculty Dismissal Proceedings* 40
Introductory comments 40
Procedural recommendations 42
Preliminary proceedings concerning the fitness of a faculty member 42
Commencement of formal proceedings 42
Suspension of the faculty member 43
Hearing committee 43
Committee proceeding 43
Consideration by hearing committee 44
Consideration by governing body 44
Publicity 45

1964 *Statement on the Standards for Notice of Nonreappointment* 46

Chapter IV. Academic Freedom and Tenure: Other Statements 47

Academic Freedom and Tenure in the Quest for National Security [1956] 47
The justification of academic freedom 47
The claims of military security 49
Vigilance against subversion of the educational process 50
Disclaimer oaths and general investigations of college and university teachers 50
Grounds of adverse action 51
Refusal to testify as ground for removal 52
Grounds for preliminary inquiry by an employing institution 53
Procedural due process in tenure cases 53
The faculty member's obligation of disclosure 55
Suspension 55
Faculty members not on tenure 56

[Supplementary] *Statement of the Committee on Academic Freedom and Tenure* [1958] 56

Committee A Statement on Extramural Utterances [1964] 64

1967 *Joint Statement on Rights and Freedoms of Students* 66
- Preamble 66
- Freedom of access to higher education 67
- In the classroom 67
- Student records 68
- Student affairs 68
- Off-campus freedom of students 71
- Procedural standards in disciplinary proceedings 72

Recommended Institutional Regulations [1957] 75

Statement of Principles on Academic Retirement and Insurance Programs [1958] 76

Statement on Recruitment and Resignation of Faculty Members [1961] 79

Statement on Preventing Conflicts of Interest in Government-Sponsored Research at Universities [1964] 82
- Conflict situations 82
- University responsibility 84

Statement on Professional Ethics [1966] 87

Statement on Government of Colleges and Universities [1966] 90
- Editorial note 90
- Introduction 92
- The academic institution: joint effort 92
- The academic institution: the governing board 96
- The academic institution: the president 97
- The academic institution: the faculty 98
- On student status 100

PART THREE. PRACTICES

Chapter V. Resolutions of the Annual Meetings 105

A. Censorship of textbooks 105
B. Foreign scholars, oppression abroad, aid here 106
C. Fulbright scholars 107
D. Legislative committee investigations 108
E. Passports for scholars 109
F. Race matters 109
G. Speakers on campuses 112
H. Teachers' oaths, opposition to 113
J. Tenure and institutional merger 118
K. Tenure and national emergency 118

Chapter VI. Advisory Letters 121

Letter No. 1. Tenure: the provision for a year's terminal appointment in cases of dismissal not involving moral turpitude 121
Letter No. 3. Challenging the members of a hearing committee 124
Letter No. 4. Tenure and change of status 125
Letter No. 6. Tenure and leave of absence 127
Letter No. 8. Loyalty to the college 128
Letter No. 10. Candor and the prospective appointee 129
Letter No. 11. Extramural utterances 132
Letter No. 12. Late resignations by faculty members 134
Letter No. 13. Stating reasons for nonreappointment 136
Letter No. 15. A charge of plagiarism 138
Letter No. 17. Questions of religious limitations 139

Chapter VII. Lists 143

A. Censured administrations 143
B. *Ad hoc* committee reports not resulting in censure 148
C. Late notice case reports 150
D. Other reports on named institutions 151

APPENDICES

Appendix A. Declaration of Principles [1915] 155
Appendix B. Fritz Machlup, "On Some Misconceptions Concerning Academic Freedom" [1955] 177
Appendix C. Clark Byse and Louis Joughin, *Tenure in American Higher Education:* "Specific Conclusions and Recommendations" [1959] 210
Appendix D. Howard Mumford Jones, "The American Concept of Academic Freedom" [1960] 224
Appendix E. Ralph F. Fuchs, "Academic Freedom—Its Basic Philosophy, Function, and History" [1963] 242
Appendix F. Louis Joughin, "Academic Due Process" [1963] 264
Appendix G. Fritz Machlup, "In Defense of Academic Tenure" [1964] 306

SUPPLEMENT TO THE 1969 EDITION

Constitution of the Association 341
1968 *Standards for Committee T Investigations in the Area of College and University Government* 343

1968 *Statement on the Role of the Faculty in the Accrediting of Colleges and Universities* 345
1968 *Statement of Policy on Representation of Economic Interests* 348
Advisory Letters 354
Letter No. 18. Safeguarding the accuracy and integrity of the Association's reports on academic freedom and tenure 354
Letter No. 19. Review by the Washington Office of the record of dismissal hearings 357
Letter No. 20. Oral agreements at the time of appointment 359
Letter No. 22. Appointment procedures 360

Index 363

PART ONE. INTRODUCTION

Chapter I
The Nature of the Association's Concern

The purpose of the American Association of University Professors, as set forth in its Constitution,[1] is "to facilitate a more effective cooperation among teachers and research scholars . . . [and] to increase the usefulness and advance the standards, ideals, and welfare of the profession." This function is to be carried out in "promotion of the interests of higher education and research." The concern of the Association with the affairs of the academic profession is thus directly related to the general good of higher education and to the ultimate objective of all educational endeavor, which is the advancement of knowledge and the arts, and thereby of the public welfare.

During the half century since its founding in 1915, the Association has enlarged the scope of its practical operation, but from the outset its main work has been in the area of academic freedom and related fields. The protection and liberties needed to safeguard the institutional integrity of colleges and universities have been left mainly to those educational associations which draw them together and represent them as corporate bodies. Association work is now both broader and more particular; it is focused on the protections and liberties of the whole academic profession and on its individual members. Nevertheless, the important fact of interdependence and unity in relation to other components of higher education has not been forgotten; in 1925, 1940, 1958, 1961, 1964, and 1966 the American Association of University Professors joined with the American Council on Education or the Association of American Colleges in sponsoring joint statements of principle and guidance. Such cooperative efforts continue.

[1] The Constitution of the Association is printed in the *AAUP Bulletin,* 53:243–45 (Summer, 1967).

In 1915 the Association formulated a "Declaration of Principles," a statement on academic freedom and tenure and professional responsibility, which concluded with a section enumerating desirable procedures. This statement was put to immediate use, by the organization's Committee A on Academic Freedom and Tenure, in dealing with particular cases. Ten years later, the American Council on Education called a conference of a number of its constituent members, among them the American Association of University Professors, for the purpose of formulating a shorter statement which would take into account a decade's experience. The product of this effort became known as the "1925 Conference Statement on Academic Freedom and Tenure"; it was endorsed by the Association of American Colleges in 1925 and by this Association in 1926. Beginning in 1934, the two endorsing organizations again joined in a series of conferences. The result was the present policy document, the 1940 *Statement of Principles on Academic Freedom and Tenure,* which in later years has been further endorsed by additional learned societies and educational associations.[2]

During the past fifty years the American Association of University Professors has received approximately three thousand complaints in the area of academic freedom and tenure and academic due process. The great majority of these complaints have been handled without public notice. Some have been withdrawn as a result of advice given the complaining teacher; others have ended by simple termination of the controversy—for a variety of reasons; and still others have been settled as a result of formal mediation—an increasingly frequent occurrence.

Reports by *ad hoc* investigating committees have been published in the *AAUP Bulletin,* and in 73 cases such reports have resulted in censure of an administration by an Annual Meeting of the Association. The 73 censure actions have been followed by Annual Meeting or Council action to withdraw censure in 54 instances; there were 19 institutions on the Summer, 1968, List of Censured Administrations. As the imposition of censure is based upon a conclusion that unsatisfactory conditions of academic freedom or tenure prevail at a given time in a particular institution, so the withdrawal of censure is grounded upon the conclusion that conditions

[2] See below pp. 34–35.

at the institution have become satisfactory and offer adequate promise of remaining so.

Each *ad hoc* investigating committee guides its inquiry into the facts of a situation by reference to the 1940 *Statement of Principles;* its conclusions on the facts are then specifically related to the standards set forth in the 1940 *Statement.* The Association's Committee A on Academic Freedom and Tenure, in studying the report of its investigating committee, in determining whether the report should be published, and in making appropriate recommendations regarding a published report, is likewise concerned with the facts and their significance in terms of the substantive and procedural standards of the 1940 *Statement.* Similar concerns govern the Annual Meeting which takes final censure action. All groups are assisted by other policy statements and guides which explain and develop the 1940 *Statement.* The most generally used among these statements are the 1958 *Statement on Procedural Standards in Faculty Dismissal Proceedings,* the 1961 *Statement on Recruitment and Resignation of Faculty Members,* and the 1964 *Statement on the Standards for Notice of Nonreappointment.* There are also more specialized policy statements, as well as policy statements covering the Association's concern in related areas.[3] The published reports by the *ad hoc* committees offer helpful guidance for the understanding of later situations confronted by the Association. However, although such reports clearly constitute implementation of Association policy, they should not be regarded as offering a stated text of such policy. Formal definition of the Association's general policy is found in the 1940 *Statement of Principles* and other documents which have been designated as policy statements at the time of their adoption.

Academic freedom requires that a professor should receive effective protection of his economic security through a tenure system which should provide at least these safeguards:

1. A probationary period of stated length, the maximum conforming to a national standard.

2. A commitment by an institution of higher education to make a decision in advance of the end of the probationary period whether a permanent relationship will be entered into; collaterally, national standards of notice for such decisions.

[3] The full texts of all basic and related statements are in this handbook.

3. Appointment to a tenure post if a person is continued beyond the limit of the probationary period.

4. Termination of a tenure appointment only because of age under an established retirement system, financial exigency, or adequate cause.

Another essential protection for the freedom of academic persons is a system of announced, orderly procedures governing internal institutional business. This protection is particularly necessary for the adjudication of charges which, if sustained, would lead to the termination of a tenure appointment or a nontenure appointment before the expiration of its limit. "Due process" in termination proceedings should provide safeguards generally similar to those afforded by due process in legal proceedings: for example, there should be right to assistance by counsel or other advisor, confrontation of adverse evidence and witnesses, appropriate opportunity to cross-examine, to present evidence, and to submit argument, the making of a record, and decision by an unprejudiced tribunal. "Academic due process" adds to the mandatory procedural minima those further characteristically academic procedures, especially participation by faculty members in decisions, which hopefully will provide an informed and just adjudication of academic controversy.

Academic freedom, tenure, and academic due process thus form a triad which brings together the deep regard of the civilized world for knowledge and the practical forms of protection needed by academic workers. This much is relatively clear and simple. But since higher education goes on at a quite complicated level of human activity, it may be helpful to note briefly two related Association concerns, some excluded areas, and some nonacademic forces which —without invitation—push their way into the picture.

Relatedly, the American Association of University Professors is concerned with questions of professional ethics; some of these are formally handled by Committee B on Professional Ethics, a standing committee of the Association. However, since many academic freedom cases involve charges against a faculty member, as well as his charges against an administration, it is often necessary for judgment on a whole situation to include opinion about the alleged misconduct of the individual. Thus questions of professional ethics are often investigated and judged by the Association's Committee A on Academic Freedom and Tenure.

Another concern of the Association is that there be adequate participation by a faculty in the government of its institution. With almost unfailing regularity, the worst violations of academic freedom occur at institutions where the faculties either occupy ignoble positions without proper jurisdiction and power, or discover that, in a time of crisis, their supposed voice has no force. In the presence of a gross denial of faculty function, but in the absence of a particular complaint, allegations regarding an unwholesome situation fall within the purview of Committee T on College and University Government, another standing committee of the Association. It is a matter of historical fact, however, that many of the reports published under the authority of Committee A reveal that the injury done an individual has taken place against the background of a faculty denied its proper role.

In two important types of personnel decision the American Association of University Professors does not ordinarily exercise jurisdiction. The first embraces the thousands of separations which occur each year as institutions or individuals decide that a nontenure relationship is not to be renewed at the conclusion of a contract period. The second embraces the even more numerous decisions made each year concerning promotions and salary. In these two kinds of personnel decisions, the Association normally takes cognizance of a situation only if a complaining person is able to make a *prima facie* case that the adverse action involves late notice of nonreappointment or a violation of academic freedom.[4] This abstention by the Association does not mean that these areas of personnel decision are outside the concern of the academic profession, and exclusively for administrative action; on the contrary, the Association believes that the areas are subject to faculty judgment within the departments and faculties at each institution.[5]

[4] The Association is unhappily aware that some nonretentions, and some failures to promote or reward, involve abuses which cannot be studied because the evidence is not available to make a case.

[5] The Association does not handle complaints relating to tenure in administrative posts except where such tenure is linked to the individual's tenure as a professor or is part of a main question of academic freedom. It has also been found impracticable to process complaints by part-time

Higher education, like any other social structure, sometimes finds itself affected by factors over which it has no significant control. In the area of the Association's concerns, the nonacademic factor most frequently encountered is legal proceedings. When litigation occurs, counsel often and normally advise their clients, institutions and teachers alike, to remain silent outside the regulated and protective forum of the courtroom. Since the Association must proceed through the cooperative assistance of the parties in an academic controversy, its action is likely to be suspended until the courts have reached their conclusion in a legal case involving the same controversy. Furthermore, it is always possible that court proceedings will result in a solution of the problem agreeable to all concerned, thus disposing of the case.

A second external influence is the substance of law. The statutory and common laws of the states govern much of the relationship between public institutions and their teaching and research staffs, and, on occasion, the relationship of the academic profession to society in general. And where statutory or common law ends, public higher education is likely to discover the complexities of administrative law. The institutions usually described as "private" will perhaps have less concern with public law, but their privileged tax-exempt position, the public standards they must meet, and the public services they perform, have with other factors created a situation where classification as public or private is evidently becoming more difficult to make. In any event, the private institutions have their own legal problem with the law of contract, particularly in regard to controversies involving appointments on the academic staff. Third among the outside influences, as both the colleges and universities and the state and federal courts are beginning to discover, is the existence of important constitutional issues which involve the liberties of individuals in the academic context.

---

employees in their role as teachers or researchers, or complaints which arise at unaccredited institutions, although action has been taken in a few such complaints at institutions where the import has been large for the academic profession. These are practical limitations, and it should not be thought that the Association is blind or indifferent to injustices which may occur in these excluded areas.

At the outset it was pointed out that the ultimate purpose of the American Association of University Professors is to promote the interests of higher education and research, mindful, as the 1940 *Statement* puts it, that "Institutions of higher education are conducted for the common good and not to further the interest of either the individual teacher or the institution as a whole." In furtherance of this purpose the statements contained in this handbook have been evolved and are now collected in a single publication.

Chapter II
Model Case Procedure

This "model case procedure," describing the stages of a proceeding, is essentially a hypothetical construction. The Association's actual operations involve colleges and universities—extremely complicated and ever-changing social organisms—and professional persons, similarly complex and variable. Each of the two hundred or more complaints received during the year by the General Secretary, the Association's chief administrative officer, soon reveals its significantly unique qualities. The individuality of a complaint becomes even more apparent if it is one of the fifty or more which each year reach "case" status by virtue of the fact that the Association formally requests the administration of an institution to comment upon the complaint. And if the final stage of report publication is attained, an actual case becomes as individual as an episode in history or a chapter in biography.

Thus, the model case procedure presented below does not show the effect of the key forces of institutional and personal individuality. The narrative is also unreal in that no single case is likely to require all the available procedures here described. This model case procedure is designed mainly to reveal the whole range of available procedural resources.

A. THE COMPLAINT; POSSIBLE MEDIATION

1. Formulation of a complaint[1]

The faculty member who believes that his academic freedom or his tenure has been infringed, or that in some important degree he

[1] For ease in reference, the headings which describe the main steps in the Model Case Procedure are numbered consecutively, 1–25, without subordination to the four group headings.

has been denied academic due process, should first define the issues present in his situation, and then consider the proof he can offer in support. In these efforts he may be helped by colleagues who are both familiar with the local scene and informed about national standards. The local chapter of the Association is likely to be a good source for such guidance. In addition to giving specific help in formulation of the complaint, the leadership of the chapter can do much to set the general tone of exchanges, with particular reference to avoiding publicity about the controversy.

The preparation of a complaint will ordinarily call for assembling the documents pertinent to a teacher's appointment and contractual history, and those institutional regulations which bear on the situation out of which the complaint arises. The teacher's own views are customarily presented in a narrative account accompanied by available proof.

A complaint may be submitted directly to the Association's General Secretary if a teacher believes that such a procedure is best suited to his interests. It is not necessary that a complainant be a member of the Association.

2. Receipt of a complaint

The General Secretary receives, on behalf of Committee A and the Association, complaints relating to actions by college or university authorities, which are alleged to have occurred or to be threatened. In addition, he takes cognizance of incidents coming to his attention through other channels, if in his judgment those incidents are likely to be of concern to the Association. Preliminary examination indicates whether a complaint is of a kind which the Association handles, whether the matter is within the jurisdiction of a committee other than Committee A, or whether the complaint appears in fact to embody an issue of academic freedom, tenure, late notice, or academic due process.

3. Acknowledgment of a complaint

In acknowledging receipt of a complaint, the General Secretary informs the writer whether the matter appears to be within the Association's purview; if so, he usually indicates whether it is a matter for Committee A or some other group. Frequently he will request further factual information, copies of written matter, or the development of the complainant's views. If it appears likely that study will go forward, the complainant will be asked to authorize communication by the Association with the administration and other knowledgeable persons. Clarification of issues and advice concerning the selection of an academic counsellor may be offered.

At this point or later, the General Secretary may explore with the complainant the risks which are inseparable from controversy and notoriety.

4. Communication with the local chapter of the Association

The chapter of the Association at the institution may already have been informed of or involved in the problem of the complainant. It may already have been in communication with the Washington Office, perhaps even being the agent of first information. At least by this point the General Secretary will in all ordinary situations communicate with the chapter. Sections on the relations of the local chapter, and of the conference, to a case conclude this review of model case procedure (see below, pp. 24–29).

5. Decisions regarding the possibility of a violation and the usefulness of mediation or investigation

In time the General Secretary has available the information necessary to determine whether adequate ground exists for pursuing the matter further. In other words, he has before him evidence which, if it stands up on further investigation, would support a conclusion that there has been a violation of the principles of academic freedom, tenure, or notice, or a significant denial of academic due process. Such a decision is reached only after appropriate consultation among staff members, and at times with the chairman of Committee A and the officers of the Association. If the decision is affirmative, action is taken under step 6 or step 7, mediation or assignment of case status.

6. Attempted mediation

If circumstances offer hope, the General Secretary may at this time attempt to bring about an adjustment through mediative efforts. He may work with the parties concerned, often through other members of the faculty at the institution, chapter members and officers, Council members and officers of the Association, members of the Association's Panel of Consultants, and all other persons who might be helpful. The interests of the academic profession will in some instances require that any agreement reached will correct a general situation or establish an important principle, as well as settling the particular issue between the parties. In other situations, it may be wiser not to involve issues of principle and to allow agreement to embrace only the material aspects of a particular complaint. In all instances the General Secretary must be reasonably well satisfied that the situation which led to the complaint will not again arise. This assurance of good prospects must be all the more firmly based when mediation takes place because in almost all instances mediation precludes publicity; it thereby also precludes alerting the profession to the possibility of academic issues of the kind raised by the complaint.

B. CASE STATUS; INVESTIGATION

7. Case status; letter from the General Secretary to the chief administrator of the institution

In attempting mediation the General Secretary may have been in direct communication with the chief administrator of the institution concerned. If there is no hopeful prospect for mediation or if such efforts fail, the General Secretary writes to the chief administrator of the institution concerned, setting forth:

(a) The fact that a complaint has been received from a member of the institution's academic professional staff.

(b) The main elements of the complaint.

(c) The principles involved and the Association policy which supports those principles.

(d) A request for the view of the administration regarding the situation, accompanied by any controlling factual information not noted by the General Secretary in his letter.

(e) An offer to assist in achieving an amicable resolution of the problem. Although the General Secretary may advance a tentative recommendation based on the facts already at hand, the chief administrator is assured that final judgment must await an opportunity to study the further information he can supply.

At this same time the General Secretary writes to the complainant and the chapter president informing them that a letter of inquiry has been written to the chief administrator.[2] The letter to the chief administrator gives the complaint "case status" in the Washington Office.

8. Decision to appoint an *ad hoc* investigating committee

The reply by the administration may result in further correspondence, interviews, or other communications which may turn the parties toward mediation or may even achieve a solution at this point. But if all such prospects fail of realization, the General Secretary must determine whether to ask an *ad hoc* committee to investigate the case. He may seek the advice of the chairman of Committee A and the officers of the Association, but the decision rests with him. He will bear in mind that an accomplished investigation more often than not leads to the publication of a report, and that such an event must be viewed in relation to the good of the whole faculty at the institution, and the general good of the academic profession, as well as the interests of the parties in a specific case.

9. Special and emergency investigations

In rare instances, where the violation of academic freedom and tenure has been admitted or where the total evidence to be considered is a matter of undisputed record, the General Secretary may proceed to have a report written by a member of the Association's professional staff without a visit to the institution by an *ad hoc* committee. In any situation, an Association representative will

[2] In the course of correspondence about a case, the General Secretary informs each party of the fact of his having been in communication with the other party, in such detail as to chronology and substance as will serve the ends of objective and fair investigation; but copies of letters received in and sent from the Washington Office are not ordinarily furnished except to the persons originally writing or receiving them, and to other persons who have "a need to know" such as the members of the *ad hoc* committee.

normally visit the campus if request is made by the complainant, the administration, or a representative faculty group such as the Association chapter.

In emergencies of great importance, Committee A itself, with the aid of preliminary inquiry by one or more of its members, may proceed to determine the facts and render a report without resort to an *ad hoc* committee.

10. Appointment of the *ad hoc* committee

One or more persons are asked by the General Secretary to serve as an *ad hoc* committee to investigate, and to report both upon a particular complaint and upon general conditions of academic freedom and tenure at the institution; in almost all instances a visit to the campus will be made. In selecting members, consideration may be given to their professional standing, their disciplines, their varieties of institutional connection, and their locations, with particular regard to the import of these elements for the complainant and the institution in the case at hand.

11. Briefing of the *ad hoc* committee

The General Secretary provides the *ad hoc* committee with these aids:

(a) An account of the facts as presented by the parties, with particular notice of factual contradictions which require investigation, or of significant gaps in the factual structure.

(b) A formulation of the issues which appear to arise from the facts as known at this point.

(c) A statement of the apparently applicable standards and procedures embodied in Association policy statements, and otherwise supported by the Association. References to published reports which may throw light on the present case.

(d) Lists of the persons who are to be interviewed; such lists are ordinarily furnished by the complainant, the administration, and the chapter officers upon the request of the General Secretary, and he may compile his own.

(e) Copies of supporting documents and relevant correspondence.

(f) A statement of Association procedures in academic freedom and tenure cases.

In addition, the *ad hoc* committee may receive advice regarding its activities and function, as follows:
(g) The *ad hoc* committee normally waits upon the president of the institution, thus expressing its respect for the college or university. If there is a local chapter one or more chapter officers usually introduce the members of the committee to the president.
(h) All expenses incurred by the *ad hoc* committee are met by Association funds, and no indebtedness to the complainant or the institution is incurred by the visiting group. However, in arranging for the visit the General Secretary may request the administration to provide rooms suitable for interview purposes; the *ad hoc* committee should also be available for interviews at its lodgings or some other off-campus place. The committee will use its judgment about accepting secretarial or other similar services which may be of help in the investigation.
(i) The *ad hoc* committee maintains effective relations with the officers of the local chapter but not of a social kind (see below, p. 27).
(j) The *ad hoc* committee refrains from publicizing its activity. If approached by representatives of the news media, the committee members will merely identify themselves and state that their function is to report to Committee A of the Association regarding conditions of academic freedom and tenure at the institution. All other questions, depending upon their nature, are referred to the president of the institution or to the General Secretary of the Association.
(k) The *ad hoc* committee is informed that its function is to present to Committee A its independent judgment on all the relevant facts it can assemble, viewed in the light of the principles and procedures supported by the Association. The *ad hoc* committee is informed that it is free to make recommendations to Committee A, but that such recommendations are advisory and should be presented in a communication separate from the report. The *ad hoc* committee is asked to note that Committee A has the official responsibility for deciding upon publication and for making recommendations, if any, for endorsement by the Council and for action by the Annual Meeting.
(l) The *ad hoc* committee is asked to bear in mind its status as a

professional group representing a professional academic association, and that its investigation should be conducted as a rigorously objective inquiry into the facts of a situation, and into those elements of community or institutional history, which have bearing on the conditions of academic freedom and tenure at the college or university.

12. The investigation

The *ad hoc* committee is usually on a campus for two or three days, but shorter or longer visits may occur depending upon the scale and complexity of the inquiry. Normally the committee interviews persons separately, but it may be useful to meet small groups. Depending upon need, interviews may be held with the complainant, administrative officers, faculty members, members of the governing board, and other persons with knowledge of the facts at first hand.

When matters are complex, or for other good reasons, the committee may read back to an interviewee its notes on their conversation in order that accuracy of understanding shall be established. The committee should, in so far as possible, give each person against whom material adverse information has been received an opportunity to rebut this information with knowledge of its source. Committees do not normally make a tape recording of their interviews; if they feel the need of an exact record, they should secure the permission of the person being interviewed before making use of a tape recorder.

On occasion, the *ad hoc* committee may, after prior consultation with the chairman of Committee A, substitute for the customary investigative procedure of holding separate interviews, a hearing procedure at which both parties are present during the examination of documentary evidence and during interviews between the *ad hoc* committee and persons giving oral testimony. The manner of conducting such a hearing will rest entirely in the hands of the *ad hoc* committee.

If the dismissed faculty member was entitled to a hearing by a faculty committee, the *ad hoc* committee should determine:

(a) whether the dismissed faculty member was accorded academic due process and, if not, whether the shortcomings in the procedure actually accorded invalidated the dismissal;

(b) whether the record of the dismissal hearing, if such was accorded, contains substantial evidence in support of the factual conclusions which led to the dismissal (not whether the committee itself would have reached these conclusions); and
(c) whether the grounds for dismissal accord with the 1940 *Statement of Principles.*
In short, the committee should determine whether the decision was fairly reached and is rationally supported in the light of the Association's principles, both procedural and substantive.

At the end of the interviews, the committee will review its experience, note such tentative conclusions as seem immediately possible, and plan for further exchange of opinion. Provision will be made for further correspondence and interviews which may be needed to check facts and to establish full understanding. Further interviews may require the return to the campus of one or more members of the *ad hoc* committee. Written questions or summaries of evidence may be submitted to key persons interviewed for their comments. The members of the *ad hoc* committee will decide upon their division of labor and establish a working schedule for the writing and submission of the report.

13. Avoidance of publicity

It is the hope of the Association that all parties to an academic controversy will refrain from publicizing their differences in order to protect the investigative procedure from the impact of uninformed or uncritical reactions and in order that the door may be held open to mediation. After publication of a report, and sometimes for special reasons at an earlier point, it may be necessary for the interested persons to address themselves to the public; such declarations should be characterized by professional restraint and accuracy.

C. THE REPORT AND ACTION THEREON

14. The received report

The report of an *ad hoc* committee, bearing the signatures of its authors, is sent in confidence to the General Secretary for trans-

mission to Committee A. A number of steps are then taken so that the report shall have as satisfactory a form as possible. Since changes are likely to occur in the text as it receives a series of approvals, the General Secretary has the special responsibility to determine whether any section, or the whole report, has at any point become so materially changed as to require resubmission to those who approved it before the material change.

As a first step, the General Secretary reviews the report to determine whether any significant unexplained omissions or conflicts exist with respect to matters of fact, the views of the interested parties, the issues, and the applicable Association principles and procedures. Style is normalized to the degree necessary for Committee A consideration and possible publication.

After significant revisions have been approved by the *ad hoc* committee, the report is sent to the members of Committee A with a request for comment and with a ballot on which a vote may be entered for or against publication of the report in the *AAUP Bulletin.*

15. Committee A consideration of the report

Committee A may criticize freely both the substance and the form of the report. It may request further consideration of the facts by the *ad hoc* committee, reject a body of evidence on a point, or take any other action which will test or illuminate the facts, the findings, and the conclusions; changes in the structure or language of the report may also be made. Significant points made by Committee A members are generally circulated for study by the group.

If the new evidence to be incorporated, or the changes to be made, relate to fundamental determinations, an individual member of Committee A may reserve his vote until he has had opportunity to study the modified report. In this connection, it should be noted that the vote of Committee A on the publication of a report is by no means a matter of a numerical majority. The General Secretary, mindful of the Association's responsibility to the broad interests of higher education, will take cognizance of both the extent and the weight of all expressed views; if there is a significant minority opinion, he will usually recommend further discussion, having as his aim the elimination of major differences and the attainment of a genuine consensus.

On occasion Committee A may disapprove publication of a report. It may decide that the facts developed in the report do not support a firm conclusion, that the case investigated has not proved sufficiently significant to be called to the attention of the academic profession, or that, because of favorable developments at the institution since the investigation, publication of the report will serve no useful purpose.

16. The submission of the report to the parties

If publication of a report is authorized by Committee A, a further substantive and editorial check occurs. When the *ad hoc* committee has agreed to the revised text, the report is sent, under confidential restrictions, to the complainant, the administration, and the chapter president; some parts of the report may be sent to interviewees whose described actions or opinions are sufficiently central to require direct confirmation, or whose personal involvement is sufficiently serious to require its being checked. A time limit for the submission of comments is determined by the General Secretary.

Those receiving the text are requested to note any error of fact or any inaccuracy in the presentation of a position taken or opinion expressed. The General Secretary gives careful study to all information and comment received in reply; he may consult the *ad hoc* committee or Committee A if necessary.

At no phase of the proceedings is it more important that confidentiality be observed.

17. Publication of the report

When all final corrections and clarifications have been accomplished, the text is given to the editor of the *AAUP Bulletin*. Ordinarily the report appears in the next issue of that journal to be published. By long tradition a report must be published four weeks or more before an Annual Meeting if it is to be considered on that occasion; this period of time is designed to give the members of the Association full opportunity for study.

The report is published over the names of the members of the *ad hoc* committee; then follow the names of the members of Committee A, the body authorizing publication. Each report carries as its first footnote this or a similar statement:

> The text of this report was written in the first instance by members of the investigating committee. In accordance with Association practice that text was submitted for consideration by (a) the Association's standing Committee on Academic Freedom and Tenure (Committee A), (b) the teacher(s) in whose interests the investigation was conducted, (c) the administration [named institution(s)]. In the light of the suggestions received, and with the editorial assistance of the Association staff, the report has been prepared for publication.

When published, copies of the report are sent to the complainant and to the chief administrator and governing board members of the institution.

18. Recommendations of Committee A before the Council and the Annual Meeting

Committee A meets immediately before the first session of the spring meeting of the Association's Council, which in turn immediately precedes the Annual Meeting. Committee A may make a recommendation based upon any report which has been published, and may request endorsement by the Council before it seeks approval by the Annual Meeting.

If a report documents a violation or unsatisfactory conditions of academic freedom and tenure, the General Secretary attempts, in the interval between the publication of the report and action upon it by the Annual Meeting, to persuade the administration to take corrective measures; if such measures are taken, Committee A weighs them when it frames its recommendation to the Annual Meeting. If a case has resulted in part from absent or inadequate regulations, advice will be available concerning appropriate innovations or changes. If redress to the dismissed faculty member is an issue, the General Secretary is available as an agent for bringing the parties together.

If a serious situation has not been corrected, Committee A's normal recommendation to the Annual Meeting is for a vote of censure. The Annual Meeting is the sole body within the Association which has the authority to take this action, and its censure is imposed only upon the administration of the institution.

19. Publication of Annual Meeting action

The action taken by the Annual Meeting is at once communicated to the institution in each case involving censure. Since the Association report and action are on behalf of the academic profession, appropriate national and local press notices are released. In the issue of the *AAUP Bulletin* which describes the Annual Meeting there is printed the report by the chairman of Committee A, which indicates actions taken thereon.

Each issue of the *Bulletin* carries a list of censured administrations;[3] the names of the institutions are arranged in the chronological order of action taken by succeeding Annual Meetings, and there are references to the *Bulletin* issue in which the *ad hoc* committeee report appeared and to the year in which censure was imposed.

20. Withdrawal of censure

The bases for a recommendation by Committee A to an Annual Meeting that censure be withdrawn are that (a) the conditions which led to censure are essentially corrected, and (b) there is reason to believe that observance and protection of academic freedom and tenure will in the future meet the standards of the academic profession. A significant factor in determining whether these conditions have been met will, in many situations, be the steps which the institution has taken to right a wrong done. Committee A proceeds to consideration of withdrawal of censure after receiving the recommendation of the General Secretary that such action be taken.

In a recommendation which leads to censure, Committee A will not ordinarily specify the grounds for the removal of censure. In extraordinary cases, as where an administration has overtly challenged and refused to comply with the provisions of the 1940 *Statement of Principles,* withdrawal of censure may have to be accomplished by a specified action which was recommended, at the time of censure, by Committee A, endorsed by the Council, and voted by the Annual Meeting.

[3] See Chapter VII, List A, Censured Administrations (below, pp. 143–47).

During the period that the name of an institution remains upon the list of censured administrations, the General Secretary endeavors to assist the administration, in every way compatible with the principles of the Association, to take action which can lead to withdrawal of censure. Each year, in the March issue of the *Bulletin,* he reports to the profession in an article entitled "Developments Relating to Censure by the Association." Also, at each Annual Meeting, the chairman of Committee A reports concerning the reasons for not recommending withdrawal of censure.

The fact that the name of an institution appears upon the list of censured administrations does not establish a boycott of a college or university, nor does it visit censure upon the faculty, student body, or alumni. The position taken by the Association with respect to appointments is set forth in language adopted by Committee A:

> Members of the Association have often considered it to be their duty, in order to indicate their support of the principles violated, to refrain from accepting an appointment to an institution so long as it remains on the censure list. Since circumstances differ widely from case to case, the Association does not consider it advisable to assert that such an unqualified obligation exists for its members; it does urge that, before accepting appointments, they seek information on present conditions of academic freedom and tenure from the Association's Washington Office and prospective departmental colleagues. The Association leaves it to the discretion of the individual possessed of the facts to make the proper decision.

D. CHAPTER ACTION IN ACADEMIC FREEDOM AND TENURE CASES

Chapter members and officers are likely to be better informed, at least in the early stages of a case, than persons outside the institution. Their status as faculty members gives them knowledge and sensitivity not immediately possible for strangers; their known membership in an organization which concerns itself with faculty protection may have brought them confidences or requests for advice from faculty colleagues. But significant intervention by chapter leaders, particularly if feelings run high, may subject them to administrative animosity. Consequently, the chapter must be prepared for possible recrimination. This fact, and other considerations, have led to a series of fairly explicit guidelines for chapter action in academic freedom and tenure cases.

21. Before case status

(a) Before the complaint. During the period in which events are taking form as an issue, and before the issue becomes a complaint, the role of the chapter can be very important. As noted on pp. 12–21, the chapter can be of great assistance to the teacher as he formulates his complaint; help can be given in the definition of issues and in the mustering of evidence and the preliminary weighing of its usefulness as supporting proof. It may offer the teacher, the faculty, and the administration advice as to standards and procedures, and should call attention to any formal institutional means for reviewing complaints. It can give guidance which will exclude irrelevant issues and minimize others, will prevent premature hardening of positions, and will direct attention to available channels of communication, mediation, and remedy. In some cases one or more members of the chapter's executive committee may be able to resolve the problem through conferences with administrative officers and the faculty member.

In this first phase, and in all later ones, the chapter should be careful to distinguish between its status as an organized group of informed academic persons and the status of the faculty and its duly constituted committees and agencies. A large measure of identity of persons may exist, but the functions, authority, and other formal characteristics of the two bodies are significantly different.

(b) The framing of a complaint; selection of counsel (see above, pp. 11–12, sects. 1 and 2). If a teacher wishes to lodge a complaint with the General Secretary, he will in many instances be helped by the chapter in the presentation of his account and the assembling of his supporting documents. At this same time it will usually be necessary for the complainant to obtain an academic advisor or counsel, who will accompany him, guide him, and represent him in various ways throughout the course of the contro-

versy. The chapter is often in an especially good position to assist in the selection of such counsel; it may be particularly helpful if a person outside the institution is needed. The chapter may also be able to offer advice, of the kind that comes from reasonable men, regarding a need for legal counsel.

(c) Communication with the General Secretary (see above, pp. 12–13, sect. 3). Before or at the time of the complaint, the chapter and the General Secretary are normally in communication about the situation. Such exchange can often continue usefully and with much variety of form throughout a case. Officers of the chapter or appropriate committee members normally serve as its agents; their frank analysis of the situation, on a confidential basis, can be of great help to the General Secretary. Also, if there is division of, or a shift in, opinion in the faculty or in the chapter, the General Secretary should be informed.

(d) Mediation (see above, p. 13, sect. 5). The circumstances of different situations are so variable that it is inadvisable to attempt to define in specific terms the part which the chapter can play if mediation is attempted. But the variety of possible action in this phase of a case does not lessen the importance of the chapter role. In some situations the mediation is largely the work of the chapter; the Association, nationally, assists the local mediators.

22. During case status (see above, pp. 14–22, sects. 6–17)

(e) Realignment of relations; chapter disengagement. When it becomes necessary for the General Secretary to communicate formally with the administration of an institution, stating that a complaint has been received and asking for information and comment, the complaint becomes a case. At this point the matter passes into the jurisdiction of Committee A, acting for the concern of the Association's members and the academic profession in terms of national and local interests. The General Secretary henceforth acts on behalf of Committee A.

Committee A ultimately performs a judicial function. Informalities permissible in the past may have to be discarded; the now visible possibility of a publicly declared judgment by the Association introduces new and weighty considerations. The new procedural phase requires concentration of authority and responsibility at the level of national action, in the hands of Committee A and the General Secretary. This transformation of a local complaint into an issue for investigation and possible report by a national professional organization also permits effective emphasis upon the gravity of the situation. For these reasons the local chapter should at the point of case status disengage itself from organizational responsibility or action.

In this same phase, it is likely that at some institutions members of the faculty will differ in their views of a situation; a variety of complicated internal faculty personal relations may grow out of a case. These developments, which are the commonplaces of controversy, are intimately related to the increasing involvement of faculty members in a time of stress. Ordinary discretion therefore presents a further reason why a chapter will refrain from organizational participation.

(f) Chapter services. Relieved of official responsibilities, the chapter is now in a position to perform services of great value to the Association and of the highest order of importance for the achieving of a sound professional judgment in the area of academic freedom and tenure. The chapter's chief responsibilities are:

1. To assist the General Secretary by reporting on significant developments which he may not hear of because they are superficially marginal or unrelated to a case.
2. To be constantly on the alert for any possibility of conciliation or mediation, and to notify the General Secretary about such prospects.
3. To assist in maintaining lines of communication.
4. To assist in the orderly conduct of an investigation by arranging interviews and providing the *ad hoc* committee with the information at its disposal.

23. Following publication of an *ad hoc* committee report

In addition to assisting in maintaining all possible lines of communication, the local chapter may be helpful to Committee A and the Association by having available considered statements of faculty opinion on the case at this critical phase. Committee A may request the view of the chapter before it gives formal consideration to the recommendation it will make to the Annual Meeting, and in especially complex cases it may invite chapter representatives to meet with it in advance of the Annual Meeting.

24. During censure status (see above, p. 22, sect. 18)

At an institution whose name appears upon the Association's list of censured administrations, the local chapter may be in a conspicuous and delicate position but also one in which it may do much good. It will probably be well advised, in the first instance, to protect itself by indicating that it ceased to act organizationally at the point where a complaint became a case and that further action lay in the hands of the Committee A, the General Secretary, and the Annual Meeting.

But the local chapter during the censure period has a great potential for effecting conditions which will make the removal of censure possible. The chapter is ordinarily in a strong position to become the chief agent for the promotion of conversations which can lead to corrective action. Such explorations are likely to be especially effective if there is need for the revision of institutional regulations.

25. The general responsibility of the chapter

The foregoing description of the role of a chapter at an institution where a case arises focuses upon particular obligations. But the most important opportunity and responsibility of a chapter in a case situation covers the entire scene and extends from the beginning to the end. It is the chapter which by precept and example can best demonstrate the fact that the American Association of University Professors is an organization of professional academic persons, and is so acting. Inflexible devotion to principle, courtesy toward colleagues and administration alike, objective and dignified utterance, have great power to create a context worthy of scholars and of institutions devoted to higher education, and in that setting to achieve a solution.

E. CONFERENCE ACTION

A state or regional conference of the Association can also play an important role in ending the censure status of an administration, and sometimes during the early stages of a complaint. It can furnish advice on Association principles and procedures to the chapter at an institution when a case has been reported, and can assist the General Secretary by calling his attention to developments relative to a complaint and by suggesting competent mediators, or advisors, for aggrieved faculty members, when these are desired. After censure has been imposed the conference can publicize in its area the burden which is placed upon the whole community by the fact of censure, it can approach the natural area concentration of the alumni of the institution concerned and ask them to use their good offices for correction, and in numerous other ways give proper interpretation and perspective to the censure situation.

PART TWO. PRINCIPLES AND PROCEDURES

Chapter III
Academic Freedom and Tenure: Basic Statements

This chapter presents those principles and procedures relating to academic freedom and tenure which are set forth in official Association statements. The first two statements have been jointly formulated and then approved by this Association and by the Association of American Colleges or the American Council on Education. The third, formulated by this Association, is a clarification of the 1940 *Statement of Principles on Academic Freedom and Tenure,* the Association's fundamental policy statement in this area. In terms of application, these statements of principle and procedure have operated as a unified and unifying force in American higher education since the beginning of the Association's work.

1940 Statement of Principles on Academic Freedom and Tenure

In 1915, at the time of the founding of the Association, a committee on academic freedom and tenure formulated a statement entitled a "Declaration of Principles." This statement set forth the concern of the Association for academic freedom and tenure, for proper procedures, and for professional responsibility. The Declaration was endorsed by the American Association of University Professors at its Second Annual Meeting, held December 31, 1915, and January 1, 1916.

In 1925, the American Council on Education called a conference of representatives of a number of its constituent members, among them the American Association of University Professors, for the purpose of preparing a statement in this area. There emerged the 1925 "Conference Statement on Academic Freedom and Tenure," which was endorsed in 1925 by the Association of American Colleges and in 1926 by the American Association of University Professors.

In 1940, following upon a series of conferences which began in 1934, representatives of the Association of American Colleges and the American Association of University Professors agreed upon a "Statement of Principles on Academic Freedom and Tenure," and upon three attached "Interpretations." The 1940 Statement, *and its Inter-*

pretations, were endorsed by the two associations in 1941. In subsequent years endorsement has been officially voted by numerous other organizations.[1]

The purpose of this statement is to promote public understanding and support of academic freedom and tenure and agreement upon procedures to assure them in colleges and universities. Institutions of higher education are conducted for the common good and not to further the interest of either the individual teacher[2] or the institution as a whole. The common good depends upon the free search for truth and its free exposition.

Academic freedom is essential to these purposes and applies to both teaching and research. Freedom in research is fundamental to the advancement of truth. Academic freedom in its teaching aspect is fundamental for the protection of the rights of the teacher in teaching and of the student to freedom in learning. It carries with it duties correlative with rights.

Tenure is a means to certain ends; specifically: (1) Freedom of teaching and research and of extramural activities and (2) a

[1] 1941 Association of American Colleges; American Association of University Professors

1946 American Library Association (adapted for librarians); Association of American Law Schools

1947 American Political Science Association

1950 American Association of Colleges for Teacher Education (endorsed by predecessor, American Association of Teachers Colleges, in 1941); Association for Higher Education, National Education Association; Eastern Psychological Association

1952 American Philosophical Association, Western Division; (Eastern Division, 1953; Pacific Division, 1962)

1953 Southern Society for Philosophy and Psychology

1961 American Psychological Association; American Historical Association; Modern Language Association of America

1962 American Economic Association; American Farm Economic Association

1963 Midwest Sociological Society; Mississippi Valley Historical Association; American Philological Association; American Council of Learned Societies; Speech Association of America; American Sociological Association; Southern Historical Association; American Studies Association; Southern Economic Association; Association of American Geographers

sufficient degree of economic security to make the profession attractive to men and women of ability. Freedom and economic security, hence, tenure, are indispensable to the success of an institution in fulfilling its obligations to its students and to society.

Academic freedom

(a) The teacher is entitled to full freedom in research and in the publication[3] of the results, subject to the adequate performance of

---

1964 Classical Association of the Middle West and South; Southwestern Social Science Association; Archaeological Institute of America; Southern Management Association; American Educational Theatre Association; South Central Modern Language Association; Southwestern Philosophical Society

1965 Council for the Advancement of Small Colleges; Mathematical Association of America; Arizona Academy of Science; Council of the Western History Association; Academy of Management; American Risk and Insurance Association

1966 American Catholic Historical Association; American Catholic Philosophical Association; Association of State Colleges and Universities; Association for Education in Journalism; Western History Association; Mountain-Plains Philosophical Conference; Society of American Archivists; Southeastern Psychological Association

1967 American Association for the Advancement of Slavic Studies; American Mathematical Society; College Theology Society; Council on Social Work Education; American Association of Colleges of Pharmacy; American Academy of Religion; American Catholic Sociological Society; American Society of Journalism School Administrators; The John Dewey Society for the Study of Education and Culture; South Atlantic Modern Language Association; American Finance Association; Catholic Economic Association

1968 United Chapters of Phi Beta Kappa; American Society of Christian Ethics; American Association of Teachers of French; Appalachian Finance Association; Association of Teachers of Chinese Language and Culture

[2] The word "teacher" as used in this document is understood to include the investigator who is attached to an academic institution without teaching duties. [*Editor's note.* In practice the term "teacher" is often replaced by "professor" because it applies to higher education and extends to both the research and the teaching function.]

[3] [*Editor's note.* There may be justification for very special limitations upon publication where the individual concerned has in advance clearly accepted them; for example, a limitation based upon the fact that the work to be accomplished will involve the efforts of several persons, who are ethically bound to publish as a group.]

his other academic duties; but research for pecuniary return should be based upon an understanding with the authorities of the institution.

(b) The teacher is entitled to freedom in the classroom in discussing his subject, but he should be careful not to introduce into his teaching controversial matter which has no relation to his subject.[4] Limitations of academic freedom because of religious or other aims[5] of the institution should be clearly stated in writing at the time of the appointment.

(c) The college or university teacher is a citizen, a member of a learned profession, and an officer of an educational institution. When he speaks or writes as a citizen,[6] he should be free from institutional censorship or discipline, but his special position in the community imposes special obligations. As a man of learning and an educational officer, he should remember that the public may judge his profession and his institution by his utterances. Hence he should at all times be accurate, should exercise appropriate restraint, should show respect for the opinions of others, and should make every effort to indicate that he is not an institutional spokesman.

Academic tenure

(a) After the expiration of a probationary period,[7] teachers or investigators should have permanent or continuous tenure, and

[4] [*Editor's note.* Some courses of study require consideration of matter on which the teacher is not in all aspects expert; thus the teacher of English composition or literature may have to deal with writings about race relations, sexual mores, or social philosophy. A teacher handling mixed responsibilities of this type ordinarily indicates the limits of his expert judgment, and should not be subject to particular scrutiny because he may deal with controversial issues.]

[5] [*Editor's note.* Problems sometimes arise through the failure of an institution to be explicit about its particular limitations at the time of appointing a teacher, or the failure of a teacher to observe limitations which he has accepted—short of waiver of his fundamental academic obligations.]

[6] [*Editor's note.* An issue has also arisen regarding the right to silence or, conversely, the obligation of disclosure. For detailed presentation of the Association position, see below, pp. 47–63.]

[7] [*Editor's note.* Appointments of an irregular or special kind may not count toward fulfillment of a probationary period if they are in fact ex-

their service should be terminated only for adequate cause,[8] except in the case of retirement for age, or under extraordinary circumstances because of financial exigencies.

In the interpretation of this principle it is understood that the following represents acceptable academic practice:

(1) The precise terms and conditions of every appointment should be stated in writing and be in the possession of both institution and teacher before the appointment is consummated.

(2) Beginning with appointment to the rank of full-time instructor or a higher rank, the probationary period should not exceed seven years, including within this period full-time service in all institutions of higher education; but subject to the proviso that when, after a term of probationary service of more than three years in one or more institutions, a teacher is called to another institution it may be agreed in writing[9] that his new appointment is for a probationary period of not more than four years, even though thereby the person's total probationary period in the academic profession is extended beyond the normal maximum of seven years. Notice should be given at least one year prior to the expiration of the probationary period if the teacher is not to be continued in service after the expiration of that period.[10]

---

ceptional and of relatively brief duration; many institutions appoint scholars for a semester or a year on a temporary basis. But such appointments may, if repeated, be regarded by the profession as in fact to have been regular appointments and to have retrospective force. Colleges and universities should have written general regulations indicating whether time on sabbatical or research leave should count as probationary service.]

[8] [*Editor's note.* The 1940 *Statement* does not define "adequate cause" in particular terms, although later references, in the section entitled "Academic Tenure, (4)," to "incompetence" and "reasons not involving moral turpitude" permit a number of inferences. A resolution adopted by the 1953 Annual Meeting states that, "The tests of the fitness of a college teacher should be his integrity and his professional competence, as demonstrated in instruction and research." Whatever the alleged "adequate cause" may be, it should be proved before a faculty hearing committee.]

[9] [*Editor's note.* Many cases involving failure to count prior service arise at institutions which have not entered into a written agreement at the time of final appointment, or lack a general rule, or both.]

[10] [*Editor's note.* The probationary period is determined by the decision of the institution not to reappoint a person. If this decision is reached dur-

(3) During the probationary period a teacher should have the academic freedom that all other members of the faculty have.

(4) Termination for cause of a continuous appointment, or the dismissal for cause of a teacher, previous to the expiration of a term appointment, should, if possible, be considered by both a faculty committee and the governing board of the institution.[11] In all cases where the facts are in dispute, the accused teacher should be informed before the hearing in writing of the charges against him and should have the opportunity to be heard in his own defense by all bodies that pass judgment upon his case. He should be permitted to have with him an adviser of his own choosing who may act as counsel. There should be a full stenographic record of the hearing available to the parties concerned. In the hearing of charges of incompetence the testimony should include that of teachers and other scholars, either from his own or from other institutions. Teachers on continuous appointment who are dismissed for reasons not involving moral turpitude should receive their salaries for at least a year from the date of notification of dismissal whether or not they are continued in their duties at the institution.

(5) Termination of a continuous appointment because of financial exigency should be demonstrably bona fide.

Interpretations

At the conference of representatives of the American Association of University Professors and of the Association of American Colleges on November 7–8, 1940, the following interpretations of the 1940 *Statement of Principles on Academic Freedom and Tenure* were agreed upon:

---

ing the first year of service, it would obviously be impossible to give a year's notice (and it is likely that the writers of the 1940 *Statement* were thinking in the context of their less hurried times). In order not to impose an unreal standard, the Association has for many years applied standards of notice more in conformity with developing practices in higher education; these standards are set forth below, p. 46.]

[11] [*Editor's note.* The 1958 *Statement on Procedural Standards in Faculty Dismissal Proceedings* is largely an elaboration and commentary upon this section of the 1940 *Statement,* which sets forth the minimum essentials for adjudication of termination situations.]

1. That its operation should not be retroactive.[12]
2. That all tenure claims of teachers appointed prior to the endorsement should be determined in accordance with the principles set forth in the 1925 *Conference Statement on Academic Freedom and Tenure.*
3. If the administration of a college or university feels that a teacher has not observed the admonitions of Paragraph (c) of the section on *Academic Freedom* and believes that the extramural utterances of the teacher have been such as to raise grave doubts concerning his fitness for his position, it may proceed to file charges under Paragraph (a) (4) of the section on *Academic Tenure.* In pressing such charges the administration should remember that teachers are citizens and should be accorded the freedom of citizens. In such cases the administration must assume full responsibility and the American Association of University Professors and the Association of American Colleges are free to make an investigation.

[12] [*Editor's note.* The proscription against retroactivity was directed to the situation in 1940; it was not intended to suggest that an institution formally adopting the 1940 *Statement* in 1966 would thereby be excused from extending its protections to a faculty member whose first appointment was, say, in 1962.]

1958 Statement on Procedural Standards in Faculty Dismissal Proceedings

The following *Statement on Procedural Standards in Faculty Dismissal Proceedings* was prepared by a joint committee representing the Association of American Colleges and the American Association of University Professors. It is intended to supplement the 1940 *Statement of Principles on Academic Freedom and Tenure* by providing a formulation of the "academic due process" that should be observed in dismissal proceedings. However, the exact procedural standards here set forth "are not intended to establish a norm in the same manner as the 1940 *Statement of Principles on Academic Freedom and Tenure,* but are presented rather as a guide. . . ." The committee members from the Association of American Colleges were President Louis T. Benezet (Colorado College), President Margaret Clapp (Wellesley College), and President Samuel B. Gould (Antioch College). The other members were Professor Ralph F. Fuchs (Indiana University), Professor Quincy Wright (University of Chicago), and Professor Helen C. White (University of Wisconsin). The Statement was approved by the Annual Meeting of the American Association of University Professors and by the Association of American Colleges in 1958.

Introductory comments

Any approach toward settling the difficulties which have beset dismissal proceedings on many American campuses must look beyond procedure into setting and cause. A dismissal proceeding is a symptom of failure; no amount of use of removal process will help strengthen higher education as much as will the cultivation of conditions in which dismissals rarely if ever need occur.

Just as the board of control or other governing body is the legal and fiscal corporation of the college, the faculty are the academic entity. Historically, the academic corporation is the older. Faculties were formed in the Middle Ages, with managerial affairs either self-arranged or handled in course by the parent church. Modern college faculties, on the other hand, are part of a complex and extensive structure requiring legal incorporation, with stewards and managers specifically appointed to discharge certain functions.

Nonetheless, the faculty of a modern college constitutes an entity as real as that of the faculties of medieval times, in terms of collective purpose and function. A necessary precondition of a strong faculty is that it have first-hand concern with its own membership.

This is properly reflected both in appointments to and in separations from the faculty body.

A well-organized institution will reflect sympathetic understanding by trustees and teachers alike of their respective and complementary roles. These should be spelled out carefully in writing and made available to all. Trustees and faculty should understand and agree on their several functions in determining who shall join and who shall remain on the faculty. One of the prime duties of the administrator is to help preserve understanding of those functions. It seems clear on the American college scene that a close positive relationship exists between the excellence of colleges, the strength of their faculties, and the extent of faculty responsibility in determining faculty membership. Such a condition is in no wise inconsistent with full faculty awareness of institutional factors with which governing boards must be primarily concerned.

In the effective college, a dismissal proceeding involving a faculty member on tenure, or one occurring during the term of an appointment, will be a rare exception, caused by individual human weakness and not by an unhealthful setting. When it does come, however, the college should be prepared for it, so that both institutional integrity and individual human rights may be preserved during the process of resolving the trouble. The faculty must be willing to recommend the dismissal of a colleague when necessary. By the same token, presidents and governing boards must be willing to give full weight to a faculty judgment favorable to a colleague.

One persistent source of difficulty is the definition of adequate cause for the dismissal of a faculty member. Despite the 1940 *Statement of Principles on Academic Freedom and Tenure* and subsequent attempts to build upon it, considerable ambiguity and misunderstanding persist throughout higher education, especially in the respective conceptions of governing boards, administrative officers, and faculties concerning this matter. The present statement assumes that individual institutions will have formulated their own definitions of adequate cause for dismissal, bearing in mind the 1940 *Statement* and standards which have developed in the experience of academic institutions.

This statement deals with procedural standards. Those recommended are not intended to establish a norm in the same manner as the 1940 *Statement of Principles on Academic Freedom and Tenure,* but are presented rather as a guide to be used according to the nature and traditions of particular institutions in giving effect to both faculty tenure rights and the obligations of faculty members in the academic community.

Procedural recommendations

1. Preliminary proceedings concerning the fitness of a faculty member. When reason arises to question the fitness of a college or university faculty member who has tenure or whose term appointment has not expired, the appropriate administrative officers should ordinarily discuss the matter with him in personal conference. The matter may be terminated by mutual consent at this point; but if an adjustment does not result, a standing or *ad hoc* committee elected by the faculty and charged with the function of rendering confidential advice in such situations should informally inquire into the situation, to effect an adjustment if possible and, if none is effected, to determine whether in its view formal proceedings to consider his dismissal should be instituted. If the committee recommends that such proceedings should be begun, or if the president of the institution, even after considering a recommendation of the committee favorable to the faculty member, expresses his conviction that a proceeding should be undertaken, action should be commenced under the procedures which follow. Except where there is disagreement, a statement with reasonable particularity of the grounds proposed for the dismissal should then be jointly formulated by the president and the faculty committee; if there is disagreement, the president or his representative should formulate the statement.

2. Commencement of formal proceedings. The formal proceedings should be commenced by a communication addressed to the faculty member by the president of the institution, informing the faculty member of the statement formulated, and informing him that, if he so requests, a hearing to determine whether he should be removed from his faculty position on the grounds stated will be conducted by a faculty committee at a specified time and place. In setting the date of the hearing, sufficient time should be allowed the faculty member to prepare his defense. The faculty member should be informed, in detail or by reference to published regulations, of the procedural rights that will be accorded to him. The faculty member should state in reply whether he wishes a hearing and, if so, should answer in writing, not less than one week before the date set for the hearing, the statements in the president's letter.

3. *Suspension of the faculty member.* Suspension of the faculty member during the proceedings involving him is justified only if immediate harm to himself or others is threatened by his continuance. Unless legal considerations forbid, any such suspension should be with pay.

4. *Hearing committee.* The committee of faculty members to conduct the hearing and reach a decision should either be an elected standing committee not previously concerned with the case or a committee established as soon as possible after the president's letter to the faculty member has been sent. The choice of members of the hearing committee should be on the basis of their objectivity and competence and of the regard in which they are held in the academic community. The committee should elect its own chairman.

5. *Committee proceeding.* The committee should proceed by considering the statement of grounds for dismissal already formulated, and the faculty member's response written before the time of the hearing. If the faculty member has not requested a hearing, the committee should consider the case on the basis of the obtainable information and decide whether he should be removed; otherwise the hearing should go forward. The committee, in consultation with the president and the faculty member, should exercise its judgment as to whether the hearing should be public or private. If any facts are in dispute, the testimony of witnesses and other evidence concerning the matter set forth in the president's letter to the faculty member should be received.

The president should have the option of attendance during the hearing. He may designate an appropriate representative to assist in developing the case; but the committee should determine the order of proof, should normally conduct the questioning of witnesses, and, if necessary, should secure the presentation of evidence important to the case.

The faculty member should have the option of assistance by

counsel, whose functions should be similar to those of the representative chosen by the president. The faculty member should have the additional procedural rights set forth in the 1940 *Statement of Principles on Academic Freedom and Tenure,* and should have the aid of the committee, when needed, in securing the attendance of witnesses. The faculty member or his counsel and the representative designated by the president should have the right, within reasonable limits, to question all witnesses who testify orally. The faculty member should have the opportunity to be confronted by all witnesses adverse to him. Where unusual and urgent reasons move the hearing committee to withhold this right, or where the witness cannot appear, the identity of the witness, as well as his statements, should nevertheless be disclosed to the faculty member. Subject to these safeguards, statements may when necessary be taken outside the hearing and reported to it. All of the evidence should be duly recorded. Unless special circumstances warrant, it should not be necessary to follow formal rules of court procedure.

6. *Consideration by hearing committee.* The committee should reach its decision in conference, on the basis of the hearing. Before doing so, it should give opportunity to the faculty member or his counsel and the representative designated by the president to argue orally before it. If written briefs would be helpful, the committee may request them. The committee may proceed to decision promptly, without having the record of the hearing transcribed, where it feels that a just decision can be reached by this means; or it may await the availability of a transcript of the hearing if its decision would be aided thereby. It should make explicit findings with respect to each of the grounds of removal presented, and a reasoned opinion may be desirable. Publicity concerning the committee's decision may properly be withheld until consideration has been given to the case by the governing body of the institution. The president and the faculty member should be notified of the decision in writing and should be given a copy of the record of the hearing. Any release to the public should be made through the president's office.

7. *Consideration by governing body.* The president should transmit to the governing body the full report of the hearing committee, stating its action. On the assumption that the governing

board has accepted the principle of the faculty hearing committee, acceptance of the committee's decision would normally be expected. If the governing body chooses to review the case, its review should be based on the record of the previous hearing, accompanied by opportunity for argument, oral or written or both, by the principals at the hearing or their representatives. The decision of the hearing committee should either be sustained or the proceeding be returned to the committee with objections specified. In such a case the committee should reconsider, taking account of the stated objections and receiving new evidence if necessary. It should frame its decision and communicate it in the same manner as before. Only after study of the committee's reconsideration should the governing body make a final decision overruling the committee.

8. Publicity. Except for such simple announcements as may be required, covering the time of the hearing and similar matters, public statements about the case by either the faculty member or administrative officers should be avoided so far as possible until the proceedings have been completed. Announcement of the final decision should include a statement of the hearing committee's original action, if this has not previously been made known.

1964 Statement on the Standards for Notice of Nonreappointment

The 1940 *Statement of Principles* (section "Academic Tenure [2]") reads: "Notice should be given at least one year prior to the expiration of the probationary period if the teacher is not to be continued in service after the expiration of that period." Committee A of the Association has always recognized that the brevity of this statement of the principle of notice did not give adequate guidance for situations where the decision not to reappoint occurred during a relatively short probationary period. Practical standards have been developed. These standards for notice are set forth in this Statement, which was approved by Committee A and the Council in 1963, and endorsed by the 1964 Annual Meeting.

The standards for notice

Notice of nonreappointment, or of intention not to recommend reappointment to the governing board, should be given in writing in accordance with the following standards:

1. Not later than March 1 of the first academic year of service, if the appointment expires at the end of that year; or, if a one-year appointment terminates during an academic year, at least three months in advance of its termination.

2. Not later than December 15 of the second academic year of service, if the appointment expires at the end of that year; or, if an initial two-year appointment terminates during an academic year, at least six months in advance of its termination.

3. At least twelve months before the expiration of an appointment after two or more years in the institution.

Chapter IV
Academic Freedom and Tenure: Other Statements

Academic Freedom and Tenure in the Quest for National Security: [1956] Report of a Special Committee, [Second Section] Relevant General Principles [and] a [1958] Statement of the Committee on Academic Freedom and Tenure, Supplementary. . . .

A special committee, appointed by authority of the Council in 1955, presented the following report to the Council in 1956. The second section of the report, "Relevant General Principles," was adopted by the Council as its own statement, and these principles were then adopted by the 1956 Annual Meeting. A preceding section was introductory in nature and a following section presented a record of particular events and a group of specific recommendations.

Subsequent to the 1956 adoption of the "Relevant General Principles" of the report of the special committee, Committee A spent much time in an effort to clarify the position to be defended when a faculty member refuses to make disclosures to his own institution. The result, printed in the Spring, 1958, issue of the *AAUP Bulletin,* was "A Statement of the Committee on Academic Freedom and Tenure, Supplementary to the 1956 Report, 'Academic Freedom and Tenure in the Quest for National Security' "; this statement is printed here immediately following the 1956 "Relevant General Principles."

---

1. The justification of academic freedom

The maintenance of freedom of speech, publication, religion, and assembly (each of which is a component of intellectual freedom) is the breath of life of a democratic society. The need is greatest in fields of higher learning, where the use of reason and the cultivation of the highest forms of human expression are the basic methods. To an increasing extent, society has come to rely upon colleges and universities as a principal means of acquiring new knowledge and new techniques, of conveying the fruits of past and present learning to the community, and of transmitting these results to generations to come. Without freedom to explore, to criticize existing institutions, to exchange ideas, and to advocate solutions to human problems, faculty members and students cannot perform their work, cannot maintain their self-respect. Society suffers correspondingly. The liberty that is needed requires a freedom of thought and expression within colleges and universities, a freedom to carry the results of honest inquiry to the outside, and a freedom to influence human affairs in the same manner as other informed and unprejudiced persons do. Nor is the value of freedom lessened because error at times arises from its exercise. Learning, intellectual development, and social and scientific progress take place on a trial-and-error basis, and even the unsound cause or hypothesis may call forth the truth that displaces it. The error of one scholar has, indeed, stimulated others to discover the correcting truth.

The demand we of the academic world make for academic freedom is not made primarily for our own benefit. We enjoy the exercise of freedom; but the purposes of liberty lie, in a democracy, in the common welfare. It has recently been said, "With regard to some occupations, it is eminently in the interest of society that the men concerned speak their minds without fear of retribution. . . . The occupational work of the vast majority of people is largely independent of their thought and speech. The professor's work *consists* of his thought and speech. If he loses his position for what he writes or says, he will, as a rule, have to leave his profession, and may no longer be able effectively to question and challenge accepted doctrines or effectively to defend challenged doctrines. And if *some* professors lose their positions for what they write or say, the effect on many other professors will be such that their usefulness to their students and to society will be gravely reduced."[1]

We ask, then, for the maintenance of academic freedom and of the civil liberties of scholars, not as a special right, but as a means whereby we may make our appointed contribution to the life of the

[1] Fritz Machlup, "On Some Misconceptions Concerning Academic Freedom," *AAUP Bulletin,* 41:753–84 (Winter, 1955).

commonwealth and share equitably, but not more than equitably, in the American heritage. Society has the power to destroy or impair this freedom; but it cannot do so and retain the values of self-criticism and originality fostered by higher education. Again, in the words of the Princeton University Chapter:

> The spirit of free inquiry is not a privilege claimed for a single profession, but the touchstone of our character as a people, the proved source of our national strength. Its defilement in any area of our society is a threat to the entire body politic. . . .
>
> As teachers, loyal to the country and to the ideal of free inquiry which has sustained our nation's material, humanitarian, and spiritual progress, we cannot fail to condemn any inimical force whether proceeding from an avowed enemy or from a misguided friend within. In doing so we take our guidance from our conscience, from our sense of justice, and from the convictions of one of our Founding Fathers, who declared: "The opinions of men are not the object of civil government, nor under its jurisdiction" and "to suffer the civil magistrate to intrude his powers into the field of opinion and to restrain the profession or propagation of principles on supposition of their ill tendency is a dangerous fallacy." This belief was purchased through centuries of struggle extending far back into history beyond the discovery of the New World, but when enacted into law in the infancy of our nation was greeted in the Old World as "an example of legislative wisdom and liberality never before known." It would be one of the supreme ironies of history and one of the greatest tragedies if the confidence we exhibited in the weakness of youth should be destroyed through fear in the strength of our maturity.

2. The claims of military security

We accept unhesitatingly the application to colleges and universities of needed safeguards against the misuse of specially classified information important for military security, to the extent to which these are applied elsewhere. We insist, however, that these safeguards should extend only to persons who have access to such information; in no degree do they justify the proscription of individuals because of their beliefs or associations, unless these persons were knowingly participants in criminal acts or conspiracies, either in the past or at present. Inquiry into beliefs and associations should be restricted to those that are relevant to the discovery of such actual or threatened offenses.

3. Vigilance against subversion of the educational process

The academic community has a duty to defend society and itself from subversion of the educational process by dishonest tactics, including political conspiracies to deceive students and lead them unwittingly into acceptance of dogmas or false causes. Any member of the academic profession who has given reasonable evidence that he uses such tactics should be proceeded against forthwith, and should be expelled from his position if his guilt is established by rational procedure. Instances of the use of such tactics in the past by secret Communist groups in a few institutions seem to have occurred, and vigilance against the danger of their occurrence in the future is clearly required.

4. Disclaimer oaths and general investigations of college and university teachers

Nothing in the record of college and university teachers as a group justifies the imputation to them of a tendency toward disloyalty to the government or toward subversive intent with respect to the nation's institutions. In this regard they are not different from all other people. We deplore the entire recent tendency to look upon persons or groups suspiciously and to subject their characters and attitudes to special tests as a condition of employing them in responsible positions. This country's greatness is founded upon a belief in the individual's importance and upon a trust in his ability and worthiness to serve his fellow-men in accordance with his capacity. Only by gross misconduct, proved by means of due process, should the right to this trust be lost, and then only to the extent necessary to defend the common interest. The confidence reposed in the individual and in his integrity, and the independence of decision and action granted him, have been vindicated throughout our history by the loyalty of our citizens, and by their willingness to make sacrifices in times of crisis. With infrequent exceptions, even those who have pursued false causes and have seemed at times to threaten the nation's fundamental principles have done so, as history generally recognizes, out of concern for the general welfare as they saw it.

For all these reasons, and because of the unhappy disruption of normal academic work which extreme actions in the name of security entail, as well as because of their evident fruitlessness, we oppose the imposition of disclaimer oaths, whereby individuals are compelled to swear or affirm that they do not advocate or have not advocated, or that they are not or have not been members of any organizations which advocate, overthrow of the government. For similar reasons, we oppose investigations of individuals against whom there is no reasonable suspicion of illegal or unprofessional conduct or of an intent to engage in such conduct. On the same grounds we oppose legislation which imposes upon supervisory officials the duty to certify that members of their staffs are free of subversive taint. We particularly object to these measures when they are directed against members of the academic profession as a special class apart from the population as a whole. Not only is the stigma of such a discrimination unjustified, but the application of these discriminatory measures denies the particular need for freedom from pressures and restrictions, which is a productive requirement of the academic profession and, for similar reasons, of lawmakers, judges, clergymen, journalists, and the members of certain other professions. We urge the academic profession not to be lulled, by the hope of possible non-enforcement or by a merely routine application of these measures, into an acquiescence in their maintenance as "paper" requirements. They should not be tolerated even as relics from which life might appear to have departed; for they would not only be an evil heritage unworthy of our traditions and our goals; their revivification would always be an ugly possibility. They should be steadfastly opposed until they are eliminated. At the same time, we cannot condemn educational institutions or teachers for yielding to the constraint of laws embodying such requirements, even though we regard the laws containing them as pernicious.

5. Grounds of adverse action

Action against a faculty member cannot rightly be taken on grounds that limit his freedom as an individual, as a member of the academic community, or as a teacher and scholar. This principle was defined in the 1940 *Statement of Principles on Academic Freedom and Tenure,* adopted by the Association of American

Colleges and the American Association of University Professors and approved since by other organizations. Implicit in that *Statement* is the proposition (rendered explicit in later reports of committees of the American Association of University Professors and resolutions of its Annual Meetings) that a faculty member's professional fitness to continue in his position, considered in the light of other relevant factors, is the question to be determined when his status as a teacher is challenged. No rule demanding removal for a specific reason not clearly determinative of professional fitness can validly be implemented by an institution, unless the rule is imposed by law or made necessary by the institution's particular religious coloration. Any rule which bases dismissal upon the mere fact of exercise of constitutional rights violates the principles of both academic freedom and academic tenure. By eliminating a decision by a faculty member's peers, it may also deny due process. This principle governs the question of dismissal for avowed past or present membership in the Communist Party taken by itself. Removal can be justified only on the ground, established by evidence, of unfitness to teach because of incompetence, lack of scholarly objectivity or integrity, serious misuse of the classroom or of academic prestige, gross personal misconduct, or conscious participation in conspiracy against the government. The same principle applies, *a fortiori,* to alleged involvement in Communist-inspired activities or views, and to refusal to take a trustee-imposed disclaimer oath.

6. Refusal to testify as ground for removal

It follows that the invocation of the Fifth Amendment by a faculty member under official investigation cannot be in itself a sufficient ground for removing him. The Amendment's protection is a constitutional privilege. The exercise of one's constitutional privilege against self-incrimination does not necessarily or commonly justify an inference of criminal guilt; and even if it were to be ruled otherwise, it would not follow that the loss of an academic position should automatically result from a legal offense, whether proved in court or established by inference, without consideration of the relation of the offense to professional fitness. Invocation of the Fifth Amendment is to be weighed with an individual's other actions in passing a judgment on him. The same may be said with regard to refusals to testify on other grounds, such as the assertion of a right of silence thought to be conferred by the free-speech provision of the First Amendment, or because of a claim of lack of authority in the investigating body, an unwillingness to inform upon other persons, or a reluctance to cooperate in an investigation deemed oppressive or dangerous to the public interest.

7. Grounds for preliminary inquiry by an employing institution

The administrations of colleges and universities should, of course, take note of indications of the possible unfitness of faculty members. If a faculty member invokes the Fifth Amendment when questioned about Communism, or if there are other indications of past or present Communist associations or activities, his institution cannot ignore the possible significance for itself of these matters. There is then a possibility of his involvement in activities subversive of education itself, or otherwise indicative, to an important degree, of his unfitness to teach. As in other instances of possible unfitness, preliminary inquiry into this possibility is warranted and can become a duty. The aid of other faculty members may be sought in such an inquiry; but the inquiry should be confidential in so far as possible, and should not be substituted for the hearing to which the faculty member has a right if formal charges are brought against him. If, after consideration of a faculty member's whole career, as well as the circumstances surrounding his invocation of the Fifth Amendment, probable cause to believe that he may be unfit is not disclosed, the matter should end at this stage; but if probable cause for belief in his unfitness is shown, charges leading to a formal hearing should be brought.

8. Procedural due process in tenure cases

The principles of procedural due process contained in the 1940 *Statement of Principles* are as applicable to instances in which a faculty member's tenure is challenged by his institution or its officials on grounds related to loyalty, national security, or alleged connections with Communism, as they are to instances of challenge on other grounds. Whenever charges are made against a faculty member with a view to his removal, he has a right to a fair hearing, to a judgment by his academic peers before adverse action is taken, and to a decision based on the evidence. The principal elements of due process in such proceedings are set forth in the 1940 *Statement of Principles,* while other procedures, the need for which appears in some of the situations this committee has reviewed, are still to be specified.

There should be adequate faculty participation in any such proceedings, although no particular form of faculty participation or means to assure it is stipulated in the principles as now stated. It is an important safeguard that whatever procedure is used should be one that the faculty of the institution has itself endorsed prior to the occurrence of the case. It is desirable to have procedural matters vested in a standing committee chosen in advance to deal with matters of academic freedom and tenure; *ad hoc* committees may be subject to manipulation or to the suspicion of it. Faculty members should be willing to accept the difficult responsibility of serving on such committees and, when cases are presented, should accept the painful need to reach decisions. On occasion, problems have arisen because faculty committees have defaulted in their responsibility to render unequivocal advice to administrative officers and trustees.

Public hearings before committees with power to recommend or decide are not regarded as desirable. The accused faculty member should be permitted, however, to have persons of his choice present along with counsel; and observers from legitimately interested outside groups, such as the American Association of University Professors, should also be permitted to attend. In accordance with established principles of justice, the burden of proof should rest upon the administrative officer bringing the charge, and should not be placed on the faculty member, whether he is being heard for invoking the Fifth Amendment or for other reasons. Because such hearings are not legal trials but are processes of a more informal sort, and the purpose is to establish clearly the fitness or unfitness of a particular person to teach, the introduction of new issues during the course of the hearings is not inconsistent with due process, provided sufficient opportunity to meet these issues is afforded. The decision should be based solely on evidence disclosed at the hearing.

9. The faculty member's obligation of disclosure

The fact that a faculty member has refused to disclose information to his own institution is relevant to the question of fitness to teach, but not decisive. If the refusal appears to be based upon evasiveness and a desire to withhold evidence of illegal conduct which would disqualify him as a member of the faculty, the refusal would be a weighty adverse factor. On the other hand, a refusal to answer questions which arises from a sincere belief that a teacher is entitled to withhold even from his own institution his political and social views should be accorded respect and should be weighed with other factors in the determination of his fitness to teach. Nevertheless, members of the teaching profession should recognize that sincerity cannot be judged objectively and that a college or university is entitled to know the facts with which it must deal. This is especially true when a faculty member's activities, whether or not they are blameworthy, have resulted in publicity hurtful to his institution. Accordingly, in any proper inquiry by his institution, it is the duty of a faculty member to disclose facts concerning himself that are of legitimate concern to the institution, namely, those that relate to his fitness as a teacher, as enumerated above in the sections, Grounds of Adverse Action, and Grounds for Preliminary Inquiry by an Employing Institution. This obligation diminishes if the institution has announced a rigid policy of dismissal in such a way as to prejudge the case.

We are aware that statements made by a faculty member to his institution are not legally privileged and that his interrogators may be compelled in a later official proceeding to testify that he made them. If such statements tend to incriminate him, he may in effect lose the protection of the Fifth Amendment. But we believe that the institution's right to know facts relevant to fitness to teach should prevail over this consideration.

10. Suspension

Suspension of a faculty member during the time of inquiry and decision by the institution is justified only in certain instances in which the reason for proceeding render it highly probable not only that he is unfit to continue as a faculty member but that his unfitness is of a kind almost certain to prejudice his teaching or research. Even in such instances, the suspension should be with full salary. By his own desire the faculty member may, of course, be temporarily relieved of his duties in order to prepare his defense.

11. Faculty members not on tenure

Academic freedom should be accorded not only to faculty members with tenure but also, during the terms of their appointments, to others with probationary or temporary status who are engaged in teaching or research. Moreover, neither reappointment nor promotion to tenure status should be denied, nor any other adverse action taken, for reasons that violate academic freedom. Dismissal or other adverse action prior to the expiration of a term appointment requires the same procedures as does the dismissal of a faculty member with tenure; but no opportunity for a hearing is normally required in connection with failure to reappoint. If, however, there are reasonable grounds to believe that a nontenure staff member was denied reappointment for reasons that violate academic freedom, there should be a hearing before a faculty committee. In such a hearing the burden of proof is on the persons who assert that there were improper reasons for the failure to reappoint. If a *prima facie* case of violation of academic freedom is made, the administration of the institution is then required to come forward with evidence in rebuttal.

A [1958] Statement of the Committee on Academic Freedom and Tenure Supplementary to the 1956 Report, "Academic Freedom and Tenure in the Quest for National Security"

Recent decisions of the United States Supreme Court, recognizing the validity of legally-based assertions of the right to remain silent under a variety of circumstances, or declaring the invalidity of official action adverse to an individual because of his refusal to yield information about his possible Communist connections, go far to justify the position taken by the Association's Special Committee on these matters in its report, "Academic Freedom and Tenure in the Quest for National Security," which was published in the Spring, 1956, issue of the *AAUP Bulletin* and was approved by the Association's Council and Forty-Second Annual Meeting. Some of these involve situations closely analogous to academic dismissal proceedings.[2]

Several of the reports of investigating committees [not published here] deal with cases in which dismissed faculty members followed their refusals to answer questions before Congressional committees with refusals to make disclosures to representatives of their own institutions, when their previous conduct gave rise to questions. These cases may be visualized as falling into a spectrum extending from a complete refusal to discuss questions dealing with political or social views or associations, to the most complete willingness to answer all such questions even in a formal, open hearing. At one end of the spectrum, that of complete refusal to answer questions of this type on the claim of principle, is found the case of Professor Stanley Moore at Reed College. To this may be added the case of Professor Horace B. Davis at the University of Kansas City, already published in the *AAUP Bulletin* (April, 1957, Supplement) but not yet acted upon by the Association. Farther down the spectrum is the stand of Professor L. R. LaVallee at Dickinson College, who seems to have answered questions relating to previous political associations in certain private conferences but bluntly refused to answer similar questions in his hearing. Two cases fall near the middle of the spectrum. One is the case of Dr. H. Chandler Davis at the University of Michigan, who answered some questions relating to his integrity, but declined to answer questions directed toward his political views. The other is that of Associate Professor Edwin Berry Burgum, at New York University, who in his hearing denied any corrupting influence of his alleged Communist connections, any advocacy of violent overthrow of the government, or any dictation of his views by an outside source; but who nevertheless refused to answer certain other questions regarding his political views and activities, and in particular concerning his

[2] See, in particular, *Slochower* v. *Board of Higher Education,* 350 U. S. 551 (1956); *Watkins* v. *United States,* 354 U. S. 178 (1957); *Sweezy* v. *State of New Hampshire,* 354 U. S. 234 (1957); *Konigsberg* v. *State Bar of California,* 353 U. S. 252 (1957).

possible engagement in recruiting students into the Communist Party. Farther toward the end marked by compliance with questioning is the special case of Professor Alex B. Novikoff, at the University of Vermont. Professor Novikoff answered frankly all questions relating to the period dating from his appointment to the University, but he refused to discuss questions directed at certain associations alleged to have existed in earlier years. Yet ultimately he offered to answer even these questions if his testimony could be made off the record in private instead of public hearing, an offer which the board of hearing did not see fit to accept. Finally, at the extreme of the spectrum, is the case of Associate Professor Mark Nickerson, at the University of Michigan. Professor Nickerson undertook to answer all questions directed to him.

It may be further noted that in the case of Mr. Andries Deinum, at the University of Southern California, no opportunity at all was given him to answer questions or charges or to have a hearing. In the early case of Associate Professor Lyman Bradley, at New York University, there was, on the other hand, a hearing on charges, but refusal to answer, or lack of candor toward college authorities, did not become an issue. These cases may be regarded as extending the two ends of the spectrum into the invisible.

Each report here published expresses the judgment of its authors upon the situation presented, when judged in the light of Association principles still undergoing refinement and application. Committee A has been charged with the function of elaborating those principles on the basis of further thought and of the experience reflected in these reports. It is first desirable to restate pertinent passages from the 1956 Report of the Special Committee, as follows:

> The administrations of colleges and universities should, of course, take note of indications of the possible unfitness of faculty members. If a faculty member invokes the Fifth Amendment when questioned about Communism, or if there are other indications of past or present Communist associations or activities, his institution cannot ignore the possible significance for itself of these matters. There is then a possibility of his involvement in activities subversive of education itself, or otherwise indicative, to an important degree, of his unfitness to teach. As in other in-

stances of possible unfitness, preliminary inquiry into this possibility is warranted and can become a duty. The aid of other faculty members may be sought in such an inquiry; but the inquiry should be confidential in so far as possible, and should not be substituted for the hearing to which the faculty member has a right if formal charges are brought against him. If, after consideration of a faculty member's whole career, as well as the circumstances surrounding his invocation of the Fifth Amendment, probable cause to believe that he may be unfit is not disclosed, the matter should end at this stage; but if probable cause for belief in his unfitness is shown, charges leading to a formal hearing should be brought.

. . . [T]he invocation of the Fifth Amendment by a faculty member under official investigation cannot be in itself a sufficient ground for removing him. The Amendment's protection is a constitutional privilege. The exercise of one's constitutional privilege against self-incrimination does not necessarily or commonly justify an inference of criminal guilt; and even if it were to be ruled otherwise, it would not follow that the loss of an academic position should automatically result from a legal offense, whether proved in court or established by inference, without consideration of the relation of the offense to professional fitness. Invocation of the Fifth Amendment is to be weighed with an individual's other actions in passing a judgment on him. The same may be said with regard to refusals to testify on other grounds, such as the assertion of a right of silence thought to be conferred by the free-speech provision of the First Amendment, or because of a claim of lack of authority in the investigating body, an unwillingness to inform upon other persons, or a reluctance to cooperate in an investigation deemed oppressive or dangerous to the public interest.

The fact that a faculty member has refused to disclose information to his own institution is relevant to the question of fitness to teach, but not decisive. If the refusal appears to be based upon evasiveness and a desire to withhold evidence of illegal conduct which would disqualify him as a member of the faculty, the refusal would be a weighty adverse factor. On the other hand, a refusal to answer questions which arises from a sincere belief that a teacher is entitled to withhold even from his own institution his political and social views should be accorded respect and should be weighed with other factors in the determination of his fitness to teach. Nevertheless, members

> of the teaching profession should recognize that sincerity cannot be judged objectively and that a college or university is entitled to know the facts with which it must deal. This is especially true when a faculty member's activities, whether or not they are blameworthy, have resulted in publicity hurtful to his institution. Accordingly, in any proper inquiry by his institution, it is the duty of a faculty member to disclose facts concerning himself that are of legitimate concern to the institution. . . . This obligation diminishes if the institution has announced a rigid policy of dismissal in such a way as to prejudge the case.
>
> We are aware that statements made by a faculty member to his institution are not legally privileged and that his interrogators may be compelled in a later official proceeding to testify that he made them. If such statements tend to incriminate him, he may in effect lose the protection of the Fifth Amendment. But we believe that the institution's right to know facts relevant to fitness to teach should prevail over this consideration.
>
> . . . Removal can be justified only on the ground, established by evidence, of unfitness to teach because of incompetence, lack of scholarly objectivity or integrity, serious misuse of the classroom or of academic prestige, gross personal misconduct, or conscious participation in conspiracy against the government. The same principle applies, *a fortiori,* to alleged involvement in Communist-inspired activities or views.

II

The most urgent need for elaboration of the principles enunciated in 1956 concerns the relative weight that may properly, in the context of all other pertinent considerations, be given, in reaching a final decision, to the reasons for the faculty member's continued refusal to make disclosures to his own institution. As the 1956 report recognizes, such refusal, in itself, may not be discreditable to the faculty member if it is based on honest adherence to principle—for example, a principle of freedom, or belief in the right of privacy—even if others disagree with his view. This is true even where such silence may follow a refusal on Fifth Amendment or other grounds to testify before a Congressional committee or other governmental agency. On the other hand, the faculty member's continued silence may reflect unfavorably upon him if his purpose is to conceal derogatory information he knows to be pertinent to the question of fitness.

The assertion by a faculty member of the right to withhold from his institution information which is pertinent to his fitness casts upon him the burden of explaining his refusal. Following such an explanation, the responsible tribunal or authorities may find it necessary to determine, as one element in gauging his fitness to continue as a teacher, what his actual reasons for silence are, even though this will not always be an easy determination to make.

Even if the tribunal finds that the faculty member's reasons for silence are discreditable to him, this adverse factor must be judged in the context of all the other available evidence as to his professional fitness, for here, as in all other aspects of dismissal proceedings, the deciding tribunal or authority is always under a duty to reach a just conclusion in the light of the faculty member's full record. The tribunal also has an obligation to state the reasoning that lies back of its decision in a manner that will show the considerations that have affected the decision and how they have been balanced. On his part, the faculty member who persists in silence within his own institution must remember that, although the burden of proof rests on those who are bringing charges against him, his withholding of information sought by his institution may well leave unchallenged other evidence tending to show him unfit. To put it somewhat differently, the institution may properly concern itself with the facts falling within the area of the teacher's silence as they bear upon the issue of his fitness, and arrive at a judgment concerning them.

The faculty member may find himself facing another dilemma. He may run the risk of losing the protection of the Fifth Amendment if he answers questions in a public hearing and on the record, or, conversely, of being misjudged if he remains silent. If, in such straits, he offers to answer privately, and off the record, questions he has previously refused to answer, the tribunal should either accept the offer or recognize that the offer is in itself some evidence of candor and sincerity on the part of the teacher. Such private, off-the-record testimony would not, in this committee's judgment, violate the requirement of the 1940 *Statement of Principles on Academic Freedom and Tenure* that "There should be a full stenographic record of the hearing available to the parties concerned." It is well to remember that a dismissal proceeding is not bound by strict legal rules, and that the aim of the tribunal is to arrive, by all fair means, at the fullest truth relevant to the charges. Off-the-record testimony is properly regarded with suspicion and therefore generally forbidden in academic dismissal proceedings, particularly for witnesses testifying against the accused faculty member. But its limited use for good cause by the faculty member, who enjoys the benefit of the doubt in the proceeding and on whom the duty of candor is being urged, may well enable the tribunal to reach a fair and just decision. In explaining its decision, it may, of course, draw inferences, whether favorable or unfavorable, from such off-the-record testimony, even though the testimony itself may not be disclosed.

If the tribunal refuses to accept an honorable reason offered by a faculty member in justification of his nondisclosure, there being no rational basis in the record for this refusal, and he is then dismissed solely because of this silence, the action is censurable because a sufficient ground for dismissal has not been established. If, on the other hand, a decision to dismiss is found to have been reached fairly and to be supportable on the record when judged by the foregoing considerations, the Association is not entitled to dispute it.

III

Further comment should be made concerning the statement in the 1956 Report that the "obligation [of a faculty member to disclose facts concerning himself that are of legitimate concern to his institution] diminishes if the institution has announced a rigid policy of dismissal in such a way as to prejudge the case." The objection here is not to the fact that an institution may wish to enumerate in a general statement justifiable grounds for the removal of members of its faculty, such as those found in the 1956 Report of the Special Committee, for it is often desirable that conduct deemed to be improper should be defined in advance. Where, however, a rigid policy, in effect predetermining the question of fitness, is based on inadequate grounds, such as invocation of the Fifth Amendment or the simple fact of membership in an organization, the faculty member may be justified in refusing to become party to an intramural form of self-incrimination.

Bentley Glass (Biology), The Johns Hopkins University, *Chairman*

Members: Robert L. Calhoun (Theology), Yale University; Robert K. Carr (Political Science), Dartmouth College and Washington Office; William P. Fidler (English), Washington Office; Ralph F. Fuchs (Law), Indiana University; Charles T. McCormick (Law), University of Texas; Douglas B. Maggs (Constitutional Law), Duke University; Walter P. Metzger (History), Columbia University; Warren C. Middleton (Psychology), Washington Office; Glenn R. Morrow (Philosophy), University of Pennsylvania; George Pope Shannon (English), Washington Office; Warren Taylor (English), Oberlin College; George C. Wheeler (Biology), University of North Dakota; Helen C. White (English), University of Wisconsin, *ex officio.*

1964 Committee A Statement on Extramural Utterances

The Statement which follows was approved by the Association's Committee A on Academic Freedom and Tenure on October 29, 1964. Its purpose is to clarify those sections of the 1940 *Statement of Principles on Academic Freedom and Tenure* relating to the faculty member's exercise of his freedom of speech as a citizen. The Statement emphasizes the essential considerations and procedures when a faculty member's utterances raise grave doubts concerning his fitness for his position.

The 1940 *Statement of Principles* asserts the faculty member's right to speak or write, as citizen, free from institutional censorship or discipline. At the same time it calls attention to the faculty member's special obligations arising from his position in the community: to be accurate, to exercise appropriate restraint, to show respect for the opinions of others, and to make every effort to indicate that he is not an institutional spokesman. An interpretation of the 1940 *Statement,* agreed to at a conference of the AAC and the AAUP held on November 8, 1940, states that an administration may file charges in accordance with procedures outlined in the *Statement* if it feels that a faculty member has failed to observe the above admonitions and believes that his extramural utterances raise grave doubts concerning his fitness for his position.

In cases involving such charges, it is essential that the hearing should be conducted by an appropriate—preferably elected—faculty committee, as provided in Section 4 of the 1958 *Statement on Procedural Standards in Faculty Dismissal Proceedings.*[1] The controlling principle is that a faculty member's expression of opinion as a citizen cannot constitute grounds for dismissal unless it clearly demonstrates the faculty member's unfitness for his position. Extramural utterances rarely bear upon the faculty member's fitness

[1] Section 4 provides:
The committee of faculty members to conduct the hearing and reach a decision should either be an elected standing committee not previously concerned with the case or a committee established as soon as possible after the president's letter to the faculty member has been sent. The choice of members of the hearing committee should be on the basis of their objectivity and competence and of the regard in which they are held in the academic community. The committee should elect its own chairman.

for his position. Moreover, a final decision should take into account the faculty member's entire record as a teacher and scholar. In the absence of weighty evidence of unfitness, the administration should not prefer charges; and if it is not clearly proved in the hearing that the faculty member is unfit for his position, the faculty committee should make a finding in favor of the faculty member concerned.

Committee A asserts that it will view with particular gravity an administrative or board reversal of a favorable faculty committee hearing judgment in a case involving extramural utterances. In the words of the 1940 *Statement of Principles,* "the administration should remember that teachers are citizens and should be accorded the freedom of citizens." In a democratic society freedom of speech is an indispensable right of the citizen. Committee A will vigorously uphold that right.

1967 Joint Statement on Rights and Freedoms of Students

In June, 1967, a joint committee, comprised of representatives from the American Association of University Professors, U.S. National Student Association, Association of American Colleges, National Association of Student Personnel Administrators, and National Association of Women Deans and Counselors, met in Washington, D.C., and drafted the *Joint Statement on Rights and Freedoms of Students.*

Since its formulation, the Joint Statement has been endorsed by each of its five national sponsors, as well as by a number of other professional bodies; AAUP approval was voted by the Council on October 27, 1967, and by the Fifty-Fourth Annual Meeting on April 26, 1968. The endorsers are: U.S. National Student Association; Association of American Colleges; American Association of University Professors; National Association of Student Personnel Administrators; National Association of Women Deans and Counselors; American Association for Higher Education; Jesuit Education Association; American College Personnel Association; Executive Committee, College and University Department, National Catholic Education Association; Commission on Student Personnel, American Association of Junior Colleges.

Preamble

Academic institutions exist for the transmission of knowledge, the pursuit of truth, the development of students, and the general well-being of society. Free inquiry and free expression are indispensable to the attainment of these goals. As members of the academic community, students should be encouraged to develop the capacity for critical judgment and to engage in a sustained and independent search for truth. Institutional procedures for achieving these purposes may vary from campus to campus, but the minimal standards of academic freedom of students outlined below are essential to any community of scholars.

Freedom to teach and freedom to learn are inseparable facets of academic freedom. The freedom to learn depends upon appropriate opportunities and conditions in the classroom, on the campus, and in the larger community. Students should exercise their freedom with responsibility.

The responsibility to secure and to respect general conditions conducive to the freedom to learn is shared by all members of the academic community. Each college and university has a duty to develop policies and procedures which provide and safeguard this freedom. Such policies and procedures should be developed at each institution within the framework of general standards and with the broadest possible participation of the members of the academic community. The purpose of this statement is to enumerate the essential provisions for student freedom to learn.

I. Freedom of access to higher education

The admissions policies of each college and university are a matter of institutional choice provided that each college and university makes clear the characteristics and expectations of students which it considers relevant to success in the institution's program. While church-related institutions may give admission preference to students of their own persuasion, such a preference should be clearly and publicly stated. Under no circumstances should a student be barred from admission to a particular institution on the basis of race. Thus, within the limits of its facilities, each college and university should be open to all students who are qualified according to its admission standards. The facilities and services of a college should be open to all of its enrolled students, and institutions should use their influence to secure equal access for all students to public facilities in the local community.

II. In the classroom

The professor in the classroom and in conference should encourage free discussion, inquiry, and expression. Student performance should be evaluated solely on an academic basis, not on opinions or conduct in matters unrelated to academic standards.

A. Protection of freedom of expression. Students should be free to take reasoned exception to the data or views offered in any course of study and to reserve judgment about matters of opinion, but they are responsible for learning the content of any course of study for which they are enrolled.

B. Protection against improper academic evaluation. Students should have protection through orderly procedures against prejudiced or capricious academic evaluation. At the same time, they are responsible for maintaining standards of academic performance established for each course in which they are enrolled.

C. Protection against improper disclosure. Information about student views, beliefs, and political associations which professors acquire in the course of their work as instructors, advisers, and counselors should be considered confidential. Protection against improper disclosure is a serious professional obligation. Judgments of ability and character may be provided under appropriate circumstances, normally with the knowledge or consent of the student.

III. Student records

Institutions should have a carefully considered policy as to the information which should be part of a student's permanent educational record and as to the conditions of its disclosure. To minimize the risk of improper disclosure, academic and disciplinary records should be separate, and the conditions of access to each should be set forth in an explicit policy statement. Transcripts of academic records should contain only information about academic status. Information from disciplinary or counseling files should not be available to unauthorized persons on campus, or to any person off campus without the express consent of the student involved except under legal compulsion or in cases where the safety of persons or property is involved. No records should be kept which reflect the political activities or beliefs of students. Provisions should also be made for periodic routine destruction of noncurrent disciplinary records. Administrative staff and faculty members should respect confidential information about students which they acquire in the course of their work.

IV. Student affairs

In student affairs, certain standards must be maintained if the freedom of students is to be preserved.

A. Freedom of association. Students bring to the campus a variety of interests previously acquired and develop many new interests as members of the academic community. They should be free to organize and join associations to promote their common interests.

1. The membership, policies, and actions of a student organization usually will be determined by vote of only those persons who

hold bona fide membership in the college or university community.

2. Affiliation with an extramural organization should not of itself disqualify a student organization from institutional recognition.

3. If campus advisers are required, each organization should be free to choose its own adviser, and institutional recognition should not be withheld or withdrawn solely because of the inability of a student organization to secure an adviser. Campus advisers may advise organizations in the exercise of responsibility, but they should not have the authority to control the policy of such organizations.

4. Student organizations may be required to submit a statement of purpose, criteria for membership, rules of procedures, and a current list of officers. They should not be required to submit a membership list as a condition of institutional recognition.

5. Campus organizations, including those affiliated with an extramural organization, should be open to all students without respect to race, creed, or national origin, except for religious qualifications which may be required by organizations whose aims are primarily sectarian.

B. Freedom of inquiry and expression. 1. Students and student organizations should be free to examine and discuss all questions of interest to them, and to express opinions publicly and privately. They should always be free to support causes by orderly means which do not disrupt the regular and essential operation of the institution. At the same time, it should be made clear to the academic and the larger community that in their public expressions or demonstrations students or student organizations speak only for themselves.

2. Students should be allowed to invite and to hear any person of their own choosing. Those routine procedures required by an institution before a guest speaker is invited to appear on campus should be designed only to insure that there is orderly scheduling of facilities and adequate preparation for the event, and that the occasion is conducted in a manner appropriate to an academic community. The institutional control of campus facilities should not be used as a device of censorship. It should be made clear to the academic and the larger community that sponsorship of guest speak-

ers does not necessarily imply approval or endorsement of the views expressed, either by the sponsoring group or the institution.

C. Student participation in institutional government. As constituents of the academic community, students should be free, individually and collectively, to express their views on issues of institutional policy and on matters of general interest to the student body. The student body should have clearly defined means to participate in the formulation and application of institutional policy affecting academic and student affairs. The role of the student government and both its general and specific responsibilities should be made explicit, and the actions of the student government within the areas of its jurisdiction should be reviewed only through orderly and prescribed procedures.

D. Student publications. Student publications and the student press are a valuable aid in establishing and maintaining an atmosphere of free and responsible discussion and of intellectual exploration on the campus. They are a means of bringing student concerns to the attention of the faculty and the institutional authorities and of formulating student opinion on various issues on the campus and in the world at large.

Whenever possible the student newspaper should be an independent corporation financially and legally separate from the university. Where financial and legal autonomy is not possible, the institution, as the publisher of student publications, may have to bear the legal responsibility for the contents of the publications. In the delegation of editorial responsibility to students the institution must provide sufficient editorial freedom and financial autonomy for the student publications to maintain their integrity of purpose as vehicles for free inquiry and free expression in an academic community.

Institutional authorities, in consultation with students and faculty, have a responsibility to provide written clarification of the role of the student publications, the standards to be used in their evaluation, and the limitations on external control of their operation. At the same time, the editorial freedom of student editors and managers entails corollary responsibilities to be governed by the canons of responsible journalism, such as the avoidance of libel, indecency, undocumented allegations, attacks on personal integrity, and the techniques of harassment and innuendo. As safeguards for the editorial freedom of student publications the following provisions are necessary.

1. The student press should be free of censorship and advance approval of copy, and its editors and managers should be free to develop their own editorial policies and news coverage.

2. Editors and managers of student publications should be protected from arbitrary suspension and removal because of student, faculty, administrative, or public disapproval of editorial policy or content. Only for proper and stated causes should editors and managers be subject to removal and then by orderly and prescribed procedures. The agency responsible for the appointment of editors and managers should be the agency responsible for their removal.

3. All university published and financed student publications should explicitly state on the editorial page that the opinions there expressed are not necessarily those of the college, university, or student body.

V. Off-campus freedom of students

A. Exercise of rights of citizenship. College and university students are both citizens and members of the academic community. As citizens, students should enjoy the same freedom of speech, peaceful assembly, and right of petition that other citizens enjoy and, as members of the academic community, they are subject to the obligations which accrue to them by virtue of this membership. Faculty members and administrative officials should insure that institutional powers are not employed to inhibit such intellectual and personal development of students as is often promoted by their exercise of the rights of citizenship both on and off campus.

B. Institutional authority and civil penalties. Activities of students may upon occasion result in violation of law. In such cases, institutional officials should be prepared to apprise students of sources of legal counsel and may offer other assistance. Students who violate the law may incur penalties prescribed by civil authorities, but institutional authority should never be used merely to duplicate the function of general laws. Only where the institution's interests as an academic community are distinct and clearly involved should the special authority of the institution be asserted.

The student who incidentally violates institutional regulations in the course of his off-campus activity, such as those relating to class attendance, should be subject to no greater penalty than would normally be imposed. Institutional action should be independent of community pressure.

VI. Procedural standards in disciplinary proceedings

In developing responsible student conduct, disciplinary proceedings play a role substantially secondary to example, counseling, guidance, and admonition. At the same time, educational institutions have a duty and the corollary disciplinary powers to protect their educational purpose through the setting of standards of scholarship and conduct for the students who attend them and through the regulation of the use of institutional facilities. In the exceptional circumstances when the preferred means fail to resolve problems of student conduct, proper procedural safeguards should be observed to protect the student from the unfair imposition of serious penalties.

The administration of discipline should guarantee procedural fairness to an accused student. Practices in disciplinary cases may vary in formality with the gravity of the offense and the sanctions which may be applied. They should also take into account the presence or absence of an honor code, and the degree to which the institutional officials have direct acquaintance with student life in general and with the involved student and the circumstances of the case in particular. The jurisdictions of faculty or student judicial bodies, the disciplinary responsibilities of institutional officials and the regular disciplinary procedures, including the student's right to appeal a decision, should be clearly formulated and communicated in advance. Minor penalties may be assessed informally under prescribed procedures.

In all situations, procedural fair play requires that the student be informed of the nature of the charges against him, that he be given a fair opportunity to refute them, that the institution not be arbitrary in its actions, and that there be provision for appeal of a decision. The following are recommended as proper safeguards in such proceedings when there are no honor codes offering comparable guarantees.

A. Standards of conduct expected of students. The institution has an obligation to clarify those standards of behavior which it considers essential to its educational mission and its community life. These general behavioral expectations and the resultant specific regulations should represent a reasonable regulation of student conduct, but the student should be as free as possible from imposed limitations that have no direct relevance to his education. Offenses should be as clearly defined as possible and interpreted in a manner consistent with the aforementioned principles of relevancy and reasonableness. Disciplinary proceedings should be instituted only for violations of standards of conduct formulated with significant student participation and published in advance through such means as a student handbook or a generally available body of institutional regulations.

B. Investigation of student conduct. 1. Except under extreme emergency circumstances, premises occupied by students and the personal possessions of students should not be searched unless appropriate authorization has been obtained. For premises such as residence halls controlled by the institution, an appropriate and responsible authority should be designated to whom application should be made before a search is conducted. The application should specify the reasons for the search and the objects or information sought. The student should be present, if possible, during the search. For premises not controlled by the institution, the ordinary requirements for lawful search should be followed.

2. Students detected or arrested in the course of serious violations of institutional regulations, or infractions of ordinary law, should be informed of their rights. No form of harassment should be used by institutional representatives to coerce admissions of guilt or information about conduct of other suspected persons.

C. Status of student pending final action. Pending action on the charges, the status of a student should not be altered, or his right to be present on the campus and to attend classes suspended, except for reasons relating to his physical or emotional safety and well-being, or for reasons relating to the safety and well-being of students, faculty, or university property.

D. Hearing committee procedures. When the misconduct may result in serious penalties and if the student questions the fairness of disciplinary action taken against him, he should be granted, on request, the privilege of a hearing before a regularly constituted hearing committee. The following suggested hearing committee procedures satisfy the requirements of procedural due process in situations requiring a high degree of formality.

1. The hearing committee should include faculty members or students, or, if regularly included or requested by the accused, both faculty and student members. No member of the hearing committee who is otherwise interested in the particular case should sit in judgment during the proceeding.

2. The student should be informed, in writing, of the reasons for the proposed disciplinary action with sufficient particularity, and in sufficient time, to insure opportunity to prepare for the hearing.

3. The student appearing before the hearing committee should have the right to be assisted in his defense by an adviser of his choice.

4. The burden of proof should rest upon the officials bringing the charge.

5. The student should be given an opportunity to testify and to present evidence and witnesses. He should have an opportunity to hear and question adverse witnesses. In no case should the committee consider statements against him unless he has been advised of their content and of the names of those who made them, and unless he has been given an opportunity to rebut unfavorable inferences which might otherwise be drawn.

6. All matters upon which the decision may be based must be introduced into evidence at the proceeding before the hearing committee. The decision should be based solely upon such matters. Improperly acquired evidence should not be admitted.

7. In the absence of a transcript, there should be both a digest and a verbatim record, such as a tape recording, of the hearing.

8. The decision of the hearing committee should be final, subject only to the student's right of appeal to the president or ultimately to the governing board of the institution.

1957 Recommended Institutional Regulations on Academic Freedom and Tenure

In 1957, Committee A approved a statement entitled "Recommended Institutional Regulations on Academic Freedom and Tenure." This statement is now undergoing extensive revision. Four paragraphs assert positions not elsewhere found in documents in this handbook. They are as follows:

5. . . . The nonrenewal of a probationary appointment with less advance notice than that specified in these regulations shall be preceded by a statement of reasons and by opportunity to be heard by the tribunal or tribunals specified in Regulation 6 [which has become the 1958 *Statement on Procedural Standards in Faculty Dismissal Proceedings*.]

8. If a tenure appointment is terminated because of a financial emergency, the released faculty member's place will not be filled by a replacement within a period of two years, unless the released faculty member has been offered reappointment and has declined.

10. If a faculty member on probationary appointment alleges that a decision not to reappoint him is caused by considerations violative of academic freedom, his allegation shall be given preliminary consideration by the following faculty committee: [here designate, or specify the composition of, the committee]. If the committee concludes that there is probable cause for the faculty member's allegation, the matter shall be heard in the manner set forth in Regulation 5, except that the faculty member will be responsible for stating the grounds on which he bases his allegations and the burden of proof will rest upon him.

11. Administrative personnel who hold academic rank are subject to the foregoing regulations in their capacity as faculty members, and shall also have available, with reference to the termination of their appointments as administrators, the rights conferred in Regulation 10.

1958 Statement of Principles on Academic Retirement and Insurance Programs

The 1958 *Statement of Principles on Academic Retirement and Insurance Programs* was approved in that year by the Association of American Colleges, and approved by the Council and endorsed by the Annual Meeting of the American Association of University Professors.

Institutions of higher education are conducted for the common good and not to further the interest of either the individual teacher or administrator, or even of the individual institution. The policy of an institution for the retirement of faculty members and administrators and its plan for their insurance benefits and retirement annuities should be such as to increase the effectiveness of its services as an educational agency. Specifically, this policy and plan should be such as to attract individuals of the highest abilities to educational work, to sustain the morale of the faculty, to permit faculty members with singleness of purpose to devote their energies to serving their institution, and to make it possible in a socially acceptable manner to discontinue the services of members of the faculty when their usefulness is undermined by age.

The following is recommended practice:

1. The retirement policy and annuity plan of an institution, as well as its insurance program, should be clearly defined and be well understood by both the faculty and the administration of the institution.

2. The institution should have a fixed and relatively late retirement age, the same for teachers and administrators. The length of training of college teachers, their longevity and their health generally are such that in the present circumstances the desirable fixed retirement age would appear to be from sixty-seven to seventy.

3. Circumstances that may seem to justify the involuntary retirement of a teacher or administrator before the fixed retirement age should in all cases be considered by a joint faculty-administration committee of the institution. This committee should preferably be a standing committee, but in the consideration of specific cases, no interested person should be permitted to participate in its deliberations. (The above is not meant to indicate that the involuntary

return of an administrator to teaching duties need be regarded as a retirement.)

4. The recall of teachers on retired status should be without tenure and on an annual appointment. Such recall should be used only where the services are clearly needed and where the individual is in good mental and physical health. It may be for part or for full time. Such recall should be rare where the retirement age is as late as 70.

5. The institution should provide for a system of retirement annuities. Such a system should:

(a) Be financed by contributions made during the period of active service by both the individual and the institution.

(b) Be participated in by all full-time faculty members who have attained a certain fixed age, not later than 30.

(c) Be planned to provide in normal circumstances and in so far as possible for a retirement life annuity (including Federal Old Age and Survivors Insurance benefits) equivalent in purchasing power to approximately 50% of the average salary over the last 10 years of service if the retirement is at 70, and a somewhat higher percentage if the fixed retirement age is younger.

(d) Ensure that the full amount of the individual's and the institution's contribution, with the accumulations thereon, be vested in the individual, available as a benefit in case of death while in service, and with no forfeiture in case of withdrawal or dismissal from the institution.

(e) Be such that the individual may not withdraw his equity in cash but only in the form of an annuity. (To avoid administrative expense, exception might be made for very small accumulations in an inactive account.) Except when they are small, death benefits to a widow should be paid in the form of an annuity.

6. When a new retirement policy or annuity plan is initiated or an old one changed, reasonable provision either by special financial arrangements or by the gradual inauguration of the new plan should be made for those adversely affected.

7. It is desirable for the insurance program of an institution to include the following:

(a) Life insurance on a group basis, in addition to survivors' benefits under Federal Old Age and Survivors Insurance.

(b) Insurance for medical expenses, including major medical (catastrophic) insurance.

(c) Disability insurance, covering long-term total disability for any occupation for which the staff member is reasonably fitted, and paying half-salary up to a reasonable maximum during disability before retirement as well as continuing contributions toward a retirement annuity.

1961 Statement on Recruitment and Resignation of Faculty Members

The *Statement on Recruitment and Resignation of Faculty Members* was adopted by the Association of American Colleges in January, 1961, with the following reservations as set forth in a preamble prepared by that Association's Commission on Academic Freedom and Tenure:

> 1. No set of principles adopted by the Association can do more than *suggest* and *recommend* a course of action. Consequently, the present statement in no way interferes with institutional sovereignty.
> 2. The Commission realizes that the diversity of practice and control that exists among institutions of higher learning precludes any set of standards from being *universally* applicable to every situation.
> 3. The statement is concerned only with *minimum* standards and in no way seeks to create a norm for institutions at which "better" practices already are in force.
> 4. The Commission recognizes the fact that "emergency" situations will arise and will have to be dealt with. However, it urges both administration and faculty to do so in ways that will not go counter to the spirit of cooperation, good faith and responsibility that the statement is seeking to promote.
> 5. The Commission believes that the spirit embodied in the proposed statement is its most important aspect.

In view of these reservations, the Council of the American Association of University Professors, in April, 1961, voted approval of the Statement without adopting it as a binding obligation. Endorsement of the Statement in this form was voted by the Forty-Seventh Annual Meeting.

Mobility of faculty members among colleges and universities is rightly recognized as desirable in American higher education. Yet the departure of a faculty member always requires changes within his institution, and may entail major adjustments on the part of his colleagues, the administration, and students in his field.[1] Ordinarily

[1] [*Editor's note.* This statement deals with a teacher's accountability to his institution; breach of the standards here set forth may under certain circumstances warrant public notice. A teacher may also have a further professional responsibility to the educational process, to his colleagues, and to his students; failure to give due recognition to the possibility or fact of such further responsibility may constitute an ethical lapse of a private but nonetheless significant nature.]

a temporary or permanent successor must be found and appointed to either his position or the position of a colleague who is promoted to replace him.

In a period of expansion of higher education, such as that already existing and promising to be even more intensified as a pattern for the coming years, adjustments are required more frequently as the number of positions and of transfers among institutions increases. These become more difficult than at other times, especially in the higher academic ranks. Clear standards of practice in the recruitment and in the resignations of members of existing faculties should contribute to an orderly interchange of personnel that will be in the interest of all.

The standards set forth below are recommended to administrations and faculties, in the belief that they are sound and should be generally followed. They are predicated on the assumption that proper provision has been made by employing institutions for timely notice to probationary faculty members and those on term appointments, with respect to their subsequent status. In addition to observing applicable requirements for notice of termination to probationary faculty members, institutions should make provision for notice to all faculty members not later than March 15 of each year of their status the following fall, including rank and (unless unavoidable budget procedures beyond the institution forbid) prospective salary.

1. Negotiations looking to the possible appointment for the following fall of persons who are already faculty members of other institutions, in active service or on leave-of-absence and not on terminal appointment, should be begun and completed as early as possible in the academic year. It is desirable that, when feasible, the faculty member who has been approached with regard to another position inform the appropriate officers of his institution when such negotiations are in progress. The conclusion of a binding agreement for the faculty member to accept an appointment elsewhere should always be followed by prompt notice to his institution.

2. A faculty member should not resign in order to accept other employment as of the end of the academic year, later than May 15 or 30 days after receiving notification of the terms of his continued

employment the following year, whichever date occurs later. It is recognized, however, that this obligation will be in effect only if institutions generally observe the time factor set forth in the following paragraph for new offers. It is also recognized that emergencies will occur. In such an emergency the faculty member may ask the appropriate officials of his institution to waive this requirement; but he should conform to their decision.

3. To permit a faculty member to give due consideration and timely notice to his institution in the circumstances defined in paragraph 1 of these standards, an offer of appointment for the following fall at another institution should not be made after May 1. The offer should be a "firm" one, not subject to contingencies.

4. Institutions deprived of the services of faculty members too late in the academic year to permit their replacement by securing the members of other faculties in conformity to these standards, and institutions otherwise prevented from taking timely action to recruit from other faculties, should accept the necessity of making temporary arrangements or obtaining personnel from other sources, including new entrants to the academic profession and faculty personnel who have retired.

5. Except by agreement with his institution, a faculty member should not leave or be solicited to leave his position during an academic year for which he holds an appointment.

1964 Statement on Preventing Conflicts of Interest in Government-Sponsored Research at Universities

A joint statement of the Council of the American Association of University Professors and the American Council on Education.

The increasingly necessary and complex relationships among universities, Government, and industry call for more intensive attention to standards of procedure and conduct in Government-sponsored research. The clarification and application of such standards must be designed to serve the purposes and needs of the projects and the public interest involved in them and to protect the integrity of the cooperating institutions as agencies of higher education.

The Government and institutions of higher education, as the contracting parties, have an obligation to see that adequate standards and procedures are developed and applied; to inform one another of their respective requirements; and to assure that all individuals participating in their respective behalfs are informed of and apply the standards and procedures that are so developed.

Consulting relationships between university staff members and industry serve the interests of research and education in the university. Likewise, the transfer of technical knowledge and skill from the university to industry contributes to technological advance. Such relationships are desirable, but certain potential hazards should be recognized.

A. Conflict situations

1. Favoring of outside interests. When a university staff member (administrator, faculty member, professional staff member, or employee) undertaking or engaging in Government-sponsored work has a significant financial interest in, or a consulting arrangement with, a private business concern, it is important to avoid actual or apparent conflicts of interest between his Government-sponsored university research obligations and his outside interests and other obligations. Situations in or from which conflicts of interest may arise are the:

a. Undertaking or orientation of the staff member's university research to serve the research or other needs of the private firm without disclosure of such undertaking or orientation to the university and to the sponsoring agency;

b. Purchase of major equipment, instruments, materials, or other items for university research from the private firm in which the staff member has the interest without disclosure of such interest;

c. Transmission to the private firm or other use for personal gain of Government-sponsored work products, results, materials, records, or information that are not made generally available. (This would not necessarily preclude appropriate licensing arrangements for inventions, or consulting on the basis of Government-sponsored research results where there is significant additional work by the staff member independent of his Government-sponsored research);

d. Use for personal gain or other unauthorized use of privileged information acquired in connection with the staff member's Government-sponsored activities. (The term "privileged information" includes, but is not limited to, medical, personnel, or security records of individuals; anticipated material requirements or price actions; possible new sites for Government operations; and knowledge of forthcoming programs or of selection of contractors or subcontractors in advance of official announcements);

e. Negotiation or influence upon the negotiation of contracts relating to the staff member's Government-sponsored research between the university and private organizations with which he has consulting or other significant relationships;

f. Acceptance of gratuities or special favors from private organizations with which the university does or may conduct business in connection with a Government-sponsored research project, or extension of gratuities or special favors to employees of the sponsoring Government agency, under circumstances which might reasonably be interpreted as an attempt to influence the recipients in the conduct of their duties.

2. *Distribution of effort.* There are competing demands on the energies of a faculty member (for example, research, teaching, committee work, outside consulting). The way in which he divides his effort among these various functions does not raise ethical questions unless the Government agency supporting his research is

misled in its understanding of the amount of intellectual effort he is actually devoting to the research in question. A system of precise time accounting is incompatible with the inherent character of the work of a faculty member, since the various functions he performs are closely interrelated and do not conform to any meaningful division of a standard work week. On the other hand, if the research agreement contemplates that a staff member will devote a certain fraction of his effort to the Government-sponsored research, or he agrees to assume responsibility in relation to such research, a demonstrable relationship between the indicated effort or responsibility and the actual extent of his involvement is to be expected. Each university, therefore, should—through joint consultation of administration and faculty—develop procedures to assure that proposals are responsibly made and complied with.

3. Consulting for Government agencies or their contractors. When the staff member engaged in Government-sponsored research also serves as a consultant to a Federal agency, his conduct is subject to the provisions of the Conflict of Interest Statutes (18 U.S.C. 202–209 as amended) and the President's memorandum of May 2, 1963, *Preventing Conflicts of Interest on the Part of Special Government Employees.* When he consults with one or more Government contractors, or prospective contractors, in the same technical field as his research project, care must be taken to avoid giving advice that may be of questionable objectivity because of its possible bearing on his other interests. In undertaking and performing consulting services, he should make full disclosure of such interests to the university and to the contractor insofar as they may appear to relate to the work at the university or for the contractor. Conflict of interest problems could arise, for example, in the participation of a staff member of the university in an evaluation for the Government agency or its contractor of some technical aspect of the work of another organization with which he has a consulting or employment relationship or a significant financial interest, or in an evaluation of a competitor to such other organization.

B. University responsibility

Each university participating in Government-sponsored research should make known to the sponsoring Government agencies:

1. The steps it is taking to assure an understanding on the part of the university administration and staff members of the possible conflicts or interest or other problems that may develop in the foregoing types of situations, and

2. The organizational and administrative actions it has taken or is taking to avoid such problems, including:

a. Accounting procedures to be used to assure that Government funds are expended for the purposes for which they have been provided, and that all services which are required in return for these funds are supplied;

b. Procedures that enable it to be aware of the outside professional work of staff members participating in Government-sponsored research, if such outside work relates in any way to the Government-sponsored research;

c. The formulation of standards to guide the individual university staff members in governing their conduct in relation to outside interests that might raise questions of conflicts of interest; and

d. The provision within the university of an informed source of advice and guidance to its staff members for advance consultation on questions they wish to raise concerning the problems that may or do develop as a result of their outside financial or consulting interests, as they relate to their participation in Government-sponsored university research. The university may wish to discuss such problems with the contracting officer or other appropriate Government official in those cases that appear to raise questions regarding conflicts of interest.

The above process of disclosure and consultation is the obligation assumed by the university when it accepts Government funds for research. The process must, of course, be carried out in a manner that does not infringe on the legitimate freedoms and flexibility of action of the university and its staff members that have traditionally characterized a university. It is desirable that standards and procedures of the kind discussed be formulated and administered by members of the university community themselves, through their joint initiative and responsibility, for it is they who are the best judges of the conditions which can most effectively stimulate the search for knowledge and preserve the requirements of academic freedom. Experience indicates that such standards and procedures should be developed and specified by joint administrative-faculty action.

1966 Statement on Professional Ethics

In March, 1965, Committee B distributed a draft of a Statement on Professional Ethics to all Association chapters and conferences for their criticism. The Statement was also published in the Summer, 1965, *Bulletin,* with a request for individual comments.

In October, 1965, the Committee reported to the Council on the membership response to the Statement, and received guidance and instructions to proceed to another draft. It met in December, 1965, and in light of both Council and membership reaction produced a new draft, which was then submitted to the members of the Council for a preliminary response. A third draft was then printed in the Spring, 1966, *Bulletin,* and again membership reaction was solicited.

In April, 1966, the Council approved the following Statement on Professional Ethics, and later that same month the Fifty-Second Annual Meeting at Atlanta adopted the Statement as Association policy.

The members of Committee B who prepared the following statement are: William H. McPherson (Labor and Industrial Relations, University of Illinois), *Chairman,* David M. Bevington (English, University of Virginia), John A. Christie (English, Vassar College), Philip Denenfeld (English, Washington Office), Kenneth E. Eble (English, University of Utah), Joseph M. Nygaard (Education, Butler University), Henry T. Yost (Biology, Amherst College).

Introduction

From its inception, the American Association of University Professors has recognized that membership in the academic profession carries with it special responsibilities. The Association has consistently affirmed these responsibilities in major policy statements, providing guidance to the professor in his utterances as a citizen, in the exercise of his responsibilities to students, and in his conduct when resigning from his institution or when undertaking Government-sponsored research.[1] The Statement on Professional Ethics that follows, necessarily presented in terms of the ideal, sets forth those general standards that serve as a reminder of the vari-

[1] 1964 *Committee A Statement on Extra-Mural Utterances* (Clarification of sec. 1c of the 1940 *Statement of Principles on Academic Freedom and Tenure)*

1966 *Proposed Statement on the Academic Freedom of Students*

1961 *Statement on Recruitment and Resignation of Faculty Members*

1964 *On Preventing Conflicts of Interest in Government-Sponsored Research*

ety of obligations assumed by all members of the profession. For the purpose of more detailed guidance, the Association, through its Committee B on Professional Ethics, intends to issue from time to time supplemental statements on specific problems.

In the enforcement of ethical standards, the academic profession differs from those of law and medicine, whose associations act to assure the integrity of members engaged in private practice. In the academic profession the individual institution of higher learning provides this assurance and so should normally handle questions concerning propriety of conduct within its own framework by reference to a faculty group. The Association supports such local action and stands ready, through the General Secretary and Committee B, to counsel with any faculty member or administrator concerning questions of professional ethics and to inquire into complaints when local consideration is impossible or inappropriate. If the alleged offense is deemed sufficiently serious to raise the possibility of dismissal, the procedures should be in accordance with the 1940 *Statement of Principles on Academic Freedom and Tenure* and the 1958 *Statement on Procedural Standards in Faculty Dismissal Proceedings.*

The statement

I. The professor, guided by a deep conviction of the worth and dignity of the advancement of knowledge, recognizes the special responsibilities placed upon him. His primary responsibility to his subject is to seek and to state the truth as he sees it. To this end he devotes his energies to developing and improving his scholarly competence. He acccepts the obligation to exercise critical self-discipline and judgment in using, extending, and transmitting knowledge. He practices intellectual honesty. Although he may follow subsidiary interests, these interests must never seriously hamper or compromise his freedom of inquiry.

II. As a teacher, the professor encourages the free pursuit of learning in his students. He holds before them the best scholarly standards of his discipline. He demonstrates respect for the student as an individual, and adheres to his proper role as intellectual guide and counselor. He makes every reasonable effort to foster honest academic conduct and to assure that his evaluation of students reflects their true merit. He respects the confidential nature of the relationship between professor and student. He avoids any exploitation of students for his private advantage and acknowledges significant assistance from them. He protects their academic freedom.

III. As a colleague, the professor has obligations that derive from common membership in the community of scholars. He respects and defends the free inquiry of his associates. In the exchange of criticism and ideas he shows due respect for the opinions of others. He acknowledges his academic debts and strives to be objective in his professional judgment of colleagues. He accepts his share of faculty responsibilities for the governance of his institution.

IV. As a member of his institution, the professor seeks above all to be an effective teacher and scholar. Although he observes the stated regulations of the institution, provided they do not contravene academic freedom, he maintains his right to criticize and seek revision. He determines the amount and character of the work he does outside his institution with due regard to his paramount responsibilities within it. When considering the interruption or termination of his service, he recognizes the effect of his decision upon the program of the institution and gives due notice of his intentions.

V. As a member of his community, the professor has the rights and obligations of any citizen. He measures the urgency of these obligations in the light of his responsibilities to his subject, to his students, to his profession, and to his institution. When he speaks or acts as a private person he avoids creating the impression that he speaks or acts for his college or university. As a citizen engaged in a profession that depends upon freedom for its health and integrity, the professor has a particular obligation to promote conditions of free inquiry and to further public understanding of academic freedom.

1966 Statement on Government of Colleges and Universities

Jointly formulated and issued by the American Association of University Professors, the American Council on Education, and the Association of Governing Boards of Universities and Colleges.

Committee T on College and University Government began in 1959 the preparation of a statement on "Faculty Participation in College and University Government"; in 1962 a draft placed before the Council was approved, and there was a minor addition in 1963.

In 1964 the American Council on Education expressed interest in a joint effort to draft a statement which would embrace the roles of the governing board and the administration, as well as that of the faculty. Later in 1964 the Association of Governing Boards of Universities and Colleges indicated a similar interest. These concerns bore fruit in the 1966 Statement which follows.

Professor Ferrel M. Heady was chairman of Committee T from 1958 to 1961; Professor John P. Dawson was chairman from 1961 to 1964; Professor Ralph S. Brown, Jr. (Law, Yale University) became chairman in 1964. Other members of Committee T at the time of adoption of the 1966 Statement were: Robert Bierstedt (Sociology, New York University), Eugene K. Chamberlin (History, San Diego City College), Warren J. Gates (History, Dickinson College), Forest G. Hill (Economics, University of Texas), Jacob D. Hyman (Law, State University of New York at Buffalo), Louis Joughin (History, Washington Office), William N. Leonard (Economics, Hofstra University), Herman Meyer (Mathematics, University of Miami), Otway Pardee (Mathematics, Syracuse University), Henry H. H. Remak (German, Indiana University), and Henry R. Winkler (History, Rutgers, The State University). Two other persons served on Committee T during the entire drafting period, although their terms expired before Council action: Professors Margaret P. Boddy (English, Winona State College) and Valerie A. Earle (Government, Georgetown University).

Editorial Note. The Statement which follows is directed to governing board members, administrators, faculty members, students, and other persons in the belief that the colleges and universities of the United States have reached a stage calling for appropriately shared responsibility and cooperative action among the components of the academic institution. The Statement is intended to foster constructive joint thought and action, both within the institutional structure and in protection of its integrity against improper intrusions.

It is not intended that the Statement serve as a blueprint for government on a specific campus or as a manual for the regulation of controversy among the components of an academic institution, although it is to be hoped that the principles asserted will lead to the correction of existing weaknesses and assist in the establishment of sound structure and procedures. The Statement does not attempt to cover relations with those outside agencies which increasingly are controlling the resources and influencing the patterns of education in our institutions of higher learning; e.g., the United States Government, the state legislatures, state commissions, interstate associations or compacts, and other inter-institutional arrangements. However, it is hoped that the Statement will be helpful to these agencies in their consideration of educational matters.

Students are referred to in this Statement as an institutional component coordinate in importance with trustees, administrators, and faculty. There is, however, no main section on students. The omission has two causes: (1) the changes now occurring in the status of American students have plainly outdistanced the analysis by the educational community, and an attempt to define the situation without thorough study might prove unfair to student interests[1] *and (2) students do not in fact presently have a significant voice in the government of colleges and universities; it would be unseemly to obscure, by superficial equality of length of statement, what may be a serious lag entitled to separate and full confrontation. The concern for student status felt by the organizations issuing this Statement is embodied in a note "On Student Status" intended to stimulate the educational community to turn its attention to an important need.*

This Statement, in preparation since 1964, is jointly formulated by the American Association of University Professors, the American Council on Education, and the Association of Governing Boards of Universities and Colleges. On October 12, 1966, the Board of Directors of the ACE took action by which the Council "recognizes the Statement as a significant step forward in the clarification of the respective roles of governing boards, faculties, and administrations," and "commends it to the institutions which are members of the Council." On October 29, 1966, the Council of the AAUP approved the Statement, recommended approval by the Fifty-Third Annual Meeting in April, 1967 [and this approval took place], and recognized that "continuing joint effort is desirable, in view of the areas left open in the jointly formulated Statement, and the dynamic changes occurring in higher education." On November 18, 1966, the Executive Committee of the AGB

[1] Note: 1950, the formulation of the *Student Bill of Rights* by the United States National Student Association; 1956, the first appearance of *Academic Freedom and Civil Liberties of Students,* published by the American Civil Liberties Union; 1961, the decision in *Dixon* v. *Alabama State Board of Education,* currently the leading case on due process for students; 1965, the publication of a tentative *Statement on the Academic Freedom of Students,* by the American Association of University Professors.

took action by which that organization also "recognizes the Statement as a significant step forward in the clarification of the respective roles of governing boards, faculties and administrations," and "commends it to the governing boards which are members of the Association."

I. Introduction

This Statement is a call to mutual understanding regarding the government of colleges and universities. Understanding, based on community of interest, and producing joint effort, is essential for at least three reasons. First, the academic institution, public or private, often has become less autonomous; buildings, research, and student tuition are supported by funds over which the college or university exercises a diminishing control. Legislative and executive governmental authority, at all levels, plays a part in the making of important decisions in academic policy. If these voices and forces are to be successfully heard and integrated, the academic institution must be in a position to meet them with its own generally unified view. Second, regard for the welfare of the institution remains important despite the mobility and interchange of scholars. Third, a college or university in which all the components are aware of their interdependence, of the usefulness of communication among themselves, and of the force of joint action will enjoy increased capacity to solve educational problems.

II. The academic institution: joint effort

A. Preliminary considerations. The variety and complexity of the tasks performed by institutions of higher education produce an inescapable interdependence among governing board, administration, faculty, students, and others. The relationship calls for adequate communication among these components, and full opportunity for appropriate joint planning and effort.

Joint effort in an academic institution will take a variety of forms appropriate to the kinds of situations encountered. In some instances, an initial exploration or recommendation will be made by the president with consideration by the faculty at a later stage; in other instances, a first and essentially definitive recommendation will be made by the faculty, subject to the endorsement of the president and the governing board. In still others, a substantive contribution can be made when student leaders are responsibly involved in the process. Although the variety of such approaches may be wide, at least two general conclusions regarding joint effort seem clearly warranted: (1) important areas of action involve at one time or another the initiating capacity and decision-making participation of all the institutional components, and (2) differences in the weight of each voice, from one point to the next, should be determined by reference to the responsibility of each component for the particular matter at hand, as developed hereinafter.

B. Determination of general educational policy. The general educational policy, i.e., the objectives of an institution and the nature, range, and pace of its efforts, is shaped by the institutional charter or by law, by tradition and historical development, by the present needs of the community of the institution, and by the professional aspirations and standards of those directly involved in its work. Every board will wish to go beyond its formal trustee obligation to conserve the accomplishment of the past and to engage seriously with the future; every faculty will seek to conduct an operation worthy of scholarly standards of learning; every administrative officer will strive to meet his charge and to attain the goals of the institution. The interests of all are coordinate and related, and unilateral effort can lead to confusion or conflict. Essential to a solution is a reasonably explicit statement on general educational policy. Operating responsibility and authority, and procedures for continuing review, should be clearly defined in official regulations.

When an educational goal has been established, it becomes the responsibility primarily of the faculty to determine appropriate curriculum and procedures of student instruction.

Special considerations may require particular accommodations: (1) a publicly supported institution may be regulated by statutory provisions, and (2) a church-controlled institution may be limited by its charter or bylaws. When such external requirements influence course content and manner of instruction or research, they impair the educational effectiveness of the institution.

Such matters as major changes in the size or composition of the student body and the relative emphasis to be given to the various elements of the educational and research program should involve participation of governing board, administration and faculty prior to final decision.

C. Internal operations of the institution. The framing and execution of long-range plans, one of the most important aspects of institutional responsibility, should be a central and continuing concern in the academic community.

Effective planning demands that the broadest possible exchange of information and opinion should be the rule for communication among the components of a college or university. The channels of communication should be established and maintained by joint endeavor. Distinction should be observed between the institutional system of communication and the system of responsibility for the making of decisions.

A second area calling for joint effort in internal operations is that of decisions regarding existing or prospective physical resources. The board, president, and faculty should all seek agreement on basic decisions regarding buildings and other facilities to be used in the educational work of the institution.

A third area is budgeting. The allocation of resources among competing demands is central in the formal responsibility of the governing board, in the administrative authority of the president, and in the educational function of the faculty. Each component should therefore have a voice in the determination of short and long-range priorities, and each should receive appropriate analyses of past budgetary experience, reports on current budgets and expenditures, and short and long-range budgetary projections. The function of each component in budgetary matters should be understood by all; the allocation of authority will determine the flow of information and the scope of participation in decisions.

Joint effort of a most critical kind must be taken when an institution chooses a new president. The selection of a chief administrative officer should follow upon cooperative search by the governing board and the faculty, taking into consideration the opinions of others who are appropriately interested. The president should be equally qualified to serve both as the executive officer of the governing board and as the chief academic officer of the institution and the faculty. His dual role requires that he be able to interpret to board and faculty the educational views and concepts on institutional government of the other. He should have the confidence of the board and the faculty.

The selection of academic deans and other chief academic officers should be the responsibility of the president with the advice of and in consultation with the appropriate faculty.

Determinations of faculty status, normally based on the recommendations of the faculty groups involved, are discussed in Part V of this Statement; but it should here be noted that the building of a strong faculty requires careful joint effort in such actions as staff selection and promotion and the granting of tenure. Joint action should also govern dismissals; the applicable principles and procedures in these matters are well established.[2]

D. External relations of the institution. Anyone—a member of the governing board, the president or other member of the administration, a member of the faculty, or a member of the student body or the alumni—affects the institution when he speaks of it in public. An individual who speaks unofficially should so indicate. An official spokesman for the institution, the board, the administration, the faculty, or the student body should be guided by established policy.

It should be noted that only the board speaks legally for the whole institution, although it may delegate responsibility to an agent.

The right of a board member, an administrative officer, a faculty member, or a student to speak on general educational questions or about the administration and operations of his own institution is a part of his right as a citizen and should not be abridged by the institution.[3] There exist, of course, legal bounds relating to defamation of character, and there are questions of propriety.

[2] See the 1940 *Statement of Principles on Academic Freedom and Tenure* and the 1958 *Statement on Procedural Standards in Faculty Dismissal Proceedings.* These statements have been jointly approved or adopted by the Association of American Colleges and the American Association of University Professors; the 1940 *Statement* has been endorsed by numerous learned and scientific societies and educational associations.

[3] With respect to faculty members, the 1940 *Statement of Principles on Academic Freedom and Tenure* reads: "The college or university teacher is a citizen, a member of a learned profession, and an officer of an educational institution. When he speaks or writes as a citizen, he should be free from institutional censorship or discipline, but his special position in the community imposes special obligations. As a man of learning and an edu-

III. The academic institution: the governing board

The governing board has a special obligation to assure that the history of the college or university shall serve as a prelude and inspiration to the future. The board helps relate the institution to its chief community: e.g., the community college to serve the educational needs of a defined population area or group, the church-controlled college to be cognizant of the announced position of its denomination, and the comprehensive university to discharge the many duties and to accept the appropriate new challenges which are its concern at the several levels of higher education.

The governing board of an institution of higher education in the United States operates, with few exceptions, as the final institutional authority. Private institutions are established by charters; public institutions are established by constitutional or statutory provisions. In private institutions the board is frequently self-perpetuating; in public colleges and universities the present membership of a board may be asked to suggest candidates for appointment. As a whole and individually when the governing board confronts the problem of succession, serious attention should be given to obtaining properly qualified persons. Where public law calls for election of governing board members, means should be found to insure the nomination of fully suited persons, and the electorate should be informed of the relevant criteria for board membership.

Since the membership of the board may embrace both individual and collective competence of recognized weight, its advice or help may be sought through established channels by other components of the academic community. The governing board of an institution of higher education, while maintaining a general overview, entrusts the conduct of administration to the administrative officers, the president and the deans, and the conduct of teaching and research to the faculty. The board should undertake appropriate self-limitation.

---

cational officer, he should remember that the public may judge his profession and his institution by his utterances. Hence he should at all times be accurate, should exercise appropriate restraint, should show respect for the opinion of others, and should make every effort to indicate that he is not an institutional spokesman."

One of the governing board's important tasks is to ensure the publication of codified statements that define the overall policies and procedures of the institution under its jurisdiction.

The board plays a central role in relating the likely needs of the future to predictable resources; it has the responsibility for husbanding the endowment; it is responsible for obtaining needed capital and operating funds; and in the broadest sense of the term it should pay attention to personnel policy. In order to fulfill these duties, the board should be aided by, and may insist upon, the development of long-range planning by the administration and faculty.

When ignorance or ill-will threatens the institution or any part of it, the governing board must be available for support. In grave crises it will be expected to serve as a champion. Although the action to be taken by it will usually be on behalf of the president, the faculty, or the student body, the board should make clear that the protection it offers to an individual or a group is, in fact, a fundamental defense of the vested interests of society in the educational institution.

IV. The academic institution: the president

The president, as the chief executive officer of an institution of higher education, is measured largely by his capacity for institutional leadership. He shares responsibility for the definition and attainment of goals, for administrative action, and for operating the communications system which links the components of the academic community. He represents his institution to its many publics. His leadership role is supported by delegated authority from the board and faculty.

As the chief planning officer of an institution, the president has a special obligation to innovate and initiate. The degree to which a president can envision new horizons for his institution, and can persuade others to see them and to work toward them, will often constitute the chief measure of his administration.

The president must at times, with or without support, infuse new life into a department; relatedly, he may at times be required, working within the concept of tenure, to solve problems of obsolescence. The president will necessarily utilize the judgments of the faculty, but in the interest of academic standards he may also seek outside evaluations by scholars of acknowledged competence.

It is the duty of the president to see to it that the standards and procedures in operational use within the college or university conform to the policy established by the governing board and to the standards of sound academic practice. It is also incumbent on the president to insure that faculty views, including dissenting views, are presented to the board in those areas and on those issues where responsibilities are shared. Similarly the faculty should be informed of the views of the board and the administration on like issues.

The president is largely responsible for the maintenance of existing institutional resources and the creation of new resources; he has ultimate managerial responsibility for a large area of nonacademic activities, he is responsible for public understanding, and by the nature of his office is the chief spokesman of his institution. In these and other areas his work is to plan, to organize, to direct, and to represent. The presidential function should receive the general support of board and faculty.

V. The academic institution: the faculty

The faculty has primary responsibility for such fundamental areas as curriculum, subject matter and methods of instruction, research, faculty status, and those aspects of student life which relate to the educational process. On these matters the power of review or final decision lodged in the governing board or delegated by it to the president should be exercised adversely only in exceptional circumstances, and for reasons communicated to the faculty. It is desirable that the faculty should, following such communication, have opportunity for further consideration and further transmittal of its views to the president or board. Budgets, manpower limitations, the time element and the policies of other groups, bodies, and agencies having jurisdiction over the institution may set limits to realization of faculty advice.

The faculty sets the requirements for the degrees offered in course, determines when the requirements have been met, and authorizes the president and board to grant the degrees thus achieved.

Faculty status and related matters are primarily a faculty responsibility; this area includes appointments, reappointments, decisions not to reappoint, promotions, the granting of tenure, and dismissal. The primary responsibility of the faculty for such matters is based upon the fact that its judgment is central to general educational policy. Furthermore, scholars in a particular field or activity have the chief competence for judging the work of their colleagues; in such competence it is implicit that responsibility exists for both adverse and favorable judgments. Likewise there is the more general competence of experienced faculty personnel committees having a broader charge. Determinations in these matters should first be by faculty action through established procedures, reviewed by the chief academic officers with the concurrence of the board. The governing board and president should, on questions of faculty status, as in other matters where the faculty has primary responsibility, concur with the faculty judgment except in rare instances and for compelling reasons which should be stated in detail.

The faculty should actively participate in the determination of policies and procedures governing salary increases.

The chairman or head of a department, who serves as the chief representative of his department within an institution, should be selected either by departmental election or by appointment following consultation with members of the department and of related departments; appointments should normally be in conformity with department members' judgment. The chairman or department head should not have tenure in his office; his tenure as a faculty member is a matter of separate right. He should serve for a stated term but without prejudice to re-election or to reappointment by procedures which involve appropriate faculty consultation. Board, administration, and faculty should all bear in mind that the department chairman has a special obligation to build a department strong in scholarship and teaching capacity.

Agencies for faculty participation in the government of the college or university should be established at each level where faculty responsibility is present. An agency should exist for the presentation of the views of the whole faculty. The structure and procedures for faculty participation should be designed, approved and established by joint action of the components of the institution.

Faculty representatives should be selected by the faculty according to procedures determined by the faculty.

The agencies may consist of meetings of all faculty members of a department, school, college, division or university system, or may take the form of faculty-elected executive committees in departments and schools and a faculty-elected senate or council for larger divisions or the institution as a whole.

Among the means of communication among the faculty, administration, and governing board now in use are: (1) circulation of memoranda and reports by board committees, the administration, and faculty committees, (2) joint *ad hoc* committees, (3) standing liaison committees, (4) membership of faculty members on administrative bodies, and (5) membership of faculty members on governing boards. Whatever the channels of communication, they should be clearly understood and observed.

On student status

When students in American colleges and universities desire to participate responsibly in the government of the institution they attend, their wish should be recognized as a claim to opportunity both for educational experience and for involvement in the affairs of their college or university. Ways should be found to permit significant student participation within the limits of attainable effectiveness. The obstacles to such participation are large and should not be minimized: inexperience, untested capacity, a transitory status which means that present action does not carry with it subsequent responsibility, and the inescapable fact that the other components of the institution are in a position of judgment over the students. It is important to recognize that student needs are strongly related to educational experience, both formal and informal. Students expect, and have a right to expect, that the educational process will be structured, that they will be stimulated by it to become independent adults, and that they will have effectively transmitted to them the cultural heritage of the larger society. If institutional support is to have its fullest possible meaning it should incorporate the strength, freshness of view and idealism of the student body.

The respect of students for their college or university can be enhanced if they are given at least these opportunities: (1) to be listened to in the classroom without fear of institutional reprisal for the substance of their views, (2) freedom to discuss questions of institutional policy and operation, (3) the right to academic due process when charged with serious violations of institutional regulations, and (4) the same right to hear speakers of their own choice as is enjoyed by other components of the institution.

PART THREE. PRACTICES

A number of Association statements, especially those directed toward specific problems, indicate the way in which policy has been applied in practice. Although these statements have not been adopted as defined policy, they are important both in themselves and in their continuing influence, and belong in this handbook. This group of statements includes resolutions of the Annual Meeting and advisory letters which have been published. Because practice is reflected in case action, a list of Association reports is included. Each year's issues of the *AAUP Bulletin* of course contribute new material for the record of "practices."

Chapter V Resolutions of the Annual Meetings

Annual meetings of the Association have passed resolutions on a number of matters relating to academic freedom and tenure; those having permanent or current force are here presented.

A. CENSORSHIP OF TEXTBOOKS

[*AAUP Bulletin,* 38:100–101 (Spring, 1952)]

Aware of a widespread and apparently growing tendency toward the censorship of textbooks by individuals and groups outside the profession of education; convinced that in many cases adverse judgments are made on the basis of slight acquaintance with the subject-matter, superficial examination of books, or passages quoted out of context, and that, in some instances, condemnation represents merely the reaction of an individual or group whose interests or prejudices are offended by the treatment of a particular topic; aware, also, that there exist organized groups which are engaged in a systematic attempt to arouse the public against the textbooks which these groups view with disfavor and to force teachers, administrators, and educational boards to adopt books favorable to their views;

Believing that the welfare of our country requires that present and future citizens be given accurate information and well-considered conclusions on all subjects, as determined by competent investigators and thinkers in accordance with tested procedures of science and scholarship; believing that the continuous discovery and evaluation of facts, the continuous reformulation of judgments, and the presentation of the results of these processes, which is the function of education, are hampered by censorship, whether deliberately partisan or merely irresponsible; believing that censorship does the greatest harm at the higher levels of education, which are more directly concerned with the discovery and presentation of new truth; and believing, finally, that the competence and integrity of the academic profession guarantee the prompt discovery, exposure, and displacement of erroneous or biased presentations, with no need for outside assistance;

This, the Thirty-Eighth Annual Meeting [1952] of the American Association of University Professors, expresses its full confidence in the integrity and ability of those professionally responsible for the selection of textbooks, and in the capacity of the academic profession to correct the occasional abuses or failure of those thus responsible; it condemns irresponsible lay censorship of textbooks, and pressure tactics with reference to the choice of textbooks; and it especially condemns the efforts of organized groups to exert pressure concerning textbooks in order to advance special interests and points of view.

[See also *AAUP Bulletin,* 39:96 (Spring, 1953); 40:118–19 (Spring, 1954); 41:97–98 (Spring, 1955); 42:351 (Summer, 1956).]

B. FOREIGN SCHOLARS: OPPRESSION ABROAD, AID HERE

[*AAUP Bulletin,* 25:6–7 (January, 1939)]

Be It Resolved: that the American Association of University Professors at its annual meeting of 1938, believing that the primary duty of the college and university is the search for and diffusion of truth, express its abhorrence at the action of totalitarian regimes which prevent the accomplishment of this duty by persecuting teachers on account of their race, religion, or political ideals; and that it express its sympathetic approval of its colleagues living under such regimes who, even in apparent silence, are protesting against the action of their governments.

[See also *AAUP Bulletin,* 26:8 (January, 1940); 27:8 (January, 1941); 28:14 (January, 1941).]

[*AAUP Bulletin,* 43:363 (Summer, 1957)]

The Forty-Third Annual Meeting [1957] of the American Association of University Professors, mindful of the Association's primary function of upholding the interests of scholarship and of scholars in the United States, notes that these are times when neither the Association nor its members can be indifferent to what happens to scholarship and scholars in other lands. When scholars are grossly abused by a repressive government, as has been happening in Hungary, or are made victims of rampant racism, as has been happening in South Africa, we are necessarily deeply concerned. In the name of the Association we extend sincere sympathy to our colleagues thus made to suffer. This we do on humanitarian impulse, but also in full awareness that the scholars of the world do indeed constitute a community, and that casualties, wherever inflicted, and a setback to scholarly endeavor on any front, damage the entire scholarly community, of which we are a part.

[See also *AAUP Bulletin,* 44:505 (Summer, 1958); 46:220 (Summer, 1960); 47:167 (Summer, 1961).]

C. FULBRIGHT SCHOLARS

[*AAUP Bulletin,* 46:220–21 (Summer, 1960)]

The Forty-Sixth Annual Meeting [resolves that]:

(a) Applicants for Fulbright appointments are entitled to know the criteria by which the choice will be made. In particular, if any nonacademic criteria are to be applied, these should be clearly specified in advance and their respective weights indicated.

(b) The screening committees, if they are to do their work efficiently, must have access to all information that is to have weight in the final selections.

(c) Applicants can best be judged by their peers. The Board of Foreign Scholarships should be composed primarily of persons experienced in productive scholarship and teaching.

D. LEGISLATIVE COMMITTEE INVESTIGATIONS

[*AAUP Bulletin,* 38:99 (Spring, 1952)]

The Thirty-Eighth Annual Meeting [1952] of the American Association of University Professors protests the present tendency, in legislative investigations relating to loyalty, toward using the professional writings, utterances, and normal personal associations of individuals to impugn their loyalty without regard to context of time or circumstances. In this connection we reassert the basic American constitutional principle that the function of the legislative branch of the government is the enactment of legislation and not the prosecution of individuals, that the prosecution of individuals is the function of the law-enforcing agencies of the government. We reassert also the basic American constitutional principle that the proper efforts of the government to protect itself against subversion, as against any other harmful actions, are limited to the enactment of legislation defining and proscribing specific acts as subversive and to the prosecution of individuals who commit legally defined subversive acts, including conspiracy to commit such acts; and does not extend to opinions, utterances, and personal relationships unless these have been legally defined and proscribed as subversive. Legislative investigations which are in fact trials of individuals based on the thoughts and opinions which they may lawfully hold and express, or on their lawful personal associations, discourage freedom of thought, of inquiry, and of expression, and are inimical to the welfare of the Nation. The study of national and international affairs in particular, upon which national policies must ultimately be based, requires freedom of thought, of inquiry, and of expression. The critical nature of our times therefore calls for more, not less, freedom of thought, of inquiry, and of expression. We affirm our belief that only by encouraging these freedoms can we in the long run, if not immediately, achieve wise decisions concerning national and international problems, and we urge that inquiring minds capable of engaging in the study of national and international affairs be officially encouraged.

[See also *AAUP Bulletin,* 39:93–94 (Spring, 1953); 39:94–95 (Spring, 1953); 40:94 (Spring, 1940); 41:95–97 (Spring, 1955); 44:505 (Summer, 1958).]

E. PASSPORTS FOR SCHOLARS

[*AAUP Bulletin,* 38:100 (Spring, 1952)]

Since the search for knowledge and the growth of international understanding are indispensable to the establishment and strengthening of a free and orderly world, American scholars should be unhampered in foreign travel. The Thirty-Eighth Annual Meeting [1952] of the American Association of University Professors therefore urges that governmental agencies facilitate the granting of passports to scholars who wish to attend meetings or to teach or to carry on research abroad. We also urge the removal of legislative and administrative barriers to the visits of foreign students and scholars to this country.

[See also *AAUP Bulletin,* 40:119 (Spring, 1954); 42:351–52 (Summer, 1956).]

F. RACE MATTERS

[*AAUP Bulletin,* 42:352–53 (Summer, 1956)]

The Forty-Second Annual Meeting [1956] of the American Association of University Professors endorses the principles set forth by the United States Supreme Court in decisions providing for the elimination of racial segregation in publicly supported institutions of higher education. In addition, the Association expresses its belief that these principles should be adhered to by privately supported institutions of higher education.

The right to teach and the right to learn are vital and inseparable aspects of academic freedom. Consequently, free access to every kind of educational opportunity, measured only by the aptitude and achievement of the individual teacher or student, must be safeguarded to all Americans of whatever race. Any interference with such access imperils the right of the teacher to teach, as well as the right of the student to learn.

The Association also calls attention to the right of every teacher to discuss the meaning and purpose of academic freedom, including the right to learn without regard to racial considerations. This includes his right, both as a teacher and as a citizen, to be active as an individual and as a member of organizations in exerting his influence with respect to problems of providing, at all levels, equal educational opportunity without racial segregation.

Finally, the Association wishes to note its satisfaction with the undoubted progress our nation has made in recent years toward implementation of the principles here under examination. It wishes also to commend those institutions, both public and private, and in all parts of the country, which have made real and substantial efforts to bring their policies and practices into conformity with the fundamental principles supported in this resolution.

[See also *AAUP Bulletin,* 43:352–63 (Summer, 1967); 44:504 (Summer, 1958)]

[*AAUP Bulletin*, 45:277 (Summer, 1959)]

The Forty-Fifth Annual Meeting [1959] of the American Association of University Professors reaffirms the resolutions of the Forty-Third and Forty-Fourth Annual Meetings endorsing the principles set forth by the United States Supreme Court in decisions providing for the elimination of racial segregation in publicly supported institutions of higher learning, and commending institutions, both public and private, which have made progress in implementing the principle that educational opportunity should be open to every individual, regardless of race.

The Annual Meeting further reaffirms the principle that every teacher has the right, both as teacher and as citizen, to be active in organizations which exert their influence toward the provision of educational opportunity without racial segregation; and it specifically condemns any legislation or administrative action which would deny to teachers or students the right to membership in any organization seeking the elimination of racial segregation in education.

In addition, the Annual Meeting deplores the apparent willingness of some governmental bodies and private groups to sacrifice public education in order to maintain racial segregation.

Finally, the Annual Meeting particularly commends those scholars and teachers in sections of the country where public pressures against desegregation are heavy, who have courageously resisted those pressures and have given their best effort to resolving the problems involved in desegregation.

[*AAUP Bulletin,* 46:219–20 (Summer, 1960)]

The Forty-Sixth Annual Meeting [1960] of the American Association of University Professors observes with sorrow and indignation the action of college and university authorities who have disciplined, suspended, or expelled students for protesting in peaceful ways against racial discrimination. Such action constitutes an abuse of academic authority. Since not every conviction under law necessarily represents an offense with which an educational institution must concern itself, it is incumbent upon educational authorities to reach their own decisions in these situations. Not to do so constitutes a failure in the exercise of academic authority. The academic community should not restrict the civil rights of students. We call upon the authorities of colleges and universities not to be misled by public pressures into punitive action which impairs the learning process and destroys the civil liberties of students.

In the face of threats to close publicly supported educational institutions or to discredit public and private institutions for the purpose of preserving racial segregation, the Forty-Sixth Annual Meeting of the American Association of University Professors reaffirms the resolutions of the three preceding Annual Meetings. It again endorses the principles set forth by the United States Supreme Court in decisions providing for the elimination of racial segregation in publicly supported educational institutions. It again commends institutions, both public and private, which have made progress in implementing the principle that race should not be a condition for educational opportunity. It condemns the willingness of some governmental bodies and private groups to sacrifice public education in order to maintain racial segregation.

The Annual Meeting further reaffirms the principle that every teacher has the right, both as teacher and as citizen, to be active in organizations which exert their influence toward the provision of educational opportunity without racial segregation; and it specifically condemns legislation or administrative action which would deny to teachers or students the right to membership in any organization seeking by constitutional means the elimination of racial segregation.

Finally, this Annual Meeting particularly commends those scholars and teachers who have courageously resisted public pressures and have continued to give their best effort to resolving the problems involved in desegregation.

[*AAUP Bulletin,* 49:189 (Summer, 1963)]

The Forty-Ninth Annual Meeting [1963] commends the increasing number of privately supported colleges and universities now selecting students on the basis of merit and without respect to race, color, or creed. Such voluntary recognition of the rights of human beings is a gratifying manifestation of the increasing sentiment in favor of equal educational opportunities for all people.

The Forty-Ninth Annual Meeting also commends those publicly supported institutions, notably represented by Clemson College, which have recognized the primacy of law and order and have accepted integration peacefully. The Forty-Ninth Annual Meeting reaffirms the resolution of the Forty-Eighth Annual Meeting that federal aid to higher education be restricted to desegregated institutions.

The Forty-Ninth Annual Meeting commends those faculty members of the University of Mississippi and those faculty members and administrators in the colleges and universities of the South who, in the face of extreme pressures of adverse public opinion and intransigent political or legal authority, have openly upheld their principles and sought to strengthen the practices of academic freedom and tenure.

[See also *AAUP Bulletin* (two resolutions), 47:167 (Summer, 1961); (two resolutions) 48:174 (Summer, 1962); 50:190 (Summer, 1964).]

G. SPEAKERS ON CAMPUSES

[*AAUP Bulletin,* 43:363 (Summer, 1957)]

The Forty-Third Annual Meeting [1957] of the American Association of University Professors asserts the right of college and university students to listen to anyone whom they wish to hear, and affirms its own belief that it is educationally desirable that students be confronted with diverse opinions of all kinds. The Annual

Meeting therefore holds that any person who is presented by a recognized student or faculty organization should be allowed to speak on a college or university campus.

H. TEACHERS' OATHS, OPPOSITION TO

[*AAUP Bulletin,* 23:7 (January, 1937)]

Whereas, twenty-two states of the union have enacted statutes requiring teachers to take loyalty oaths, and whereas, there is continuing pressure for the enactment of such measures in other states; and whereas loyalty oaths laws for teachers are futile in effecting the legitimate aims of such laws, that is, an understanding of and loyalty towards American ideals; and whereas, these laws can easily be used as an instrument to promote intolerance, restrict our civil liberties and the freedom of teaching, and to accentuate propaganda against democratic ideals; and whereas, these laws cast an undeserved aspersion on the integrity and loyalty of the teaching profession;

Be it *Resolved,* therefore, [by the Twenty-Third, 1937 Annual Meeting] that our chapters and all citizens are urged to oppose the enactment of such laws, and to work for their repeal in states where such laws are already on the statute books.

[*AAUP Bulletin,* 36:13–15 (Spring, 1950)]

Our democracy is founded upon the principles of freedom of thought, speech, and conscience, and any invasions of these civil liberties not necessitated by direct governmental responsibilities of the persons involved or by their access to secret information vital to national security threatens to bring about those very totalitarian restrictions which we are most concerned to avoid. We recognize that safeguards against espionage by such persons must be maintained; but to subject the members of the teaching profession to tests and prescriptions of loyalty beyond those which bind other citizens is a particularly grave blow to the intellectual freedom and moral integrity that are the greatest heritage of our educational system.

Be it therefore *Resolved,* By this the Thirty-Sixth Annual Meeting [1950] of the American Association of University Professors, that:

1. We are opposed to the requirement, by any authority, political or academic, that teachers, students, or research fellows, except those who have direct governmental responsibilities or access to officially secret (classified or restricted) information, shall take special loyalty oaths or shall disclaim membership in organizations listed as subversive.

2. We express our disapproval of singling out for special investigation the personal convictions or the political beliefs and connections of teachers or students who do not have access to officially secret information.

Such practices are ineffective to identify dangerous individuals, who may not hesitate to comply falsely; and the imposition of such requirements, or resort to such investigations, casts unjustified suspicion upon the teaching profession. Their true gravity lies, however, in their tendency to sap the strength of American education, American thought, and American institutions by requiring conformity to official orthodoxy of opinion and conduct.

. . . .

We believe that a sound national program of education and research in basic science will be in the national interest and in the interest of humanity only if the best minds can be attracted to it, and we believe that freedom of thought and action is inherent in the American tradition. We recognize also that the establishment of a National Science Foundation should aid in training scientists and in prosecuting research in areas of science not connected with problems which must be classified as secret for reasons of national security.

Be it therefore *Resolved,* By this the Thirty-Sixth [1950] Annual Meeting of the American Association of University Professors, that:

1. We urge the Congress of the United States not to include in any bill designed to establish a National Science Foundation any mandatory general requirement for investigation into the personal life and opinions of those who may receive grants or benefits from such a Foundation except that the Foundation should assure itself,

by all proper means, of the loyalty of those persons who may be required by their duties to have access to information the revelation of which to unauthorized persons would be harmful to national security.

2. We express our disapproval of any proposal for the establishment of a National Science Foundation under conditions that will require the Federal Bureau of Investigation to investigate all persons who might receive scholarships and fellowships and we urge the President of the United States to withhold approval of such legislation should it be enacted by the Congress.

. . . .

The principles of academic freedom and tenure long maintained by the American Association of University Professors and other organizations have consistently been interpreted and applied according to the conception that guilt of misconduct warranting dismissal from a college or university teaching position must be personal and may not be established according to the formula of guilt by association. Continued adherence to this interpretation is essential to the maintenance of free thought and instruction and of educational opportunity in a democratic society.

Be it therefore *Resolved,* By this the Thirty-Sixth Annual Meeting of the American Association of University Professors, that:

We affirm our belief in the principles of academic freedom and tenure as previously applied, and oppose the substitution of any doctrine whereby membership of a college or university teacher in any lawful political party or other organization could become in itself a proper ground of dismissal from his post.

[See also *AAUP Bulletin,* 37:67–68 (Spring, 1951).]

[*AAUP Bulletin,* 38:97–99 (Spring, 1952)]

The Thirty-Eighth Annual Meeting [1952] of the American Association of University Professors reaffirms the views concerning loyalty oaths, academic freedom, and professional status which were developed by Committee A on Academic Freedom and Tenure and by the Council of the Association, and endorsed in statements adopted by the Thirty-Sixth and the Thirty-Seventh Annual Meetings of the Association. The reaffirmation of these views is with a full awareness that, in recent history, state legislation has gone far in imposing nondisloyalty oaths upon teachers in the public schools and in publicly controlled colleges and universities, and that the tendency in legislation is strong to disqualify persons from teaching, as well as from other public employment, because of their past or present organizational affiliations, and that the Supreme Court of the United States has sustained the constitutionality of such legislation. Yet the Supreme Court, although it has affirmed the powers of legislatures to determine factors relevant to the fitness of teachers in publicly controlled educational institutions, has been careful to withhold approval of any action whereby membership in a lawful organization, even when relevant to the question of professional fitness, becomes in itself a ground for disqualification.

None of these developments lends validity to any departure from the principle that, in the interest of the welfare of society, higher education must be free from imposed conformity or bias, to the end that it may continue to discover and impart truth—new truth, as well as old—through untrammeled inquiry and unintimidated utterances. The tests of the fitness of a member of the academic profession should be his professional competence, his integrity and character, and his ability and willingness to engage in vigorous, objective instruction and research; these to be measured by the accepted principles and standards of the profession. A teacher who is guilty of misusing his classes or his other relationships with his students for biased partisan propaganda, or is guilty of a legally defined subversive act, is responsible as an individual for the violation of professional principles or the law of the land, as the case may be, and should be dismissed, provided his guilt is established by evidence adduced in a proceeding in which he is given a full measure of due process. Experience has abundantly demonstrated that neither the organizational affiliations of a teacher, if lawful, nor his social, economic, political, or religious opinions, however difficult for others to understand and however distasteful to others they may be, are sufficient evidence of disqualification for work in the academic profession. The acceptance of the contrary view leads logically to nondisloyalty test oaths, and to inquisitions into the beliefs of individuals and into the affairs of colleges and universities, both of which are inimical to the American way of life and our institutions of higher education. Such consequences make clear the importance of the observance of the principle that unprofessional conduct or unlawful acts which might disqualify one for academic work are personal, and can be dealt with justly only in a proceeding directed to the individual teacher.

The movement to impose ideological tests upon teachers has done, and will continue to do, serious harm to education and to the nation. As Dr. Oliver C. Carmichael, President of the Carnegie Foundation for the Advancement of Teaching, has said recently, in commenting on this movement: "The climate of opinion which permits such folly is designed to stifle academic freedom and thus to abrogate one of the great traditions. If regimentation should ever replace real freedom in teaching either through legislation or intimidation, not only would the dynamics of education be lost but one of the chief bulwarks of freedom would be removed."

[See also *AAUP Bulletin,* 39:91–93 (Spring, 1953); 40:115–17 (Spring, 1954); 41:92–93 (Spring, 1955).]

[*AAUP Bulletin,* 45:275–76 (Summer, 1959)]

The Forty-Fifth Annual Meeting [1959] of the American Association of University Professors, while grateful for the concern of Congress with the welfare of higher education, as expressed in the National Defense Education Act, wishes to record its objection to the disclaimer affidavit requirement in Section 1001(f), Title X, of that Act. This Act requires that any individual, including students, who benefit under the National Defense Education Act, shall not receive payment unless he has "executed and filed with the Commissioner [of Education] an affidavit that he does not believe in, and is not a member of and does not support any organization that believes in or teaches the overthrow of the United States Government by force or violence or by any illegal or unconstitutional methods." Like all test oaths this oath is repugnant to the American tradition; it vaguely and improperly inquires into persons' beliefs, and it invidiously singles out for attention the academic community, thus casting doubt upon the integrity of an honorable and respected segment of the American public. When it considers that truly subversive persons will sign such an oath, and that many highly principled persons, whose participation in the National Defense Education Act would benefit the nation, may refuse to sign it, this Annual Meeting particularly deplores the effort and money required for the administration of a provision which cannot be expected to accomplish the purpose for which it was intended, and which must help to defeat the purpose of the Act as a whole.

[See also *AAUP Bulletin,* 46:220 (Summer, 1960); 47:166–67 (Summer, 1961); 48:162–63 (Summer, 1962); 49:188–89 (Summer, 1963).]

J. TENURE AND INSTITUTIONAL MERGER

[*AAUP Bulletin,* 37:69–70 (Spring, 1951)]

The Thirty-Seventh Annual Meeting [1951] of the American Association of University Professors calls attention to the problems of academic tenure which arise when colleges or universities merge or come under new control, with continuance of the previous programs. In such circumstances the tenure rights of members of all affected faculties should be respected.

K. TENURE AND NATIONAL EMERGENCY

[*AAUP Bulletin,* 37:69 (Spring, 1951)]

Recognizing that the national emergency may produce conditions in some colleges and universities necessitating drastic economy, and that proposed measures of economy may include reductions in faculty personnel; and recognizing that in these circumstances there is danger that the principles of academic tenure may be ignored or minimized, this, the Thirty-Seventh Annual Meeting [1951] of the American Association of University Professors, affirms its belief that the continued observance of these principles is essential to higher education in this period of emergency, and recommends the following policy as according with these principles: (1) It is the joint responsibility of administration and faculty to economize by all means possible without resort to the reduction of faculty personnel; (2) if reduction of faculty personnel is unavoidable, it should be confined to faculty members who have not acquired tenure status; and (3) if teachers entitled to tenure are called into the armed forces, or if by agreement with their respective administrations they voluntarily enter the armed services or accept positions in government or industry during the period of emergency, they should be granted bona fide leaves of absence, to protect their professional status.

Chapter VI
Advisory Letters

A chief function of the Washington Office staff is to answer questions from members about the application of established Association policy to particular situations or essentially new kinds of problems. In reply it is customary first to state the applicable governing principle or procedure, and then to offer such analysis, comment, and advice as is possible and reasonable. These later remarks are not, of course, policy, but a gloss upon policy.

Committee A, believing that some of these advisory letters would be of general interest and usefulness, has authorized the publication of selected excerpts. Selection is approved by a committee consisting of the President of the Association, the Chairman of Committee A, and the General Secretary.

LETTER NO. 1. TENURE: THE PROVISION FOR A YEAR'S TERMINAL APPOINTMENT IN CASES OF DISMISSAL NOT INVOLVING MORAL TURPITUDE

[*AAUP Bulletin,* 48:394 (Winter, 1962)]

The year's notice rule—its history

Of the several rules which protect the teacher in his sought for or achieved tenure status, one of the most important is the provision that he shall receive a year's notice if he is not being reappointed (applicable to nontenure status teachers), or if he is dismissed (tenure status teachers). The need for such a rule has been seen from the beginning of the American Association of University Professors in 1915 to the present moment. . . .

The first major policy statement by this Association, the 1915 *Declaration of Principles,* stated that "No university teacher of any rank should, except in cases of grave moral delinquency, receive notice of dismissal or of refusal of reappointment later than three months before the close of any academic year, and in the case of teachers above the grade of instructor, one year's notice should be given." Ten years later there emerged from a conference called by the American Council on Education a statement which was endorsed by the Association of American Colleges and by this Association. The 1925 *Conference Statement* eliminated the consideration of rank and tied the notice principle to tenure. It said: "Dismissal for reasons other than immorality or treason should not ordinarily take effect in less than a year from the time the decision is reached." Fifteen years later, the 1940 *Statement of Principles,* likewise endorsed by the Association of American Colleges and this Association, extended the right to a year's notice to all. It said: "Notice should be given at least one year prior to the expiration of the probationary period if the teacher is not to be continued in service after the expiration of that period. . . . Teachers on continuous appointment who are dismissed for reasons not involving moral turpitude should receive their salaries for at least a year from the date of notification whether or not they are continued in their duties at the institution." (Since the one-year provision places the burden of an unrealistic procedure upon an institution at the beginning of its acquaintance with a teacher, Committee A of the Association in its 1957 *Recommended Institutional Regulations* authorized the Washington Office to relax the requirement to this extent: during the first year of a teacher's service, notice is adequate if given by March 1; during the second year of service, notice should be given six months before the end of the academic year.)

The year's notice rule in practice

The provision requiring a year's notice protects the whole profession, except a teacher proved to be gravely immoral. It is true that this protection covers the very small group of individuals who could at some moment be charged with irresponsibility or incompetence. But the protection also covers several hundred thousand unquestionably competent professional men and women. It is not the first social regulation which properly bestows a vital protection upon a whole group, even though that group may contain a few persons who are less than desirable in the opinion of some.

The argument for the year's notice provision, on the logical ground just cited, is simple. It is equally obvious and equally strong on historical grounds.

Who in fact are the college and university teachers who are not reappointed in any particular year, or are actually dismissed? Who, in other words, actually benefits by the provision of a year's notice? The answer is revealing of the real need for protection.

(a) Each year perhaps fifty thousand teachers who have not yet acquired tenure are simply not reappointed for a host of reasons: the institution has found or hopes to find a person more to its purpose, the institution has changed its program, the institution must retrench. . . . No one can object to an institution doing its best to solve its staffing problems by its own lights. Likewise, no one can object to a year's notice for a professional man who has been busy doing his work and has had no time to arrange for next year. . . .

(b) Each year an extremely small but extremely important group of teachers, some with and some without tenure, are dismissed for cause not involving moral turpitude. This group is *not* mainly made up of teachers charged with incompetence; in fact, the charge of incompetence is about the rarest heard in these critical situations. The teachers dismissed are those who have become subjects of public controversy, those who have displeased their institutions, those who are the figures in academic freedom complaint cases. The Association is bound to note the considerable coincidence between the institutions involved in this group of dismissals and the institutions regarding whom the Association has been compelled to make inquiry—and in the worst situations to vote censure of the administration.

The American Association of University Professors has no intention of abandoning or relaxing a regulation which is essential for the protection of academic freedom as well as tenure, and which in the cases that are our chief concern have revealed the close bonds which unite freedom and tenure.

LETTER NO. 3. CHALLENGING THE MEMBERS OF A HEARING COMMITTEE

[*AAUP Bulletin,* 49:78 (Spring, 1963)]

You refer to one section of the proposed regulations of your university which has given some cause for worry. There are precedents for the disqualification of an elected member to a faculty hearing committee, particularly when the issue in question has arisen in that committee member's department, or when that committee member has previously expressed judgments on the merits of the case or with respect to the colleague involved. Obviously, the burden of disqualification should be borne by the committee member himself. The inclusion of a regulation on disqualification for cause is to take care of any situation in which the committee member has not himself taken the initiative. I recognize, of course, that animosities might be aroused by the use of challenges; on the other hand, more severe animosities might be aroused if the right is not available to the faculty member under charges, and disqualification seems desirable.

I dare say that you are more troubled by the substance of the paragraph concerning peremptory challenges. Those proposing this provision are probably doing so by analogy with the privilege of peremptory challenges in selecting juries. There are arguments on both sides of the question: peremptory challenges do affect the principles underlying *faculty election* of a hearing committee; on the other hand I think we can agree that even though all parties approach a dismissal proceeding in complete good faith, there are situations in which considerable embarrassment would result from a requirement that reasons for a challenge must be openly argued. An academic community is composed of individuals who have worked closely together, and must continue to do so, and biases inevitably develop which could serve as a reasonable basis for disqualification but which would serve no useful purpose to have extracted for open discussion. Also, in some instances where the concern of the faculty member involved is reasonable or bona fide although mistaken, it may be desirable to have disqualification of the committee member. This is not, of course, intended to suggest that the right to peremptory challenges should be without reasonable limitation, and it is on this specific assumption that these comments are made. I note in this connection that the draft [of your regulations] limits such challenges to two, and I am wholly in agreement with this kind of limitation. I wonder also whether the problems you suggest in connection with peremptory challenges are not perhaps of greatest concern in connection with their exercise by the President, particularly in the case of a faculty-selected committee. It is quite possible therefore that these problems can largely be obviated by limiting the right to such challenges to the person who is actually under charges.

Frankly, I could not agree that the principle of challenge and disqualification should be ruled out completely in formulating a set of standards on dismissal proceedings. The principal document on this subject, *Statement on Procedural Standards in Faculty Dismissal Proceedings,* includes the following relevant clauses (section 4, "Hearing Committee, . . . an elected standing committee *not previously concerned with the case. . . .*" [and] "The choice of members of the hearing committee should be on the basis of their objectivity. . . ." [emphasis supplied] Where the Committee member in question clearly has a *previous concern* in the case or has spoken or acted in such a manner as to call his *objectivity* into question, he should be disqualified from serving on the hearing committee, preferably at his own suggestion, but by challenge if necessary. The question is, what is the most logical manner of inserting this principle into a set of tenure regulations without seriously injuring the concept of *faculty election* of a standing committee?

LETTER NO. 4. TENURE AND CHANGE OF STATUS

[*AAUP Bulletin,* 49:79 (Spring, 1963)]

Your confidential letter raises several complicated problems, seldom occurring in academic circles, for which individual negotiation between you and the administration appears to be necessary. If you are dissatisfied with the results of such negotiation, you may wish to give the Association all details for review, and we shall consider appropriate steps in the light of our understanding of the rights of all parties.

First, I should like to comment on what appears to be the basis for the proposal to change your status: the bona fide elimination of the department in which you hold the rank of full professor with tenure. I would advise that the administration should seek to find an assignment for you, for which you are professionally fitted, and apparently such an effort is being made in continuing you in the post of Director of ———. I cannot speak to the point of the appropriateness of assigning to this post at ——— College the additional status of membership on the faculty, but I do know that numerous institutions give academic rank to directors of various kinds of bureaus; in most instances, I believe, the director is available for course assignments when needed. Your case is exceptional in that the department of your discipline is being eliminated, and therefore no opportunity would arise for assigning teaching to you, unless you are qualified to teach in an area other than ———. Possible research assignments might appropriately accompany the directorship, and if this is true a faculty status would appear to be justified. In making the comments immediately above, you will understand that I am speaking in general terms, in the light of my understanding of common practices, and perhaps my remarks may not be applicable to the situation in which you find yourself at ——— College. In any event, you are well advised to negotiate for professional status; as to the Association's position on this issue, I repeat that the issue is so highly specialized that I cannot cite a principle or precedent that applies directly to the facts in your case as I understand them, but I shall be glad to continue our discussion of the problem in the light of the special circumstances surrounding your situation and with regard to what appears to be professionally sound procedure.

I raise the following point which is possibly relevant to your special interest: if the administration of ——— College offered you *tenure* in the Directorship, and if in your judgment this post is not in danger of being eliminated, would you not consider such tenure to be an adequate substitute for retaining a professional rank without teaching assignments? And further, if you are doubtful of the permanence of the post of Director, would not a promise from the administration that you could remain on the staff until your retirement, with an assignment which is satisfactory to both parties, be a suitable guarantee of tenure? From the information contained in your letter, I have no means of knowing the likely reasons for denying you professorial status, with continuing tenure, and possibly your request will be approved by the administration.

As indicated earlier in this letter, the Association will be glad to continue its interest in your case, and to take appropriate steps if you place a formal complaint with it. I hope you will pardon me for commenting on your phrase, ". . . would the AAUP defend me?" Actually, we do not "defend" or enter investigations "in the interest of" any particular party, whether the complaining teacher is or is not a member of the Association. To put it more appropriately, we investigate cases in the light of principles enunciated by the Association usually in collaboration with other associations, or if the cases are so individually specialized that adopted principles do not clearly offer guidance, we investigate in terms of what our Committee A and the Council consider fair practice in the special circumstances. The judgments of the Association have been widely respected, and we have confidence in the diligence, accuracy, and fair play of our investigating committees. But I repeat: we seek to arrive at just conclusions, even though the complainant's contentions might be rejected in whole or in part, and an examination of our published reports will show that the Association does not always agree with the position taken by a complaining teacher.

Let me know if you wish further counsel in your situation, which certainly poses grave consequences for your professional future.

LETTER NO. 6. TENURE AND LEAVE OF ABSENCE

[*AAUP Bulletin,* 49:202 (Summer, 1963)]

With regard to your specific problem, leaves of absence sometimes present special difficulty for those seeking to acquire tenure or to maintain it. The Association has not formalized its policy because of the variety of circumstances governing particular cases. But at least the following observations are possible:

1. An institution should cooperate in arranging leaves of absence for staff members who wish to perform significant profes-

sional duties or render special kinds of public service in other locations.

2. A professor seeking leave should recognize that he owes a very important obligation to the institution where he has his regular connection; he should be mindful of the problems which a leave of absence can create for his administration, his colleagues, and his students.

3. A leave of absence which satisfies all practical considerations should not affect in any way the status of a person who has achieved tenure.

4. A leave of absence for a person who does not have permanent tenure is treated differently in different institutions: (a) one college will simply not count the leave period as part of the probationary period of the professor's service, while (b) another college will, if the services performed elsewhere are significant for judgment of the teacher's work at his home base, consider the leave of absence period to accrue to the teacher's benefit as probationary service.

In all situations, both administrations and professors should be advised to have clearly set forth in writing their understanding of all the terms related to leave of absence and its effect upon the status of the person involved.

LETTER NO. 8. LOYALTY TO THE COLLEGE

[*AAUP Bulletin,* 49:202 (Summer, 1963)]

Thank you for sending me copies of the old and new policies respecting faculty rank at ——— College. It seems to me that, in the new policy, the addition at three points of the qualifications of "Demonstrated usefulness and loyalty at the college" is both redundant and undesirable. Quite obviously if the faculty member has furnished "Evidence of professional growth, continued scholarly effort and superior teaching," he has succeeded in demonstrating his usefulness to the College, and a specific qualification of "usefulness" becomes superfluous. As for loyalty to the College, I see no reason why this should be made a qualification for promotion; such loyalty is very difficult to define, and a provision of this sort is readily open to abuse.

It seems to me that a faculty member's loyalty to the College is one of those things always to be assumed in the absence of clear evidence to the contrary. Certainly a faculty member should not have to give evidence of "cheerful . . . performance of assigned duties" in order to be considered loyal. This is too much. Some of the most crotchety faculty members known have unquestionably had the best interests of their institutions at heart. And I hardly need point out the anomaly of assuming that assigned duties, no matter how trivial, ought by their very nature to inspire cheerfulness.

LETTER NO. 10. CANDOR AND THE PROSPECTIVE APPOINTEE

[*AAUP Bulletin,* 49:295 (Autumn, 1963)]

The Association has adopted no policy concerning the issues which a college or university may properly consider when it is contemplating the appointment of a new faculty member, and I know of no previous situation comparable to that which in general terms you have described in your letter. Consequently, we are able to give you nothing more than the informal reaction you have requested.

You indicate that the candidate has stated that he is not now a member of the Communist Party and has not been a Party member since he went to the University as a student some ten years ago. He has, however, refused to state whether or not he was a Party member previous to that period, even though the university has stated that it will probably appoint him whether he was or not. The university feels, however, that it is entitled to an answer covering the earlier period, not for political reasons but "as part of hiring procedures."

Before commenting on your hypothetical case, I feel that I should indicate my difficulty in understanding the distinction you are making between "a political matter" and "hiring procedures." If it is customary to ask all prospective Research Associates about Communist Party membership, past and present, and to expect informative answers, I would say that such an inquiry may be considered part of the university's hiring procedures. But I wonder if the inquiry is not unavoidably political, unless of course the candidate, if appointed, will be working in an area concerned with national security. (In that case, however, I would assume that the inquiry into his associations would be conducted by an agency of the federal government.) In any event, it seems to me that, whatever the candidate's answer—unless it is a refusal to discuss the matter—the university has learned something about his political orientation, past or present, and it would be difficult, if not impossible, to avoid making some political judgment about him.

Although the university insists upon an answer to the question concerning previous Party membership, you indicate that the appointment will probably be made whatever answer is given. I assume this to mean that if the candidate replies that he has never been a member he will certainly be appointed, and that if he replies that he has been a member he will probably be appointed. His failure to reply, of course, leaves both possibilities open. At worst then, the university can assume Party membership, a development which you have said would nonetheless leave it probably disposed to appoint.

Since the university is not presently disposed to appoint, however, its real concern seems to be, not that it may have a former Communist in its midst, but that it will have someone who has failed to answer all questions during his appointing interviews—who has, in the university's view, appeared less than candid. Yet I wonder if sufficient reason has been established for not making an appointment the university otherwise seems to favor.

The university is wrestling here, in another context, with a problem that the Association's Committee A on Academic Freedom and Tenure has spent countless hours debating: the problem of what information a university has a right to expect its faculty members unequivocally to provide it. Committee A has concluded that a faculty member may have sound reasons based upon principle for withholding certain information, and that the institution should respect these reasons, although it has always the right to try to determine whether the faculty member is sincere in taking his stand upon principle. If it doubts his sincerity, this adverse judgment should not be decisive in itself, since the faculty member is entitled to the consideration of his whole record, which may contain nothing to support the institution's doubts. In short, refusal to answer should not be equated with lack of candor.

This policy, I should make clear, applies to faculty members already appointed, although I think parts of it are relevant to the case you have described. And I should make clear also that the question of candor has always arisen, at least to my knowledge, when a faculty member has refused to discuss his present political affiliations. The university's problem, I think, is somewhat less serious. The candidate has answered for the last ten years, and his refusal to answer for a previous period—thus avoiding any imputation that he would lie about it—lends at least some credence to his response about the more recent period.

I of course doubt that it is standard practice at the university to ask such questions of candidates for faculty positions. The practice is rare, even at much less renowned institutions, and has I would say very little to recommend it. I suspect therefore that it is being followed in this case because someone has raised questions about the candidate which make the line of inquiry relevant. Distressing though the candidate's refusal to answer about an earlier period may be, is it not possible that he has one or more reasons for his refusal which deserve to be respected? For example, he may fear a legislative inquiry which, on the basis of his reply to the university, may compel him to inform upon friends who in his judgment have done nothing execrable. Whether or not he was ever a Party member, he may look upon his politics before his student days at the university as beyond the university's concern. He may simply wish to close off, even from his nearest friends, the memory of a foolishness long since outgrown. Perhaps everyone is entitled to that much privacy.

In conclusion I would ask again—if the university is truly satisfied with his qualifications and his past ten years—whether that ought not to suffice. Ten years are a long time, particularly in a young man's life, and the candidate you are considering may bear only a superficial resemblance to the young person he was ten years before. At any rate, I would think it proper for the university to base its decision, not upon his refusal to answer, but upon his explanation of his refusal. The explanation may itself meet the university's test of candor.

LETTER NO. 11. EXTRAMURAL UTTERANCES

[*AAUP Bulletin,* 49:393 (Winter, 1963)]

Your inquiry concerns a section in the 1940 *Statement of Principles on Academic Freedom and Tenure* which delineates the rights of faculty members as citizens. That section, as you know, states that

> The college or university teacher is a citizen, a member of a learned profession, and an officer of an educational institution. When he speaks or writes as a citizen, he should be free from institutional censorship or discipline, but his special position in the community imposes special obligations. As a man of learning and an educational officer, he should remember that the public may judge his profession and his institution by his utterances. Hence he should at all times be accurate, should exercise appropriate restraint, should show respect for the opinions of others, and should make every effort to indicate that he is not an institutional spokesman.

Two questions are raised relating to the application of the term "appropriate restraint" to the extramural utterances of a faculty member in the above admonition: (1) does the term "appropriate restraint" relate only to manner or mode of expression, and (2) is there a special obligation on the part of the faculty member to refrain from extramural utterances that may embarrass the institution in its relationships with the community, alumni, legislature, and Board of Trustees? Although the second question may be answered categorically in the negative, i.e., there is no special obligation to refrain from extramural utterances that may "embarrass" these groups, the first question requires some explanation.

It is the view of this Office that the term "appropriate restraint," as used above, refers solely to choice of language and to other aspects of the manner in which a statement is made. It does not refer to the substance of a teacher's remarks. It does not refer to the times and place of his utterance.

This interpretation is not only supported by the legislative history of the 1940 *Statement of Principles* but also by the language of earlier official pronouncements, including the 1915 *Declaration of Principles* and the 1925 *Conference Statement on Academic Freedom and Tenure*. The most explicit recent statement on this question has been provided by Professor Ralph F. Fuchs, one of the most eminent leaders of the Association, in a comment appearing in the Committee A statement published in the report on "Academic Freedom and Tenure: The University of Illinois," *AAUP Bulletin* (March, 1963). In his statement, Professor Fuchs emphasized

> that institutional discipline for an utterance allegedly violating the "standard of academic responsibility" in the 1940 *Statement of Principles* cannot validly call in question the facts or opinions set forth by a faculty member. A violation may consist of serious intemperateness of expression, intentional falsehood, incitement of misconduct, or conceivably some other impropriety of circumstance. It may not lie, however, in the error or unpopularity, even though gross, of the ideas contained in an utterance.

It thus appears that a determination concerning alleged violation of the standard of academic responsibility may not be made except on the basis of the criteria elaborated above.

In addition, it is important to understand that the requirements of due process outlined in the 1940 *Statement of Principles* should be provided in every instance, as indicated in the "Interpretation" of the 1940 *Statement of Principles* agreed upon at a conference of representatives of the Association of American Colleges and the American Association of University Professors on November 7-8, 1940. This "Interpretation" states this obligation in specific terms:

> If the administration of a college or university feels that a teacher has not observed the admonitions of Paragraph (c) of the section on *Academic Freedom* and believes that the extramural utterances of the teacher have been such as to raise grave doubts concerning his fitness for his position, it may proceed to file charges under Paragraph (a) (4) of the section on *Academic Tenure*. In pressing such charges the administration should remember that teachers are citizens and should be accorded the freedom of citizens. In such cases the administration must assume full responsibility and the American Association of University Professors and the Association of American Colleges are free to make an investigation.

In brief, the above "Interpretation" requires that academic consideration of the extramural utterances of a faculty member shall occur only when the remarks raise "grave doubts" concerning his fitness for his position; the "Interpretation" also specifies that no judgment should be made without academic due process. Oversight by the Association in this sensitive area includes examination and review of faculty as well as administrative action. Disciplinary action, of course, may follow only upon proper judgment.

In conclusion, this Office wishes to stress the fact that the disciplining of a faculty member for exercising the rights of free speech guaranteed to him as a citizen by the Constitution of the United States necessarily raises such fundamental issues that institutions are cautioned to take such action only under extraordinary circumstances. Neither the error nor the unpopularity of ideas or opinions may provide an adequate basis for such disciplinary action, whatever temporary embarrassment these views may bring to the institution. Moreover, and generally speaking, college and university professors ought not to be disciplined for failure to adhere to any narrowly defined or absolute standard of conduct. A careful distinction should be drawn at all times between those common instances of relatively insignificant disregard of the admonitions cited above and those rare instances which do in fact raise "grave doubts" about a faculty member's fitness to teach.

LETTER NO. 12. LATE RESIGNATIONS BY FACULTY MEMBERS

[*AAUP Bulletin,* 49:394 (Winter, 1963)]

Two or three times in the course of each year we receive letters from administrative officers of colleges and universities calling our attention to the fact that persons who have signed contracts appear to have unilaterally abrogated them at an unconscionably late date. For your guidance regarding the Association's previous official position I enclose our 1929 *Statement* of policy on resignations. More recently, recognizing that the 1929 *Statement* may be somewhat out of date, a less binding but more detailed statement has been published; to this we give general adherence. You will notice that this 1961 *Statement* provides the faculty member more time than the 1929 *Statement;* this liberalization, it should be emphasized, met with the approval of the administrative representatives on the joint group.

You will recognize, I am sure, the complexities of these situations, particularly the fact that not two but three parties are usually involved: the institution losing out, the teacher leaving or withdrawing, and the institution which offered the new appointment. In other words, not always but very often, a case embodies the known practice of "raiding." Finally, I need hardly tell an experienced administrator how the situation is likely to change in its main aspects throughout the years, as one sees oscillation from a buyer's to a seller's market and back and forth.

To my knowledge we do not receive complaints from institutions which are themselves in error by giving very late notice. For such institutions there is little that can be done when a teacher leaves late, except to observe that good institutional standards are a necessary prerequisite to a pattern of fair dealing at the hands of those who receive appointment.

Parenthetically we note the human aspect of the situation. A professor contracted to perform duties for a particular sum at a particular place suddenly discovers an opportunity to increase greatly his income in the modest world of education, or sometimes to obtain appointment at a famous institution. Perhaps these seductive forces would be less powerful if all institutions had a declared policy indicating willingness to consider renegotiation in the face of significantly more attractive firm offers, provided that all aspects of the situation are essentially ethical.

And so we come to the final and very important question: what should be done about a professional person who has unquestionably acted improperly by late cancellation of his contract. We can assure you that the American Association of University Professors, in dealing with a case of established wrongdoing in this area, would regard such behavior as clearly and seriously unethical. It is unfair to students who may find themselves dealing with a makeshift arrangement or an inferior teacher. It is unfair to colleagues who may be required to make unhappy late adjustments in their schedules or to carry unexpected additional burdens. It is unfair to the administrative officers of the institution who are entitled to be free to turn to other important matters, confident that they have a settled arrangement based upon agreement between professional persons. And of course it is unfair to the institution.

Last year we made inquiry of two administrators who complained but neither supplied us with specific details. This year we have just received another complaint, already in somewhat greater detail, and we have written asking for the full story and supporting documents. If there are one or more cases regarding persons who have recently "canceled out" at ——— College, we are ready to receive from you names, the full story, and supporting documents. We would then pursue our usual course and ask the faculty members involved for their comments upon the situation. With both accounts before us it would be the responsibility of the General Secretary and his colleagues to determine whether the matter should be put before the Council or some other appropriate group.

We have replied to you at length because we want to make clear our concern about these matters. For your information I also enclose a copy of the 1915 *Declaration of Principles* (the founding document of the AAUP). You will, I think, find there genuinely respectful consideration of the problem of the teacher's responsibility.

LETTER NO. 13. STATING REASONS FOR NONREAPPOINTMENT

[*AAUP Bulletin,* 50:85 (Spring, 1964)]

You ask why we consider that an institution has no obligation to provide probationary faculty members with a statement of reasons for their nonreappointment. Before giving you a direct answer to that question, I think I should make clear that we do not advise institutions *not* to inform faculty members why they are not to be retained. It seems obvious that a young faculty member can be much assisted in his career if senior members of his department, the chairman of his department or division, the dean, or the president, will counsel with him from time to time about the quality of his teaching. The beginning faculty member is serving a kind of internship or clerkship, and while he may be trying to model his teaching after the various excellent examples he has encountered, he may not always be the best judge of his own effectiveness. An occasional word of caution, advice, or encouragement from experienced colleagues can therefore be very salutary. If the time comes that the department, division, and administration conclude that his connection with the institution should be severed, we would say that responsible officials of the institution should feel completely free to explain to the faculty member the basis of their decision. We could not agree, however, that if reasons are given for the non-reappointment the institution assumes a burden of demonstrating the validity of its reasons. To be sure, the faculty member may question whatever reasons are given him. But unlike the tenure teacher, he does not as a probationer have what can be considered a claim to his position, and it would thus seem unreasonable to compel the institution to account for this exercise of its prerogative, much less to carry the burden of justifying its decision.

These remarks are made, I am sure you understand, on the assumption that the faculty member has had an appropriate evaluation by his colleagues and that he is not being given notice for reasons which violate his academic freedom. And I believe that I have come above to a direct answer to your question. I think I must say further that our purpose is to permit the institution, within the limits of academic freedom, very great latitude in determining who will be retained for tenure appointments. Because the granting of tenure is an important institutional decision, we feel that the institution should be reasonably satisfied with respect to the faculty member's qualifications for tenure before it reaches a favorable decision. But what appears reasonable to those responsible for the decision may not appear reasonable to the faculty member concerned, for there are often grounds for a decision that are either very difficult to discuss frankly or which the faculty member cannot appreciate (very often, of course, they do not reflect adversely on him). As a result, if an institution is compelled to state its reasons, it may find that it is raising more problems than it has solved; it may grasp at the inconsequential or the unfounded simply to lend support to its decision, or it may place itself in the position of granting tenure by default. Such expedients are regrettable, but the granting of tenure by default is likely to have serious consequences for the faculty and the institution, and it is just these consequences we seek to avoid. In short, we believe that tenure—and thus the institution and the profession—are well served by the policy which we pursue.

LETTER NO. 15. A CHARGE OF PLAGIARISM

[*AAUP Bulletin,* 51:71 (Spring, 1965)]

You state that you intend to lodge formal charges of plagiarism against a member of the academic profession and request specific advice.

I imagine the one point on which everyone would agree is the fact that a charge of plagiarism is a serious matter which, whatever the outcome, has considerable potential for injury to the reputation of the institution and the welfare of its staff and student body. And to the degree that the charges are aired and judged publicly, the harm done clearly increases. Consequently, those making the charges, those offering defense, and those sitting in judgment, should weigh most carefully: (1) the possibility of clarifying a situation satisfactorily by the use of any available alternative procedures of an appropriate kind, and (2) if a trial of the plagiarism issue is unavoidable, the need for constant reference to the general good of the academic community.

If the situation must inescapably continue to develop, at least these cautions and safeguards should be observed:

1. Recourse should be had to existing local procedures. In detail this would ordinarily mean taking the matter up privately with the chairman or head of the department involved; if this is not feasible, the matter could be discussed with the dean of the school or college concerned. From the beginning in informal discussion, possibly later in formal hearing, and finally at any appellate level, two needs should be fully met: it is essential that a thorough and full hearing of the charges be given, and that full procedural due process should be given the individual charged.

2. If in some degree an institution lacks appropriate machinery for the hearing of a charge of plagiarism, the faculty and administration should be given adequate opportunity to devise an appropriate *ad hoc* procedure.

3. If it seems that an appropriate procedure does not exist or cannot be devised within the institution, it would not be wrong to turn to an outside agency. Since it is almost certain that a charge of plagiarism will require the opinion of authorities in the involved subject matter, the indication is that the appropriate learned society or subject matter society be the outside agent whose help

should be sought with respect to the merits of the situation. This Association would, of course, be particularly available for advice on procedure.

Please let me emphasize that this Association is open to request for guidance and expert study from the complainant, the person who might be complained of, the faculty or faculty committee involved, and the administration. You will wish to consider that you have available not one but two sources of consultation. We can do what we can do on the basis of our general experience in the Washington Office. But we hope that you will give serious consideration to the fact that the local chapter of the Association at —— College surely contains among its members persons of experience and wisdom. I therefore conclude this reply both with the offer of further comment if you wish to submit additional material, and with the expression of a strongly felt belief that you would be well-advised to discuss the situation privately with the chapter president.

LETTER NO. 17. QUESTIONS OF RELIGIOUS LIMITATIONS

[*AAUP Bulletin,* 51:72 (Spring, 1965)]

Your inquiry states a concern lest a religious vow, long required of all full professors at your institution be henceforth required of new appointees at any rank and of all present faculty members who are to be promoted to assistant professors or associate professors. There are, I think, three questions of regulation and a general question.

Undoubtedly under the terms of the 1940 *Statement of Principles* some degree of limitation of academic freedom "because of religious or other aims of the institution" is admissible, "provided that such limitations are clearly stated in writing at the time of the appointment." This provision, in a statement of academic principles, is designed to do for higher education what well-established principles of law do for the general community. The provision is intended to insure exactness of understanding so that the teacher will know as well as he can what he may do and what he may not do with respect to certain areas of his teaching which touch on the religious concerns of the institution; collaterally and as good practice, it is stated that this important relationship should be established in writing. Presumably this provision governs full professors at ——— College.

I do not find in the words quoted from the 1940 *Statement of Principles* any indication whether an institution may limit new appointments to persons specifically of its religious belief or denomination.

With respect to present faculty members who may be promoted to ranks below full professor, I find in the 1940 *Statement* language an implication which is present in the whole pattern of administrative justice; no *ex post facto* regulation should abridge the freedom or privilege of persons who entered any kind of situation in good faith. Consequently, I think the main question you present is one which actually goes beyond the special concerns of the Association and relates to a principle which is universally applicable to every aspect of American society where justice and fair dealing have effective force. Faculty members who have been appointed at ——— College have made certain commitments to the College. But the College has made certain commitments to them, for example, that on the basis of an academic evaluation unfettered by additional religious requirements they may be retained from year to year, promoted to the level of assistant or associate professor, and given tenure. The action contemplated by the Board would therefore change the ground rules which governed faculty service when the appointments were agreed upon and may thus reasonably be thought unjust to present members of the faculty. Please let me know if I have adequately answered your question.

During the past three years we have received complaints in this office relating to two religiously oriented colleges where actual denominational membership or doctrinal subscription was an important issue. Such inquiries raise a general question of importance. We have had to consider whether an exceedingly rigid demand might not mean that an institution was in fact more a religious organization than an educational organization. One would not expect any religious faith to accept as a specific instrumentality of its particular interests a completely secular college; conversely, the occasion may some day arise when American higher education may question whether its specific interest in education can adequately be carried out by an instrument preponderantly inclined toward a doctrinally defined religious function. So far, happily, there has been a broad enough range of give and take to permit hundreds of institutions to maintain two standards and to perform multiple functions. Many of us would regret to see polarization occur to the extent which might cause religion and education to draw apart.

Chapter VII Lists

A. CENSURED ADMINISTRATIONS, 1930–1968, ALPHABETICAL LIST, *AAUP BULLETIN* REFERENCES

Institution	Ad hoc *committee report*	*Censured*	*Censure withdrawn*
Adelphi College (New York)	1941 (27:494–517)	1941 (28:11)	1952 (38:104)
Agricultural and Mechanical College	1930 (16:551–53)	1930 (17:140–41)[1]	1932 (19:8)
Alabama Polytechnic Institute	1958 (44:158–69)	1958 (44:503, 661)	1964 (50:133)
Alabama State College	1961 (47:303–9)	1962 (48:162–63)	. . .
Alcorn Agricultural and Mechanical College	1962 (48:248–52)	1963 (49:133)	. . .
Allen University	1960 (46:87–104)	1961 (47:144)	1962 (48:162)
Amarillo College	1967 (53:292–302)	1968 (54:172–73)	. . .
University of Arizona	1963 (49:336–43)	1965 (51:246–47)	1966 (52:125)
Arkansas Agricultural, Mechanical and Normal College	1964 (50:36–43)	1964 (50:133–34)	1965 (51:245–46)
Arkansas Agricultural and Mechanical College	1967 (53:385–90)	1968 (54:173)	. . .
University of Arkansas	1963 (49:344–51)	1964 (50:134)	1968 (54:177–78)
Battle Creek College		1932 (19:8)	1933 (19:299)
Benedict College	1960 (46:87–104)	1961 (47:144)	. . .

[1] Mississippi State institutions, on recommendation by the Council.

Institution	Ad hoc *committee report*	*Censured*	*Censure withdrawn*
Brenau College	1934 (20:10)	1933 (20:10)	1943[2]
University of California	1956 (42:64–66)	1956 (42:341)	1958 (44:503, 665)
Catawba College	1957 (43:196–224)	1957 (43:360)	1964 (50:132–33)
Central Washington College of Education	1940 (26:471–75)	1940 (27:6)	1948 (34:11)
Cheyney State College	1967 (53:391–99)	1968 (54:173)	. . .
DePauw University	1934 (20:295–302)	1934 (21:133)	1936 (23:249–50)
Dickinson College	1958 (44:137–50)	1958 (44:503, 661)	1963 (49:133)
Evansville College	1949 (35:74–111)	1950 (36:16–17)	1956 (42:340)
Fisk University	1959 (45:27–46)	1959 (45:274, 393)	1966 (52:125)
Grove City College	1963 (49:15–24)	1963 (49:134)	. . .
Harris Teachers College	1933 (19:111)	1932 (19:111)	1935 (22:101)
University of Illinois	1963 (49:25–43)	1963 (49:134)	1967 (52:125; 53:6, 122–23)
The Jefferson Medical College	1956 (42:75)	1956 (42:342)	1968 (54:178–79)
The University of Kansas City	1941 (27:478–93)	1941 (28:11)	1957 (43:533)
Lincoln College	1964 (50:244–50)	1965 (51:246)	1968 (54:178)
Livingstone College	1958 (44:188–91)	1958 (44:503, 661)	1960 (46:228)
Lorain County Community College	1968 (54:49–58)	1968 (54:175–76)	. . .
Lowell Technological Institute	1959 (45:550–67)	1960 (46:229)	. . .
Memphis State College	1943 (29:550–80)	1944[3]	1949 (35:11)
Mercy College of Detroit	1963 (49:245–52)	1964 (50:134)	1968 (54:178)

[2] By action of the Council on May 28, 1943.

[3] By action of the Council; no Annual Meeting this year.

Institution	Ad hoc *committee report*	*Censured*	*Censure withdrawn*
University of Michigan	1958 (44:53–101)	1958 (44:503, 661–62)	1959 (45:273–74, 398–99; 46:228–29)
University of Mississippi[4]	1930 (16:551–53)	1930 (17:140–41)	1932 (19:8)
University of Missouri	1945 (31:278–315)	1946[5]	1952 (38:104)
Montana State University	1940 (26:73–91)	1939 (26:290)	1945[6]
University of Nevada	1956 (42:530–62)	1957 (43:360)	1959 (45:273, 395)
New York University	1958 (44:22–52)	1959 (45:274, 393–94)	1961 (47:144)
North Dakota Agricultural College	1938 (24:585–97)	1938 (25:238)	1939 (26:289–90)
———	1956 (42:130–60)	1956 (42:340)	1964 (50:132)
Ohio State University	1956 (42:81–83)	1956 (42:341–42)	1959 (45:273, 394–95)
University of Oklahoma	1956 (42:69–70)	1956 (42:341)	1957 (43:359–60)
College of the Ozarks	1963 (49:352–59)	1964 (50:134–35)	. . .
University of Pittsburgh	1935 (21:224–66)	1935 (22:99)	1947 (33:7)
Princeton Theological Seminary	1959 (45:47–57)	1960 (46:229)	1961 (47:144)
Rollins College	1933 (19:416–39)	1933 (20:10)	1938 (25:238)
Rutgers University	1956 (42:77–78)	1956 (42:342)	1958 (44:503, 665–66)
St. John's University (New York)	1966 (52:12–19)	1966 (52:100, 124)	. . .
St. Louis University	1939 (25:514–35)	1939 (26:290)	1947 (33:7)
———	1956 (42:108–29)	1956 (42:339–40)	1957 (43:360)

[4] Mississippi State institutions, on recommendation by the Council.
[5] By action of the Council; no Annual Meeting this year.
[6] By action of the Council; no Annual Meeting this year.

Institution	Ad hoc *committee report*	*Censured*	*Censure withdrawn*
St. Mary's College (Minnesota)	1968 (54:37–42)	1968 (54:174)	. . .
Sam Houston State College	1963 (49:44–51)	1963 (49:134)	. . .
South Dakota State University	1961 (47:247–55)	1962 (48:163)	. . .
University of South Florida	1964 (50:44–57)	1964 (50:133)	1968 (54:178)
Southern University and Agricultural and Mechanical College	1968 (54:14–24)	1968 (54:173–74)	. . .
Southwestern Louisiana Institute	1956 (43:718–33)	1958 (44:503, 662)	1960 (46:228)
State College of Arkansas	1963 (49:5–14)	1963 (49:133–34)	1968 (54:177)
State Teachers College (Tenn.)	1942 (28:662–77)	1943[7]	1956 (42:340)
State College for Women (Miss.)	1930 (16:551–53)	1930 (17:140–41)[8]	1932 (19:8)
John B. Stetson University	1939 (25:377–99)	1939 (26:290)	1949 (35:11)
Temple University	1956 (42:79–80)	1956 (42:342)	1961 (47:143)
University of Tennessee	1939 (25:310–19)	1939 (26:290)	1947 (33:7)
Texas A & M University	1967 (53:378–84)	1968 (54:176)	. . .
Texas Technological College	1958 (44:170–87)	1958 (44:503, 662–63)	1967 (53:123)
University of Texas	1946 (32:374–85)	1946[9]	1953 (39:100)
Trenton State College	1968 (54:43–48)	1968 (54:174–75)	. . .
United States Naval Academy	1934 (20:25–31)	1933 (20:10)	1938 (24:301)
Wayne State College	1964 (51:347–54)	1965 (51:246)	. . .

[7] By action of the Council; no Annual Meeting this year.
[8] Mississippi State institutions, on recommendation by the Council.
[9] By action of the Council; no Annual Meeting this year.

Institution	Ad hoc *committee report*	*Censured*	*Censure withdrawn*
West Chester State Teachers College	1939 (25:44–72)	1939 (26:290)	1959 (45:273, 395–96)
Western Washington College of Education	1941 (27:48–60)	1941 (28:11)	1944[10]
Winthrop College	1942 (28:173–96)	1943[11]	1957 (43:360)
Wisconsin State University—Whitewater	1968 (54:25–36)	1968 (54:175)	. . .

[10] By action of the Council; no Annual Meeting this year.
[11] By action of the Council; no Annual Meeting this year.

B. *AD HOC* COMMITTEE REPORTS NOT RESULTING IN CENSURE, 1917–1967, ALPHABETICAL LIST, *AAUP BULLETIN* REFERENCES

Institution	Ad hoc *committee report*	*Action noted*
Adelphi University	1967(53:278–91)	1968(54:177)
Allegheny College	1917 (3; 8:19–22)	...
Bethany College	1919 (5; 5:26–61)	...
Boston University	1929 (15:270–76)	...
Centre College	1933 (19:440)	...
Clark University	1924 (10:412–79)	1932 (18:349–50)
Colorado College	1919 (5; 7–8:51–130)	1920 (6; 4:20)
Colorado School of Mines	1920 (6; 5:19–40)	...
University of Colorado	1916 (2; 2; 2:3–72)	...
———	1956 (42:67–69)	...
Columbia University	1918 (4; 2–3:11–12)	1922 (8; 7:21–41)
Converse College	1934 (20:434–47)	...
Culver-Stockton College	1935 (21:592–95)	...
Dean Junior College	1967(53:64–69)	1967(53:122)
Eastern Washington College of Education	1957 (43:225–41)	...
George Washington University	1962 (48:240–47)	1963 (49:135)
Gonzaga University	1965 (51:8–20)	1965 (51:247)
Illinois Wesleyan University	1934 (20:447–49)	...
The University of Kansas City	1957 (43:177–95)	1958 (44:663)
Kansas State Teachers College	1938 (24:115–28)	...
Kansas State Teachers College at Emporia	1956 (42:70–71)	...
Lincoln Memorial University	1931 (17:409–13)	1932 (18:355–56)
C. W. Post College of Long Island University	1962 (48:5–9)	1962 (48:163)
University of Louisville	1927 (13:429–69)	1932 (18:350–51)
Middlebury College	1921 (7; 5:28–37)	...
University of Montana	1917 (3; 5; 2:3–52)	1932 (18:348)
———	1919 (5; 5:13–25)	...
———	1924 (10:154–62)	...
New York City Municipal Colleges	1956 (42:71–74)	...
New York University	1956 (42:75–77)	1958 (44:663–64)
State College of Agriculture and Engineering of North Carolina	1932 (18:224–32)	...
Northwestern University	1962 (48:332–43)	1963 (49:135)
Oklahoma Agricultural and Mechanical College	1929 (15:513–19)	1932 (18:352)
Oregon State College	1956 (42:66–67)	...
University of Oregon	1935 (21:389–404)	...

Institution	Ad hoc *committee report*	*Action noted*
Park College	1937 (23:631–41)	. . .
University of Pennsylvania	1916 (2; 3; 2:7–57)	. . .
Reed College	1956 (42:92–96)	1958 (44:664)
Rensselaer Polytechnic Institute	1936 (22:15–20)	. . .
Rhode Island State College	1932 (18:492–99)	. . .
Rocky Mountain College	1956 (42:292–309)	. . .
San Angelo College	1947 (33:153–58)	. . .
San Diego State College	1956 (42:74–75)	. . .
Simpson College	1940 (26:607–19)	. . .
Smith College	1946 (32:107–48)	. . .
University of South Carolina	1940 (26:476–89)	. . .
University of Southern California	1958 (44:151–57)	1959 (45:399)
University of Tennessee	1924 (10:213–60)	1925 (11; 2:70)
Texas Christian University	1933 (19:472–76)	. . .
University of Utah	1915 (Special Issue)	. . .
University of Vermont	1956 (42:83–85)	. . .
———	1958 (44:11–21)	1958 (44:665)
Washburn College	1921 (7; 1–2:66–137)	. . .
Washington State College	1937 (23:19–21)	. . .
University of Washington	1917 (3; 4:13–16)	. . .
———	1956 (42:61–64)	1956 (42:379–80)
Washington and Jefferson College	1922 (8; 1:53–84)	. . .
Wayne University	1956 (42:87–89)	. . .
Wesleyan University	1916 (2; 2; 2:75–76)	. . .
West Virginia University	1924 (10:92–104)	1932 (18:348)
———	1940 (26:315–49)	. . .
University of Wichita	1935 (21:549–57)	. . .
William Jewell College	1930 (16:226–44)	1932 (18:355)
Wooster College	1917 (3; 5; 1:13–150)	1919 (5; 6:11)
Yale University	1937 (23:353–82)	. . .

C. LATE NOTICE CASE REPORTS, 1959–1967, ALPHABETICAL LIST, *AAUP BULLETIN* REFERENCES

Institution	*Report*
Four Institutions (unnamed)	1959 (45:58–61)
The Agricultural and Technical College of North Carolina	1962 (48:369)
Central Missouri State College	1965 (51:22)
Central State College (Oklahoma)	1965 (51:22)
College of Osteopathic Medicine and Surgery	1960 (46:408)
Dillard University (Louisiana)	1962 (48:369)
Florida Agricultural and Mechanical University	1962 (48:369–70)
Florida Southern College	1960 (46:406–7)
Fort Lewis Agricultural and Mechanical College	1960 (46:407)
Maryland State College	1960 (46:407)
University of Maryland	1965 (51:22)
Menlo College (California)	1965 (51:22)
Mississippi Valley State College	1965 (51:22–23)
Montana State University	1962 (48:370)
North Central College (Illinois)	1965 (51:23)
Northrop Institute of Technology	1962 (48:370–71)
St. Francis College (Pennsylvania)	1965 (51:23)
Savannah State College	1965 (51:23)
Southern University (Louisiana)	1962 (48:371)
———	1965 (51:23–24)
State Teachers College (Bowie, Maryland)	1962 (48:371)
State University College at New Paltz (New York)	1962 (48:369)
West Virginia Wesleyan College	1960 (46:407)
Westminster College (Pennsylvania)	1965(51:304–9)

D. OTHER REPORTS ON NAMED INSTITUTIONS, 1917–1967, ALPHABETICAL LIST, *AAUP BULLETIN* REFERENCES

Institution	*Report*
Alabama State Institutions	1936 (22:453–54)
American University	1930 (16:308)
American University of Beirut	1966 (52:32–41)
Arkansas Polytechnic College	1959 (45:342–45)
University of Arkansas	1959 (45:342–45)
Bard College	1935 (21:595)
Battle Creek College	1933 (19:8)
Butler University	1931 (17:405–7)
———	1934 (20:141–42)
California State College at Long Beach	1968 (54:64–77)
University of California	1920 (6; 5:8–9)
———	1923 (9:382–84)
———	1934 (20:470–71)
———	1950 (36:237–48)
———	1950 (36:585–87)
———	1951 (37:92–101)
———	1956 (42:100–7)
University of Chicago	1921 (7; 3:11–13)
Clark University	1932 (18:349)
Colorado College	1918 (4; 6:10–12)
Colorado School of Mines	1921 (7; 3:7–11)
Dartmouth College	1917 (3; 6:5–6)
———	1921 (7; 3:13–16)
DePauw University	1935 (21: 133)
Des Moines University	1927 (13:544–47)
Elon College	1932 (18:235–36)
University of Georgia	1936 (22:376)
Hamline University	1929 (15:127–28)
Harris Teachers College	1932 (18:429)
Harvard University	1938 (24:598–608)
———	1954 (40:9–17)
Louisiana State University	1931 (17:593–94)
Marshall College	1929 (15:433–34)
Michigan State College	1929 (15:434–35)
Mills College	1931 (17:510–11)
Milwaukee State Teachers College	1932 (18:302–3)
University of Minnesota	1938 (24:222–29)
Mississippi Agricultural and Mechanical College	1931 (17:140–41)
Mississippi State College for Women	1931 (17:140–41)
Mississippi Woman's College	1932 (18:34–36)
University of Mississippi	1932 (17:140–41)

Institution	*Report*
University of Montana	1939 (25:578–84)
———	1940 (26:90–91)
———	1940 (26:602–6)
Morningside College	1931 (17:511)
Muhlenberg College	1927 (13:547)
New York City College	1940 (26:369–77)
New York University	1931 (17:268–70)
Ohio State University	1917 (3; 6:6–11)
Oklahoma Agricultural and Mechanical College	1932 (18:303–4)
Oklahoma College for Women	1927 (13:547–48)
University of Omaha	1935 (21:505–6)
Pacific University	1936 (22:375–76)
Princeton University	1966 (52:41–45)
St. Lawrence University	1933 (19:307–8)
Smith College	1936 (22:480–81)
Tennessee State Teachers College	1942 (28:662–77)
University of Tennessee	1925 (11:70)
Texas Christian University	1931 (17:511–12)
University of Texas	1945 (31:462–65)
Transylvania College	1931 (17:416)
Temple University	1933 (19:477)
———	1934 (20:31)
———	1934 (20:449–50)
United States Naval Academy	1925 (11:71)
———	1934 (20:10)
———	1934 (20:203)
University of Utah	1916 (2; 2:20)
———	1917 (3; 4:8–12)
Central Washington College of Education	1940 (26:471–75)
West Chester Normal School	1928 (14:401–2)
West Chester State Teachers College	1928 (14:401)
West Texas State Teachers College	1931 (17:593–94)
University of West Virginia	1932 (18:348)
Wesleyan University	1935 (21:571–73)
Western Washington College of Education	1940 (26:619)
Wooster College	1917 (3; 3:3–5)

APPENDICES

Appendix A

THE 1915 DECLARATION OF PRINCIPLES

Editor's Note[1]*: Throughout its history the American Association of University Professors has sought the formulation, the recognition, and the observance of principles and procedures conducive to freedom of thought, of inquiry, and of expression in colleges and universities. At the organizational meeting of the Association on January 1 and 2, 1915 it was voted that the Association form a Committee on Academic Freedom and Academic Tenure, which should include members of a joint Committee on Academic Freedom and Tenure of the American Economic Association, the American Political Science Association, and the American Sociological Society, which had been constituted in 1913 to study and report on problems of academic freedom and tenure in teaching and research in economics, political science, and sociology. Pursuant to this action Dr. John Dewey, the Association's first President, appointed a Committee of fifteen members as follows: Edwin R. A. Seligman (Economics), Columbia University,* Chairman; *Charles E. Bennett (Latin), Cornell University; James Q. Dealey (Political Science), Brown University; Edward C. Elliott (Education), University of Wisconsin; Richard T. Ely (Economics), University of Wisconsin; Henry W. Farnam (Political Science), Yale University; Frank A. Fetter (Economics), Princeton University; Guy Stanton Ford (History), University of Minnesota; Charles A. Kofoid (Zoology), University of California; James P. Lichtenberger (Sociology), University of Pennsylvania; Arthur O. Lovejoy (Philosophy), The Johns Hopkins University; Frederick W. Padelford (English), University of Washington; Roscoe Pound (Law), Harvard University; Howard C. Warren (Psychology), Princeton University; Ulysses G. Weatherly (Sociology), Indiana University.*[2]

The Association's first Committee on Academic Freedom and Academic Tenure was established primarily to formulate principles and

[1] The "Editor's Note," here printed with minor omissions, was written for a 1954 reproduction of the *Declaration of Principles (AAUP Bulletin,* 40:89–112, Spring, 1954).

[2] In view of the necessity of investigating an incident at the University of Pennsylvania, Professor Lichtenberger resigned in August, 1915, and was replaced by Professor Franklin H. Giddings (Sociology), Columbia University. Professor Elliott, having been elected Chancellor of the University of Montana, resigned in October. Professor Ford resigned in December, on account of inability to attend the meetings of the committee.

procedures, the observance of which would insure intellectual freedom in colleges and universities. It was not anticipated that the Committee would be called upon to engage in extensive investigatory work. In this connection it is pertinent to note Dr. Dewey's statement as Chairman of the organizational meeting of the Association in reference to the Association's interest in academic freedom:

> *The defense of academic freedom and tenure being already a concern of the existing learned societies will not, I am confident, be more than an incident in the activities of the Association in developing professional standards.*

The Committee had scarcely been formed, however, when a number of alleged infringements of academic freedom were brought to its attention. Eleven such cases were considered during 1915. These cases were diverse in character, viz., *dismissal of individual professors, resignation of professors in protest of dismissals of colleagues, dismissal of a university president, and a complaint of a university president against the institution's governing board. Apropos of these unanticipated demands that were made on the Association during 1915, Dr. Dewey spoke as follows in his Presidential Address to the Annual Meeting of that year:*

> *In concluding I wish to say a word about the large place occupied in this year's program by the question of academic freedom in its relation to academic tenure. I have heard rumors of some criticism on this point. Some have expressed to me fear lest attention to individual grievances might crowd out attention to those general and "constructive" matters which are the Association's reason for existence. Let me say for the reassurance of any such that none of the officers of the Association, least of all those who have been overwhelmed by the duties incident to these investigations, regard this year's work as typical or even as wholly normal. . . . The investigations of particular cases were literally thrust upon us. To have failed to meet the demands would have been cowardly; it would have tended to destroy all confidence in the Association as anything more than a talking body. The question primarily involved was not whether the Council should authorize the investigation of this or that case, but whether the Association was to have legs and arms and be a working body. In short, as conditions shape themselves for us, I personally feel that the work done on particular cases this year turned out to be of the most constructive sort which could have been undertaken. . . . The amount and quality of energy and the time spent upon these matters by our secretary and by the chairman of our committee of fifteen are such as to beggar thanks. These gentlemen and the others who have labored with them must find their reward not only in the increased prosperity of this Association in the future, but, above all, in the enhanced security and dignity of the scholar's calling throughout our country.*

Despite the unexpected volume of work incident to the investigation of individual cases during its first year, the Committee was able to complete a comprehensive report concerning academic freedom, which was approved by the Annual Meeting of the Association held in Washington, D.C., December 31, 1915 and January 1, 1916. In presenting this report to the meeting the Committee said:

> *The safeguarding of a proper measure of academic freedom in American universities requires both a clear understanding of the principles which bear upon the matter, and the adoption by the universities of such arrangements and regulations as may effectually prevent any infringement of that freedom and deprive of plausibility all charges of such infringement. This report is therefore divided into two parts, the first constituting a general declaration of principles relating to academic freedom, the second presenting a group of practical proposals, the adoption of which is deemed necessary in order to place the rules and procedure of the American universities, in relation to these matters, upon a satisfactory footing.*

Largely as a result of the interest in the principles enunciated in the 1915 Declaration of Principles, *the American Council on Education in 1925 called a conference for the purpose of discussing the principles of academic freedom and tenure, with a view to formulating a succinct statement of these principles. Participating in this conference were representatives of a number of organizations of higher education. At this conference there was formulated a statement of principles known to the profession as the 1925* Conference Statement on Academic Freedom and Tenure. *In the formulation of this statement, the participants were not seeking to formulate new principles, but rather to restate good academic custom and usage as these had been developed in practice over a long period of time in institutions whose administrations were aware of the nature of the academic calling and the function of academic institutions.* [*In both*] *the 1925* Conference Statement *and the subsequent adaptation of the principles set forth therein—the 1940* Statement of Principles, . . . *the principles set forth in the Declaration of 1915 are adhered to, adapted, and strengthened* . . . .

A. GENERAL DECLARATION OF PRINCIPLES

The term "academic freedom" has traditionally had two applications—to the freedom of the teacher and to that of the student, *Lehrfreiheit* and *Lernfreiheit*. It need scarcely be pointed out that the freedom which is the subject of this report is that of the teacher. Academic freedom in this sense comprises three elements: freedom of inquiry and research; freedom of teaching within the university or college; and freedom of extra-mural utterance and action. The first of these is almost everywhere so safeguarded that the dangers of its infringement are slight. It may therefore be disregarded in this report. The second and third phases of academic freedom are closely related, and are often not distinguished. The third, however, has an importance of its own, since of late it has perhaps more frequently been the occasion of difficulties and controversies than has the question of freedom of intra-academic teaching. All five of the cases which have recently been investigated by committees of this Association have involved, at least as one factor, the right of university teachers to express their opinions freely outside the university or to engage in political activities in their capacity as citizens. The general principles which have to do with freedom of teaching in both these senses seem to the committee to be in great part, thought not wholly, the same. In this report, therefore, we shall consider the matter primarily with reference to freedom of teaching within the university, and shall assume that what is said thereon is also applicable to the freedom of speech of university teachers outside their institutions, subject to certain qualifications and supplementary considerations which will be pointed out in the course of the report.

An adequate discussion of academic freedom must necessarily consider three matters: (1) the scope and basis of the power exercised by those bodies having ultimate legal authority in academic affairs; (2) the nature of the academic calling; (3) the function of the academic institution or university.

Basis of Academic Authority

American institutions of learning are usually controlled by boards of trustees as the ultimate repositories of power. Upon them finally it devolves to determine the measure of academic freedom which is to be realized in the several institutions. It therefore becomes necessary to inquire into the nature of the trust reposed in these boards, and to ascertain to whom the trustees are to be considered accountable.

The simplest case is that of the proprietary school or college designed for the propagation of specific doctrines prescribed by those who have furnished its endowment. It is evident that in such cases the trustees are bound by the deed of gift, and, whatever be their own views, are obligated to carry out the terms of the trust. If a church or religious denomination establishes a college to be governed by a board of trustees, with the express understanding that the college will be used as an instrument of propaganda in the interests of the religious faith professed by the church or denomination creating it, the trustees have a right to demand that everything be subordinated to that end. If, again, as has happened in this country, a wealthy manufacturer establishes a special school in a university in order to teach, among other things, the advantages of a protective tariff, or if, as is also the case, an institution has been endowed for the purpose of propagating the doctrines of socialism, the situation is analogous. All of these are essentially proprietary institutions, in the moral sense. They do not, at least as regards one particular subject, accept the principles of freedom of inquiry, of opinion, and of teaching; and their purpose is not to advance knowledge by the unrestricted research and unfettered discussion of impartial investigators, but rather to subsidize the promotion of the opinions held by the persons, usually not of the scholar's calling, who provide the funds for their maintenance. Concerning the desirability of the existence of such institutions, the committee does not desire to express any opinion. But it is manifestly important that they should not be permitted to sail under false colors. Genuine boldness and thoroughness of inquiry, and freedom of speech, are scarcely reconcilable with the prescribed inculcation of a particular opinion upon a controverted question.

Such institutions are rare, however, and are becoming ever more rare. We still have, indeed, colleges under denominational auspices; but very few of them impose upon their trustees responsibility for the spread of specific doctrines. They are more and more coming to occupy, with respect to the freedom enjoyed by the members of their teaching bodies, the position of untrammeled institutions of learning, and are differentiated only by the natural influence of their respective historic antecedents and traditions.

Leaving aside, then, the small number of institutions of the proprietary type, what is the nature of the trust reposed in the governing boards of the ordinary institutions of learning? Can colleges and universities that are not strictly bound by their founders to a propagandist duty ever be included in the class of institutions that we have just described as being in a moral sense proprietary? The answer is clear. If the former class of institutions constitute a private or proprietary trust, the latter constitute a public trust. The trustees are trustees for the public. In the case of our state universities this is self-evident. In the case of most of our privately endowed institutions, the situation is really not different. They cannot be permitted to assume the proprietary attitude and privilege, if they are appealing to the general public for support. Trustees of such universities or colleges have no moral right to bind the reason or the conscience of any professor. All claim to such right is waived by the appeal to the general public for contributions and for moral support in the maintenance, not of a propaganda, but of a nonpartisan institution of learning. It follows that any university which lays restrictions upon the intellectual freedom of its professors proclaims itself a proprietary institution, and should be so described whenever it makes a general appeal for funds; and the public should be advised that the institution has no claim whatever to general support or regard.

This elementary distinction between a private and a public trust is not yet so universally accepted as it should be in our American institutions. While in many universities and colleges the situation has come to be entirely satisfactory, there are others in which the relation of trustees to professors is apparently still conceived to be analogous to that of a private employer to his employees; in which, therefore, trustees are not regarded as debarred by any moral restrictions, beyond their own sense of expediency, from imposing their personal opinions upon the teaching of the institution, or even from employing the power of dismissal to gratify their private antipathies or resentments. An eminent university president thus described the situation not many years since:

> In the institutions of higher education the board of trustees is the body on whose discretion, good feeling, and experience the securing of academic freedom now depends. There are boards which leave nothing to be desired in these respects; but there are also numerous bodies that have everything to learn with regard to academic freedom. These barbarous boards exercise an arbitrary power of

> dismissal. They exclude from the teachings of the university unpopular or dangerous subjects. In some states they even treat professors' positions as common political spoils; and all too frequently, both in state and endowed institutions, they fail to treat the members of the teaching staff with that high consideration to which their functions entitle them.[3]

It is, then, a prerequisite to a realization of the proper measure of academic freedom in American institutions of learning, that all boards of trustees should understand—as many already do—the full implications of the distinction between private proprietorship and a public trust.

The Nature of the Academic Calling

The above-mentioned conception of a university as an ordinary business venture, and of academic teaching as a purely private employment, manifests also a radical failure to apprehend the nature of the social function discharged by the professional scholar. While we should be reluctant to believe that any large number of educated persons suffer from such a misapprehension, it seems desirable at this time to restate clearly the chief reasons, lying in the nature of the university teaching profession, why it is to the public interest that the professional office should be one both of dignity and of independence.

If education is the cornerstone of the structure of society and if progress in scientific knowledge is essential to civilization, few things can be more important than to enhance the dignity of the scholar's profession, with a view to attracting into its ranks men of the highest ability, of sound learning, and of strong and independent character. This is the more essential because the pecuniary emoluments of the profession are not, and doubtless never will be, equal to those open to the more successful members of other professions. It is not, in our opinion, desirable that men should be drawn into this profession by the magnitude of the economic rewards which it offers; but it is for this reason the more needful that

[3] From "Academic Freedom," an address delivered before the New York Chapter of the Phi Beta Kappa Society at Cornell University, May 29, 1907, by Charles William Eliot, President of Harvard University.

men of high gifts and character should be drawn into it by the assurance of an honorable and secure position, and of freedom to perform honestly and according to their own consciences the distinctive and important function which the nature of the profession lays upon them.

That function is to deal at first hand, after prolonged and specialized technical training, with the sources of knowledge; and to impart the results of their own and of their fellow-specialists' investigation and reflection, both to students and to the general public, without fear or favor. The proper discharge of this function requires (among other things) that the university teacher shall be exempt from any pecuniary motive or inducement to hold, or to express, any conclusion which is not the genuine and uncolored product of his own study or that of fellow-specialists. Indeed, the proper fulfillment of the work of the professoriate requires that our universities shall be so free that no fair-minded person shall find any excuse for even a suspicion that the utterances of university teachers are shaped or restricted by the judgment, not of professional scholars, but of inexpert and possibly not wholly disinterested persons outside of their ranks. The lay public is under no compulsion to accept or to act upon the opinions of the scientific experts whom, through the universities, it employs. But it is highly needful, in the interest of society at large, that what purport to be the conclusions of men trained for, and dedicated to, the quest for truth, shall in fact be the conclusions of such men, and not echoes of the opinions of the lay public, or of the individuals who endow or manage universities. To the degree that professional scholars, in the formation and promulgation of their opinions, are, or by the character of their tenure appear to be, subject to any motive other than their own scientific conscience and a desire for the respect of their fellow-experts, to that degree the university teaching profession is corrupted; its proper influence upon public opinion is diminished and vitiated; and society at large fails to get from its scholars, in an unadulterated form, the peculiar and necessary service which it is the office of the professional scholar to furnish.

These considerations make still more clear the nature of the relationship between university trustees and members of university faculties. The latter are the appointees, but not in any proper sense the employees, of the former. For, once appointed, the scholar has professional functions to perform in which the appointing authorities have neither competency nor moral right to intervene. The responsibility of the university teacher is primarily to the public itself, and to the judgment of his own profession; and while, with respect to certain external conditions of his vocation, he accepts a responsibility to the authorities of the institution in which he serves, in the essentials of his professional activity his duty is to the wider public to which the institution itself is morally amenable. So far as the university teacher's independence of thought and utterance is concerned—though not in other regards—the relationship of professor to trustees may be compared to that between judges of the Federal courts and the Executive who appoints them. University teachers should be understood to be, with respect to the conclusions reached and expressed by them, no more subject to the control of the trustees than are judges subject to the control of the President with respect to their decisions; while of course, for the same reason, trustees are no more to be held responsible for, or to be presumed to agree with, the opinions or utterances of professors than the President can be assumed to approve of all the legal reasonings of the courts. A university is a great and indispensable organ of the higher life of a civilized community, in the work of which the trustees hold an essential and highly honorable place, but in which the faculties hold an independent place, with quite equal responsibilities—and in relation to purely scientific and educational questions, the primary responsibility. Misconception or obscurity in this matter has undoubtedly been a source of occasional difficulty in the past, and even in several instances during the current year, however much, in the main, a long tradition of kindly and courteous intercourse between trustees and members of university faculties has kept the question in the background.

The Function of the Academic Institution

The importance of academic freedom is most clearly perceived in the light of the purposes for which universities exist. These are three in number.

A. To promote inquiry and advance the sum of human knowledge.

B. To provide general instruction to the students.

C. To develop experts for various branches of the public service.

Let us consider each of these. In the earlier stages of a nation's intellectual development, the chief concern of educational institutions is to train the growing generation and to diffuse the already accepted knowledge. It is only slowly that there comes to be provided in the highest institutions of learning the opportunity for the gradual wresting from nature of her intimate secrets. The modern university is becoming more and more the home of scientific research. There are three fields of human inquiry in which the race is only at the beginning: natural science, social science, and philosophy and religion, dealing with the relations of man to outer nature, to his fellowmen, and to ultimate realities and values. In natural science all that we have learned but serves to make us realize more deeply how much more remains to be discovered. In social science in its largest sense, which is concerned with the relations of men in society and with the conditions of social order and well-being, we have learned only an adumbration of the laws which govern these vastly complex phenomena. Finally, in the spiritual life, and in the interpretation of the general meaning and ends of human existence and its relation to the universe, we are still far from a comprehension of the final truths, and from a universal agreement among all sincere and earnest men. In all of these domains of knowledge, the first condition of progress is complete and unlimited freedom to pursue inquiry and publish its results. Such freedom is the breath in the nostrils of all scientific activity.

The second function—which for a long time was the only function—of the American college or university is to provide instruction for students. It is scarcely open to question that freedom of utterance is as important to the teacher as it is to the investigator. No man can be a successful teacher unless he enjoys the respect of his students, and their confidence in his intellectual integrity. It is clear, however, that this confidence will be impaired if there is suspicion on the part of the student that the teacher is not expressing himself fully or frankly, or that college and university teachers in general are a repressed and intimidated class who dare not speak with that candor and courage which youth always demands in those whom it is to esteem. The average student is a discerning observer, who soon takes the measure of his instructor. It is not only the character of the instruction but also the character of the instructor that counts; and if the student has reason to believe that the instructor is not true to himself, the virtue of the instruction as an educative force is incalculably diminished. There must be in the mind of the teacher no mental reservation. He must give the student the best of what he has and what he is.

The third function of the modern university is to develop experts for the use of the community. If there is one thing that distinguishes the more recent developments of democracy, it is the recognition by legislators of the inherent complexities of economic, social, and political life, and the difficulty of solving problems of technical adjustment without technical knowledge. The recognition of this fact has led to a continually greater demand for the aid of experts in these subjects, to advise both legislators and administrators. The training of such experts has, accordingly, in recent years, become an important part of work of the universities; and in almost every one of our higher institutions of learning the professors of the economic, social, and political sciences have been drafted to an increasing extent into more or less unofficial participation in the public service. It is obvious that here again the scholar must be absolutely free not only to pursue his investigations but to declare the results of his researches, no matter where they may lead him or to what extent they may come into conflict with accepted opinion. To be of use to the legislator or the administrator, he must enjoy their complete confidence in the disinterestedness of his conclusions.

It is clear, then, that the university cannot perform its threefold function without accepting and enforcing to the fullest extent the principle of academic freedom. The responsibility of the university as a whole is to the community at large, and any restriction upon the freedom of the instructor is bound to react injuriously upon the efficiency and the *morale* of the institution, and therefore ultimately upon the interests of the community.

The attempted infringements of academic freedom at present are probably not only of less frequency than, but of a different character from, those to be found in former times. In the early period of university development in America the chief menace to academic freedom was ecclesiastical, and the disciplines chiefly affected were philosophy and the natural sciences. In more recent times the danger zone has been shifted to the political and social sciences—though we still have sporadic examples of the former class of cases in some of our smaller institutions. But it is precisely in these provinces of knowledge in which academic freedom is now most likely to be threatened, that the need for it is at the same time most evident. No person of intelligence believes that all of our political problems have been solved, or that the final stage of social evolution has been reached. Grave issues in the adjustment of men's social and economic relations are certain to call for settlement in the years that are to come; and for the right settlement of them mankind will need all the wisdom, all the good will, all the soberness of mind, and all the knowledge drawn from experience, that it can command. Toward this settlement the university has potentially its own very great contribution to make; for if the adjustment reached is to be a wise one, it must take due account of economic science, and be guided by that breadth of historic vision which it should be one of the functions of a university to cultivate. But if the universities are to render any such service toward the right solution of the social problems of the future, it is the first essential that the scholars who carry on the work of universities shall not be in a position of dependence upon the favor of any social class or group, that the disinterestedness and impartiality of their inquiries and their conclusions shall be, so far as is humanly possible, beyond the reach of suspicion.

The special dangers to freedom of teaching in the domain of the social sciences are evidently two. The one which is the more likely to affect the privately endowed colleges and universities is the danger of restrictions upon the expression of opinions which point toward extensive social innovations, or call in question the moral legitimacy or social expediency of economic conditions or commercial practices in which large vested interests are involved. In the political, social, and economic field almost every question, no matter how large and general it at first appears, is more or less affected with private or class interests; and, as the governing body of a university is naturally made up of men who through their standing and ability are personally interested in great private enterprises, the points of possible conflict are numberless. When to this is added the consideration that benefactors, as well as most of the parents who send their children to privately endowed institutions, themselves belong to the more prosperous and therefore usually to the more conservative classes, it is apparent that, so long as effectual safeguards for academic freedom are not established, there is a real danger that pressure from vested interests may, sometimes deliberately and sometimes unconsciously, sometimes openly and sometimes subtly and in obscure ways, be brought to bear upon academic authorities.

On the other hand, in our state universities the danger may be the reverse. Where the university is dependent for funds upon legislative favor, it has sometimes happened that the conduct of the institution has been affected by political considerations; and where there is a definite governmental policy or a strong public feeling on economic, social, or political questions, the menace to academic freedom may consist in the repression of opinions that in the particular political situation are deemed ultra-conservative rather than ultra-radical. The essential point, however, is not so much that the opinion is of one or another shade, as that it differs from the views entertained by the authorities. The question resolves itself into one of departure from accepted standards; whether the departure is in the one direction or the other is immaterial.

This brings us to the most serious difficulty of this problem; namely, the dangers connected with the existence in a democracy of an overwhelming and concentrated public opinion. The tendency of modern democracy is for men to think alike, to feel alike, and to speak alike. Any departure from the conventional standards is apt to be regarded with suspicion. Public opinion is at once the chief safeguard of a democracy, and the chief menace to the real liberty of the individual. It almost seems as if the danger of despotism cannot be wholly averted under any form of government. In a political autocracy there is no effective public opinion, and all are subject to the tyranny of the ruler; in a democracy there is political freedom, but there is likely to be a tyranny of public opinion.

An inviolable refuge from such tyranny should be found in the university. It should be an intellectual experiment station, where new ideas may germinate and where their fruit, though still distasteful to the community as a whole, may be allowed to ripen until finally, perchance, it may become a part of the accepted intellectual food of the nation or of the world. Not less is it a distinctive duty of the university to be the conservator of all genuine elements of value in the past thought and life of mankind which are not in the fashion of the moment. Though it need not be the "home of beaten causes," the university is, indeed, likely always to exercise a certain form of conservative influence. For by its nature it is committed to the principle that knowledge should precede action, to the caution (by no means synonymous with intellectual timidity) which is an essential part of the scientific method, to a sense of the complexity of social problems, to the practice of taking long views into the future, and to a reasonable regard for the teachings of experience. One of its most characteristic functions in a democratic society is to help make public opinion more self-critical and more circumspect, to check the more hasty and unconsidered impulses of popular feeling, to train the democracy to the habit of looking before and after. It is precisely this function of the university which is most injured by any restriction upon academic freedom; and it is precisely those who most value this aspect of the university's work who should most earnestly protest against any such restriction. For the public may respect, and be influenced by, the counsels of prudence and of moderation which are given by men of science, if it believes those counsels to be the disinterested expression of the scientific temper and of unbiased inquiry. It is little likely to respect or heed them if it has reason to believe that they are the expression of the interests, or the timidities, of the limited portion of the community which is in a position to endow institutions of learning, or is most likely to be represented upon their boards of trustees. And a plausible reason for this belief is given the public so long as our universities are not organized in such a way as to make impossible any exercise of pressure upon professorial opinions and utterances by governing boards of laymen.

Since there are no rights without corresponding duties, the considerations heretofore set down with respect to the freedom of the academic teacher entail certain correlative obligations. The claim to freedom of teaching is made in the interest of the integrity and of the progress of scientific inquiry; it is, therefore, only those who carry on their work in the temper of the scientific inquirer who may justly assert this claim. The liberty of the scholar within the university to set forth his conclusions, be they what they may, is conditioned by their being conclusions gained by a scholar's method and held in a scholar's spirit; that is to say, they must be the fruits of competent and patient and sincere inquiry, and they should be set forth with dignity, courtesy, and temperateness of language. The university teacher, in giving instruction upon controversial matters, while he is under no obligation to hide his own opinion under a mountain of equivocal verbiage, should, if he is fit for his position, be a person of a fair and judicial mind; he should, in dealing with such subjects, set forth justly, without suppression or innuendo, the divergent opinions of other investigators; he should cause his students to become familiar with the best published expressions of the great historic types of doctrine upon the questions at issue; and he should, above all, remember that his business is not to provide his students with ready-made conclusions, but to train them to think for themselves, and to provide them access to those materials which they need if they are to think intelligently.

It is, however, for reasons which have already been made evident, inadmissible that the power of determining when departures from the requirements of the scientific spirit and method have occurred, should be vested in bodies not composed of members of the academic profession. Such bodies necessarily lack full competency to judge of those requirements; their intervention can never be exempt from the suspicion that it is dictated by other motives than zeal for the integrity of science; and it is, in any case, unsuitable to the dignity of a great profession that the initial responsibility for the maintenance of its professional standards should not be in the hands of its own members. It follows that university teachers must be prepared to assume this responsibility for themselves. They have hitherto seldom had the opportunity, or perhaps the disposition, to do so. The obligation will doubtless, therefore, seem to many an unwelcome and burdensome one; and for its proper discharge members of the profession will perhaps need to acquire, in a greater measure than they at present possess it, the capacity for impersonal judgment in such cases, and for judicial severity when the occasion requires it. But the responsibility cannot, in this committee's opinion, be rightfully evaded. If this profession should prove itself unwilling to purge its ranks of the incompetent and the unworthy, or to prevent the freedom which it claims in the name of science from being used as a shelter for inefficiency, for superficiality, or for uncritical and intemperate partisanship, it is certain that the task will be performed by others—by others who lack certain essential qualifications for performing it, and whose action is sure to breed suspicions and recurrent controversies deeply injurious to the internal order and the public standing of universities. Your committee has, therefore, in the appended "Practical Proposals" attempted to suggest means by which judicial action by representatives of the profession, with respect to the matters here referred to, may be secured.

There is one case in which the academic teacher is under an obligation to observe certain special restraints—namely, the instruction of immature students. In many of our American colleges, and especially in the first two years of the course, the student's character is not yet fully formed, his mind is still relatively immature. In these circumstances it may reasonably be expected that the instructor will present scientific truth with discretion, that he will introduce the student to new conceptions gradually, with some consideration for the student's preconceptions and traditions, and with due regard to character-building. The teacher ought also to be especially on his guard against taking unfair advantage of the students' immaturity by indoctrinating him with the teacher's own opinions before the student has had an opportunity fairly to examine other opinions upon the matters of question, and before he has sufficient knowledge and ripeness in judgment to be entitled to form any definitive opinion of his own. It is not the least service which a college or university may render to those under its instruction, to habituate them to looking not only patiently but methodically on both sides, before adopting any conclusion upon controverted issues. By these suggestions, however, it need scarcely be said that the committee does not intend to imply that it is not the duty of an academic instructor to give to any students old enough to be in college a genuine intellectual awakening and to arouse in them a keen desire to reach personally verified conclusions upon all questions of general concernment to mankind, or of special significance for their own time. There is much truth in some remarks recently made in this connection by a college president:

> Certain professors have been refused re-election lately, apparently because they set their students to thinking in ways objectionable to the trustees. It would be well if more teachers were dismissed because they fail to stimulate thinking of any kind. We can afford to forgive a college professor what we regard as the occasional error of his doctrine, especially as we may be wrong, provided he is a contagious center of intellectual enthusiasm. It is better for students to think about heresies than not to think at all; better for them to climb new trails, and stumble over error if need be, than to ride forever in upholstered ease in the overcrowded highway. It is a primary duty of a teacher to make a student take an honest account of his stock of ideas, throw out the dead matter, place revised price marks on what is left, and try to fill his empty shelves with new goods.[4]

It is, however, possible and necessary that such intellectual awakening be brought about with patience, considerateness, and pedagogical wisdom.

There is one further consideration with regard to the classroom utterances of college and university teachers to which the committee thinks it important to call the attention of members of the profession, and of administrative authorities. Such utterances ought always to be considered privileged communications. Discussions in the classroom ought not to be supposed to be utterances for the public at large. They are often designed to provoke opposition or arouse debate. It has, unfortunately, sometimes happened in this country that sensational newspapers have quoted and garbled such remarks. As a matter of common law, it is clear that the utterances of an academic instructor are privileged, and may not

[4] William T. Foster, President of Reed College, in *The Nation*, November 11, 1915.

be published, in whole or part, without his authorization.[5] But our practice, unfortunately, still differs from that of foreign countries, and no effective check has in this country been put upon such unauthorized and often misleading publication. It is much to be desired that test cases should be made of any infractions of the rule.

In their extramural utterances, it is obvious that academic teachers are under a peculiar obligation to avoid hasty or unverified or exaggerated statements, and to refrain from intemperate or sensational modes of expression. But subject to these restraints, it is not, in this committee's opinion, desirable that scholars should be debarred from giving expression to their judgments upon controversial questions, or that their freedom of speech, outside the university, should be limited to questions falling within their own specialties. It is clearly not proper that they should be prohibited from lending their active support to organized movements which they believe to be in the public interest. And, speaking broadly, it may be said in the words of a nonacademic body already once quoted in a publication of the Association, that "it is neither possible nor desirable to deprive a college professor of the political rights vouchsafed to every citizen."[6]

It is, however, a question deserving of consideration by members of this Association, and by university officials, how far academic teachers, at least those dealing with political, economic, and social subjects, should be prominent in the management of our great party organizations, or should be candidates for state or national offices of a distinctly political character. It is manifestly desirable that such teachers have minds untrammeled by party loyalties, unexcited by party enthusiasms, and unbiased by personal political ambitions; and that universities should remain uninvolved in

[5] The leading case is Abernathy *vs.* Hutchinson, 3 L.J., Ch. 209. In this case, where damages were awarded, the court held as follows: "That persons who are admitted as pupils or otherwise to hear these lectures, although they are orally delivered and the parties might go to the extent, if they were able to do so, of putting down the whole by means of shorthand, yet they can do that only for the purpose of their own information and could not publish, for profit, that which they had not obtained the right of selling."

[6] Report of the Wisconsin State Board of Public Affairs, December 1914.

party antagonisms. On the other hand, it is equally manifest that the material available for the service of the State would be restricted in a highly undesirable way, if it were understood that no member of the academic profession should ever be called upon to assume the responsibilities of public office. This question may, in the committee's opinion, suitably be made a topic for special discussion at some future meeting of this Association, in order that a practical policy, which shall do justice to the two partially conflicting considerations that bear upon the matter, may be agreed upon.

It is, it will be seen, in no sense the contention of this committee that academic freedom implies that individual teachers should be exempt from all restraints as to the matter or manner of their utterances, either within or without the university. Such restraints as are necessary should in the main, your committee holds, be self-imposed, or enforced by the public opinion of the profession. But there may, undoubtedly, arise occasional cases in which the aberrations of individuals may require to be checked by definite disciplinary action. What this report chiefly maintains is that such action cannot with safety be taken by bodies not composed of members of the academic profession. Lay governing boards are competent to judge concerning charges of habitual neglect of assigned duties, on the part of individual teachers, and concerning charges of grave moral delinquency. But in matters of opinion, and of the utterance of opinion, such boards cannot intervene without destroying, to the extent of their intervention, the essential nature of a university—without converting it from a place dedicated to openness of mind, in which the conclusions expressed are the tested conclusions of trained scholars, into a place barred against the access of new light, and precommitted to the opinions or prejudices of men who have not been set apart or expressly trained for the scholar's duties. It is, in short, not the absolute freedom of utterance of the individual scholar, but the absolute freedom of thought, of inquiry, of discussion, and of teaching, of the academic profession, that is asserted by this declaration of principles. It is conceivable that our profession may prove unworthy of its high calling, and unfit to exercise the responsibilities that belong to it. But it will scarcely be said as yet to have given evidence of such unfitness. And the existence of this Association, as it seems to your committee, must be construed as a pledge, not only that the profession will earnestly guard those liberties without which it cannot rightly render its distinctive and indispensable service to society, but also that it will with equal earnestness seek to maintain such standards of professional character, and of scientific integrity and competency, as shall make it a fit instrument for that service.

B. PRACTICAL PROPOSALS

As the foregoing declaration implies, the ends to be accomplished are chiefly three:

1. To safeguard freedom of inquiry and of teaching against both covert and overt attacks, by providing suitable judicial bodies, composed of members of the academic profession, which may be called into action before university teachers are dismissed or disciplined, and may determine in what cases the question of academic freedom is actually involved.
2. By the same means, to protect college executives and governing boards against unjust charges of infringement of academic freedom, or of arbitrary and dictatorial conduct—charges which, when they gain wide currency and belief, are highly detrimental to the good repute and the influence of universities.
3. To render the profession more attractive to men of high ability and strong personality by insuring the dignity, the independence, and the reasonable security of tenure, of the professorial office.

The measures which it is believed to be necessary for our universities to adopt to realize these ends—measures which have already been adopted in part by some institutions—are four:

Action by faculty committees on reappointments. Official action relating to reappointments and refusals of reappointment should be taken only with the advice and consent of some board or committee representative of the faculty. Your committee does not desire to make at this time any suggestion as to the manner of selection of such boards.

Definition of tenure of office. In every institution there should be an unequivocal understanding as to the term of each appointment; and the tenure of professorships and associate professorships, and of all positions above the grade of instructor after ten years of service, should be permanent (subject to the provisions hereinafter given for removal upon charges). In those state universities which are legally incapable of making contracts for more than a limited period, the governing boards should announce their policy with respect to the presumption of reappointment in the several classes of position, and such announcements, though not legally enforceable, should be regarded as morally binding. No university teacher of any rank should, except in cases of grave moral delinquency, receive notice of dismissal or of refusal of reappointment, later than three months before the close of any academic year, and in the case of teachers above the grade of instructor, one year's notice should be given.

Formulation of grounds for dismissal. In every institution the grounds which will be regarded as justifying the dismissal of members of the faculty should be formulated with reasonable definiteness; and in the case of institutions which impose upon their faculties doctrinal standards of a sectarian or partisan character, these standards should be clearly defined and the body or individual having authority to interpret them, in case of controversy, should be designated. Your committee does not think it best at this time to attempt to enumerate the legitimate grounds for dismissal, believing it to be preferable that individual institutions should take the initiative in this.

Judicial hearings before dismissal. Every university or college teacher should be entitled, before dismissal or demotion, to have the charges against him stated in writing in specific terms and to have a fair trial on those charges before a special or permanent judicial committee chosen by the faculty senate or council, or by the faculty at large. At such trial the teacher accused should have full opportunity to present evidence, and if the charge is one of professional incompetency, a formal report upon his work should be first made in writing by the teachers of his own department and of cognate departments in the university, and, if the teacher concerned so desires, by a committee of his fellow-specialists from other institutions, appointed by some competent authority.

The above declaration of principles and practical proposals are respectfully submitted by your committee to the approval of the Association, with the suggestion that, if approved, they be recommended to the consideration of the faculties, administrative officers, and governing boards of the American universities and colleges.

EDWIN R. A. SELIGMAN (Economics), Columbia University, *Chairman*
CHARLES E. BENNETT (Latin), Cornell University
JAMES Q. DEALEY (Political Science), Brown University
RICHARD T. ELY (Economics), University of Wisconsin
HENRY W. FARNAM (Political Science), Yale University
FRANK A. FETTER (Economics), Princeton University
FRANKLIN H. GIDDINGS (Sociology), Columbia University
CHARLES A. KOFOID (Zoology), University of California
ARTHUR O. LOVEJOY (Philosophy), The Johns Hopkins University
FREDERICK W. PADELFORD (English), University of Washington
ROSCOE POUND (Law), Harvard University
HOWARD C. WARREN (Psychology), Princeton University
ULYSSES G. WEATHERLY (Sociology), Indiana University

Appendix B

ON SOME MISCONCEPTIONS CONCERNING ACADEMIC FREEDOM[1]

By Fritz Machlup[2]
Princeton University

Recent discussions have shown that there is much confusion about the meaning, the purposes, the scope, and the implementation of academic freedom. Lifelong champions of academic freedom who have been in agreement on the formulation of its principles now find themselves divided in their interpretation.

Perhaps the smallest of the troubles is that it is difficult or impossible to formulate an unambiguous definition of academic freedom. If confined to the most general idea, the definition will be too broad for practical purposes; if it includes many qualifications, it may be subject to such narrow interpretations by unsympathetic interpreters as to become almost useless. One must not expect to find a definition from which a course of action for implementing the principles of academic freedom can be safely inferred.

If freedom in general is defined as the absence of, or protection from, restraints and interferences, the definition of a particular

[1] First printed in *AAUP Bulletin,* 41:753–84 (Winter, 1955); Professor Machlup was in 1955 on the faculty of The Johns Hopkins University.

[2] This statement was approved by a committee of the Association's chapter at The Johns Hopkins University, and later by the chapter, which, at a regular meeting, voted "to consider Dr. Machlup's essay an excellent exposition of the freedom that society should grant to members of the academic profession if they are to fulfill their function most effectively." The author gratefully acknowledges criticisms and suggestions received from G. Heberton Evans, Jr., Hans W. Gatzke, H. Bentley Glass, Kemp Malone, Richard H. Shryock, and Abel Wolman; also from J. D. H. Donnay, Ludwig Edelstein, Ward Edwards, Evelyn Howard, Victor Lowe, Edith Penrose, and David Riesman. However, responsibility for the views expressed is solely the author's.

kind of freedom will have to specify whose protection from whose interferences of what sort and with what kind of activity it refers to. The following definition attempts to make these specifications, if only tentatively and subject to clarification later in this paper:

> Academic freedom consists in the absence of, or protection from, such restraints or pressures—chiefly in the form of sanctions threatened by state or church authorities or by the authorities, faculties, or students of colleges and universities, but occasionally also by other power groups in society—as are designed to create in the minds of academic scholars (teachers, research workers, and students in colleges and universities) fears and anxieties that may inhibit them from freely studying and investigating whatever they are interested in, and from freely discussing, teaching, or publishing whatever opinions they have reached.

Faithful to the original meaning of academic freedom, this definition comprises the freedom to learn as well as the freedom to teach. There have been countries and times in which the students' freedoms were more debated than the professors'. Where all institutions of higher learning are operated by the state and a student has no alternative place to study, the problem of his freedom is indeed of prime importance. In the present-day United States, the only important issue regarding the freedom to learn is linked with possible restrictions on the freedom to teach: the opportunities to learn are restricted if certain subjects or ideas are excluded from the curriculum or if teachers of certain persuasions are excluded from the faculty. In this country, freedom to teach has always been the more important problem, so much so that the American dictionary definitions of academic freedom confine themselves to the professors' side of it. All the public discussions in recent years have, in fact, dealt with the professors' freedom, and so will the reflections in this paper.

Efforts to cast a better definition or to formulate more ringing pronouncements of the principles of academic freedom are unlikely to produce the clarifications that are needed at the present time. Since the positive meaning of a proposition is not clear as long as doubt is left concerning what it negates, attempts at clarification should critically analyse the logical status of supposed corollaries which may actually contradict the proposition if correctly understood. In this sense, a critical or negative statement will serve the purpose better than a reiteration of positive contentions. The following comments are offered as a contribution to the clarification of some of the issues on which dissension appears to be most bewildering. Each section of comment is introduced by a negative, critical, questioning, or actually erroneous statement concerning academic freedom or its application to a given situation.

I. Merely an aspect of freedom of speech?

It has been said that academic freedom should not be conspicuously advertised, lest it be resented, and that it should be presented simply as an aspect of general freedom of speech.

Those who propose that we had better be silent about "academic freedom" and talk only about "freedom of speech" apparently fear that the people at large, who have long since been suspicious of the "intellectual"—and particularly of the professor—will resent granting special liberties to the teachers of their children. Thus, they disclaim that there is any special freedom for the professor, and declare that there is nothing beyond the general freedom of thought and expression which holds good for every citizen.

Granted, of course, that academic freedom is a part of the general category of freedom of thought and expression, it is useful to recall the significant differences in their history, their legal status, their social functions, and their institutional safeguards. Academic freedom antedates general freedom of speech by several hundreds of years, and its development was quite separate and independent. In the United States, academic freedom is not a right that professors or students have under the Constitution[3] or under any law of the land, whereas general freedom of speech is one of the civil liberties protected by the Bill of Rights in our Constitution. While violations of this right can be taken to the courts of law, infringements of academic freedom can be protected only by appealing to the conscience of individuals and groups in society; there is no recourse to the courts except where contractual relations are involved. Finally, academic freedom requires special safeguards

[3] The Prussian Constitution of 1850 contained a provision that "Science and its teaching shall be free."

quite different from those provided by the freedom of speech guaranteed in the Constitution.

The Constitutional guarantee of free speech implies only that one who says unpopular or supposedly dangerous things will not be punished by the government, and that the Congress will not make any laws to interfere with free speech. Professors need more than this absence of governmental sanctions, more than a guarantee that they will not be jailed for the expressions of their thoughts. If they are to be encouraged to pursue the truth wherever it may lead, to "follow out any bold, vigorous, independent train of thought," braving the criticism, ridicule, or wrath of their colleagues, they need protection from all more material sanctions, especially from dismissal. The dismissal of a professor from his post not only prevents him from performing his function in society, but, by intimidating thousands of others and causing them to be satisfied with "safe" subjects and "safe" opinions, it also prevents the entire profession from effectively performing its function.

With regard to some occupations, it is eminently in the interest of society that the men concerned speak their minds without fear of retribution. Lawmakers, judges, professors, researchers, clergymen, journalists are in occupations of this type. But these very same occupations are quite sensitive to pressures and fears unless they are granted special immunities (as the law provides in the cases of legislators and judges). A factor contributing to the sensitiveness of these professions is that a member's competence or integrity is made suspect if his services are terminated. More than in most other occupations, the dismissal of a professor jeopardizes or destroys his eligibility for another position in his occupation. The occupational work of the vast majority of people is largely independent of their thought and speech. The professor's work *consists* of his thought and speech. If he loses his position for what he writes or says, he will, as a rule, have to leave his profession, and may no longer be able effectively to question and challenge accepted doctrines or effectively to defend challenged doctrines. And if *some* professors lose their positions for what they write or say, the effect on many other professors will be such that their usefulness to their students and to society will be gravely reduced.

In brief, freedom of speech has a very special function in the case of those whose job it is to speak.

II. A favor to a special interest group?

It has been said that academic freedom is claimed by professors as special privilege solely in their own interest.

Academic freedom comprises not only freedom of teaching, research, and publication, but also freedom of learning; thus it concerns itself not only with the rights of professors, but also with the rights of students. But even the freedom of professors is not defended for the professors' sake, and does not mainly work for their benefit. Indeed, it can be argued that, as a group, professors are made to pay, in terms of lower incomes, for their "privilege" of unrestricted inquiry and speech. Academic freedom cannot be secured without academic tenure. Tenure, or job security, tends to reduce mobility; and reduced mobility, in the long run, tends to depress the salary levels of the group concerned (particularly because movement to alternative occupations is discouraged). Whereas low salary levels obtain for almost all professors, it is only a small fraction of all teachers and scholars that are at all likely ever to disseminate ideas critical of the opinions held by the professional, political, or ecclesiastical authorities, and are thus in any danger of incurring serious disapprobation, and therefore in need of the protection accorded by the rules of academic freedom and tenure.

The fact that perhaps only three or four of every thousand professors would ever have occasion to say or write things that would bring them into conflict with the authorities, or with power groups in society, explains why it is sometimes difficult to rally all faculty members to the vigorous support of academic freedom. There are always a good many professors in "safe" subjects or with "safe" ideas who resent the activities of the "trouble makers" on the faculty. We can understand if they refuse to regard themselves as "beneficiaries" of the "privilege" of academic freedom. For, it is in the interest of society at large, not just in the interest of the professors, that academic freedom is defended.

Society as a whole has much to gain from academic freedom. Since academic freedom promotes intellectual innovation and, indirectly, material as well as intellectual progress, to safeguard it is in the social interest. It is important that the few potential trouble makers are encouraged to voice their dissent, because on such dissent, however unpopular, the advancement of our knowledge and the development of material, social, or spiritual improvements may depend. Materially, professors as a group gain from their freedom only as members of society, and at best in proportion to the gains accruing to society.

Ultimately, then, academic freedom is a right of the people, not a privilege of a few; and this situation is not affected by the fact that most people know little about it. It is the people at large who have a right to learn what scholars may succeed in finding out if they are left free and secure from reprobation. It is the people at large who have a right to the cultural and material benefits that may flow from the teaching and the inquiries of scholars who have nothing to fear when they make honest mistakes.

III. Who threatens, who protects?

It has been said that academic freedom concerns only the relationship between the scholar and the members of the board of trustees of his college or university.

In some recent comments on the pressures exerted by congressional committees, the opinion has been expressed that these pressures, because they did not come from the trustees, did not raise any issue of academic freedom. The explanation of this view lies obviously in the fact that, in the brief history of academic freedom in the United States, it has been chiefly from the boards of trustees that pressures have been exerted upon professors. However, this view overlooks the fact that outside the United States most universities have no boards of trustees; that historically most pressures have come from the state and from the church; and that the atmosphere of academic freedom can be created only by an absence of deliberate pressures of any sort, no matter what their source may be.

A stereotyped view of infringements of academic freedom always sees professors as the oppressed, and governments or trustees as the oppressors. Yet there are many examples in history in which the rôles were reversed, and the state or university authorities acted to protect the professors' freedom. In several German principalities of the 17th and 18th centuries the sovereign was protector of the professor's freedom against the restraints and pressures exerted by narrow-minded colleagues.[4] In the late 1920's and early 1930's in Germany and Czechoslovakia the administration protected professors from students who used violence to prevent non-nationalistic teachers from giving their lectures. Some fifteen years ago, an American university head protected a rabble-rousing Marxist professor not only from the wrath of the trustees but also from the pressure of an action committee of the faculty which had set out to obtain the resignation of their troublesome colleague.

Far from seeing boards of trustees as the main sources of infringements of academic freedom in the United States, one may regard them ideally as the chief protectors of academic freedom against pressures from the outside, from political or ecclesiastical quarters, from civic organizations, or from private interest groups. There have been many instances in which boards of trustees have understood and carried out this function and have protected members of their teaching staff from interference from the outside. When trustees have abdicated their function of protecting the faculty, professors have felt impelled to take action to secure recognition of academic freedom; and even where trustees are fully conscious of their function as protectors and conscientious in the execution of it, they can be greatly aided by a faculty united in the support of these principles and vigilantly guarding their freedoms of teaching and research.

The function of trustees as protectors of academic freedom against outside pressures has probably never been more forcefully stated than by the head of a university when, speaking to professors, he complained about the "most difficult problems" created by the "exhibitionist" on the faculty, "actually unworthy of defense":

> Nevertheless—and now I speak as an administrator—we must defend him, of that I am profoundly convinced; defend him at the risk of our official lives if need be. The reason, of course, is plain. If those who control a professor's employment attempt to place any metes and bounds whatsoever to academic freedom there is no academic freedom. Within the limits imposed by the law of the land it is absolute, or it is non-existent. Therefore trustees and

[4] See G. Kaufmann, *Die Lehrfreiheit an den deutschen Universitäten im neunzehnten Jahrhundert* (Leipzig: Hurzel, 1898).

> presidents must interpose themselves between a justly outraged community and individuals whom they do not respect. They must at least condone platform behavior which fills them with disgust. They must allow their institutions to be disgraced and derided. These things they must do for the sake of a cause which often seems very remote and abstract, and which the public does not understand. It is a hard assignment.[5]

Thus, trustees and administrators, no less than sovereigns and governors, should share with professors and students in the defense of academic freedom. And such defense may be needed against pressures from all quarters—including professors themselves. In short, academic freedom implies protection from pressures and from attempts to intimidate, no matter whence they come.

IV. No other threats but dismissal?

It has been said that academic freedom means protection from dismissal, and that the principles of academic freedom can be identified with rules for academic tenure.

Undoubtedly, most of the publicized issues of academic freedom have had to do with attempted dismissals of professors. Undoubtedly, continuous or permanent tenure is a most important means of protecting the principles of academic freedom. Yet we must recognize that there are many ways, in addition to the threat of dismissal, in which the scholar may be intimidated. Many of the fears gripping the nonconforming scholar, besides the fear of losing his position, can and reasonably should be removed or reduced in order to maintain that atmosphere free from intimidation that is the essence of academic freedom.

A scholar who, through his writing, speeches, or lectures, offends the sensibilities of others—his colleagues, department chairmen, university authorities, interest groups, or large parts of the community—may thereby jeopardize the realization of several of his claims and prospects. Among those may be reappointment in a non-permanent position, promotion to a better position, an increase in his salary, the maintenance of his salary, a moderate teaching load, approval of his course offerings, security clearance

[5] Samuel P. Capen, former Chancellor, University of Buffalo, "Privileges and Immunities," *AAUP Bulletin*, 23:198 (1937).

for access to documents important for his research, undisturbed privacy, freedom from harassment and vilification, freedom from hostile investigation expensive of money, time, and nervous energy.

Ideally, all these threats would have to be removed if academic freedom were to be secured absolutely. In practice this cannot be achieved. In practice a scholar cannot prove that he would have received an increase in his salary had he not voiced his dissent from authoritative opinion. In practice he cannot prove that he would have been given other courses to teach had he not by his teaching or publications incurred the antagonism of his superiors. In practice he cannot prove that he would have been promoted to a better position had he not published or taught certain ideas disliked by others, who found them too radical or too conservative. In practice it is difficult to prove that an appointment was made on the basis of political affiliation, religious background, or national or racial descent.

In spite of these difficulties, the implementation of academic freedom should not be narrowed to the observance of set procedures or "due process" principles in the termination of professors' appointments. It should be recognized that all these and other ways of discriminating against a scholar may be used to intimidate him or to bar him from freely disseminating his views. Academic freedom committees of the faculties in colleges and universities could well take account of complaints along all the lines mentioned and, by objective investigation of such cases, might prevent many attempts to abridge academic freedom.

We do not entertain illusions concerning the effectiveness of machinery designed to strengthen the principles of academic freedom in matters not related to tenure. Even under ideal conditions, the standards applied to the selection of a scholar for a new appointment must be different from the standards applied in the termination of tenure. To be sure, competency and integrity ought to be the paramount criteria in either case. But there is no reliable way of separating a judgment of *comparative* competence and integrity from judgments of many other personal traits, social graces, congeniality, professional likemindedness; and undoubtedly, *comparative* evaluation is the basis of decisions on new appointments and promotions. This is not so, however, with regard to the termination of the tenure of a college or university teacher. In this situation the problem is no longer one of comparing different qualities of achievements, but of finding that certain *minimum* standards have not been met—that is, of finding that the incumbent is *incompetent* or *dishonest.* Such a finding can and should be subjected to certain procedural tests, and these tests are the essence of tenure rules.[6] It would hardly be practicable or desirable to devise strict procedural tests for all the other possible questions in respect to which academic freedom may be violated.

Yet, despite all these difficulties, conceptual as well as procedural, it would be a mistake to restrict the scope of academic freedom to the implementation of tenure rules and to overlook all other ways by which sanctions and undue pressures may be applied to dissenting professors.

V. What about academic responsibility?

It has been debated whether or not academic freedom has a "counterpart" in some particular responsibilities on the part of those to whom the freedom is granted.

Any such statement, affirmative or negative, can become meaningful only after it is made clear just what the term "responsibility" means in the context. Responsibility may mean legal accountability, with the implied risk of legal sanctions for transgressions of some sort, *de facto* accountability with the risk of *de facto* sanctions, or simply conscientiousness in the exercise of certain moral obligations. Moreover, referring to a group of men, responsibility may be individual or collective.

Individual responsibility in the sense of being *de jure* or *de facto* accountable, for actions or omissions, to the state or university authorities can exist only with regard to matters regulated by the law

[6] It may be worth pointing to the difference between legal tenure and merely *de facto* or moral tenure. The former gives the incumbent in an academic position a legal claim enforceable in the courts of law. The latter gives him merely a hope that the college or university authorities will live up to an implied promise and, should they be inclined to go back on it, that his colleagues and the American Association of University Professors will rally to his defense and apply effective moral suasion.

of the land or stipulated by the contract with the institution at which the individual scholar holds an appointment. Individual responsibility in the sense of moral obligation exists with regard to the performance of the scholar's professional functions. This responsibility, however, is less to the appointing authorities than "to the public itself, and to the judgment of his own profession."[7] In a version proposed by a university president for incorporation in a conference statement by the Association of American Colleges and the American Association of University Professors it was stated that the teacher should be the sole judge of what constitutes fulfillment of his responsibilities.[8] This was superseded by a recognition of a measure of faculty responsibility; indeed the American Association of University Professors, from its beginning, had declared that the profession had a "responsibility for the maintenance of its professional standards," and "that university teachers must be prepared to assume this responsibility for themselves."[9]

What is involved here is *moral* responsibility of the members of a faculty as a *body;* it is recognized that such responsibility is indeed a necessary counterpart of academic freedom; but the question of its scope has yet to be answered. Undoubtedly, the faculty has a moral obligation to *select and recommend* for appointment only scholars of assured integrity and competence in their profession. Does faculty responsibility go beyond this?

If death, permanent disability, or the reaching of a stipulated retirement age were the only possible grounds for termination of a teacher's services, the faculty as a group would have no further responsibilities. They could let conscience be the sole guide of the individual teacher's actions. But if dismissal on grounds of professional incompetence or moral turpitude or perhaps other disqualifications is possible under the accepted rules of tenure, then faculty responsibility must extend to the reexamination of a member's fitness to teach whenever facts become known that cast grave doubt on his fitness.

[7] "The 1915 Declaration of Principles," *AAUP Bulletin,* 40:98(1954).

[8] Proposed by Henry Wriston, President of Brown University, in one of the conferences that preceded the agreement on the 1940 *Statement of Principles.*

[9] "The 1915 Declaration of Principles," *op. cit.,* p. 105.

But this responsibility must be cautiously circumscribed lest it become a negation, rather than a complement, of academic freedom. For, let us repeat it, a scholar's intellectual freedom can also be restricted by a narrow-minded group of his own peers. As a matter of fact, it has recently been suggested that professors set up some kind of investigatory agency to probe the political reliability of their colleagues.[10] This suggestion, to be sure, was advanced in order to ward off improper and indiscreet interferences by committees of the Congress and of State legislatures. But the idea of offering, as a substitute for the encroachments on academic freedom "from the outside," more tactful encroachments "from the inside" must be rejected. If college and university faculties were to take it upon themselves suspiciously to watch their members, to investigate alleged "security risks," and to recommend the dismissal of those judged to espouse "wrong" ideas or to be disloyal to the "right" causes, academic freedom would be gone.

The accepted formulations of the principles of academic freedom and tenure provide for the termination of a teacher's services for cause, judged by a duly constituted committee of the faculty after a fair hearing on charges with the safeguards of "due process."[11] Dismissal by the governing board of a college or univerity, without or against the advice of a faculty committee, is a flagrant violation of the principles of academic freedom; and, it should be emphatically stated, a faculty that acquiesces in such a discretionary action by its governing authorities is negligent in its moral obligations to the academic community and to society as a whole.

A judgment whether a scholar is fit or unfit to teach can be made only on the basis of an evaluation of those of his professional and moral qualifications that are relevant to his particular professional activities. Such an evaluation can be made only by his

[10] The creation of a "central educational investigation service" was proposed by a group of educators to the American Council on Education. See "Plan Bids Colleges Police Subversives," *The New York Times,* October 10, 1953, p. 19.

[11] *Editor's Note:* The 1940 *Statement of Principles* provides that dismissal "should, *if possible,* be considered by both a faculty committee and the governing board of the institution." [Emphasis supplied.]

professional colleagues. In hearings on charges of incompetence, the testimony should include that of his professional colleagues in his own institution and others, preferably of scholars nominated by the professional association of his field of specialization. When the charges are related to violations of the law, or to activities creating the presumption of such violations, the faculty committee has to decide whether such violations carry with them strong implications bearing on the teacher's fitness to teach. Where religious or political affiliations or beliefs appear to be part of the charges, it is the responsibility of the faculty to ensure that the judgment about the teacher's fitness to teach is not affected by any disapproval of his opinions and associations, and rests only on evidence concerning his actual professional (or professionally relevant) activities.

The faculty has a moral obligation to remove a member who, for personal gain or on orders from political authorities, deliberately and dishonestly distorts the truth in the presentation of verified or readily verifiable facts. In other words, the faculty has a moral responsibility to initiate action against the scoundrel who fakes evidence in research experiments, forges records to support his alleged findings, deliberately gives false testimony as a paid expert witness in private litigation, fabricates reports and figures, or disseminates what he knows to be fabrications, for the purpose of deceiving.

If such cases ever occur, they certainly are extremely rare. They are listed here as "illustrations" in order to point out that there are cases in which the removal of a teacher is appropriate; that in such cases the faculty has a moral responsibility to take action against the offending teacher; that the charges preferred must be heard and investigated with all the safeguards of due process; that the charges must refer to offenses bearing on his fitness to teach; and that the charges must not refer to his political, philosophic, or religious opinions, beliefs, and associations.

VI. How much immunity for dissenters?

It has been said that academic freedom need not be so far-reaching as to protect dissenters from the usual consequences of their unpopularity.

A judgment on this statement depends on what is regarded as a "usual" consequence of unpopularity. Surely, no one would call it an infringement of academic freedom if a faculty member whose views are disliked is not invited to social gatherings; nor would any scholar in his right mind claim immunity from criticism, however acid and from whatever quarters, academic or non-academic. Indeed, a free flow of critical exchanges is precisely what academic freedom is designed to encourage.

But we are told that more serious retributions should also be tolerated as "usual consquences" of unpopularity. Supposedly, great men will not be easily discouraged; and professors

> must learn to take the bad with the good and to accept the pains that are always inflicted upon those who disturb the present order and the persons who are entrenched therein. It has always been so, from Christ to Galileo, from Galileo to the teachers who dared to espouse the teachings of Darwin, and to offend established beliefs.[12]

This view, we believe, reveals a fundamental misunderstanding of the primary purpose which academic freedom is designed to serve. It is the purpose of academic freedom to create in institutions of higher learning an atmosphere conducive to the critical examination of all accepted doctrines and to the development of new thought, as well as to the defense of old views that have fallen out of fashion; an atmosphere in which scholars and students, however timid or unwilling to make sacrifices, will feel encouraged to question the teachings of authorities and to express freely and vigorously their dissenting views, however unpopular.

Christ and Galileo, we agree, were courageous and self-denying, prepared to sacrifice their lives to their ideals. That they had no freedom of teaching, no protection against persecutions by a world hostile to their messages, is mankind's lasting shame. But, apart from the moral issue, the world should not have to depend for its progress on teachers possessing that kind of courage and self-denial; and for that reason, societies have found it wise to create

[12] Morris A. Soper, "A Layman Looks at the Professors," *The Johns Hopkins Magazine,* May, 1953, p. 16.

an atmosphere in which timid souls and "practical realists" are willing to voice their dissent.[13]

Great scholars, great discoverers, great inventors, great teachers, great philosophers may be timid men, or they may not care enough to face vilification, or they may be too "realistic" to invite trouble. A society that wishes to avail itself of the fruits of their intellectual enterprise must give them as much immunity as possible. Assuming as a fact that scholars may be timid or too "realistic," society has developed the institution of academic freedom in order to reduce the penalties on unpopular unorthodoxy or on unfashionable orthodoxy and to encourage scholars to say whatever they feel that they have to say.

VII. Freedom also for those who abuse freedom?

It has been said that academic freedom must not be granted to those who abuse it.

The question when a "use" becomes an "abuse" is, as a rule, a matter of judgment, and sometimes a matter of prejudice. An appeal to the principles of academic freedom becomes necessary only when protection is demanded against some who are outraged by a professor's opinions and activities and who are therefore inclined to make the charge of an "abuse" of academic freedom. Thus, without in the least denying the important responsibilities of professors or denying the possibility that a few might misuse their positions of trust, we must realize that the charge of "abuse" of freedom often expresses the view that freedom should be denied in some respects or to some persons.

Charges that a professor has misused his position in a dishonest way or for illegitimate purposes must be clearly specified and should not be expressed in vague generalities. We shall presently have to deal with several general grounds on which, according to some widely held points of view, academic freedom should be denied; we shall have to consider the question of whether there are

[13] "Who can compute what the world loses in the multitude of promising intellects combined with timid characters, who dare not follow out any bold, vigorous, independent train of thought lest it should land them in something which would admit of being considered irreligious or immoral" [or subversive]? John Stuart Mill, *On Liberty* (London, 1859; New York: Appleton-Century-Crofts, 1947), p. 33.

definable limits of academic freedom. On the general charge of "abuse" of freedom, however, we should understand, first, the logic of the relationship between used and abused freedom. There are two senses in which it may be said that *use* is being made of academic freedom: in a subjective sense, when a professor acts in a way which he thinks may appear offensive to others but does so in reliance on his immunity from sanctions; in an objective sense, when the principles of academic freedom are invoked in order to forestall sanctions against a professor who has acted in a way which actually did appear offensive to others. Now, since the principles of freedom have to be invoked only under attack and are attacked only on the charge of *abuse,* every "use" of academic freedom—in the objective sense—is an "abuse" in the eyes of some.

Contrary to the view that academic freedom cannot exist if it is abused, it should be recognized that so-called abuses are the only proofs that the freedom really exists; as long as the professors do not say things that impress those who have power to interfere as dangerous or loathsome, there is no way of telling whether academic freedom is only a sham and illusion or something real. Only when the university authorities or others in power are sorely tempted to silence a professor, to threaten him, dismiss him, or "go after" him in any way, and when they resist the temptation out of respect for academic freedom—only then can we see that such freedom exists.

In other words, academic freedom is purely "academic"—hypothetical, imaginary—as long as it is not tested. There is only one possible test of its real existence: when some scholars, through their writings, teachings, speeches, or associations, offend the sensibilities of people in power, or of pressure groups, so potently that complaints of "abuse" of academic freedom are made and interventions against the perpetrators of the "abuse" are demanded; and when these pressures and temptations to interfere are resisted and the offenders are assured of their immunity, then, and only then, is academic freedom shown to be a reality.

Thus, the occurrences of so-called abuses of academic freedom, far from being incompatible with the existence of academic freedom, are the only proofs of its existence.

VIII. Freedom beyond the scholar's area of competence?

It has been said that academic freedom should be confined to the recognized area of the individual scholar's competence and must not be extended to writings or utterances "outside his field."

This view, formulated in the definitions or pronouncements of many sincere advocates of freedom of teaching and research, was perhaps suggested by the fact that competence is the chief factor in the selection of scholars for academic posts, and incompetence the chief ground on which separation from academic posts can be justified. But what this means is that no one should be appointed unless he is competent in the field in which he is expected to search and teach, and that no one should be allowed to hold a post in a field in which he is clearly incompetent. It does not follow, however, that a scholar must be silent on questions pertaining to fields for which he was not appointed, or that he must avoid expressing himself on matters which even he himself may consider outside his area of competence. Still less does it follow that a professor should be reprimanded or dismissed if he expresses his opinions in fields that lie beyond the area assigned to him by the terms of his academic appointment.

Recognition of incompetence as a cause for separation—recognition that the dismissal of a teacher incompetent in his specialty does not violate academic freedom—implies absolutely nothing regarding the freedom of a teacher, whose competence in his specialty is not questioned, to expound on matters outside his specialty. Is it perhaps possible to deduce from the "presuppositions" of the principles of academic freedom whether that freedom should be confined by the boundaries of a scholar's area of competence or should have no such boundaries?

There are at least five different ways in which professors engage in "extra-curricular" speech:

1. Although appointed as a teacher or researcher in a particular subject, a professor may have scholarly interests in one or more other fields of learning, cognate or quite apart, and may engage in research, lecturing, and writing in these fields.

2. Although thoroughly trained only in particular fields, a professor may have intellectual curiosity about matters in other disciplines and may freely express his views on these matters in and out of his classroom and in and out of his university.

3. A professor may be interested in political or religious issues and hold forth on them without inhibitions, both in the classroom and on the public platform.

4. A professor may find it necessary or desirable in his lectures to expatiate on ramifications of the problems he discusses which lie outside his field of competence.

5. As a counsellor and adviser to his students, a professor may discuss their personal problems with them and may take positions on questions for which he has no special qualifications.

Should any of these "invasions of foreign areas" be condemned as improper? All have been so regarded at one time or another. The first of the five kinds of "transgression," incidentally, is different from the other four in that the trespassing scholar would not consider himself as unqualified in the areas into which he has expanded; if some professors in the invaded fields call for "border control" to keep out the men from other university departments, we may suspect that professional jealousy is behind their complaints. The other four kinds of professorial sorties are admittedly into territories which they do not master; thus, if professors warn their colleagues against such sorties, their caution can be attributed to the modesty and conscientiousness which are typical of most scholars. Typically, scholars have serious inhibitions against talking about things of which they know little, inhibitions they acquired when they realized how hard it is to achieve valid generalizations in their own specialty. Not all scholars, of course, have these inhibitions. The question with which we are concerned, however, is not whether professors should be encouraged to overcome their scholarly inhibitions—we believe that they should not—but rather whether areas other than those of certified competence should be considered "out of bounds" and whether a "transgressing" professor should be dismissed.

Against the restrictionist view, let us recall that almost all great thinkers, originators, and developers of great ideas were polyhistors, not narrow specialists. Will anyone seriously contend that Leibnitz should have "specialized" instead of freely holding forth on philosophy, mathematics, law and theology? that Newton should not have been free to lecture and write on theological problems? that Kant should have stayed away from law and politics?

that the mathematician Cournot, the logician Jevons, the astronomer Newcomb, should not have felt free to expound the principles of economics?

It is not only difficult but dangerous to define a scholar's "area" of competence, because such an area ought not to be a static but a continually enlarging one. Interdisciplinary thinking and discussion, on problems for which perhaps no one has a satisfactory answer, is precisely what is most needed in our time, if not at all times. Progress is chiefly made by those who continually press forward to enlarge their areas of competence and to question all certified competences.

All this, perhaps, will be thought by many to be beside the point, for what the limitists nowadays really have in mind when they object to extensions of academic freedom beyond the area of competence is the scholar's taking part in public discussions of current political problems. For several centuries it was the area of religious controversy which many wanted to declare as "out of bounds"; now it is chiefly the area of social, economic, and political controversies from which the professors are to be scared away. And for professors not in the fields of social, economic or political science, this would be achieved through the area-of-competence clause in the definition of academic freedom.

From its very beginning the American Association of University Professors has rejected such limitations of academic freedom. The Association's 1915 *Declaration of Principles* stated that it was not desirable

> that scholars should be debarred from giving expression to their judgments upon controversial questions, or that their freedom of speech, outside the university, should be limited to questions falling within their own specialties. It is clearly not proper that they should be prohibited from lending their active support to organized movements which they believe to be in the public interest.[14]

In other words, while the recognition of academic freedom entails academic responsibilities, particularly a moral obligation of the professor to refrain from "intemperate and sensational modes of

[14] *AAUP Bulletin,* 40:108(1954).

expression," it does not entail a reduction of his civil liberties. It is possible, of course, that there is a point of view from which it can be argued that a professor who exercises his freedom of speech as a citizen in discussing political questions thereby foregoes his tenure rights, and that the trustees, if they dislike his ideas, may dismiss him from his post; but this point of view can hardly be reconciled with the fundamental principles on which academic freedom rests.

A definition of academic freedom which tends to discourage the academic scholar from discussing controversial questions is not consistent with the objectives of academic freedom. The restriction of academic freedom to "areas of competence" is obviously designed to act as such a discouragement.

IX. Freedom to teach subversive ideas?[15]

It has been said that academic freedom must not include the right to advocate or teach "subversive ideas."

Any one informed about the history of academic freedom knows that the most serious interferences with the freedom of teaching have been interferences on the part of authorities fearful of what they regarded as subversion. While in the past many of the ideas condemned as subversive were in the fields of religion or in the natural sciences, where new ideas challenged religious dogma, it is now in the fields of politics and economics that "subversive" ideas are most feared.

In the past, it was exactly the teaching of allegedly subversive ideas in the universities that needed protection from interference. It was exactly the issue of subversion which demonstrated the need for academic freedom. Free enterprise and free markets for the products of the human mind required immunity for the writer and teacher who tried to overturn religious dogma or economic orthodoxy or the belief in a particular form of government. It was through the overturn—i.e., the subversion—of accepted dogmas that we have progressed as far as we have; and it was through sub-

[15] This section was revised after the article had been submitted to The Johns Hopkins University Chapter. The revisions were designed merely to clarify the exposition, and not to alter the meaning.

version of an accepted government that we established the one under which we now live.

That society approves almost all past subversions of doctrine and many past subversions of government need not mean that it should always welcome new subversions and grant immunity to those who promote them. But in any case, confusion must be avoided between the overthrow of doctrines or beliefs—even beliefs in a form of government—and the actual overthrow of a government; the one is in the sphere of thought, the other in the sphere of action.

A discussion of "subversive teaching" must appear rather unrealistic, inasmuch as substantiated charges that a particular professor has been teaching subversive ideas are extremely rare in our times. The facts usually established are the past associations of the professor; from this his accusers deduce his beliefs; from this they deduce that his teaching may have reflected his beliefs; and from this they deduce that he has taught subversive ideas. Obviously, on the basis of such conjectures no charges of subversive teaching can be brought. But the issue, however hypothetical, merits examination. In view of the fact that vigilantes are inclined to mark as "subversive" what others would consider only as radical, is it possible to draw a line where real subversiveness begins? And should some degree of subversiveness be regarded as definitely outside the protection of academic freedom?

Speaking first of the subversion or violent overthrow of government, it may be worth remembering the position of the founding fathers of our republic. Thomas Jefferson, in his Inaugural Address in 1801 said:

> If there be any among us who would wish to dissolve this Union or to change its republican form, let them stand undisturbed as monuments of the safety with which error of opinion may be tolerated where reason is left free to combat it.[16]

Others went further and recognized a basic "right to revolt." Indeed, the right to subvert the government was written into several

[16] From the Inaugural Address of March 4, 1801. Reprinted in *The Writings of Thomas Jefferson* (Thomas Jefferson Memorial Association, 1903), III, 319.

state constitutions.[17] And this principle was reaffirmed by Abraham Lincoln when he said:

> Whenever [the people] shall grow weary of the existing government, they can exercise their constitutional right of amending it or their revolutionary right to dismember or otherthrow it.[18]

But if we should have lost this confidence, if a majority of us should feel insecure under a freedom to overthrow the government, we should at least be intelligent enough to make some significant distinctions. There are important differences among (1) a teacher who organizes a violent uprising, tells his students what actions they should take, what weapons wield, what buildings occupy at an appointed time or signal; (2) a teacher who harangues his students, urging them to participate in a revolutionary conspiracy; (3) a teacher who presents to his students the "need" or "desirability" of a violent overthrow of the government;[19] (4) a teacher who, in his comparative description of alternative social, political, and economic systems, is disparagingly critical of the present system and full of praise for a substitute system; (5) a teacher who, in his comparative description of social, political, and economic institutions within the present system, shows a decided preference for radical changes.

Can the term "subversive" be legitimately applied to all these cases? With due respect for differences in semantic taste, the indiscriminate use of the term for such different situations would be misleading, to say the least. Most of us would probably propose a demarcation line before or after the third of these cases. Should some or all of them be beyond the protection of academic freedom? Some of us may propose the same demarcation line; others, though inclined to draw the line to include the third case among those of

[17] The Constitution of the State of Maryland declared that: "the people . . . have, at all times, the inalienable right to alter, reform or abolish their Form of Government in such manner as they may deem expedient."

[18] Abraham Lincoln, First Inaugural, March 4, 1861.

[19] If he presents the "probability" or "inevitability" of the overthrow, he might be expressing an opinion, based on Marxian or similar arguments, free of any value judgment.

"subversive teaching," may prefer not to regard it as a revolutionary act, but as an "error of opinion" which "may be tolerated where reason is left free to combat it."

Concerning hostile criticism of our present systems and institutions, there should be no doubt that such teaching can be offset by the more objective or contrarily biased presentation of other teachers. Indeed, the teachers who understand the operations of the capitalistic system will be more effective in their exposition if they can take issue with the "subversive" views to which their students may have been exposed in the lectures of its enemies.

To say that teachers must be "scientifically objective" is well enough; but it is neither possible nor desirable for a good teacher always to be "neutral" and to suppress his value judgments. Perhaps "objectivity" in teaching is always a matter of degree. Commitment is always present, at least as regards premises. Almost all our teachers in the social sciences share the preference of the American people for democracy and for capitalism. It would be hypocrisy to call a favorable appraisal "objective" and an adverse one "biased." We all condemn communist countries for suppressing academic freedom when they silence the critics of communism and the friends of capitalism. In any case, academic freedom does not stop this side of "dangerous" beliefs. We must not, as cowards, allow ourselves to brand as "conspiracy violently to overthrow the government" the teaching of ideas that can be answered by reasoned argument.

X. Freedom only for loyal citizens?

It has been said that academic freedom should be granted only to scholars loyal to the present form of government and "diligent and loyal in citizenship."

A requirement of loyalty, one has to assume, is something different from—and probably much wider in scope than—the prohibition of subversive actions or subversive teaching, or acts of treason, sabotage, or espionage. According to the dictionary, loyalty means "faithful adherence" or "enthusiastic devotion." Can we demand that scholars be faithful and devoted, not only to the ideals of learning and scholarship, but to the government or its form?

This indeed was the view of certain Prussian kings,[20] it was the view of the Italian Fascists and the German Nazis; it has been the view of the Russian Communists; and it has recently been proclaimed in a statement by a group of American educators, who, however, at the same time, somewhat inconsistently, emphasized the value of "independence" of thought.[21]

Against this view it should be stated with stark emphasis that colleges and universities are not agencies for the support or preservation of the government or its form. To make them such agencies is in the program of totalitarian states, but is not consistent with the principles of democracy.

In the words of a great thinker, "Thought knows no nation." Only a totalitarian government judges "truth" relative to its helpfulness to the state. Most of us have had contempt and pity for the Russian, German, and Italian university professors who accepted the supremacy of the state and swore loyalty to their governments even where this meant disloyalty to the ideals of independent thinking. Most of us have admired the few—all too few—courageous professors in totalitarian countries who chose retirement or exile rather than submit to the demands of "loyalty" to their governments.

Now some of our own educators have taken to waving the flag and pronouncing the professors' "obligation of being diligent and loyal in citizenship."[22] The absurdity of such an obligation is especially obvious in the case of non-citizens serving as professors in American universities. Several of our best universities, selecting scholars primarily on the basis of competence, have filled some positions with nationals of foreign countries. Should these scholars be required to renounce allegiance to their countries? Should American professors teaching in foreign universities accept allegiance to

[20] The Prussian Minister of Education, in 1899, declared that every professor, in his lectures and otherwise, must uphold and protect the political and legal authority, and defend it against all attacks. See *Die Aktenstücke des Disziplinarverfahrens gegen den Privatdozenten Dr. Arons* (Berlin: Georg Reimers, 1900).

[21] *The Rights and Responsibilities of Universities and their Faculties:* A Statement by the Association of American Universities, March 24, 1953.

[22] *Ibid.*

foreign governments? The answers, surely, are "no." Let us add that nationality and nationalism are not positive elements in the qualifications of a scholar; they contribute nothing to his competence or his integrity.

Those insisting on expressions or declarations of loyalty to the present form of government might with advantage reflect on what such requirements would mean in various foreign countries or would have meant in our past. They might recall that in Spain "loyalists" were the defenders of a government which not long before had violently replaced a different one, and was shortly to be violently overthrown by another. They might recall the presence of royalists in republican France and Italy, and the presence of republicans in monarchist Greece and Belgium; of men, therefore, openly opposed—not loyal—to their form of government. (We would justly be horrified if academic freedom were denied to professors of such persuasions). They might recall that patriotism often meant disloyalty to the existing form of government; that some of the greatest patriots in history—including the history of the United States—fought against the system of government to which they were supposed to be loyal; that love for their country compelled them to be disloyal to the government of the time.

But let us not confuse loyalty and law obedience. Needless to say, as citizens we have obligations to the government, and the government may and will enforce the fulfillment of such obligations. But *as scholars* professors have only one obligation: to search for truth and speak the truth as they see it. Where a conflict of obligations may chance to arise, they may have to choose between loyalty to the government and integrity as scholars; but *such a conflict can arise only in countries whose governments have abridged the freedoms of thought, expression, and conscience.* In a truly free society there is no reason why professors should not "render unto Caesar the things which are Caesar's" and yet pursue their teaching and research without restriction or encumbrance by "loyalty" to the government.

As members of an academic community our loyalty is undivided: it is only to our conscience as seekers and teachers of the truth as we see it. Loyalties to governments, enemy, allied, or our own, should not enter our thoughts as scholars; if university authorities insist on judging the fitness of a professor in terms of an "obligation of being diligent and loyal in citizenship," this is clearly inconsistent with the truly essential requirement of "integrity and independence" of scholars. And, incidentally, unceasing insistence on freedom of thought, unrestricted by demands of loyalty to the government, is perhaps the highest loyalty to the ideas fundamental to our American form of government.

The proposal to retain in academic positions only those who show diligence and loyalty in citizenship is a limitation on academic freedom which in effect may negate it. To say this is not to defend disloyalty to the government, but only to point out that the professors' loyalty to the government is none of the business of university authorities. Treason, espionage, or other criminal acts will be punished by the state, and the faculty may decide that a convicted felon, if his motives or methods were dishonorable, is not fit to hold a teaching position. But appraisals by university authorities or faculties of a professor's loyalty to the government should not enter into the determination of his academic tenure.

XI. Freedom for those without independence of thought?

It has been said that academic freedom does not include the freedom to teach—or even to hold—doctrines dictated by some outside authority and slavishly accepted by a teacher who has surrendered his own independence of thinking.

We agree with this rejection of propagandists who follow the party line or preach the articles of faith of a political or ecclesiastical authority, inasmuch as they may hold the doctrines in question not as a result of an honest search for truth but in blind submission to authority. Rarely, however, will a practical course of action follow from this point of view; for it is hardly possible to ascertain whether or not a teacher is truly convinced of the validity of the conclusions which he presents to his students or on what grounds his convictions are based.

There are those who take a scholar's membership in an organization devoted to the propaganda for a certain faith as evidence of a lack of integrity and independence of his thought. While some may regard such evidence as persuasive with regard to a member of the Communist Party, one can quickly realize the iniquity of this procedure when one applies it to other organizations or associations, professional, political, or religious. And we must not apply to one group a principle which we would reject for another. We must not impugn the motives of any one merely on the ground of his associations. Even if we knew with absolute certainty that most members of a certain association or party have in effect surrendered their freedom of thought, we have no right to conclude that all members have done so.

Of course, if manifest untruths and patent distortions of firmly established facts were presented to students or the public in conformance with orders emanating from notorious sources of propaganda, it would be possible to prove that a propagandizing teacher or researcher was deliberately disseminating what he knew to be untrue. Where such proof is conclusive, action by the faculty against the offender is called for. But rarely will a case be that simple. For as a rule the teacher cannot himself verify the truth or falsity of all that he teaches. No scholar could possibly have tested personally all the findings and conclusions in his own field of competence, let alone those in other fields. He must needs accept a large amount of findings and conclusions reached by other specialists; indeed, he must accept probably the bulk of his knowledge on the authority of others. Who can say that his faith in such authority is not genuine, not honest? Who can prove that a scholar's acceptance of truths pronounced by others indicates a surrender of his independence?

Since a scholar's affiliation or association is not acceptable as conclusive evidence and since confession will hardly be obtained without intolerable inquisition, there is, apart from proofs of deliberate distortions of verifiable facts, no simple and acceptable way of establishing that a professor lacks independence of thought; where such lack cannot be established, it is useless as a criterion for judging his continued fitness as a college or university teacher.

XII. Freedom for those who would destroy freedom?

It has been said that academic freedom must be denied to those who conspire to destroy it.

It is cogently argued that, if we treasure freedom, we must not grant freedom to work for the abolition of freedom. There are at least four categories of persons to whom this argument may apply: those who openly denounce unrestricted intellectual freedom as "licence," unwholesome to a good society; those who are members of a group or party known to be hostile to the free institutions of democratic-capitalist nations; those who advocate the adoption of institutions or policies incompatible with the maintenance of intellectual freedom, but who deny this incompatibility; and those who advocate these institutions or policies while frankly admitting their incompatibility with full freedom of speech.

The debate about the distinction between liberty and licence, and about the alleged need for limits to intellectual freedom in a good society, has been going on for at least 2500 years. Although several conspiracies to restrict intellectual freedom have had temporary success, champions of unrestricted freedom refuse to be inconsistent and to silence their opponents. He who believes in full freedom of speech cannot consistently restrict the freedom of those who disparage such liberty by calling it licence, and ask for the imposition of restrictions.

The question of "implied advocacy of the destruction of freedom," inferred from party membership, is most controversial at the present time. The argument runs as follows: It is an established fact that the Communists have abolished academic freedom wherever they are in political power; it is reported on good authority that members of the Communist party are pledged to support its objectives by fair means or foul; it follows that membership in the Communist party is sufficient evidence of conspiracy to destroy freedom, and that such membership "extinguishes the right to a university position."

The logic of this argument is obviously faulty if we accept the fundamental principle of American justice, that guilt is personal and cannot be established by opinion and association; we cannot make party membership a decisive criterion. The number of known exceptions is too large to permit us to generalize even for purposes of presumptive evidence. There are many who joined the Communist party and left it again, disillusioned.[23] Thus there must

[23] There were others who were expelled by the Communist Party because they were not sufficiently subservient to its programs or directives. The Party cannot possibly be so efficient that a member's lacking or failing faith is always

have been, at any given time, members of the party who did not believe in the supposed objectives of the party, but had to "find out"; many members may be finding out at present, experiencing their enlightenment and disillusionment. There may be others who joined the party and signed all sorts of pledges without intending to serve its revolutionary aims, or without recognizing that such aims are pursued or, if pursued, are incompatible with the maintenance of intellectual freedom. One may blame such people for being shockingly naïve; but one cannot honestly make safe inference from membership to belief in the destruction of freedom. (Indeed, there are those who joined the party in order to report its activities to the security agencies of our government.) Thus, party membership, past or present, does not prove that a member is a participant in a conspiracy to destroy freedom.

The third category of implicit foes of intellectual freedom consists of those who advocate the adoption of institutions or policies incompatible with the maintenance of intellectual freedom but who deny this incompatibility. If we, on empirical and analytical grounds, are convinced of this incompatibility while they deny it, we are bound to conclude that they are either naïve or dishonest. The toleration of honest error, however naïve, is surely the essence of intellectual freedom. If we can prove that they are dishonest, we can and should eliminate them from their academic positions. But the proof, as has been explained before, is difficult, because evidence that some one speaks and writes what he knows to be untrue is hard to come by.

There remain—if they exist in colleges and universities—the avowed totalitarian communists about whose beliefs one need not make any questionable inferences. They frankly admire the political institutions of the Soviet Union, and openly advocate the adoption in our country of these institutions, including the abolition or restriction of most political freedoms. If such a man can be found in an academic position, trying to impart his honest convictions to his students, should we let him go on teaching? Before we

detected without delay and an expulsion order executed immediately. Indeed, evidence exists indicating that the Party officials have sometimes preferred to be "lenient" and to retain certain members despite known defects in their submission to party discipline.

give in to an impulse, let us be conscious of one clear fact: if we silence him, *we* have *actually* abrogated freedom of speech, whereas *he* has merely talked about doing so.

XIII. Freedom not abridged by prescribed oath?

It has been said that the requirement of a prescribed oath for academic teachers is consistent with, and no abridgment of, academic freedom.

This view is peculiarly at variance with historical tradition. A large part of the history of academic freedom is the history of battles against oath requirements. Oaths have been imposed by ecclesiastical authorities, by sovereigns and state governments, by university authorities, or by academic senates and other bodies of the professors themselves. The oaths required of professors and resisted by those who fought for academic freedom have been of several kinds: oaths of belief in certain doctrines, of renunciation of certain doctrines, of allegiance to a sovereign, of support of a constitution, of non-affiliation with certain groups. One of the "milestones" in the history of academic freedom was the case of the seven professors of the University of Göttingen—the "Göttingen Seven"—who, in 1837, were ousted from their positions after they refused to take an oath of loyalty to a new state constitution.

Even the least dangerous of oaths required of academic teachers, the oath to support—though not necessarily to believe in—the constitution, is on principle inconsistent with real freedom of teaching, especially because the meaning of "supporting" is not unambiguous. "An oath to 'support' the Constitution . . . may be construed as a pledge to refrain from advocating changes in these laws. It is clearly with this sense in mind that many of the proponents of teachers' oath bills favor them. . . . The bills . . . when thus construed . . . are themselves, in their apparent intent, negations of the essential spirit of the Federal Constitution and of the constitutions of most, if not all, of the States."[24]

These oaths to support the Constitution can become acutely dangerous to academic freedom when they are construed as giving

[24] A. J. Carlson and A. O. Lovejoy, "Teachers' Oath Laws: Statement of Committee B," *AAUP Bulletin,* 23:27–29(1937).

to "the governing boards of executives of colleges and universities a quasi-legal ground for dismissing any teacher whose political opinions, affiliations, or activities are regarded by these officials as inconsistent with 'support of the Constitution'—in any sense which they may put upon this equivocal expression."[25] And it is "evident that some supporters of these [teachers' oath] statutes do not really aim at the restriction of teachers' general civic rights, but at some sort of control over the content of instruction or over the teachers' methods in the classroom."[26]

The oaths most inimical to academic freedom are the belief oaths, or test oaths, by which an academic teacher has to swear adherence to or rejection of certain doctrines or opinions. "Test oaths are notorious tools of tyranny. When used to shackle the minds they are, or at least they should be, unspeakably odious to a free people."[27]

The imposition of loyalty or non-disloyalty test oaths in several States has not been met with the appropriate resistance on the part of most professors. Many have argued, with disarming simplicity: "Since I am not a Communist, why should I not say so under oath?" These teachers have not thought through the implications of a test oath for academic scholars.

A thinker and teacher who has taken an oath binding him positively to allegiance to, or negatively to renunciation of, any doctrine or system, is no longer a disinterested scholar. It will be to his interest to avoid any thoughts that might lead him to conclusions deviating from those to which he has sworn; it will be to his interest to avoid utterances which could make him suspected of deviationist ideas or actions.

Needless to say, this loss of disinterestedness may be largely irrelevant if the scholar's field of inquiry and instruction is far removed from the doctrine or system which he is bound, by his

[25] *Ibid.*, p. 28.

[26] *Ibid.*, p. 29.

[27] *Wieman et al.* v. *Updegraff et al.* 344 U.S. 183, 193. This is a case against the State of Oklahoma. In unanimous decision the Supreme Court of the United States declared that the Oklahoma Loyalty Oath was unconstitutional. The quoted sentences are part of a concurring opinion by Justice Black. See *AAUP Bulletin*, 41:93(1955).

oath, to proclaim or renounce; and this is probably the reason why professors in these "safe" fields are often insensible of or indifferent to the moral and intellectual dangers of a test oath. But in some subjects, freedom of thought and expression is necessarily restricted by a test oath. Oaths on religious doctrine or affiliations may restrict the intellectual freedom of theologians, philosophers, biologists, astronomers, geologists, sociologists; and oaths on political doctrine or affiliations may restrict the intellectual freedom of political scientists, sociologists, economists, historians, philosophers.

A teacher who is firmly convinced that his own views are true and right, and also in conformance with the required test oath, may be unable to see the implications of his taking the oath, because he cannot imagine that his views may change; indeed, he does not want them to change. But this is precisely where the loss of his impartiality manifests itself. If we detest fascism, communism, despotism, cannibalism, Molochism, or genocide, we have the right to say so, but we ought not, as honorable men, to derive material profit from the fact that public opinion agrees with us, nor ought we, as intellectually honest scholars, to preclude developments in our thinking which would make us accept any of these tenets. A loyalty or non-disloyalty oath as a condition of employment might not be objectionable to us when we seek or accept a government position not connected with academic teaching; but in the capacity as academic teachers we ought not to give up our complete impartiality.

If teachers are bound by oath to adherence to, or rejection of, certain ideas, students will be deprived of the freedom to learn about those controversial matters which teachers will avoid discussing. But worse than that, even if teachers are willing to enter the danger zone of controversial ideas prescribed or proscribed by their oath, their effectiveness will be sorely weakened. The better students will not have respect for the teachers' opinions on questions about or around the ideas controlled by the oath. These students have confidence only in what they consider the honest opinion of their teacher, and they will not believe that an opinion can be completely honest if it is prescribed or controlled by a compulsory oath.

Those who insist on non-communist oaths for teachers obviously do not realize that they ruin the best and often only chance of straightening out the intellectual twists of a youth leaning toward communist ideas, but groping in the fog of his thoughts, and willing to examine an honest argument. An intelligent teacher whose sincerity is trusted by the youth can guide him toward saner views. But whatever a teacher bound by a non-communist oath can say to his student will be discounted, or even scornfully shrugged off with the comment: "Oh, well, that's what he is sworn to say."

We conclude that an oath which restricts teaching in any respect is inconsistent with the principles of academic freedom, abridges both the freedom to learn and the freedom to teach, and obstructs the attainment of the very objectives which its proponents mean to serve.

Appendix C

TENURE IN AMERICAN HIGHER EDUCATION: "SPECIFIC CONCLUSIONS AND RECOMMENDATIONS."[1]

By Clark Byse and Louis Joughin

The recommendations that follow do not propose action by state or federal legislative bodies. Nor do they call for the use of outside arbitrators to resolve differences. The prime need is not for extramural intervention, but for each institution of higher learning to engage in systematic discussion and analysis and to take appropriate action to make tenure as positive a force as possible for the good of education. Particularly, trustees, administrators, and faculties should participate in this process in order to reach agreement concerning the proper distribution among them of the powers and responsibilities which relate to matters of tenure. If this basic question can be rightly settled, there will be little need for intercession by outside forces.

The recommendations, which derive from study of a multitude of concrete facts, take the form of generalizations for consideration wherever they may be pertinent. But all generalizations are tentative and subject to correction or replacement in light of new data and fresh analysis. The advantages of diversity and experimentation and the differences in the customs and traditions of the colleges and universities in this country suggest the limitations of any single approach. The proposals thus are not advanced as a uniform code for indiscriminate adoption. They can, however, serve to focus attention on particular issues; and it is hoped they will not be rejected except after careful deliberation.

1. The tenure idea is almost universally recognized; of the [80] institutions here surveyed, all but three state they have conferred

[1] From *Tenure in American Higher Education*, pp. 132–47, © 1959 by Cornell University. Used by permission of Cornell University Press.

tenure on some of their teachers. Since the idea is so firmly established, the practical need is for further study of the coverage, provisions, and legal significance of various plans and practices.

Recommendation

Because of the values of tenure, outlined in Chapter I, those institutions which have not yet given full recognition to tenure should adopt plans and procedures under which faculty members may achieve tenure. If governing boards and administrators do not inaugurate action, faculty members might appropriately take the initiative, first by local suasion and then, if necessary, by inviting the American Association of University Professors or other organizations to note the institution's failure in this regard. Indeed, professional organizations—such as the Association of American Law Schools and the associations in the subject-matter areas—might well assume a more active role in bringing about sound conditions of tenure in American higher education.

2. Tenure is embodied in a bewildering variety of policies, plans, and practices; the range reveals extraordinary differences in generosity, explicitness, and intelligibility. Large or small, public or private, nonsectarian or religiously affiliated, there is no consensus concerning either the criteria or the procedures for acquiring and terminating tenure.

The variety encountered probably results from the differences among the institutions in financial resources, in concepts of educational function, and in particular historical development. This diversity is healthy to the degree that it represents imaginative individuality and reflects the rich variety of free institutions in a democratic society. But it should be harmonized with the characteristics of the teaching profession as a group of experts.

The faculties of American colleges and universities are made up of men and women whose primary allegiance is to knowledge as a universal value and to teaching as a universal art. Furthermore, teachers are a fairly mobile group and seek appointments in a "national labor market," at least in the years up to the point of achieving tenure. These professional and economic attributes of the teaching group transcend the policies and customs of any particular institution, and teachers are aware of this fact. The college or university which takes a markedly narrow or parochial view of the key idea of tenure is likely to meet frustration or irritation among its faculty, and, on occasion, sharp conflict at the level of a "tenure case." Conversely, the institution which handles tenure in general conformity with the professional status of the persons it appoints will have a more effective faculty and strengthen its power to recruit.

Recommendation

An institution which entertains any doubts about its tenure policy, plan, or practice should examine the whole question; trustees, administrative officials, and the faculty should participate in the process; comparative study should be made of the institution's own handling of tenure and that of other appropriate institutions; and full use should be made of consultative resources of the American Association of University Professors and other groups which have a national perspective.

3. Many institutions, some of unquestioned liberal reputation and tradition, fail to incorporate all of their tenure policy into a written plan. Some that have a fully developed plan choose to leave it in a limbo of unofficial sanction. In those instances where the inadequacy is the result of inertia, there is simply a need for a job to be done. In those instances where there is conscious or subconscious antipathy toward the tenure idea, the faculty has an important educational responsibility to perform.

But the absence of a full, written plan may also result from a conviction that custom and tradition, sometimes referred to as the "common law" of academic affairs, are preferable to written regulations. Thus, President Lowell expressed his belief to the Harvard Board of Overseers: "Tradition has great advantages over regulations. It is a more delicate instrument: it accommodates itself to things which are not susceptible of sharp definition: it is more flexible in its application."[2] It has also been urged that written pro-

[2] President A. Lawrence Lowell's report, 1919–20, quoted by Charles P. Dennison, *Faculty Rights and Obligations* (1955), p. 10.

visions involve an element of inflexibility which is avoided by reliance on custom and tradition.[3]

Unquestionably, an occasional institution may over a long span of years develop a tradition with respect to tenure which is both substantively desirable and clearly defined. At such a college or university sound principles of academic freedom and tenure may obtain despite the absence of an explicit, written tenure plan. But since a happy outcome of this kind has only occasionally been achieved, most institutions would benefit from an attempt to state policy in explicit detail.[4]

Such an endeavor would very likely disclose gaps which need to be filled and, by focusing trustee, administrative, and faculty attention on the problem, would also bring about improvement in tenure policy. A written plan provides a greater degree of legal protection. It also gives faculty members, particularly junior and newer members, information concerning their position. And a written plan guaranteeing academic freedom and tenure rights can be used advantageously to meet attacks by pressure groups in times of stress.[5]

Recommendation

Tenure plans, with possible rare exceptions, should be formally set forth in explicit detail.

4. Legal protection of tenure is insubstantial. Judicial reluctance to decree specific performance of "personal service" con-

[3] Dennison (note 2 above), p. 107.

[4] Even the institution governed by a proper tradition may be somewhat handicapped because it cannot be assumed that its tenure policy and practice will be easily perceived by teachers at other places and by the profession at large.

[5] "If a professor, for example, were propounding unpopular views and causing an irresponsible minority in the community to demand his dismissal, a legal commitment regarding the professor's rights and obligations might be a more effective defense of the college's action than an effort to present the merits of the case to an excited public." Dennison (note 2 above), p. 103. Pages 101–18 of the Dennison book contain an excellent discussion of the general problem "Written Commitments vs. Less Formal Understandings" in academic government.

tracts, charter provisions authorizing discharge at will, disclaimer and finality clauses, confusing uncertainty in the written plans of some institutions, the complete absence of formal plans in others, the vagueness and inclusiveness of termination criteria, and retention of ultimate decisional authority by most governing boards—all underscore the hazards of reliance on judicial protection of tenure.

Recommendation

Because of the importance of enforcement by an independent judiciary, those institutions with charters and plans containing provisions which hinder legal enforcement should adopt corrective amendments eliminating or clarifying authorizations to discharge at will, disclaimer clauses, finality provisions, confusing ambiguities, and vague termination criteria which only remotely bear upon a faculty member's fitness to teach, to engage in research, or to associate with students.

5. The role of the courts in reviewing dismissal determinations by institutions which have sound, written tenure plans should be quite conventional and relatively simple. It would be the court's responsibility to determine whether the requirements of the plan had been complied with. Was there failure to follow the stated procedure? Were the facts proved by a preponderance of the evidence? Did the proved facts constitute disqualifying conduct within the meaning of the plan?

Courts reviewing dismissal determinations made under plans which did not conform to sound principles would have a more difficult task. For if the institution had not accorded the faculty member academic due process or if it had discharged the faculty member for reasons other than professional unfitness, the tenure principle would have been infringed and academic freedom undermined. But traditional doctrine would say that in the absence of a contractual limitation on the institution's power of appointment and termination, the faculty member in a private institution, at least, had no legally protectible interest. The answer to this argument is that, as important as it is, the social interest in freedom of contract may in some instances be subordinated to a more important social interest—academic freedom.

Recommendation

The creative judge, recognizing the vital importance of academic freedom in our society and its customary acknowledgment in long-established usage, should feel free to hold that in the absence of a specific disclaimer or finality clause, the faculty member of long service has acquired a *status* and that an incident of this status is protection from discharge except for good cause and after proceedings which comply with the principles of academic due process.[6] The remedy for infringement of tenure should include an order of reinstatement.

6. All faculty members, particularly those having tenure, should recognize that membership in the community of scholars of American higher education entails particular obligations. Foremost and best recognized is conscientious discharge of research, teaching, and assigned administrative responsibilities. In addition, the faculty member must remember that as "a man of learning and an educational officer . . . the public may judge his profession and his institution by his utterances. Hence he should at all times be accurate, should exercise appropriate restraint, should show respect for the opinion of others, and should make every effort to indicate that he is not an institutional spokesman."[7] He should be scrupulous in giving reasonable advance notice of an intention to resign, for the process of replacing faculty members, especially those with tenure, is time-consuming and difficult.

Recommendation

The obligation to discharge one's primary responsibilities with fidelity and diligence, to give advance notice of intention to resign, to act with restraint, to show respect for the opinions of others, and to avoid giving the impression of being an institutional spokesman should be recognized by faculty members. Faculty groups, such as the American Association of University Professors, might ap-

[6] See materials cited in Chapter III [of *Tenure in American Higher Education*], notes 104–6. Consult also the provocative essay by Professor Thomas A. Cowan, "Interference with Academic Freedom: The Pre-Natal History of a Tort," *Wayne L. Rev.* 4:205(1958).

[7] 1940 *Statement of Principles,* from *AAUP Bulletin,* 44:291(1958).

propriately assume a greater initiative in this respect than has been customary in the past.

7. Religious freedom is one of the preferred American freedoms. It accounts for the hospitable reception accorded sectarian colleges and universities by our society. But sectarian colleges and universities are nonetheless educational institutions; and as such they must recognize the legitimate demands of academic freedom and tenure.

Recommendation

The principles of academic freedom and tenure here recommended should be applicable to educational institutions conducted by religious groups, with the proviso that reasonable limitations because of the religious objective of the institution may be imposed by agreement entered into between the institution and the faculty member at the time of his appointment.[8]

8. Some institutions, particularly those which grant tenure on an *ad hoc* basis, object to the "automatic" provision of some tenure plans. This objection is based on a misapprehension. The only automatic element in these plans is the fixing of the date at which an institution must distinguish between its hitherto unrestricted right not to appoint and its now imminent obligation. A college or university is privileged, under the standards of the profession, to release with adequate notice any teacher in any rank during his probationary period. But once that period has been served and it is decided that a teacher shall be retained, privilege should yield to obligation. Refusal to grant tenure to a teacher who has served his probation and is reappointed constitutes failure on the part of the

[8] The precise character of the "reasonable limitations" presents an extremely difficult problem, which deserves further study. For opposing viewpoints on the general subject of academic freedom and the denominational university, see Robert M. MacIver, *Academic Freedom in Our Time* (1955), 285–89; Journet Kahn, "The Threat to Academic Freedom," *Proceedings of the American Catholic Philosophical Association,* 30:160(1956).

institution fully to confirm its judgment. Such a failure is unjust to the teacher and harmful to institutional morale.

Recommendation

Tenure plans should provide that retention of a teacher beyond a stated probationary term confers tenure.

9. A teacher who has completed his professional training, served at an institution for something like seven years, and has been reappointed is in some institutions required further to qualify for tenure by achieving a particular rank. The difficulty with this criterion is that promotion is often conditioned by the financial and actuarial picture in an institution.[9] As for the argument that an all-rank tenure plan is conducive to an all-tenure staff, it fails to recognize that any rank or any post can be kept fluid by not retaining personnel beyond the probationary period.

Recommendation

Tenure plans should be of the all-rank type; achievement of rank should not be a condition of tenure.

10. A few institutions go no further than to state that tenure must or may be "considered" after a specified probationary period. Such a provision does not constitute a tenure plan. A loose commitment of this kind, happily often stronger in practice than in promise, is an unnecessary aberration from general tenure principle, harmful to staff morale and a handicap upon recruiting.

Recommendation

Provisions requiring consideration of tenure at the conclusion of the probationary period should be replaced by provisions requiring the granting of tenure.

[9] [George Pope Shannon], "The 1940 Statement of Principles does not associate tenure with rank, nor is it morally defensible that a man or woman of proved competence should have to wait for tenure on the happy accident of death in the superior ranks. Security of tenure and opportunity for promotion are two different things and their confusion has been and is the cause of much injustice." "Editor's Notes," *AAUP Bulletin,* 42:585(1956).

11. Tenure is based in part on retention; retention is based in part on the meeting of evaluative standards. Yet only thirty-eight of the institutions surveyed state the grounds upon which teachers are judged for promotion and tenure, and some of these statements are inadequate.

Recommendation

The best practices with regard to standards for acquisition of tenure should be studied and generally embodied with appropriate local modifications.

12. Only twenty-six of the eighty institutions studied provide for faculty action on recommendations for tenure. Thus only one-third of these colleges and universities require responsible action by the best-informed group on the most important kind of personnel decision made on the campus. Under these circumstances the teaching profession is not likely to feel that acquisition of tenure is governed by genuinely professional standards; nor will trustees and administrators benefit by the considered and official advice of the experts who do the institution's work.

Recommendation

Tenure plans should provide for official action by the faculty, at one or more levels, on all decisions about acquisition of tenure.

13. Only thirty-five of the institutions offer procedure governing appeal from denial of tenure, and of this group of thirty-five only thirteen permit such an appeal to an all-faculty group. This means that 84 per cent of these institutions have not provided procedures whereby a faculty member who believes himself unjustly or wrongly denied tenure may obtain a judgment by his peers. This situation demeans the teaching profession.

Recommendation

Provision should be made for appeal from denial of tenure which at some stage permits judgment by a standing committee of the faculty.

14. Once a faculty member has acquired tenure, his appointment should be terminated only for professional unfitness or perhaps because of financial exigencies. The standard for dismissal because of actions within the academic institution should be incompetence in teaching or research or gross personal misconduct which unfits the faculty member for association with students. External affairs only become relevant if they involve "grave moral delinquencies which unfit him for contact with young men and women."[10] As President Conant stated in his final annual report to the Board of Overseers of Harvard University:

> If the trustees or administrative officers of a university were to engage in any investigation of a professor's activities as a citizen, the life of the university would be destroyed. Of that I am sure. Outside of his classroom a professor speaks and acts as a private citizen. What his views may be or how wisely or foolishly he speaks is no concern of the university administration, provided he is not acting illegally as determined by due process of law.[11]

Dismissing a faculty member for external actions is an extremely delicate process involving unusual hazards. For the temptation is to base such a decision on the adjudicator's moral code rather than upon the more explicit standard of illegal conduct. Yet to remove a faculty member with tenure because he exercised a choice within the law is to open the way for discharges for other lawful actions, because purges once begun often know no stopping place. This is not to imply that discharge is appropriate in every instance in which a faculty member has violated the law. It is only when the violation involves a serious criminal offense that the extreme sanction of banishment from the teaching profession is appropriate. Here the counsel of Judge Charles E. Wyzanski, Jr., one of the nation's most distinguished judges and then-President of the Board of Overseers of Harvard University, deserves emphasis:

[10] Zechariah Chafee, Jr., Foreword to Alan Barth, *The Loyalty of Free Men* (1952), xxvi.

[11] President James Bryant Conant's report, 1951–52, p. 21.

A University is the historical consequence of the mediaeval *studium generale*—a self-generated guild of students or of masters accepting as grounds for entrance and dismissal only criteria relevant to the performance of scholarly duties. The men who become full members of the faculty are not in substance our employees. They are not our agents. They are not our representatives. They are a fellowship of independent scholars answerable to us only for academic integrity.

We undertake the responsibility for handling infractions of university codes occurring within the times and places where our certificate operates. On these matters we possess the best available evidence, we have familiar canons to apply, and we have established processes of judgment and punishment.

What faculty members do outside their posts, we should leave to outside authority. . . .

[A university] is not and must not become an aggregation of like-minded people all behaving according to approved convention. It is the temple of the open-minded. And so long as in his instruction, his scholarship, his relations with his associates and juniors a teacher maintains candor, and truth as *he* sees it, he may not be required to pass any other test.[12]

Recommendation

The standard for dismissal of a faculty member with tenure should be incompetence in teaching or research or gross personal misconduct which unfits the faculty member for association with students.

15. Neither specially qualified personnel nor due process procedures may be needed to ascertain simple facts pertaining to narrowly defined problems of relative unimportance. But when factual issues relate to a particular area of knowledge, when the decisional body is vested with great discretion in interpreting and applying the standards of decision, and when the ultimate decision will directly affect an individual's reputation and livelihood, the constituency of the decisional body and the procedures it follows in reach-

[12] Charles E. Wyzanski, Jr., "Sentinels and Stewards," *Harvard Alumni Bulletin*, Jan. 23, 1954, p. 316.

ing its decision are of the greatest consequence. This, of course, is the situation in tenure dismissal proceedings. The adverse effects of a dismissal on the individual's career are extremely grave. The ultimate issues of incompetence or misconduct which unfits the faculty member for association with students can best be resolved by individuals whose training and experience gives them the insight needed to make these determinations intelligently and whose professional status is sufficiently secure to make it likely that they will apply objective standards of judgment, unaffected by political or public relations pressures.

Notwithstanding the vital importance of fair procedure and of faculty participation in proceedings to terminate a tenure appointment, the provisions in most tenure plans dealing with these matters are rudimentary in character. Perhaps this is an area in which custom and tradition are more significant than formal structure. Wholesale revision of plans which have proved their merit in actual operation would certainly be unwise. But in the absence of a demonstrated effective tradition, there is need in most institutions for careful delineation of procedural rights and of the role of the faculty in dismissal proceedings.

Once attention has been focused on the procedure problem, it should not be difficult to reach general agreement concerning minimal procedural safeguards. For legal due process is a generally accepted ideal, and it has a hard core of content that can readily be incorporated into academic due process.

More difficult will be the problem of allocating decisional responsibility among the trustees, the administration, and the faculty. For nearly forty years the American Association of University Professors through its Committee on the Place and Function of Faculties in Colleges and University Government has wrestled with the general problem.[13] Although the Committee has noted progress in some respects, the fact remains that there is no consensus concerning either the constituency of the hearing group or the extent of faculty participation in the decisional process. Whatever the

[13] See "Report of Committee on the Place and Function of Faculties in College and University Government," *AAUP Bulletin,* 39:300(1953); 41:62(1955).

merits of faculty participation in other areas of academic government, the faculty should have the primary responsibility to determine who shall be appointed to the faculty and who shall be removed therefrom. The reasoning underlying this conclusion is that governing boards, "being composed for the most part of busy men of affairs,"[14] do not have the time and probably do not have the competence to reach carefully considered, fully informed judgments concerning academic personnel.

It is particularly important that the faculty be given primary responsibility in dismissal cases. The president usually is the one who initiates and supervises presentation of the charges against the faculty member; therefore he should be disqualified from adjudicating the case—although he is quite free to state his opinion as the chief administrative officer. Not only do the trustees as a rule not possess any particular competence to judge a faculty member's professional fitness, but their usual reliance on, and deference to, the president's advice[15] tends to make his disqualification their own. In any event, they are less impartial judges and less qualified to reach intelligent decisions concerning matters of professional fitness than experienced members of the faculty. The senior faculty members with tenure do more than anything or anyone else to determine the quality, character, and strength of the institution. They have devoted years of service to the institution, and they have an abiding interest in its welfare. They, rather than busy lay trustees, have the ability, experience, and time to reach fair and informed judgments concerning professional fitness.

[14] "Report of Committee on the Place and Function of Faculties in College and University Government," 1920, quoted in *AAUP Bulletin,* 39:301(1953).

[15] *Ibid.,* 301–2: "Boards of trustees, being composed for the most part of busy men of affairs frequently possessing no special competence to pass judgment on matters of educational policy rely chiefly upon the president for information and advice as to how things are going and what things should be done. . . . Thus, the powers actually exercised by university presidents are, to a very great extent, not powers legally conferred upon the office by charters, but exercised by the incumbent of the office as surrogates for groups of busy men who are not educational experts, and, fortunately, in most cases know that they are not."

Recommendation

Institutions should revise their tenure plans so as (1) to provide for adequate due process protection in dismissal proceedings and (2) to vest in the faculty or its elected representatives primary responsibility for deciding whether the accused faculty member is professionally unfit.

Appendix D

THE AMERICAN CONCEPT OF ACADEMIC FREEDOM

By Howard Mumford Jones[1]

It must bewilder academic visitors from abroad to observe how loosely our educational vocabulary is used in the United States. I sometimes think that all our key terms in education are ambiguous. Take, as an illustration, the words we employ to designate the heads of our institutions of higher learning. In this country, the head is commonly called a president, but sometimes he is not, and in these cases he may be called a chancellor. Often an American president has one or more chancellors under him, but sometimes a chancellor presides over several presidents. One American university has eight presidents and no chancellor. Many universities have a battery of vice-presidents, most of whom have nothing to do with the educational process. Some universities have a vice-president and also a provost. One or two universities have a vice-chancellor, whose function and dignity, however, in no way resemble the function and dignity of a British vice-chancellor. An academic provost, on the other hand, is a sort of administrative maid-of-all-work who, far from fulfilling the dictionary definition of the provost as the head of something and therefore an independent, or at least an autonomous, official, is simply a substitute for a head too busy to do all he is supposed to do. To add to the confusion, we have colleges in the United States fulfilling all or many of the functions of a

[1] Howard Mumford Jones is professor of English at Harvard University. He prepared this statement for Fulbright scholars visiting this country for the first time and participating in a conference at Cornell University in the summer of 1958. It is reprinted from *The American Scholar,* Vol. 29, Number 1, Winter 1959–60. Copyright © 1959 by the United Chapters of Phi Beta Kappa. By permission of the author and of the publishers.

university, and we have ambitiously entitled universities that are in fact scarcely good junior colleges. The distribution of academic titles in such institutions makes an interesting subject for speculation.

The term "academic freedom" is obviously a key term in education, one which shares in the general ambiguity. The phrase has not the same significance to Americans that it has in other parts of the world; and perhaps the best way to begin distinguishing its local meaning is to analyze this difference. We have been told many times that the concept of academic freedom, although some of its components go far back in our history, owes much to the admiration of an intellectual minority among us for the nineteenth-century German university. This is true enough, but Americans adopted only part of the German conception.

That conception included two complementary elements: *Lernfreiheit* and *Lehrfreiheit*—freedom of learning and freedom of teaching. On the whole, the Americans have not accepted wholeheartedly the idea of *Lernfreiheit,* at least as the Germans defined or understood it; and in our present mood of revulsion from the elective system of undergraduate training we are further away from the original concept than we were when Eliot was president of Harvard. In their magisterial history of academic freedom in the United States, Professors Hofstadter and Metzger describe the *Lernfreiheit* dear to nineteenth-century Germans as "the absence of administrative coercion in the learning situation." The German word, they say, referred to the fact that German students "were free to roam from place to place, sampling academic wares; that wherever they lighted, they were free to determine the choice and sequence of courses, and were responsible to no one for regular attendance; that they were exempted from all tests save the final examination; that they lived in private quarters and controlled their private lives." Even American experimental colleges scarcely go this far, and the common pattern of student life in the United States is rather more restricted than is this description of German student life.

II

American institutions have had to accept a quality of responsibility for student learning that differs significantly from the old German theory. They have had to do this for at least four important reasons. The first is that in the eyes of the law the school, college, or university stands *in loco parentis* with reference to its students, especially if the students are in point of law minors. This means that the college is compelled to accept a parietal responsibility for student welfare unknown to the German system. If the American professor no longer concerns himself with the cow in the belfry or student absence from compulsory chapel, this is principally because he has turned the problem of student behavior over to a dean, proctor, counselor or psychiatrist. But the college is still responsible.

The second reason arises out of the deliberate cultivation by American institutions of learning of active parental interest in the life of the college or university. Fathers and mothers are encouraged to visit the campus and attend classes, the alumni reunion is an annual event, and appeals are made to the domestic pocketbook for money that will make the college a home away from home. The American dormitory, the American student union, the American health center, the boast of the college or university that it supports or is adjacent to religious organizations, the interest of the institution in initiating, guiding and controlling extracurricular activities —all these move in exactly the opposite direction from institutional indifference to student welfare; and, admirable in themselves, they create innumerable regulations by the college that actually restrict student freedom. You cannot do this or that on the campus unless you are up in your studies; you cannot remain enrolled unless you maintain a minimum competence in a minimum number of courses; you connot leave the institution at will; and you cannot wander from university to university, since transfer of credits from one institution to another in America demands formal approval in the shape of legal papers that are signed and sealed by a registrar or dean conveying to the receiving institution your status at the time you left the dismissing institution.

A third powerful reason for American inability to accept the total concept of *Lernfreiheit* lies in the ambiguous attitude of the students themselves to the idea. On the one hand, they demand freedom; on the other hand, they do not especially like the responsibility freedom entails. American students want a pattern to adhere to so that they will know when they are done; they want, having paid out their money or their parents' money, to receive tangible wares in return, and these tangible wares take shape as courses and grades and curriculums and the assurance that, if all goes well, at the end of *x* years they will receive *y* degrees. Even our graduate schools, which come closer to the European university concept than does the undergraduate college, follow, if in fainter degree, this formula. A quasi-contractual relationship develops between the student and the department of his specialization. Getting a doctor's degree sometimes appears to run on the anthropological analogue of *do ut des,* in which the graduate faculty are cast in the role of gods who are required, whenever proper offerings are made, to bless the worshippers with due rewards. Less anagogically, the American student sometimes feels that to be denied a Ph.D. degree after the appropriate fulfillment of formal patterns up to the final examination can only result from a gross breach of confidence on the part of the examining committee; and many a doctoral candidate has been passed, despite grave doubts concerning his real command of the subject, because he has been faithful, has tried hard, has fulfilled the pattern, and has all the negative virtues. Were he or the undergraduate compelled tomorrow to live the unconditioned life of the German university student of fragrant pipe-smoking memory, he would be likely to exclaim with the poet: "Me this uncharter'd freedom tries."

The fourth difference lies in the constitutions of the American university. The Continental university often gives only the Ph.D. and confines itself mainly to what in American parlance is advanced or graduate work. The British university, of course, has traditionally been composed of undergraduate colleges, and there the university function has been federal, in some sense, rather than independent. But the American university is Janus-faced. The same faculty members teach in both the undergraduate college and the graduate school of arts and sciences; and the undergraduate college, particularly the freshman and sophomore years of the undergraduate college, are more like the American high school than they are like European university instruction. The responsibility of the teacher toward the immaturities he faces in elementary instruction is different from his responsibility toward mature students. This is tacitly recognized in the organization of course work; an example would be the necessary difference between introducing freshmen to, say, the ideas of Karl Marx and the study of *Das Kapital* in the graduate school. Freshman and sophomore work lies in a rather more sensitive area than does graduate work in metaphysics or economic theory; and in consequence not only is the *Lernfreiheit* of the student, so far as it exists, one thing when he begins, fresh from high school, to wrestle with the problems of the world, and another thing when he is writing a doctoral dissertation, but the *Lehrfreiheit* of his instructor is from an absolute point of view also, and I think properly, restricted.

I have hitherto spoken of the restrictions evident in the American concept of *Lernfreiheit.* There are, however, powerful countercurrents. Compulsory class attendance is no longer as widespread as it once was. Student self-government, although a government of limited powers liable to be revoked at any time by the academic administration, nevertheless revives a concept of student autonomy as old as the Middle Ages. The American undergraduate actively resents attempts by the administration of the college or university to censor the student paper, the student magazine or the student yearbook, nor does the administration always win in such contests. Students also contest the censoring of speakers who are to appear before student groups. The student does not hold his professors in the same reverence as professors are sometimes held in other lands, and he is quite capable of shrewd questioning and vigorous dissent. Moreover, when academic freedom is invaded on the American campus, students are commonly among its stoutest defenders; and student papers like the *Harvard Crimson* and the *Daily Texan* have been notable champions of intellectual liberty.

Student independence would probably go further were it not for the American system of course examination, grades and honors. The canny student is not unaware of the relation between academic regularity and job-getting, and he is therefore sometimes accused of giving back to the professor on his examination paper what the professor, or the professor's assistant, wants him to give back. The American system of awarding student honors—undertaken from the purest of motives, to be sure, and involving such things as a place on the dean's rank list, election to Phi Beta Kappa or Sigma Xi, and recommendations for fellowships—commonly depends more upon a record of grades than upon the examination of individuality. All this shrinks the area of absolute freedom in learning. I cannot forget a student in a great Midwestern university who refused to take Professor So-and-So's course because she wasn't going to spoil a Phi Beta Kappa record for anybody.

III

So much in brief compass, for *Lernfreiheit.* If we turn to the area of *Lehrfreiheit,* or freedom of teaching, we note that this concept in the United States seems to be mainly valued in higher education. The public school teachers, including the high school teacher and the teacher in the American junior college, do not enjoy the kind of community respect the teacher enjoys in other countries. The American public school system, or systems, are locally controlled, and local politics can on occasion be a grave threat to honest teaching. From the point of view of the school board or the school committee, the teacher is an employee hired by another employee, the superintendent of schools, and the law backs them up in this theory. The teacher, paid to teach a certain grade or a certain number of subjects in the high school, has only a minor voice regarding what she teaches; and in the past the teacher, in a wide variety of localities, has been forced to sign a wild variety of contracts that often invade her personal freedom. Stipulations have ranged from the length of her skirt to compulsory teaching of Sunday school classes, if called upon, and even her right to go to parties on occasion has been predetermined. The more absurd of these restrictions are now not common, but the power to make them, or others like them, continues to reside with the school authorities. If systems of tenure have come in, tenure commonly turns upon questions of seniority and the like, issues resembling those involved in agreements made between industry and a labor union rather than the unconditional right to teach one's subject matter in one's own fashion. Teacher resistance to restriction has been less well organized and less vigorous than has academic resistance, partly because the turnover in public school teaching is far more rapid than it is in the academic world, partly because the teachers have wavered between organizing themselves on the labor union pattern and organizing themselves on the professional pattern represented by the National Education Association, and partly because the teacher, hired to teach somebody else's textbook, has not the same interest in the advancement of new interpretations and the discovery of new thought as has the research professor in the university.

All this may seem an irrelevant excursion, since our principal interest is in the academic freedom of university personnel. I do not regard the public school situation as irrelevant, because it profoundly influences public opinion about all instruction. The branch of education most Americans know most about is the public schools, including the public high school. These are, so to speak, immediate institutions, whereas the college or university in most cases is far off. The public schools are involved in local politics, their budgets are mainly local budgets, if not wholly so, their administrative heads belong to the local Rotary Club or this or that local church. Inevitably, therefore, an irresistible public tendency exists to think about universities and university teachers on the analogy of value patterns locally known, especially if a state-supported institution of higher learning is in question. If the community has the right through elections to determine what the personnel of the school board shall be and what that personnel, being elected, shall direct to be done, including determining the nature of the curriculum to be taught and the regulations for those who are to teach it, the inference is irresistible that the public has the same right, through a board of regents or through a state legislature, directly or indirectly to determine the policy and the personnel of academic institutions. If the argument is sound that the board hired Miss Smith to perform such and such tasks in the school system and therefore has the right to discharge Miss Smith because it does not like the way she does or fails to do her appointed tasks, or because Miss Brown can do it better, the argument is also irresistible that a board of regents has the same power with respect to college or university personnel. The parent who complains of bad teaching or bad treatment of his offspring in the high school can see no good reason why, should the offspring complain of bad teaching or bad treatment in the university, he should not seek and find a like remedy. Finally, in this regard, almost all discussion of academic freedom is conducted in academic language, not in the vernacular, the consequence being the relative failure of the public to understand the essential difference between the concept of the school and the concept of the university. An informational job needs to be done that has never been properly performed.

IV

But it is time to come to the central concept of academic freedom. The formal definition of it in American terms is still by common consent that of the American Association of University Professors, to which even the courts now turn when the issue becomes moot. In condensed version the statement is this: Institutions of higher learning exist for the common good, not to further the interest of either the individual teacher or the institution. The common good depends upon the free search for truth and its free exposition. Academic freedom, essential to these purposes, therefore covers both teaching and research. It is fundamental for the protection of the rights of the teacher in teaching and of the student in learning, and carries with it correlative duties.

Tenure, or the right, after a probationary period, to hold one's professional post continuously until the age of retirement, is the bulwark of academic freedom. It guarantees freedom of teaching, freedom of research, and freedom in extramural activities. Tenure also requires a sufficient degree of economic security to make the profession attractive to able persons. In any event the teacher is entitled to freedom in the classroom, in discussing the subject of his special learning and its relevant implications, but he may not introduce into his teaching controversial matter not germane to his topic. Of course he must be intellectually free to pursue research work and to make known the results of his researches, the value of which is to be judged in the first instance by his colleagues, and not by outside agencies.

The college or university teacher, by becoming a member of the academic world, does not thereby cease to be a citizen. When he speaks or writes as a citizen, he should be free from institutional censorship or discipline, but he must remember that his special position in society carries with it special obligations. As a man of learning and as an educational officer, he should remember that the public may judge his profession and his institution by his utterances. Hence he should at all times be accurate, he should exercise appropriate restraint, he should show respect for the opinions of others, and he should make very effort to indicate that he is not an institutional spokesman.

After the expiration of a probationary period, teachers or investigators should have permanent or continuous tenure, and their services should be terminated only for adequate cause. When accusations are brought and facts are in dispute, the accused professor should be informed, prior to any hearing, in writing, of the charges against him and should have the opportunity to be heard in his own defense by all bodies having the power to pass judgment upon his case. Such, in brief, is the theory.

To us who live in the academic universe all this is self-evident; and the language in which I have set forth the doctrine will seem to many of you absurdly oversimplified. To the common man even this oversimplified version is more unintelligible than not. To him it appears that arrogant professors are claiming exemption from responsibility to those who pay them and demanding privileges they do not deserve. Who are these professors that they should protest against loyalty oaths and deny the right of trustees or regents or presidents or legislators or congressmen to inquire into their doings? If we as citizens, taxpayers, and donors send our children to them to be taught, we have a right to find out what they are teaching and to get rid of them in any lawful way if we do not like either what they teach or the way it is taught. This is what we citizens do with congressmen or governors or park commissioners we do not want; we should have the same right in the case of professors. He who pays the piper calls the tune. The professors talk a great deal about their right to do as they please; they do not talk at all about their responsibility to us as taxpayers or donors who support the institutions that hire them. Such, or something like it, is, I think, the response of the common man in emotional moments to the theory of academic freedom in the United States.

I am not sure that I can translate the theory of academic freedom into more vernacular language, but since part of the difficulty lies in a failure of the professors to make their case intelligible to the common man, I wish at least to try: The professor has a job to do. Getting ready to do this job has been a long and expensive process, and doing the job in most cases does not bring in much money. The job he does is important to the country because its welfare depends on having this job well done. The professor is a scientist or a scholar; as a scientist he finds out all sorts of new things we can use later on in industry or medicine or defense; and as a scholar he finds things out about the past that make clear what our country is and what other countries are, so that we can all understand each other better. Now since the professor is never going to make a lot of money, we ought to be sure that he has steady employment and that nobody fires him merely because he doesn't like something the professor says or does. Why shouldn't we do this? You can't tell the lawyer what the law is, can you? You don't take a vote to determine whether a doctor should prescribe medicine or a surgeon perform an operation, do you? You don't tell a priest or a preacher or a rabbi what he is allowed to believe, do you? The lawyer and the physician and the minister have studied their subjects and ought to know what they are talking about, and the same thing is true of the professor. Of course, if any of these men violate the law, they ought to be treated like anybody else, but it is not fair to penalize them just for being professors. All we ask is that they keep in mind that when they talk as professors, they make that clear; and that when they talk as private citizens, they make that clear also.

I am not sure my colloquial approach is necessarily the right approach, but the attempt suggests at least that the problem of academic rights and academic responsibilities is inextricably involved with the problem of democratic values. Of course from time to time the integrity of institutions of higher learning in this country has been attacked by special interest groups—by theologians in one period, by business interests in another, by political demagogues in a third, by educational reformers in a fourth; but there is an irresistible tendency to view these episodes as melodrama on a high plane. In this melodrama, villainy in the shape of Calvinism or McCarthyism or special creationism or economic privilege assaults, as it were, from ambush the little band of intrepid explorers who are pushing into the unknown wilderness and there discovering and organizing new areas of order for the benefit of mankind. The little band is for a time defeated and thrown back, and some of its members taken captive; but by and by, righteousness appears, like the United States Cavalry, rescues the beleaguered altruists, defeats villainy, and all is well again until the next ambush. As I am myself on the side of virtue and have published from time to time books or essays directed against villainy and denouncing ambush, I trust you will not misunderstand me. Academic freedom must always be defended. But I suggest that our interest in the dramatic detail of cases presented in the American Association of University Professors' *Bulletin* or in television shows of Congressional investigations into possibly disloyalty obscures the complexity of the issue in America by reducing the cultural problem to a simple black-and-white, either-or situation. Such famous cases as that of the dismissal of the entire economics department of the Kansas State Agricultural College in 1896 because it would not accept the Populist version of economic theory, or voiding the appointment of Bertrand Russell to a professorship at CCNY in 1940 because the presiding judge thought Russell's prose was full of "immoral and salacious doctrines," present with such startling clarity the naked issue of unwarranted interference that we naturally incline to the view that Satan still finds some mischief for idle minds. The recurrence of these well-meant interferences with academic freedom in successive generations in this country also suggest that, however pleasing it may be to interpret such contests as a battle between the children of darkness and the children of light, some deeper cultural issue is involved. And the deeper issue seems to me, at least, to be the problem of popular control of what is essentially an aristocratic enterprise.

The enterprise of higher education is essentially aristocratic. The academic hierarchy from teaching fellows up through the august body of full professors is something we commonly discuss in terms of rank—a word we also use about aristocratic society. It is not too fantastic to say that tenure implies aristocratic privilege—privilege not too unlike the privilege of a nobility—and academic nobility has the power, and alone has the power, to recruit its numbers through a scale of ceremonies significantly a scale of degrees, culminating through higher degrees in any case of special distinction in something called an honorary degree. The ceremonial of commencement is intended to impress onlookers with the validity of our aristocratic values, partly social, partly intellectual; and I think it significant that on court occasions we of the academic world invariably break out our ceremonial robes and hoods and gold tassels, marching not higgledy-piggledy or in alphabetical order, but in due academic dignity. We explain that we are only maintaining an ancient tradition; we explain that the doctor's gown is merely an outward and visible sign of inward and spiritual accomplishment; we declare that the ceremonial hood, like the baton of a marshal of France, lies potentially rolled up in the diploma of anybody who will take a first degree in the arts. But all our explanations cannot deny the patent truth that a professorial appointment is not for everybody, a doctoral degree is not something you acquire by mere morality and application, or that, in the academic world, many are called but few are chosen. The disparity between the thousands of entering freshmen of any given year and the lesser number of seniors graduating four years later is, if you like, evidence of a necessary sifting process, just as the disparity between the numbers who enter the graduate schools and the numbers who finally achieve the Ph.D. is evidence of a second such process. The process is, moreover, necessary, and I think that in the course of it rough justice is done; but it is a process of educational selectivity that unconsciously violates a deep instinctual American belief that anybody who wants any kind of education ought to have it.

The patterns by which we select and organize superior brains into a university faculty represent what I may call the Jeffersonian concept of democracy. They are essentially what Jefferson worked out in his scheme of education for Virginia. But they contradict what I dare to call a Jacksonian concept of democratic education, evident in much of the state legislation governing our public schools, including the high school, as well as our publicly supported universities.

The Jacksonian theory, for example, through a misunderstanding of the principles of John Dewey, declares that no child in the public schools should fail and that, if he fails, the fault lies rather with the teacher than with the family or with the child. This, in turn, rests upon the kindly theory that there is some sort of talent in everybody. When the theory comes to deal with the high school, it transforms the older concept of the high school as a college preparatory institution into the concept of the high school as a popular training school for whatever the people want; and simultaneously throws out of the high school, often by legislation, what the people do not want. For example, Greek has disappeared, Latin has diminished, and about 47 per cent of American high schools now teach no foreign languages whatever. The point is not to argue the validity of foreign language instruction; the point is that foreign languages have diminished in obedience to the expression of popular will. The theory, turning to higher education, sometimes results in legislation requiring the state university to accept graduates of the state high schools regardless of what the pupils studied; and in respect of the state universities, these institutions are compelled by law to require every student graduating from them to be exposed to a course in American history or swimming or citizenship or something else dear to the legislative heart. Again, an increase in student population leads to immediate general demands for college expansion rather than to a thoughtful analysis of the question whether an increase in the number of teenagers ought not rather permit the colleges, given this wider range of choice, to perfect better devices for greater selectivity among candidates, so that the nation may hereafter be served by superior rather than by average brains. In sum, an admirable moral belief in education for everybody moves in one direction, and an academic belief in more and more rigorous selectivity moves in another; and the problem of academic freedom and responsibility may perhaps lie at the crossing of these two tendencies.

We of the academic universe are, in respect of my two symbolic epithets, inevitably Jeffersonians. We do not believe in an aristocracy of birth, but we do believe in an aristocracy of brains. We struggle to perfect means of ascertaining from an early age those who have promise of intellectual power; we devise ways of pushing such persons forward into higher and higher realms of specialization; and we invent modes of giving them special protection against the risks of a laissez-faire educational philosophy. We say to the public in effect: If you will trust us, we will put into your hands knowledge and instruments of knowledge that will, we believe, make for a richer life and a happier nation. But to do this we must be let alone. As evidence of what we can accomplish we point to the vast industrial society created by the application of our findings, to the increased span of life and greater degree of health of the average American, to the security of the country vis-à-vis powerful Communist forces, and to the treasures of art and wisdom we have stored up for you in museums and libraries and in the printed word. If you will send your children to us, we will select from among them, through the instruments we have created, those who seem to us best fitted to become the future intellectual and cultural leaders of the United States.

Such, or something like it, is another and, in a sense, more ironic statement of the philosophy of academic freedom. Put in these terms, the statement has embarrassing parallels. Those of you who remember Professor Ralph Henry Gabriel's brilliant synopsis of the philosophy of laissez-faire capitalism will be struck by certain echoes. Those of you who have read civic philosophy from Plato to H. G. Wells will note an analogue in the notion of an elite of philosophers, a samurai class. I suggest that an understandable suspicion of a samurai class on the part of a Jacksonian-oriented populace underlies a good many attacks on academic freedom. The demagogue always appeals to the crowd, it is true, but careful reading of some scores of cases of violation of academic freedom will also reveal how frequently the interference complained of is a confused, but sincere, desire to stand up to the rights of the populace as opposed to the claims of a minority. Academic man argues that his responsibility is to a nonnational, nonsectarian, nonpolitical body of truth discovered or discoverable; a Jacksonian inevitably holds that the primary duty of the professor, since his is a public function, is to the public, the populace, the people.

I use these three terms advisedly. They are frequently interchanged in political and educational discussion, but obviously they fall into two groups: on the one hand, the public; on the other, the populace or the people. When, under the doctrine of academic freedom, the professors declare that their primary duty is to find out and present the truth, they have from their point of view discharged their principal public duty. That duty is the duty of all honest craftsmen, the duty of performing one's special function fully and fairly in the light of the special axioms that govern the specialty. Any attempt of the unenlightened to interfere with the operations of the craft, or to direct these operations to some ulterior end, not merely damages the craft and the craftsman but also damages the state. This is evident whether, as in Russia, a scientist interprets his findings according to a political theory of biology, or whether, as in the United States, a literary scholar becomes a mere popularizer of books, pretending that the austerities of art are as simple as A B C. A modern state is an even more complicated mechanism than was Plato's ideal republic, but it cannot be improved when the politician attempts to do the professor's job or the naïve parent tells the expert how to teach. *Crede experto:* that is, if you will put up with a little mistranslation, Trust the expert, or, in Western parlance, Don't shoot the pianist—he's doing his best.

The demagogue on behalf of the populace and the democrat on behalf of the people have their replies. And their most telling argument is not one I have already referred to—namely, that he who pays the piper calls the tune—but one that strikes deeper, although I suspect neither demagogue nor democrat has employed it in my terms. The argument is simply the argument of inconsistency. How in an open society can minority groups sustain closed societies of their own? We do not permit doctors to practice except when they are licensed by the state, nor lawyers, nor dentists, nor clergymen, nor undertakers. We regulate banks and railroads and insurance companies and fraternal orders by law. We expect departments of government that are quite esoteric in their interests to come forward and make public declaration of what they are doing. We require judges to live up to a code we impose upon them; we determine by law when proprietary medicines are improper; we make up our minds through our legislatures whether chiropractors are to be licensed; and so on and so on. We had thought that through the charters we, the sovereign people, granted to private colleges, and through boards of regents to govern the tax-supported institutions we ourselves created, we had also determined by law the proper functioning of a university faculty; but we now find that the professors in effect have established a private code through an organization from which regents and trustees and presidents and deans are excluded (or have been). We protest that, although there may be nothing illegal in this code, it is at least extra-legal, an *imperium in imperio,* a private and powerful league that questions the operation of the way legal bodies are supposed to control university and college. The professors claim a privilege essentially contrary to the interests of a democratic state, and the proof is that when, through public committees, we try to find out whether there are any traitors among them, the academic population rises up to deny our right to make these inquiries or seriously interferes with the work of our investigators.

I suspect it is extremely difficult for the professor to show much sympathy for what I may call the extreme Jacksonian point of view. Jacksonian or not, however, it may be well to recall one or two leading facts in the history of American education. From the founding of Harvard College in 1636 to the present day, academic institutions in the United States have been directly or indirectly the creatures of government. The picture of a confraternity of scholars spontaneously gathering together and resolving to assure the continuity of knowledge through a system of apprenticeship, whatever is elsewhere true, has virtually no relation to the American problem. The American people, passionately desiring education for their children, have gone about securing it much as they have gone about securing anything else they wanted for public use—through the creation of legal agencies to get them what they want. When they wanted a state university, they established a committee of men charged with the duty of creating one; and when this board, commonly called the regents, went to work, discovering they could not as a body determine whom to hire to teach for the proposed university, they in turn employed an agent of their own, a president, expert as they believed in academic matters, and bade him go to work to assemble a faculty. *Pari passu,* the same thing has been true of our private colleges. The picture of scholars assembling and petitioning the state for a charter is simply unhistorical. On the contrary, the charter has had to go out and hunt up the scholars. It was, in a sense, as simple as that. To this day, in point of law, a college or university is not the faculty; a college or university is a governing board, of which, in most cases, not even the president of the institution is a member. I suggest that the extraordinary difference between the American institution of higher learning and the institution of higher learning in other countries can be best understood in historical terms.

The code of academic freedom put forth by the American Association of University Professors is an effort to reserve both the implications of legal theory and the uses of three earlier centuries of educational growth. Inevitably it postulates an opposition between the administration of the American university and the true professional interests of the faculty members. That opposition has often taken dramatic form.

The professional code is not only justified in itself but is slowly winning some standing in law as courts have turned to it for an understanding of the contractual relation between a professor and his employers where suit has been brought for reinstatement. But the popular mind does not as yet either understand or accept it. I believe the popular mind can be brought to accept it, just as the popular mind accepts the implications of the Hippocratic oath in medicine, or the relations of a lawyer to his client, or the seal of the confessional; but acceptance of the code by the people at large will require an educational process not yet attempted by the profession.

Since in other parts of the world university faculties govern themselves to a degree unparalleled in the United States, and in view of what I have called the melodramatic quality in famous instances of violation of the code, it is fatally easy for the academic mind to nourish an inveterate suspicion of governing boards. To my way of thinking, however, the astonishing thing is not the occasional blindness of trustees or the failure of a dean or president here and there to protect academic freedom; the astonishing thing is the patient dedication of most trustees and most regents to the job they have undertaken. Individual members of a board may begin by assuming that a university is like a corporation having so many employees to be paid or discharged as the directors or the president see fit, but they do not long retain this simple view.

V

The code of academic freedom has made astonishing progress since World War I. It has survived even McCarthyism, but if it is to prevail, it must be translated out of academese into simple terms. As Professor Robert MacIver puts it at the conclusion of his study, *Academic Freedom in Our Time:* "The more direct instruction of the citizen concerning the meaning and service of the university can be conducted on a broader scale, utilizing all the major agencies of communication. The subject should be approached along lines that carry it home to him. For example, he has a high respect for science—the relation between the growth of science and the struggle for intellectual liberty is clear. He believes in 'fair play'—how this applies to the scholar, and to those who traduce him, can be shown in chapter and verse. He believes in democracy —how it depends on the liberty of the mind can well be demonstrated. He believes in America—what the spirit of repression does to its great traditions, to its well-being, and to its standing among the nations can be given simple and effective illustration . . . what is most important is that the people should come to appreciate the university, should learn how much of great and lasting worth it contributes to society, and how essential it is that its freedom be sustained and its standards advanced, should recognize how devoted and how disinterested the work of the true scholar is, and should look upon the institution of learning, not with suspicion from a distance, but from near at hand with affection, so that they, too, will become the guardians of its integrity."

Appendix E

ACADEMIC FREEDOM—ITS BASIC PHILOSOPHY, FUNCTION, AND HISTORY

Ralph F. Fuchs[1]

I. The scope of academic freedom

Academic freedom is that freedom of members of the academic community, assembled in colleges and universities, which underlies the effective performance of their functions of teaching, learning, practice of the arts, and research. The right to academic freedom is recognized in order to enable faculty members and students to carry on their roles. It is not sought as a personal privilege, although scholars enjoy the activities it permits,[2] and the tenure rights of faculty members, which are conferred after a period of probation, bestow economic security as well as forestall restrictions on freedom that might stem from the power to dismiss. In relation to tenure the position of the faculty member resembles that of the

[1] A.B., LL.B. 1922, Washington University; Ph.D. 1925, Robert Brookings Graduate School; J.S.D. 1935, Yale University. Professor of Law, Indiana University. President, American Association of University Professors, 1960–62. The article is reprinted, with permission, from a symposium, Academic Freedom, appearing in *Law and Contemporary Problems,* Vol. 28, No. 3, Summer 1963, published by the Duke University School of Law, Durham, N.C. Copyright © 1963, by Duke University.

The definition in the first sentence of Part I and the first paragraph of Part II of this article are largely quoted, with the kind permission of the publishers of the *Encyclopaedia Britannica,* from the author's article on "Academic Freedom" in the current edition of the Encyclopaedia, *Encyc. Brit.* I:57(1963). The bibliography attached to that article contains additional references on the subject.

[2] "Academic Freedom and Tenure in the Quest for National Security, Report of a Special Committee," *AAUP Bulletin,* 42:51, 54–55(1956). [Reprinted above, in part, pp. 47–56.]

judge who holds office during good behavior to safeguard his fearlessness and objectivity in the performance of his duties.[3]

The conception of academic freedom which is dominant in colleges and universities in the United States today rests mainly on three foundations:

(1) the philosophy of intellectual freedom, which originated in Greece, arose again in Europe, especially under the impact of the Renaissance, and came to maturity in the Age of Reason;

(2) the idea of autonomy for communities of scholars, which arose in the universities of Europe; and

(3) the freedoms guaranteed by the Bill of Rights of the federal constitution as elaborated by the courts.

Academic tenure is protected by procedural safeguards in proceedings to dismiss faculty members for cause, which are academically maintained and modelled to a significant extent on procedural due process of law.[4] Academic freedom, in addition, has its correlative in academic responsibility in the use of freedom, which there may or may not be recognized means of enforcing against faculty members.[5]

Student freedom is a traditional accompaniment to faculty free-

[3] Machlup, "On Some Misconceptions Concerning Academic Freedom," *AAUP Bulletin,* 41:753(1955). [Reprinted above, pp. 177–209.]

[4] Rudimentary procedural safeguards are required by the 1940 *Statement of Principles on Academic Freedom and Tenure,* drafted and supported by educational organizations and published at intervals by the American Association of University Professors (AAUP). See above, pp. 33–38, for the text and a list of supporting organizations. Institutional regulations provide specific procedural rules to a varying extent. See Clark Byse and Louis Joughin, *Tenure in American Higher Education* (1959), for the results of a three-state survey of such regulations. A model set of regulations is provided in "Recommended Institutional Regulations on Academic Freedom and Tenure," approved by the Committee on Academic Freedom and Tenure of the AAUP on August 4, 1957, and published in mimeographed form by the Association. In discussions of academic procedural problems, legal due process of law is often referred to. See also below, pp. 264–305.

[5] See "Academic Freedom and Tenure: The University of Illinois," *AAUP Bulletin,* 49:25(1963), for a discussion of the question whether a faculty member's alleged breach of responsibility in public utterance can be a basis of disciplinary proceedings against him.

dom as an element of academic freedom in the larger sense; but in the United States it has on the whole received secondary consideration until recently.[6] Now students are organized to some extent to assert their right to it,[7] and recent court decisions have enforced procedural protections, based on due process of law, against dismissals by state institutions on account of student exercise of off-campus rights of free speech and assembly.[8]

Exclusion from the academic community because of race has, also, been stated of late to be a violation of academic freedom;[9] and exclusion of students or teachers from public institutions on this ground or discrimination against them for this reason, is, of

[6] Teacher freedom and student freedom, *Lehrfreiheit* and *Lernfreiheit,* are companion concepts. In Europe the freedom of students to visit other institutions and to govern their own personal conduct is much wider on the whole than in this country. Here the idea has contributed to the policy of elective courses; but no generally recognized code of student freedom has arisen. See Richard Hofstadter and Walter P. Metzger, *The Development of Academic Freedom in the United States* (1955), 383–98.

[7] The United States National Student Association, composed of the student bodies of nearly 400 colleges and universities, the student governments of which have adhered to the organization, devotes a considerable portion of its attention to academic freedom and in particular to student freedom. See its *Codification of Policy* (1962–63), esp. 28–29, 38–41, 97–112. See also Am. Civil Liberties Union pamphlet, *Academic Freedom and Civil Liberties of Students in Colleges and Universities* (1961), reprinted in *AAUP Bulletin,* 48:110 (1962). See also above, pp. 66–74.

[8] Dixon v. Alabama State Board of Education, 294 F. 2d 150 (5th Cir. 1961), *cert. denied,* 368 U.S. 930 (1961); Knight v. State Board of Education, 200 F. Supp. 174 (M.D. Tenn. 1961). Like some earlier cases, the opinions support rights to due procedure in connection with dismissals for any kind of misconduct. See Byse, "Procedure in Student Dismissal Proceedings: Law and Policy," *J. College Student Personnel,* 4:130(1963).

[9] Resolution of the Forty-Third Annual Meeting, *AAUP Bulletin,* 43:362 (1957): "The right to teach and the right to learn are vital and inseparable aspects of academic freedom. Consequently, free access to every kind of educational opportunity, measured only by the aptitude and achievement of the individual teacher or student, must be safeguarded to all Americans, of whatever race. Any interference with such access imperils the right of the teacher to teach, as well as of the student to learn."

course, a violation of federal constitutional right.[10] Choice of those who shall participate in higher education (which must be an institutional choice) is, along with determination of curricula and of areas of research, among the elements of that academic autonomy which is one of the bases of academic freedom and may be looked upon as its essence.[11] It is, however, itself subject to constitutional requirements, which may on occasion protect the individual student or faculty member from action by his institution as well as by outsiders.[12]

Inroads upon autonomy in respect to research are a leading cause of concern in American colleges and universities at present, because grants from government and industry for designated projects may influence the directions of inquiry. Here institutional in-

[10] Brown v. Board of Education, 347 U.S. 483 (1954); Bolling v. Sharpe, 347 U.S. 497 (1954); Alston v. School Board of Norfolk, 112 F. 2d 992 (4th Cir. 1940); Davis v. Cook, 80 F. Supp. 443 (N.D. Ga. 1948). *Cf.* United Public Workers v. Mitchell, 330 U.S. 75, at 100 (1947).

[11] Lennard, "The Threat to Academic Freedom," *Hibbert Journal,* Oct. 1948, p. 21. Robert M. MacIver in his book, *Academic Freedom in Our Time* (1955), stresses the autonomy of the faculty within an institution in matters lying within its competence as basic to academic freedom. See especially pp. 94–95. Russell Kirk, *Academic Freedom* (1955), stresses the inherent right of the academic community to maintain its own standards in that search for truth which is its reason for being.

[12] The AAUP Annual Meeting resolution, *supra* note 9, asserts that individual rights to teach and to learn are superior to restriction by any authority on ground of race; and of course judicial judgments which strike down segregation in education are typically directed against educational authorities. If the policy which excludes a student or faculty member is based on such allowable grounds as competence or prior training, or perhaps age or sex, the right to maintain it might be claimed as an incident to institutional academic freedom. In Hamilton v. Regents of the University of California, 293 U.S. 245 (1934), the Regents' policy of excluding male students who would not submit to compulsory military training was sustained; but in Board of Education v. Barnette, 319 U.S. 624 (1943), the policy of requiring a salute to the flag (in an elementary school) had to yield to the right of pupils who refused to take part and whose parents would be punished for their nonattendance at school if they were expelled for refusing.

tegrity and individual self-direction both stand in need of protection—not from hostile action but from temptation.[13]

Notwithstanding the increasingly broad reach of academic freedom and the current emphasis on the essentiality of autonomy for academic institutions, the freedom of individual faculty members against control of thought or utterance from either within or without the employing institutions remains the core of the matter. If this freedom exists and reasonably adequate academic administration and methods of faculty selection prevail, intellectual interchange and pursuit of knowledge are secured. A substantial degree of institutional autonomy is both a usual prerequisite and a normal consequence of such a state of affairs. Student freedom will follow—unless, indeed, individual faculty members or departmental groups are permitted to tyrannize over particular students, as occasionally happens. Hence the main concern over developing and maintaining academic freedom in this country has focused upon encouragement and protection of the freedom of the faculty member. Institutional autonomy, constitutional freedoms, and the basic ideology of intellectual freedom have been invoked mainly to this end.

II. Development of academic freedom

European universities began during the Middle Ages as self-constituted communities of scholars, whether teachers or learners. The institutions they founded came under the sponsorship of the medieval church and to some degree under its authority; and the faculties, of course, were composed largely of clerics. Before the eighteenth century the Roman church and in some areas its Protestant successors exerted sporadic controls against which the universities or members of their faculties found it necessary at times to con-

[13] See American Council on Education, Committee on Research Policy, *Report on Sponsored Research Policy of Colleges and Universities* (1954); Am. Civil Liberties Union pamphlet, *Statement Concerning the University and Contract Research* (1959), reprinted in *AAUP Bulletin,* 46:52 (1960); *Harvard and the Federal Government: A Report to the Faculties and Governing Boards of Harvard University* (1961); "Twenty-six Campuses and the Federal Government," *Educational Record,* 46:95, 108–13 (1963); Goheen, "Federal Financing and Princeton University," *id.,* 168.

tend. Scholars outside of the universities, including early scientists, engaged in the same struggles, however, and the total story is one of the effort of the human intellect to escape from bondage, rather than simply of university faculties and students to be free of external control. Within the universities a considerable censorship by dominant groups, giving rise to internal controversies, prevailed for a long time. The boundaries to learning maintained by this censorship receded on the whole, even though vestiges remained for long.[14] At Oxford and Cambridge religious tests and restrictions for students were not removed until the latter half of the nineteenth century.[15]

In the eighteenth and nineteenth centuries the political state became the sponsoring authority for most universities throughout the world—although some under religious auspices remained and in the United States particularly, independent private colleges and universities have continued to exist alongside the public ones. Instances of actual or attempted political interference with public institutions have continued to arise in various countries down to the present time.[16] In the United States political control by state governments remains a danger which assumes reality under demagogic governors from time to time,[17] despite the generally good record of

[14] Hofstadter and Metzger, *op. cit. supra* note 6, ch. I.

[15] *Id.*, 393.

[16] For examples of successful resistance to attempts of this kind in the face of strong traditions of academic freedom, see instances reported in Richard H. Shryock, *The Status of University Teachers* (International Association of University Professors and Lecturers, 1961), 77 (France) and 159 (Egypt). In India the interaction of administrations, faculty groups, students, and state officials, each invoking political forces in varying degree, gives rise to government intervention from time to time, as it did in the universities of Uttar Pradesh in 1960–61.

[17] The latest of the interventions of this variety was that of the Governor of Mississippi in the crisis over admission of a Negro to the University there in September-October 1962, followed by a similar attempt in Alabama. For the response in educational circles, see Resolution adopted by the American Council on Education, Oct. 5, 1962, *Educational Record,* 44:85 (1963), also printed in *AAUP Bulletin* 48:318 (1962). An earlier Mississippi episode involving gubernatorial assumption of the control of state institutions is told about in Hudson, "The Spoils System Enters College," *New Repub.*, 64:123 (1930). For the actions of educational organizations in the matter, see *AAUP*

the states in relation to the colleges and universities they maintain. In Europe dictatorships of several varieties have supplied object-lessons of the extent to which political control can regiment and distort intellectual endeavor even while stimulating the development of learning along selected lines.[18] In some other countries, political influence may play a significant although unmeasurable role in the appointment of staff members. There is a genuine interaction between academic freedom and healthy political democracy, causing each to strengthen the other. It would be too much to say, however, that the former is wholly dependent upon the latter; for given enlightenment on the part of an autocratic government, academic freedom in a genuine sense may coexist with it, as it did in nineteenth century Germany.[19]

It was, indeed, in nineteenth century Germany that the modern conception of academic freedom came to be formulated. The idea of the university as a place where scholars are to pursue truth, as well as to formulate and transmit it to students, who at the same time learn to pursue truth for themselves, came to be dominant there. Especially in an age of science, knowledge grows as individuals ferret it out; and the free interplay of ideas is the means of purifying it. Intellectual discipline over the members of the university community is excluded, lest it distort their search. Attracted by this conception and its results, distinguished young scholars from abroad, especially from the United States, went to the German universities in numbers.[20] There they were imbued with the

Bulletin, 17:140 (1931). As to the control of Louisiana State University by Governor Huey P. Long a few years later, see Don Wharton, "Louisiana State University," *Scribner's Magazine,* Sept. 1937, p. 33. State coercion of private colleges appears in "Academic Freedom and Tenure: Allen University and Benedict Colege," *AAUP Bulletin,* 46:87 (1960).

[18] The control of fascism over the universities is exemplified by conditions which continue in Spain. See the account by Professor Tierno Galvan in Shryock, *op. cit. supra* note 16, at 133. For an account of tight Communist Party control over institutions of higher education in Russia, see I. N. Shumilin, *Soviet Higher Education,* ch. VI (1962).

[19] Hofstadter and Metzger, *op. cit. supra* note 6, at 383–92.

[20] Leo N. Rockwell, "Academic Freedom—German Origin and American Development," *AAUP Bulletin,* 36:225 (1950); Walter P. Metzger, "The German Contribution to the American Theory of Academic Freedom," *id.,* 41:214 (1955).

conception, an enlargement of which has since been dominant in this country.

Professor Friedrich Paulsen of the University of Berlin formulated systematically in 1902, in his book on *The German Universities and University Study,* the conception of academic freedom which had arisen in his country during the preceding decades. "It is no longer, as formerly," he wrote,

> the function of the university teacher to hand down a body of truth established by authorities, but to search after scientific knowledge by investigation, and to teach his hearers to do the same. . . . For the academic teacher and his hearers there can be no prescribed and no proscribed thoughts. There is only one rule for instruction: to justify the truth of one's teaching by reason and the facts.[21]

Paulsen, however, introduced a qualification. The professor of philosophy must be absolutely free; but the professor of theology "must assume a positive relation to religion and the church in general," and the professor of political and social science in a state institution must do so toward "the people and the state." The professor "who can find absolutely no reason in the state and in law, who, as a theoretical anarchist, denies the necessity of a state and legal order . . . may try to prove his theory by means of as many good arguments as he can, but he has no call to teach the political sciences at a state institution." The state, for example, is not bound to tolerate adherence to the "principles of the *social-democracy*" on the part of professors of political science. To permit such theories to be taught would indicate that "the authorities regarded the lectures of professors as harmless and insignificant. . . . So long as the state takes the universities seriously, such a form of political science as has been described will be impossible in its institutions of learning."[22]

Paulsen also expressed the view that political partisanship on the part of a faculty member is a disqualification, notwithstanding the fact that professors may be "men of noble discontent" who sow "the thoughts for future acts." The things which universities "are

[21] Translation by F. Thilly and W. W. Elwang (1906), 228–31.
[22] *Id.,* 233–38, 243–54.

called upon to cultivate transcend the boundaries of countries and nations. . . . The German universities dwell in their own world, outside of politics, and their highest achievements are in science." Hence the professors, "the representatives of science, should not engage in politics, but should reflect upon the state and the law."[23] Academic freedom, in other words, is internal to institutions of higher education, and does not apply to external activities of academic personnel.[24]

The conception of academic freedom which is dominant in American colleges and universities and in other countries today has discarded the limitations that remained in nineteenth century Germany. It accepts, rather, another statement of Paulsen's that "a people," who establish and maintain a university,

> cannot as such have an interest in the preservation of false conceptions. Its ability to live depends in no small measure upon its doing that which is necessary from a proper knowledge of actual conditions. And hence the people and the state . . . can have no desire to place obstacles in the way of an honest search for truth in the field of politics and social science, either by forbidding or favoring certain views.[25]

It follows that a society will be strengthened by permitting honest condemnation as well as defense of the state in institutions of higher learning, whether publicly or privately maintained. As to participation by professors in politics, specialization and attention to duty will ordinarily keep the faculty member from an active role; but he cannot be barred from testing his views or gathering data in action, or from urging his conclusions in the world of affairs, whether relevant to his academic subject or not, by joining organizations or by other means. In addition to "full freedom" in

[23] *Id.*, 254–62.

[24] The German university tradition involved a sharp separation between the academic community and the general one, with the former devoted to science and philosophy and hence "utterly indifferent to the turmoils and ambitions of the outer-world." See excerpts from James Morgan Hart, *German Universities: A Narrative of Personal Experience* (1874), as printed in Richard Hofstadter and Wilson Smith, *American Higher Education*, 2:569, 576 (1961).

[25] Paulsen, *supra* note 21, p. 244.

research and publication and "freedom in the classroom in discussing his subject," the faculty member in any field of study, speaking or writing as a citizen, "should be free from institutional censorship or discipline."[26]

According to the position taken by some Americans within the academic profession and outside who subscribe to broad principles of academic freedom, certain specific limitations upon that freedom may nevertheless be imposed for reasons of special urgency. During World War I some of the staunchest proponents of academic freedom sanctioned the muzzling of anti-war professors and even of those whose ancestry and utterances gave "reasonable ground for belief that they contemplate[d]" acts to aid the enemy or hamper the war effort.[27] Many today and during the past thirty years have urged that membership in the Communist Party disqualifies an individual for faculty membership without reference to sincerity or circumstances, because of the Party's discipline and the existence of a basic conflict between its purposes and freedom itself.[28] The professional charter of academic freedom which is currently followed concedes more generally that a college or university may insist upon "limitations of academic freedom because of religious or other aims of the institution," provided the limits are clearly stated in advance.[29] This concession recognizes the church sponsorship of many institutions in this country and the civil liberty of individuals and groups, including those who form academic institutions, to gov-

[26] 1940 *Statement of Principles, supra* note 4.

[27] *AAUP Bulletin,* vol. 4, Feb.-March 1918, pp. 29, 41.

[28] Association of American Universities, *The Rights and Responsibilities of Universities and Their Families,* Pt. IV (1953); Arthur O. Lovejoy, "Communism Versus Academic Freedom," *American Scholar* 18:332 (1949); Sidney Hook, "Should Communists Teach?". *N.Y. Times Magazine,* Feb. 27, 1949, p. 7; Kirk, *op. cit. supra* note 11, at 114–15. Compare Alexander Meiklejohn, "Should Communists Teach?", *N.Y. Times Magazine,* Mar. 27, 1959, p. 10; and see Hook and Fuchs, "A Joint Statement on a Matter of Importance," *AAUP Bulletin,* 42:692 (1956). For brief accounts of events at the University of Washington and the University of California which followed the implementation by those institutions of the policy of barring Communist Party members from the faculties, see *AAUP Bulletin,* 42:61–66, 100–7 (1956).

[29] 1940 *Statement of Principles, supra* note 4.

ern their own affairs. At some point in the scale of self-imposed restrictions a college or university that comes under them may, of course, cease to be an institution of higher education according to the prevailing conception;[30] and an institution that does not expressly limit itself assumes an obligation to adhere to the principles inherent in an academic community. As generally understood today, these principles do not sanction the proscription of any idea or honest means of communicating or effectuating them, on the part of academic personnel, within an institution or outside.

The present American conception of academic freedom did not, of course, spring full-blown from the soil in which higher education grew in this country. It evolved, rather, along with specific protections to academic freedom, from the organizational forms and educational policies that arose in colleges and universities, and from struggles over recurring infringements of freedom or tenure, which sometimes took the form of faculty dismissals. These infringements were committed by governing boards or administrative officers, moved in the typical case by opinion outside the institutions, which the institutional authorities ordinarily shared. At first the pressures that resulted in these incidents were the product of demands for religious conformity;[31] later they involved objections to the economic or political views of faculty members.[32] Most recently, nonconforming utterances in matters of sex, or literary works which have been deemed offensive, have produced faculty dismissals raising issues of freedom.[33]

[30] The *Declaration of Principles* formulated in 1915 by the first Committee on Academic Freedom and Tenure of the AAUP distinguished in this regard between "proprietary institutions" espousing particular ideas and those which exercise a "public trust" and "have no moral right to bind the reason or the conscience of any professor." Reprinted in *AAUP Bulletin,* 40:90, 94–97 (1954) [and in this volume, pp. 155–76].

[31] Hofstadter and Metzger, *op. cit. supra* note 6, pp. 155–77, 286–303, 320–45. Views on slavery which were out of accord with those in the academic or surrounding community were also the cause of dismissals or of hostility to individual administrators or faculty members. *Id. at* 253–61.

[32] *Id.*, ch. IX.

[33] "Academic Freedom and Tenure: The University of Illinois," *supra* note 5; "Academic Freedom and Tenure: Southwestern Louisiana Institute," *AAUP Bulletin,* 42:718 (1956). Instances of dismissal on account of publi-

III. Professional formulation and support of principles of academic freedom

Because of concern among professors over dismissals that had taken place, coupled with the belief that it would be desirable to have a national organization of college and university teachers similar to the associations of physicians and lawyers, the American Association of University Professors (AAUP) was formed in 1915 by a group of prominent faculty members in leading institutions. Those who joined as charter members came from sixty institutions. Although the purposes of the new Association were broadly professional, its most noteworthy early pronouncement was the 1915 *Declaration* of its Committee on Academic Freedom and Tenure, specifically directed to that subject.[34] The officers of the Association quickly became absorbed in efforts to cope with recurring dismissals of faculty members at institutions in various parts of the country.[35] The Association has continued in conjunction with the Association of American Colleges (AAC) to formulate basic principles of academic freedom and tenure.[36] It has also provided means of vindicating these principles by directing professional attention to academic administrations which are found to have violated them,[37] and has spelled out its policies in decisions on

---

cation of literary works have been the subject of recent complaint to the AAUP. Another recent factor contributing to violations of freedom and tenure has been, of course, a wave of dismissals from institutions in the Deep South because of views or utterances in favor of racial desegregation. For recent summaries, see *AAUP Bulletin,* 48:159, 167–69 (1962). As to the intimidating effect of the climate of opinion in which southern institutions operate today, see C. V. Woodward, "The Unreported Crisis in the Southern Colleges," *Harper's,* Oct. 1962, p. 82.

[34] 1915 *Declaration of Principles, supra* note 30.

[35] Metzger, "The First Investigation," *AAUP Bulletin,* 47:206 (1961).

[36] The two associations formulated a joint statement in 1925, now superseded by the 1940 *Statement.* See 1925 Conference Statement, *AAUP Bulletin,* 43:116 (1957). A joint *Statement on Procedural Standards in Faculty Dismissal Proceedings* received final approval in 1957–58. *AAUP Bulletin,* 44:270 (1958); see text above, pp. 40–45.

[37] These means typically consist of an cn-the-scene inquiry by a special committee of professors into a challenged dismissal that has not been resolved by negotiation, the publication of its report after approval for publication

particular cases and in annual reports of the Committee on Freedom and Tenure, carrying forward the 1915 *Declaration.*[38]

These group measures have involved only partial collaboration between the professors, represented by their association, and administrators and trustees. The AAC has shared in what might be called the legislative process; but mediation in on-campus disputes, investigation into challenged dismissals, determinations of whether violations of the principles of freedom and tenure have occurred, and the application of sanctions have fallen to the AAUP acting alone. In its investigations, reports, and use of sanctions, the Association prides itself on proceeding with scrupulous objectivity through processes judicial in character. Its conclusions as to facts have not been challenged, except very rarely by an immediate party.

In the reports it has been necessary to develop through interpretation the rather brief joint statements which underlie the conclusions. As to tenure, for example, the "acceptable academic practice" the 1940 *Statement* sets forth, of limiting the faculty member's probationary period to seven years, has been translated into a mandatory rule.[39] With respect to academic freedom during the probationary period, for which the 1940 *Statement* provides, it has been held that the faculty member may not be made to suffer non-

---

by the Committee on Academic Freedom and Tenure of the Association, "censure" of the responsible administration (including governing board) where deemed warranted by the Council and an Annual Meeting of the Association, and subsequent negotiations looking to removal of the censure. The list of censured administrations, which originated in 1938 as a substitute for previous removals of institutions from an "eligible list," is regularly published in the *Bulletin*. See above, pp. 143–47.

[38] These reports are published in the *Bulletin* after their presentation at Annual Meetings. See especially the report for 1950, *AAUP Bulletin,* 37:72 (1951). The report of the Special Committee on Academic Freedom and Tenure in the Quest for National Security, *supra* note 2, reformulated the applicable general principles with special reference to the issues presented by the national effort to combat communism. *AAUP Bulletin,* 42:50–61 (1956). A supplementary statement of the Committee on Academic Freedom and Tenure was published in 1958; see texts above, pp. 47–63.

[39] "Academic Freedom and Tenure: Princeton Theological Seminary," *AAUP Bulletin,* 45:47 (1959).

renewal of his appointment or denial of tenure because of his exercise of freedom.[40] The freedom of the faculty member to speak as a citizen, which is secured "from institutional censorship or discipline," has been taken to include his privilege of refusing on constitutional grounds to answer questions in an official investigation.[41] The judgment of unfitness to continue in a faculty position, which may be reached in a dismissal proceeding, may not be based merely on conduct, such as simple membership or honest activity in a suspected organization, which is within the ambit of academic freedom.[42] This type of development of the principles of freedom and tenure, although *ex parte,* has implicitly been accepted—in part, no doubt, because of the sheer necessity for it, and to some extent, perhaps, because of the soundness of the interpretations reached.

The extent of the actual acceptance of these interpretations by the academic community as a whole cannot be gauged with precision. The decisions by the AAUP to which they have led—and, indeed, the decisions establishing clear-cut violations of explicit principles—have not secured the reinstatement of faculty members found to have been wrongfully dismissed. The regulations of the offending institutions have, however, typically been made to conform subsequently to the stated principles, as those of many other institutions do, without dissent from the interpretations of the AAUP.[43]

Of central importance in the implementation of the principles of freedom and tenure is the assurance of participation by faculty members in decisions when the dismissal of colleagues is proposed. The 1940 *Statement* provides that "termination for cause of a continuous appointment, or the dismissal for cause of a teacher previous to the expiration of a term appointment, should, if possible, be considered by both a faculty committee and the governing

[40] "Alabama Polytechnic Institute," *AAUP Bulletin,* 44:158 (1958); see also "Academic Freedom and Tenure: Evansville College," *AAUP Bulletin,* 35: 74 (1949).

[41] "The Effects of Refusal to Testify," *AAUP Bulletin,* 42:75 (1956).

[42] University of Washington, *id.,* 61.

[43] The administration is not required to assent affirmatively to an interpretation which is disputable and which does not have the approval of the Association of American Colleges, although it sometimes does assent.

board of the institution."[44] Often characterized as a means of securing a judgment of the faculty member by his peers in the first instance, this provision draws its chief value from the assurance it gives that academic considerations will enter into decisions and from the likelihood it provides that professionally accepted principles will be given effect. Without such faculty participation, the prospects for thoroughgoing maintenance of academic freedom in American institutions of higher learning would be considerably less than they are.

IV. Legal impairment and protection of academic freedom

In addition to the contribution which constitutional law has made to the substantive and procedural aspects of academic freedom as professionally defined and maintained, the law of the land may bear directly on academic freedom in at least three ways: through the impairment of freedom by legislative restrictions on it; through judicial enforcement of constitutional barriers to such impairments; and through judicial protection of the right to freedom as against limitation by academic authorities themselves. In rendering decisions in cases arising in any of these areas the courts, especially the Supreme Court of the United States under the Bill of Rights and the fourteenth amendment, may do much to define the effective scope of academic freedom.

Legislation which attaches ideological tests to the eligibility of students or faculty to participate in higher education obviously impairs academic freedom by imposing the alternative of either outward conformity or exclusion for refusal to submit. Statutory oaths of allegiance aroused much opposition among administrators and professors in the 1930's.[45] Even though the required oaths could be taken in good faith and construed according to the subjective loyalties of the takers, they were recognized as efforts to impose conformity on education.[46] These laws remain on the books[47] and

[44] Note 4 *supra*.

[45] The index to volume 22 of the *AAUP Bulletin* (1936), under the caption "Loyalty Oaths," leads to published accounts of protests against such oaths.

[46] See Carl Becker, "In Support of the Constitution," *AAUP Bulletin,* 21: 327 (1935), reprinted from *The Nation* 140:13 (1935); J. R. Angell, address

have been augmented by a loyalty oath requirement that conditions federal aid to students and scholars under the National Science Foundation and National Defense Education Acts.[48] There have also been added the more recent requirement of disclaimers of subversive associations and beliefs, including such a requirement in the same two federal acts prior to their amendment in 1962.[49] The principal objections to such disclaimers are that they operate somewhat *in terrorem* when their terms are not wholly clear and that the exclusion of any genuinely held ideas whatsoever from colleges and universities is inconsistent with the nature of higher education. In addition, they are invidious when academic personnel are singled out for attention, and can lead easily to inquisitions when false swearing is suspected.[50] Similar in effect are statutory requirements for disclosure of memberships, accompanied by express or implied threats of dismissal if unfavorable affiliations are brought to light.[51]

---

to Yale Alumni, *AAUP Bulletin,* 22:260 (1936); "Statement on Freedom of Speech—Teachers' Oath Laws," *AAUP Bulletin,* 23:26–32 (1937).

[47] Walter Gellhorn, *The States and Subversion* (1952), 410–11.

[48] 64 Stat. 156, as amended, 42 U.S.C.A. § 1874(d)(I)(A) (Supp. 1963); 72 Stat. 1962, as amended, 20 U.S.C.A. § 581(f) (Supp. 1963).

[49] Notes 47 and 48, *supra,* prior to amendment. The requirement of the two acts was that the affiant swear "he does not believe in, and is not a member of and does not support any organization that believes in or teaches, the overthrow of the United States Government by force or violence or by any illegal or unconstitutional methods."

[50] Among many published protests against the disclaimer affidavit requirement of the National Defense Education Act, possibly the most eloquent and comprehensive is that written by President A. Whitney Griswold of Yale University and published in the *New York Times Magazine* of December 20, 1959, p. 18. For a record of opposition among educators, see "Repealing the Disclaimer Affidavit," *AAUP Bulletin,* 46:55 (1960). For the result and a final list of protesting institutions, see H. I. Orentlicher, "The Disclaimer Affidavit: A Valedictory," *id.* 48:524 (1962).

[51] See the Arkansas act involved in Shelton v. Tucker, 364 U.S. 479 (1960). Although the decision invalidating the statute was placed on the ground of undue breadth of the required disclosure (*infra* text at note 66), the legislature of the state was clearly seeking to provide a means of identifying members of the National Association for the Advancement of Colored People (NAACP), and of discouraging membership in that organization. See also

Statutes requiring investigations to ferret out individuals adhering to proscribed organizations or beliefs operate with, if anything, still more drastic effect.[52] Simple prohibitions, enforceable by criminal prosecutions, operate more sporadically. The one which has now replaced the disclaimer requirement in the National Science Foundation and National Defense Education Acts is quite tightly drawn.[53]

Investigations not required by statute and having no prescribed effects under existing law may nevertheless operate *in terrorem* and may lead to loss of reputation by those who are subject to inquiry, if their beliefs and associations are gone into. Therefore, the possible effect of such investigations in limiting the freedom of students and faculty is recognized, and specific justification for each inquiry must be shown.[54] When justification is shown and the inquiry goes forward, the restriction that may result is a consequence of the conduct of academic institutions in society. Inquiry into the substance of the teaching in an institution seems, however, to be forbidden on constitutional grounds.[55] The character and incidental activities of those who participate in the educational process, in so far as they are deemed relevant to national security, are, on the other hand, subject to scrutiny.[56]

NAACP v. Alabama, 357 U.S. 449 (1958); Bates v. Little Rock, 361 U.S. 516 (1960); Louisiana v. NAACP, 366 U.S. 293 (1961).

[52] See Adler v. Board of Education, *infra* note 62. The Association of American Law Schools (AALS) condemned sweeping investigations into the loyalty of university faculties in a resolution adopted in 1951, dealing also with other aspects of academic freedom in relation to national security. *Proceedings* (1951), 61–62, 98–101. For comprehensive reports of the Association's Committee on Academic Freedom and Tenure in this area, see *id.,* 102–36; *Proceedings* (1953), 97–125; *Proceedings* (1954), 20–22, 115–20.

[53] Under the provision, it becomes a criminal offense for a knowing member of an organization which is registered or has been required by a final order of the Subversive Activities Control Board to register, under the Internal Security Act, to apply for a federal loan or grant.

[54] Sweezy v. New Hampshire, 354 U.S. 234 (1957); see Gibson v. Florida Legislative Investigating Committee, 372 U.S. 539 (1963).

[55] *Infra,* text at note 64.

[56] Barenblatt v. United States, *infra* note 65.

Judicial enforcement of constitutional barriers to the impairment of academic freedom by governmental action, centering in the Supreme Court of the United States, has resulted in predominantly split decisions, falling now on one side of the line separating validity from invalidity and then on the other.[57] Most of the decisions involving faculty members have not turned on issues related specifically to academic affairs, but rather on such questions as whether a dismissal for past invocation of the fifth amendment violated the personal rights of the individual,[58] whether an oath law might require dismissal from any kind of public employment because of innocent membership in a proscribed organization,[59] whether a mandatory oath was invalidly vague in its terms,[60] or whether procedural due process was accorded in a legislative investigation.[61] The permissible scope of governmental inquiries into academic affairs and the permissible bases for excluding persons from teaching positions have, however, been considered; and in the opinions to which these questions have given rise the Justices of the Supreme Court have uttered formulations of academic freedom that will be enduringly influential.

The leading case is *Adler v. Board of Education,*[62] involving the Feinberg Law of New York. The statute and regulations under it by the State Board of Regents required the Board of Education of the city of New York to list organizations found, after hearing, to advocate or teach overthrow of the Government by force or violence or other unlawful means, and further required that persons

[57] See R. K. Carr, "Academic Freedom, the American Association of University Professors, and the United States Supreme Court," *AAUP Bulletin,* 45:5 (1959); Fuchs, "The Barenblatt Decision and the Academic Profession," *id.* at 333 (1959). For a penetrating discussion of restrictions on the freedom of teachers and the means of combating them, see "Racial Integration and Academic Freedom," *N.Y.U.L. Rev.* 34:725, 899 (1959) (part one of a study by the Arthur Garfield Hays Memorial Fund, School of Law, New York University).

[58] Beilan v. Board of Education, 357 U.S. 399 (1958); cf. Nelson v. County of Los Angeles, 362 U.S. 1 (1960).

[59] Wieman v. Updegraff, 344 U.S. 183 (1952).

[60] Cramp v. Board of Public Instruction, 368 U.S. 278 (1961).

[61] Sweezy v. New Hampshire, *supra* note 54.

[62] 342 U.S. 485 (1952).

teaching or advocating overthrow of the Government by these means, or knowingly belonging to organizations so teaching or advocating, should not be appointed or retained as teachers in public institutions. Hearings were to be accorded before denial of appointment or dismissal under the law, with membership in an organization listed by the Board constituting prima facie evidence of disqualification. The Supreme Court sustained the statute in an opinion by Mr. Justice Minton which upholds the authority of the state to exclude from the "sensitive area" of the schoolroom persons of the kind proscribed. The Court cited a decision the preceding year, in which a disclaimer oath requirement for Los Angeles municipal employees was upheld on the ground that public servants may be examined "as to matters that may prove relevant to their fitness and suitability for the public service."[63] Justices Douglas and Black dissented, emphasizing the intimidation caused by such legislation and by the principle of guilt by association of which the New York statute made use. "Where suspicion fills the air," said Mr. Justice Douglas, "and holds scholars in line for fear of their jobs, there can be no exercise of the free intellect."

In *Sweezy v. New Hampshire,* the decision reached by four concurring Justices turned in the end on a denial of due process through failure to show that the questions asked of a visiting lecturer at the University of New Hampshire about his lectures and party affiliations, during an official investigation, came within the authorized scope of the inquiry. The opinion of these four Justices, by Chief Justice Warren, expressed special concern over academic freedom. "The essentiality of freedom in the community of American universities is almost self-evident," he wrote:

> No one should underestimate the vital role in a democracy that is played by those who guide and train our youth. To impose any strait jacket upon the intellectual leaders in our colleges and universities would imperil the future of our Nation. No field of education is so thoroughly comprehended by man that new discoveries cannot yet be made. Particularly is that true in the social sciences, where few, if any, principles are accepted as absolutes. Scholarship

[63] Garner v. Los Angeles Board of Public Works, 341 U.S. 716 (1951).

> cannot flourish in an atmosphere of suspicion and distrust. Teachers and students must always remain free to inquire, to study and to evaluate, to gain new maturity and understanding; otherwise our civilization will stagnate and die.

Here, "We believe that there unquestionably was an invasion of petitioner's liberties in the areas of academic freedom and political expression—areas in which government should be extremely reticent to tread."[64]

The same view was elaborated in a concurring opinion by Justices Frankfurter and Harlan, basing the decision on the freedom issue. As a result, in the later *Barenblatt* case, the majority of the Court stated in an opinion by Mr. Justice Harlan that,

> . . . broadly viewed, inquiries cannot be made into the teaching that is pursued in any of our educational institutions. When academic teaching-freedom and its corollary learning-freedom, so essential to the well-being of the Nation, are claimed, this Court will always be on the alert against intrusion by Congress into this constitutionally protected domain.[65]

In the eyes of the Court majority in this case, however, the coercive effect of investigations into communist associations and activities of students and teachers is outweighed by the public interest in discovering such conduct, where there is reason to suspect it. A broadscale disclosure of all organizational affiliations cannot, however, be required of teachers in public institutions.[66]

On the frontier of legal protection to academic freedom lies the possible availability of judicial remedies to aggrieved faculty members or students against impairment of their freedoms by actions of the institutions. Breach of contract, violation of an applicable regulation of a public institution, or unconstitutional use of public power (exercised by officers of a public institution as state officials or exercised by a private institution pursuant to delegation) might be the basis of relief. The same analysis as may justify recovery

[64] 354 U.S. 234, 250 (1957).
[65] Barenblatt v. United States, 360 U.S. 109, 112 (1959).
[66] Shelton v. Tucker, 364 U.S. 479 (1960).

against violation of procedural or tenure rights[67] applies here; but the precise meaning of institutional documents securing the right to freedom is often subject to considerable doubt. The Illinois Court of Appeals has recently rejected a claim that institutional regulations securing faculty freedom provided anything more than due consideration within the university of a claim that freedom had been violated by a dismissal on account of a letter published in the student newspaper.[68] Courts will be reluctant in any event to review the determinations of academic authorities in such matters, and there is no strong demand that they do so.[69] Professional means of vindicating academic freedom against institutional action remain the chief reliance of faculties.

V. By way of summary

It should be apparent from even so brief an account as the one in the preceding pages that academic freedom rests on a variety of cultural and institutional factors; that it changes from time to time and from place to place; and that in the United States today it embraces more sweeping claims to independence, as well as a vastly greater range of educational activities, than ever before in history. Originating as a condition of scholarly endeavor in institutions that performed highly specialized functions closely related to philosophy, and restricted until recently to freedoms within those institu-

[67] See Nostrand v. Little, 58 Wash. 2d 111, 361 P.2d 551 (1961), *appeal dismissed,* 368 U.S. 436 (1962); Clark Byse, "Academic Freedom, Tenure, and the Law," *Harv. L. Rev.* 73:304 (1959).

[68] Koch v. Board of Trustees of the University of Illinois, 39 Ill. App. 2d 51, 187 N.E. 2d 340 (1962).

[69] Article 5(3) of the German Constitution reads: "Art and science, research and teaching, shall be free. Freedom of teaching shall not absolve from loyalty to the constitution." Even so explicit a provision might mean only that specified freedoms are guaranteed against interference by non-academic authority. The self-government of academic institutions is included in the guaranty, and is secured as well by state constitutional provisions. *Entscheidungen des Bundesverfassungsgerichts* 3:58, 143 (1953); Mangoldt-Klein, *Das Bonner Grundgesetz* (2d ed., 1957), 1:253. It seems unlikely, therefore, that an alleged denial of academic freedom by academic authority would be reached by the guaranty.

tions, it has been expanded in the United States to cover faculty members in a great variety of institutions "beyond the high school,"[70] and to protect the liberty to participate in extramural as well as intramural activities. To render this expanded academic freedom secure, impressive professional enforcement machinery has been established and the law of the land has been invoked to a significant extent.

[70] The German constitutional guaranty of teaching freedom (*Lehrfreiheit*) is not deemed by commentators to extend to instruction that does not depend upon independent investigation. Hence it is confined to academic institutions and does not apply to those that prescribe the content of courses to be taught or the textbooks to be used. Mangoldt-Klein, *op. cit. supra* note 69, 1:257, 258.

Appendix F

ACADEMIC DUE PROCESS

By Louis Joughin[1]

Introduction

Academic due process is brand new as a term, young as an idea having formal dimensions, but of venerable antiquity in some elements of its practice. The difference in age among these aspects is obvious when one considers the sparse use which has thus far been made of the chief approaches commonly applied to the study of a socially operative principle:

1. The concept of academic due process does not appear as yet to have received preliminary attention by writers on the history of ideas.

2. In the growing literature of academic freedom, reference is customarily made to academic due process as a chief instrument, but there is little critical analysis.

3. Studies of the college or university as an institution sometimes refer to the procedures which constitute due process, but these are not subjected to much scrutiny. Social studies of a more general kind, such as those dealing with the major forces at work in human arrangements, do not deal especially with academic due process.

[1] A.B. 1927, A.M. 1930, Ph.D. 1932, Harvard University. Associate Secretary, American Association of University Professors. The article is reprinted, with permission, from a symposium, Academic Freedom, appearing in *Law and Contemporary Problems* (Vol. 28, No. 3, Summer 1963), published by the Duke University School of Law, Durham, N.C. Copyright © 1963, by Duke University.

In this article the writer speaks only for himself; the Association is in no way responsible for the views expressed. References to AAUP materials are limited to published documents.

4. Due process in law offers a conspicuously available analogue. The kinship is often noted, but there seems to be no sibling study.

5. Fortunately, there is a solid body of case history in the record of controversies between administrations and faculty members. Most of the record is in an academic context, but there is some legal material.

6. Happily, there are five more or less explicit and detailed policy statements. Of the four by the American Association of University Professors (AAUP), that of 1915 has single sponsorship, while those of 1925, 1940, and 1958 have been jointly promulgated by the AAUP and the Association of American Colleges (AAC). The fifth statement, *Academic Due Process,* first gave the thing a name in a document designed for wide circulation; it was published by the American Civil Liberties Union (ACLU) in 1954.

The present article is mainly a systematic analysis bringing together the elements of recent case history and the elements noticed in the policy statements just referred to. However, the unexplored approaches just remarked upon are not lost sight of; from time to time there is introduced an observation, a suggestion, or even an *obiter dictum.*

There exists one further introductory obligation. The policy statements involved are due their own brief history as entities before they are dismembered and their parts distributed for purposes of comparative study.

In 1915, the newly-formed American Association of University Professors received from its Committee on Academic Freedom and Tenure a *Declaration of Principles*[2] which based its discussion of academic freedom upon consideration of: "(1) the scope and basis

[2] The Committee members preparing the report were: Edwin R. A. Seligman (Economics), Columbia University, *Chairman;* Charles E. Bennett (Latin), Cornell University; James Q. Dealey (Political Science), Brown University; Edward C. Elliott (Education), University of Wisconsin; Richard T. Ely (Economics), University of Wisconsin; Henry W. Farnam (Political Science), Yale University; Frank A. Fetter (Economics), Princeton University; Guy Stanton Ford (History), University of Minnesota; Charles A. Kofoid (Zoology), University of California; James P. Lichtenberger (Sociology), University of Pennsylvania; Arthur O. Lovejoy (Philosophy), The Johns Hopkins University; Frederick W. Padelford (English), University of Washington;

of the power exercised by those bodies having ultimate legal authority in academic affairs; (2) the nature of the academic calling; (3) the function of the academic institution or university." The document, it should be noted, gives much attention to academic responsibility, as well as to academic freedom. The final section of the *Declaration of Principles* is entitled "Practical Proposals," and discusses briefly the "formulation of grounds for dismissal" and "judicial hearings before dismissal." It is here that the AAUP first lists procedures: (1) charges should be in writing and "formulated with reasonable definiteness"; (2) there should be a fair trial before a "special or permanent judicial committee chosen by the faculty senate or council, or by the faculty at large"; (3) the teacher should have "full opportunity to present evidence" with adequate provision for expert testimony if his competence is at issue.

In effect the 1915 *Declaration of Principles* proposed that a responsible profession police itself, and practical suggestions about procedure are offered. From the vantage point of fifty years' experience, it is significant that the procedures mentioned are not given a name, and that there is no indication whether they are considered minimal, reasonably complete, or actual good practice. There is, of course, much implication of due process in such phrases as "suitable judicial bodies" and "fair trial." And it should not be forgotten that the *Declaration of Principles* was drafted during the first year of life of the Association, a year during which no less than eleven specific cases alleging infringement of academic freedom were brought to the new organization. Even though the document has little to say about procedures, a great deal of attention to some kind of due process must have been going on because of the case situation.

In 1925, the American Council on Education called a conference to discuss the principles of academic freedom, and the AAUP was largely involved. Emphasis fell upon the restatement of "good

---

Roscoe Pound (Law), Harvard University; Howard C. Warren (Psychology), Princeton University; Ulysses G. Weatherly (Sociology), Indiana University. The report was received by the first president of the Association, John Dewey. Professors Elliott, Ford, and Lichtenberger became dissociated before the report was signed.

academic customs and usage" rather than upon the development of new principles.[3] In any event, the 1925 *Conference Statement* was within a year endorsed by the AAUP and the Association of American Colleges.

The 1925 *Conference Statement* is a much shorter document than that of 1915. With respect to due process, it emphasizes the principles of confrontation, as its predecessor had not done; but it yields ground in suggesting that the limit of faculty strength is to present a useful expert opinion on a case, in contrast to 1915 when it had been strongly indicated that the judgment of a faculty hearing committee should be essentially conclusive. The due process section is short, and only a few specifics are noted.

In 1940, after a quarter of a century of experience in the handling of numerous cases, the Association again addressed itself to the problem—in few words but with enlarged import—and published the 1940 *Statement of Principles.* Dismissal for cause is frankly made the issue, but there is a sharp line drawn between the teacher on tenure and the teacher on term appointment. For the tenure professor, the burden of proof rests upon the administration; for the teacher on limited appointment, the situation is reversed and it is he who must make a prima facie case of violation of academic freedom. As to specific safeguards, some are emphasized, some are less certainly present, but the sum total of recommended procedural protection is unquestionably larger. Furthermore, as Metzger says: "The tendency . . . is clear: it is to make the faculty hearing as much as possible like a criminal court room and to protect, by legal rule, the rights of the teacher at the bar."[4]

[3] This brief history of the development of the AAUP policy statements rests upon the occasional editorial notes which have accompanied their printings in the *AAUP Bulletin;* independent historical research has not been undertaken by the writer. In addition to the classic apologies about lack of space and time, it is necessary to take into account the fact that a comprehensive history of the AAUP is presently [1967] being written by Professor Walter P. Metzger of the History Department of Columbia University; the Metzger study will provide ample context and guidance for further study.

[4] Letter from Professor Walter P. Metzger to the author, Feb. 14, 1963. The Metzger letter presents an analysis of the controlling forces which over the years have shaped the due process aspects of the AAUP policy state-

Then, in 1958, stimulated by the apparent need for more detailed guidance, and perhaps spurred by the friendly competition offered by the 1954 *Academic Due Process* of the ACLU, the AAUP and the AAC, working together, produced a *Statement on Procedural Standards in Faculty Dismissal Proceedings.* The foreword notes that the *Statement* is a supplement to the 1940 *Statement of Principles* providing a "formulation of the 'academic due process' that should be observed in dismissal proceedings." The standards, however, are a "guide" and "not intended to establish a norm."

Meanwhile, in 1954, the American Civil Liberties Union had published *Academic Due Process,* prepared by its Academic Freedom Committee. This document appears to be the first comprehensive statement of the elements of the subject, and, as has been noted, brings the term into common use.[5] The subtitle reads "A statement of desirable procedures applicable within educational institutions in cases involving academic freedom." This restriction to academic freedom cases was quite in keeping with the limitation the ACLU imposes upon itself as a civil liberties organization. But there is certainly nothing in *Academic Due Process* which makes it inapplicable to the trial of issues other than academic freedom.

---

ments. It is impossible to indicate the degree to which these pages are indebted to Mr. Metzger, who wrote at length and most thoughtfully to a colleague at the very time he himself was deeply engaged in his own research and writing.

[5] When opportunity permits, the present writer hopes to explore, as a matter of semantic interest, the origin of the term "academic due process." He knows that at some time between his first Academic Freedom Committee work with the ACLU in 1946 and his becoming the executive officer of the ACLU Academic Freedom Committee in 1951, he began to use the term; he was certainly responsible for the title of the 1954 document. But among the distinguished persons at work on academic freedom in the ACLU from 1946 to 1954 were such figures as Karl Llewellyn, Walter Gellhorn, and Alonzo F. Myers; it would be well to study the record of the exchanges heard on Olympus before jumping to conclusions. The first reference to "academic due process" in AAUP literature appears to be in the "Report of Committee A, 1956–57," signed by Professor H. Bentley Glass as chairman, *AAUP Bulletin,* 43:515, 519 (1957).

I. The rationale of academic due process

Basically, academic due process is a system of procedures designed to produce the best possible judgments in those personnel problems of higher education which may yield a serious adverse decision about a teacher. What is sought after is a "clear, orderly, fair" way of making a decision; it is desirable to provide the individual with "procedural safeguards" or "procedural guarantees"; more pallidly, there should be "normal dismissal proceedings"; or going back to earlier usage, the need is for "due process." But the matter is somewhat more complicated than these phrases suggest.

For example, the immediate institutional context, or the broader general social context, can change in ways that will affect procedure. If the main principles being applied, those of academic freedom, are distorted by pressures from without, let us say pressures resulting from fear about national security, then the procedural instrument is likely to bend under stress. For example, the ebb and flow of American devotion to the principles of democracy is bound to affect a procedure which in so many ways depends upon fair application of the power of the people. For example, mere excitement and resulting publicity, *i.e.*, the psychological milieu, the mob spirit, may limit the use of academic due process—a system of procedures which cannot return even a single "be damned to you" without contradicting its own principle.

Consequently, the rationale of academic due process must take into account more than the central fact of its intrinsic nature. At least this much:

1. Academic due process, hopefully and in its best moments, is a system which controls positive as well as negative academic action. Twenty years ago, Professor E. C. Kirkland, writing soon after the adoption of the 1940 *Statement of Principles,* indicated the fullness of the coverage: "The work of everyone would be eased if only due process became an integral part of academic procedures and standards relating to faculty personnel."[6] More recently, a study of tenure in American higher education, in describing the desirable procedures for this important area of decisions, gives

[6] E. C. Kirkland, "Annual Report for Committee A," *AAUP Bulletin,* 29: 64 (1943).

as much attention to those which are affirmative in nature and award tenure as to the painful, negative decisions which involve dismissal.[7]

2. Academic due process is analogous to legal due process, but only that and often different. Authorities in the field are careful to point out that identity of the two cannot be maintained, and that it is also incorrect to think of the academic as a variant of the legal type. As Professor John M. Maguire says:

> For many years the AAUP has labored . . . to establish the propositions that there ought to be an accepted uniform academic law of customary nature . . . and that this law can be best administered without the often heated publicity of ordinary court trials before tribunals cognizant of the presuppositions of our vast American educational enterprise. . . . The judicial tendency is to squeeze education into a common mold with other working relationships.[8]

Likewise, Professor Robert K. Carr notes that "The Association has been properly reluctant to see the development and enforcement of standards of academic freedom and tenure tied too closely to the law-making and law-enforcement processes."[9] Professor Carr does go on to say that there is a duty to "try to acquaint judges and courts with the principles in these areas that the academic profession views as correct," but that is quite a different approach. And the 1958 *Statement on Procedural Standards,* in commenting on the vital matter of procedure in a hearing, notes that "Unless special circumstances warrant, it should not be necessary to follow formal rules of court procedure."[10]

It would probably be correct to say that academic due process has evolved its own recognizable optimum—less of the certainty which derives from constitutional, statutory, or other legal guarantees, and more of the flexibility in approach which leads to a de-

[7] Clark Byse and Louis Joughin, *Tenure in American Higher Education* (1959). The sections on the law, understandably, are more concerned with dismissal actions.

[8] J. M. Maguire, book review, *AAUP Bulletin,* 47:270 (1961).

[9] R. K. Carr, "Report of Committee A, 1958–59," *id.,* 45:392 (1959).

[10] *Id.,* 44:270, 273 (1958).

sired academic solution. As Walter Gellhorn notes: "I prefer a much freer approach to what is in the end a search for the best possible procedures to be utilized in the academic world. 'Due process' always speaks in terms of the minimum necessities, whereas our concern is with the best."[11]

3. Academic due process shares with its master, academic freedom, the special capacity of making an important contribution to all who are involved. By its fairness, it seeks to protect not only the career of the individual but also the reputation of the institution. It offers the public some assurance that hasty or unprincipled action will not find it easy to wash down the drain the heavy investment by society in the powers of a costly expert.

4. Lastly, academic due process is able to teach something important about the nature of learning itself, because its action is so much like that which created the educational treasury it guards. Academic due process is a precision instrument; it has a specific applicability or jurisdiction; it operates by established rules; it concerns itself with testable facts, and tests them. It is a demonstration of the human intellect at work, submitting tentative conclusions to comparison with controls (through the consideration of evidence) and, while moving forward with a particular proceeding, it tests its own working hypotheses by constant reference to the burden of proof. A full-scale application of academic due process demonstrates powerfully the nature and use of the scholarly mind.

II. Systematic analysis

In the pages that follow, the analysis will move forward from point to point in the procedural management of a disputed decision by the administration of a college or university to dismiss a teacher from his post for cause. At each point there will be brought together the main contributions of the five policy statements[12] which

[11] Letter from Professor Walter Gellhorn to the author, Feb. 21, 1963.

[12] Among the AAUP documents, the 1915 and 1925 statements have only historical status, having been superseded as policy by the 1940 *Statement of Principles.* The 1958 *Procedural Standards* are "presented . . . as a guide" but "are not intended to establish a norm in the same manner as the 1940 *Statement of Principles.*" The 1954 ACLU *Academic Due Process* is an official policy statement of that organization.

have been referred to, and a variety of related case material. Of course, no single actual controversy would be likely to involve every procedural matter here discussed.

1. Informal conciliation. This first phase of a situation which may become a "case" is likely to bring a startled or unprepared faculty member face to face with the more or less firm determination of an administration to carry out a decision to dismiss him. There is present an ill-defined mixture of information, fear, inclination, resolution and opposition; in short, all the jumbled ingredients of a human dispute at that early stage where the adversary positions have not been occupied or even clearly perceived. In one case, a teacher may reasonably expect, and in fact discover, that his administration is willing to talk with him in a fair way, or that the administration is even willing to be convinced that it has seen things in the wrong light. Here lies the opportunity for genuine informal conciliation. But in another case, it is possible that the same early external aspects of the matter will in fact conceal an irreversible determination to achieve dismissal at any cost; here lies the danger for the possibly ignorant defendant.

But the effort at informal conciliation should be made; even a victim whose sacrifice has been determined upon may achieve a favorable tactical position by the very fact of his demonstrated early innocence. And certainly society is due the effort.

> It is therefore especially desirable that the administrative authorities and the teacher (accompanied by an adviser) sit down together in a conciliatory session, confronting the charges and the evidence squarely, and sincerely attempting a solution of their common problems. A statement of the facts may clarify the situation; exposition of the teacher's point of view may persuade an administration not to review his competence and integrity; exposition of the administration's point of view may persuade a teacher to recognize his duty to cooperate with his institution, and to indicate how he may do so without sacrifice of principle. Any one of these developments, or all of them together, may yield a solution if the participants in the discussion are moved by genuine good will.[13]
>
> When reason arises to question the fitness of a college

[13] *Academic Due Process,* 4–5 (1954).

> or university faculty member who has tenure or whose term appointment has not expired, the appropriate administrative officers should ordinarily discuss the matter with him in personal conference. The matter may be terminated by mutual consent at this point. . . .[14]

Such a conference must, of course, be in good faith. In the University of Nevada-Richardson case, five professors were charged with being members of "a small dissatisfied group"; a request for clarification brought from the president only this: "My letter of March 31 states all I have to say on the matter. The [half-hour] period [before the governing board] from—to—is granted to you to explain your position."[15] A peremptory notice of this kind is hardly suggestive of conciliation.

In the recent George Washington University-Reichard case, seven members of the department and two deans met with the teacher in an extended session where an attempt was made to determine his opinion on certain matters. It is possible to regard this meeting as in some degree aimed at conciliation, even though the occasion was formalized by the making of a stenographic record. But procedural problems of a more serious nature almost at once developed and conciliation was clearly no longer a main interest.[16]

Even though the lines of opposition may not yet be clearly drawn in this conciliatory phase, and consequently controlling procedures are likely to be minimal, two special cautions should be remembered.

First, care should be taken lest the exploration of conciliation yield information or argument which will be embodied in later formal charges against the faculty member. In an actual case of the mid-fifties, conversation regarding possible past Communist involvement disclosed the teacher to be a religious agnostic; that fact then became fixed in the mind of the governing board as an element of disqualification. One is tempted to recommend that nothing disclosed in a conciliatory session should be introduced in a

[14] "Statement on Procedural Standards in Faculty Dismissal Proceedings," *AAUP Bulletin,* 44:272 (1958) [hereinafter cited as *Statement on Procedural Standards*].

[15] *Id.,* 42:534 (1956).

[16] *Id.,* 48:240, 242 (1962).

disciplinary proceeding. But what if the revelation concerns the very heart of the educational process—let us say, attempted indoctrination of students by the teacher. Can an institution of higher learning ignore evidence clearly raising grave doubts about fitness to teach students? One possible principle would be to limit the use of the new knowledge to serve as an indicator of the direction in which the administration could seek independent evidence, but not to allow the disclosures of the conciliatory session to be used as evidence.

The second caution relates to suspension. The American Association of University Professors states that suspension "is justified only if immediate harm to himself or others is threatened by his continuance."[17] This is an important point because the entire later proceedings may be colored by implications of the act of suspension, or by the language used. That was certainly true in the New York University-Burgum case,[18] and in the very recent University of Illinois-Koch case.[19] Perhaps an extreme of impropriety and denial of academic due process occurred in the Dickinson College-LaVallee case where suspension was first announced in open faculty meeting.[20] The AAUP position cannot be emphasized too strongly: suspension as an act necessary to prevent harm must surely seldom be unavoidable; suspension for any other reason profoundly affects, at least in the public mind, the placing of the burden of proof.

2. *Procedure preliminary to a hearing or preliminary proceedings concerning the fitness of a faculty member; commencement of formal proceedings.* The differences between the treatment of this phase by the ACLU and the AAUP are significant and merit attention.

Academic Due Process asks the administration to present the teacher with "a statement meeting the demands of the principle of confrontation." It should embody:

a. Relevant legislation, board or trustee by-laws and rulings, administrative rulings, faculty legislation, and so forth.

[17] *Statement on Procedural Standards,* 272.
[18] *AAUP Bulletin,* 44:38 (1958).
[19] *Id.,* 49:28 (1963).
[20] *Id.,* 44:140 (1958).

b. The charges in the particular case.

c. A summary of the evidence upon which the charges are based, and a first list of witnesses to be called.

d. The procedure to be followed, including a statement of the nature of the hearing body.

e. A formal invitation to attend with adviser or counsel.[21]

The ACLU statement then goes on to suggest that the teacher also bears responsibility at this stage of the proceedings. He may supplement the statement of governing rules applicable to the situation, or suggest modifications in the charges or proposed procedure. He should indicate the evidence by which he expects to refute the charges and should furnish a first list of witnesses he desires to call. Then, finally, administration and teacher "should, as completely as possible . . . arrive at agreement on formulation of charges, governing rules, and procedure." Such agreement "will clarify the issues and make unnecessary at the hearing, or upon appeal, argument as to the *form* of the controversy, thereby permitting full attention to be given to matters of *substance*."[22]

The Statement on Procedural Standards in Faculty Dismissal Proceedings calls for the teacher's being informed of the applicable procedural regulations, but does not require the providing of other relevant regulations and governing principles and standards; it calls for written charges, and for formal invitation to attend. The Association document does not refer to a summary of the evidence to be presented, or the first list of witnesses, which obligations in the ACLU statement rest upon both administration and teacher.

A most significant element in the Association *Statement* reads as follows:

> . . . if an adjustment does not result, a standing or *ad hoc* committee elected by the faculty and charged with the function of rendering confidential advice in such situations should informally inquire into the situation, to effect an adjustment if possible and, if none is effected, to determine whether in its view formal proceedings to consider his dismissal should be instituted.[23]

[21] *Academic Due Process,* 5.

[22] *Ibid.*

[23] *Statement on Procedural Standards,* 272.

A doubt arises whether a committee so charged may not have dual functions which are essentially incompatible. "To effect an adjustment, if possible" calls for a mediative and conciliatory spirit; incidentally, the committee so acting may receive confidences and explore compromises. So far so good. But this same committee, failing in mediation or conciliation, also finds itself charged with the duty of a grand jury—to determine whether a hearing on dismissal should occur. In one unreported case (where, however, this aspect of the situation became public knowledge), a committee so dually charged in a forced retirement situation strongly protested to the administration against the nature of its mixed duty; in fact, it felt uncertain whether it was on one side or the other, or in the middle. It would seem desirable to clarify this matter as soon as possible, perhaps by recommending the separation of functions and their assignment to different groups. Mediation and indictment do not belong together.

The 1940 *Statement of Principles* does not touch on these preliminary matters, but the silence may accurately be characterized as one of economy, and the procedural requirements listed for the actual hearing clearly assume good procedure in the preliminary stages. The 1915 *Declaration of Principles,* interestingly, twice mentions the standard of "grounds . . . formulated with reasonable definiteness" and "charges . . . in specific terms."[24] This standard was "lost" until the 1954 *Academic Due Process* where it is loosely embodied and the 1958 *Statement on Procedural Standards* where it emerges clearly as "a statement with reasonable particularity of the grounds proposed for the dismissal."

In the Catawba College cases of 1952, orderly development of the administration's view that one or more dismissals were required was adversely affected by the self-constitution and meetings of an alumni "Fact-Finding Committee" to examine the causes of student unrest. At the time institutional controversy was going on, this committee came up with a report to the Board of Trustees which included the view that "a few disgruntled professors, who had personal grievances against the college . . . took advantage of this confused situation in an attempt to discredit the administration

[24] 1915 *Declaration of Principles, AAUP Bulletin,* 40:111 (1954).

and the trustees."[25] Such an intrusion, and it was given weight, proved most harmful to the professors involved in the Catawba College cases.

3. *An interim matter; the psychological bridge.* Somewhere in the two phases so far examined, the period of informal conciliation and the period of preliminary proceedings, one discovers that the usual academic case has developed the recognizable characteristics of an adversary proceeding. The customary benevolent and fraternal exchanges of campus life become infrequent or terminate abruptly; conversation with those not on one's side becomes guarded, lest advantage be lost or vulnerability disclosed; in talking with one's supporters thought tends to be given to tactics and strategy. The teacher is advised that:

> Communications, as a general rule, should be in writing, with copies retained. Oral discussion should be followed by an exchange of memoranda indicating the understanding which each party has of the conversation.[26]

Unusual problems may arise. In the Fisk University-Lorch case, the probable cause which had so deeply disturbed the president as to result in confused and unwise action on his part, was thrust aside when the teacher appeared before the board—and a new cause of action was announced by that body.[27] In the Princeton Theological Seminary-Theron case, it was difficult to establish the nature of some of the points to be examined because the teacher had never received any kind of written appointment during his ten years of service.[28] By contrast, in the Allen University cases, the teachers in due course discovered that the administration had in its possession, and may even have assembled, elaborate dossiers on non-academic aspects of their lives.[29]

The faculty member, in the whole time before the receiving of formal charges, is subject to hazards known and unknown. Therefore, not the least difficult of his choices will be that of a psycholo-

[25] *Id.,* 43:210, 214–15 (1957).
[26] *Academic Due Process,* 5–6.
[27] *AAUP Bulletin,* 45:27, 36–37 (1959).
[28] *Id.,* 45:50–51 (1959).
[29] *Id.,* 46:89 (1960).

gy for the situation; (1) friendly, freely communicative, and open to adjustment, or (2) advisedly self-protective, communicative only in formalities fit for a record, and rejective of overtures which have not been approved by counsel.

4. Counsel. It is of considerable historical import that neither the 1915 *Declaration of Principles* nor the 1925 *Conference Statement* states that a teacher may be assisted by counsel. It is not until 1940 that the Association says: "He should be permitted to have with him an adviser of his own choosing who may act as counsel."[30] Eighteen years later, in the 1958 *Statement on Procedural Standards,* it is said that the functions of this counsel should be similar to those of a representative of the president who will "assist in developing the case."[31] These provisions cover the ground, at least by implication. However, the ACLU *Academic Due Process* takes into account two other kinds of unfortunate situations: (1) those where academic advice proved insufficient, and the lack of legal counsel permitted injury to the teacher, and (2) those unhappy cases where the ignorance of a lawyer adviser about academic procedures led to failure in seizing upon possible academic solutions to the case. Consequently, the ACLU statement recommends:

> The teacher should select from among his colleagues a person of established position, wisdom, and judicial temper, who will act as his official academic adviser, or should select counsel to advise him on legal matters. He may, in his discretion, be assisted by both an academic adviser and a legal counselor. The teacher should inform the administration of the identity of his adviser or counsel and should obtain written agreement to his appearance on the teacher's behalf.[32]

Generally speaking, institutions have permitted a teacher to have counsel, although some faculty members have had to go outside their own institutions for help, and a few have failed to provide themselves through ignorance of their own need. Generally, counsel has been helpful, although there have been instances of a

[30] 1940 *Statement of Principles,* 109.

[31] *Statement on Procedural Standards,* 273.

[32] *Academic Due Process,* 5.

legalistic attitude (chiefly by nonlawyer counsel) which has irritated a hearing committee.

However, two main problems raised by the presence of counsel are of a broader nature than the question of choice or the degree of receptivity of the administration. First of all, it is undeniable that the presence of some kind of counsel means that now, for sure, there are adversaries present, and this may affect the further development of the situation. Significantly, in terms of its experience, the ACLU, on balance, recommends that the adviser be present even in the period of informal conciliation. In short, anyone, from the start, is in danger.

The second problem results from the extremely limited supply of adequate legal counsel. Many practicing attorneys confronted by a dismissal case will find themselves for the first time dealing professionally with the customs and principles of academic life. Conversely, few academic advisers will feel themselves competent to assist the faculty member, when there is likelihood that legal issues will develop, and the president or board is assisted by the college or university legal adviser. These deficiencies suggest why law professors, who know both law and Academia, are often drawn into academic trials. If this demand is unavoidable, possibly the Association of American Law Schools could at least contribute to a solution of the supply problem by developing and organizing a pool of legal professorial talent, so that the maximum of help might be had without allowing too heavy a burden to fall upon those law professors who have become known for their willingness to help and, consequently, are sought out more often than is fair to them.

One further caution is necessary about the influence which the presence of legal counsel may have on a hearing. Probably, the University of Vermont-Novikoff case became involved in legal tangles mainly because of complicated and confusing procedures. But an important contributory cause was the participation of an attorney, for the administration, who is reported to have played "the role of a determined prosecutor"; it is difficult to imagine how to meet such a challenge except by response of the same partisan sort.[33]

[33] *AAUP Bulletin,* 44:11–21 (1958).

5. *The constitution and creation of the hearing committee.* The demand of the 1915 *Declaration of Principles* for "suitable judicial bodies," *i.e.*, "a special or permanent judicial committee chosen by the faculty senate or council, or by the faculty at large," established the idea of the hearing by expert colleagues at the outset. The demand has been repeated with varying degrees of clarity and force by the succeeding Association statements. The 1940 *Statement of Principles,* like the 1925 *Conference Statement,* merely requires that the issue should "be considered by both a faculty committee and the governing board of the institution"; nothing is said of the formal relationship or cooperative practice of these two groups, or the manner of selection of the faculty committee. This curious gap in statement of fundamental procedure is partly filled by the language found in the *Statement on Procedural Standards,* which calls for:

> . . . an elected standing committee not previously concerned with the case or a committee established as soon as possible after the president's letter to the faculty member has been sent. The choice of members of the hearing committee should be on the basis of their objectivity and competence and of the regard in which they are held in the academic community.[34]

The ACLU statement reads:

> The hearing committee should be a standing or special group of full-time teaching colleagues, democratically chosen by and representative of the teaching staff, and selected by pre-established rules. The administration should dissociate itself from those performing a judicial function at the hearing.[35]

The difficulty is simple and ominous; plainly many institutions do not grant a hearing before a faculty committee. Of the forty-six cases reported in the *AAUP Bulletin* since 1948,[36] only four-

[34] *Statement on Procedural Standards,* 273.

[35] *Academic Due Process,* 6.

[36] Three reports are not considered; two because they relate to investigations in which there was no trial of an individual; the other report was based on a hearing which, procedurally, concerned charges brought by a teacher against a defendant institution.

teen have been adjudicated by a committee wholly or substantially faculty in composition; of the fourteen cases reported since 1958, only one has witnessed a faculty committee hearing with genuine judicial authority for the group—and in that one case the governing board set aside the unanimous faculty judgment calling for reprimand, and dismissed the teacher. The picture is not totally black: some board committees or administrative hearing bodies have rendered verdicts which appear to be just, and, of course, there have been cases in which faculty committees have judged, and been sustained, and which are unreported. But the general scene is certainly somber; there is only weak indication that the run-of-the-mill dismissal action will have in its history the one absolute essential for assurance that the faculty of an institution is charged with governing its own status and membership. Those who will admit subjective impressions may take consolation in the fact that the "better" institutions usually come through, and that the failure to use the faculty hearing committee procedure is more prevalent at places which are undeveloped or are under despotic rule.

A main question has always been the makeup of the faculty hearing committee. Ideally it should be all-faculty, and faculty-elected; not because of the greater wisdom of the faculty but because a faculty point of view and judgment is needed, by itself and untinged by the proper but different context and value system which the governing board may, in its wisdom, apply. At Catawba College the committee was made up of five trustees and five faculty members appointed by the president of the Board.[37] At the University of Kansas City the committee included five board members, the president, three deans, and five elected faculty members.[38] At North Dakota Agricultural College the committee consisted of eleven administrative officers, and two elected faculty members—one a division chief and the other a candidate for a deanship.[39] Such weird combinations tell us nothing conclusive about a particular judgment or the judicial capacity of the persons serving on

[37] *AAUP Bulletin,* 43:217–18 (1957).
[38] *Id.,* 43:185 (1957).
[39] *Id.,* 42:145–46 (1956).

these committees. They do, however, suggest that some one, some time, was afraid to hear a straight faculty opinion.

On the question of closed or private hearings, the AAUP statements of 1915, 1925, and 1940, and the ACLU statement of 1954 are silent. The 1958 *Statement on Procedural Standards* advises that the hearing committee, "in consultation with the president and the faculty member, should exercise its judgment as to whether the hearing should be public or private."[40] Another view is that the hearing should be private unless the faculty member requests otherwise.[41]

A strong argument can be made for placing the decision about an open or closed hearing in the hands of the faculty member. His professional life, perhaps the whole future for himself and his family, may be at stake; these are great concerns and outweigh any consideration of possible embarrassment or pain to a witness.

Should the committee be standing or *ad hoc?* The specially selected committee may make it possible to bring into play the judgment of particularly qualified persons for a particular situation; the standing committee has the advantage of being chosen by a sober assessment of the judicial disposition of its members, not in a time of crisis. Should the committee be appointed or elected? Either may do quite well, provided that it is the faculty or its agent which acts. No one can regard as fair the appointment of a faculty hearing committee by the administration which is to present the charges; it is essential that "the administration . . . dissociate itself from those performing a judicial function at the hearing."[42]

One procedural question is raised rather often, by obvious analogy with the law: What about challenges? Challenges for cause should certainly be permitted at any appropriate point, even at the end; the judgment in the New York University-Burgum case would have been better based if a member of the committee had not missed eleven of the eleven hearing sessions and two of the four deliberative sessions; this person did not disqualify himself and

[40] *Statement on Procedural Standards,* 273.

[41] Clark Byse and Louis Joughin, *Tenure in American Higher Education* (1959), 148–49.

[42] *Academic Due Process,* 6.

probably could not be challenged.[43] Challenge for known involvement or prejudice needs no discussion. With respect to peremptory challenges, the difficulty is that they may raise procedural problems regarding replacement, especially in a small institution. Perhaps the best working rule is to permit a wide latitude of challenge, without too much specificity as to criteria of unsuitability, and then to leave the decision, and the consequences of the decision, to the hearing committee itself.[44]

In any event, the members of the hearing committee should be "individuals of known independence and objectivity," and in support of these qualifications it is desirable that they have tenure.[45]

6. The charges. Charges are so generally important for all human controversy and so essential to any judicial proceeding that one can well understand why it has not seemed necessary to provide an elaborate analysis of their function or nature in the several formulations of academic due process. The 1915 AAUP statement refers to "grounds which will be regarded as justifying . . . dismissal . . . [and they] should be formulated with reasonable definiteness . . . stated in writing in specific terms."[46] The silence of 1925 is succeeded by the 1940 requirement that "the accused teacher should have been informed before the hearing in writing of the charges against him."[47] In the AAUP series 1958 returns full circle to 1915 and asks for written, particular charges.[48]

Academic Due Process of the ACLU calls for a good deal more. In addition to the charges themselves, there is to be an accompanying summary of the evidence upon which the charges are based and a first list of witnesses to be called. To make possible the best kind of defense the charges are to be accompanied by a full statement of the regulations pertinent to the issue and a description of

[43] *AAUP Bulletin,* 44:41–42 (1958).

[44] A thoughtful and suggestive consideration of the question of challenges is found in letter No. 3 of a new series of "Advisory Letters from the Washington Office," *id.,* 49:78–79 (1963). [See above, pp. 124–25.]

[45] Byse and Joughin, *Tenure in American Higher Education,* 148.

[46] 1915 *Declaration of Principles,* 111.

[47] 1940 *Statement of Principles,* 109.

[48] *Statement on Procedural Standards,* 272.

the procedures to be followed.[49] These further related elements to the central fact of charges were not brought in by the ACLU to increase resort to something like legal forms. On the contrary, it was felt that this full display of "the case" might lessen the game of attack and defense and help prepare for unimpassioned consideration the main points in dispute.

In the face of a principle so simple and fundamental as that which calls for charges, it is something of a shock to observe the frequent and gross failure of American administrations in higher education to provide this elementary device for achieving justice. In the Rutgers University-Fifth Amendment cases a Board of Review undertook to examine the matter in great detail, even though there were no charges before it, and even though agreement had been reached with the administration that charges would be made after the Board of Review report. But this apparently seemed slow business for an impatient governing board; the professors were given short notice to answer a congressional committee or be dismissed.[50] At Rutgers, dismissal preceded the promised charges, and that would seem to be as anticipatory as it is possible to be.

At Fisk University there were no charges until the faculty member faced his governing board, and then, vague as they were, they did not clearly relate to the objections the administration had been raising.[51] Charges were absent in the Southern California-Deinum case, and the AAUP investigating committee succinctly remarked that "there cannot be a determination that the facts are not in dispute unless there is first a determination of charges that enables the faculty member to determine what facts are alleged."[52] At the University of Nevada all five teachers received blanket charges of a very general nature; only the supreme court of the state rescued the men, by an order for a bill of particulars—and rescued them a second time when it threw out new charges not mentioned in the bill of particulars.[53] In the recent Arkansas State Teachers College-

[49] *Academic Due Process,* 5.

[50] *AAUP Bulletin,* 42:77–78 (1956).

[51] *Id.,* 45:36, 42 (1959).

[52] *Id.,* 44:156 (1958).

[53] *Id.,* 42:553–54 (1956). State *ex rel.* Richardson v. Board of Regents, 70 Nev. 144, 261 P.2d 515 (1953), 70 Nev. 347, 269 P.2d 265 (1954).

Higgins case, repeated requests for charges met no response;[54] and the report of the investigating committee makes clear that only three likely interpretations seem possible in such situations: (1) there are no charges which can be made, (2) charges if made would be irrelevant to the academic context, or (3) the charges if made would be proved false.

Other variations include the Catawba College type of broadside, so ample as to fail in particularity: disloyalty to the administration, incitement of unrest and suspicion, and failure to support the administration and the objectives of the college.[55]

At New York University in the Bradley case, a clear enough charge derived from conviction of contempt of Congress, but as the institutional proceedings went on, the charge became the different matter of identification with the Communist Party.[56] In the University of Michigan-Nickerson and Davis cases, a faculty hearing committee did all its work with witnesses and defendants and documents without making any real effort to extract from the material before it charges "set forth with reasonable particularity." Then, in its report, it made an "Analysis of Charges."[57]

An amorphous but genuine problem arises from the 1958 *Statement on Procedural Standards* recommendation that the faculty member, after receiving from the administration the charges and relevant regulations, "should answer in writing, not less than one week before the date set for the hearing, the statements in the president's letter [which presents the charges]."[58] If this requirement means no more than (1) a duty to acknowledge the receiving of the charges, or (2) acceptance of those charges which are true, or (3) response by a general denial, or (4) response by a demurrer, or (5) a summarizing of the defense evidence to be presented, or (6) a presenting of a first list of witnesses—then no harm should come. But the faculty member must not, under any circumstances, feel constrained to state, in advance of his formal hearing, any part

[54] *Id.*, 49:12 (1963).
[55] *Id.*, 43:218 (1957).
[56] *Id.*, 44:33–35 (1958).
[57] *Id.*, 44:68 (1958).
[58] *Statement on Procedural Standards*, 272.

of his reasoned defense if he feels that by doing so he might prejudice his position at the hearing itself.

In the dangerously undefinable proceedings of the George Washington University-Reichard case, counsel for the teacher asked for charges and standards; he was told he might submit a memorandum. Later the administration asserted that the teacher involved knew full well the nature of the University's concern; but the professor involved said he did not know. As the investigating committee said in its report: "It appears . . . unsatisfactory that a man should be tried for shortcomings (a) which are alleged by the University authorities to be understood by all parties, and (b) which the University authorities are unwilling to state."[59]

In the light of the record, it may correctly be said that the single most prevalent defection from academic due process is in the absence of charges, or charges of such distorted, vague, or shifting quality that no proper defense can be made. The answer, of course, is not far to seek. Not many cases involve failures in professional responsibility or gross misbehavior of the kind which permit specific charges. The usual offense is to arouse the sensitivities and angers of the community and the fears of the administration; and in such a situation a formulation of specific charges would also disclose the standards which administrations apply to such dismissal cases.

7. *Governing standards and procedures.* There is great variation in the fullness and precision of the statements under which different institutions conduct their dismissal proceedings. Some colleges and universities which offer little by way of stated fair rules and genuine academic standards are deficient in this area of academic law simply because no case has arisen to require statement of principles and machinery. However, in other institutions the standards and procedures are weak or nonexistent because of unwillingness to confront the possibility of an unpleasant affair. It is in such institutions that the AAUP discovers a most difficult task; it is not easy to persuade an angry and determined institution to take pause to discover whether it has proper criteria and procedure for the hot business in hand. At these colleges and univer-

[59] *AAUP Bulletin,* 48:243 (1962).

sities lies a strong challenge to the fraternal sense of faculty members; they are perhaps the only group which at a point of crisis can with much hope press for a well-grounded and well-ordered trial of a professor.

An interesting way of handling the rules was established by the Board of Trustees of the Lowell Institute of Technology when in the Snitzer and Fine cases it ruled at the outset that

> . . . all questions relating to the propriety of any interrogation or argument shall be determined by the Chairman or, at his request, by an Assistant Attorney General [who was conducting the case against the teachers], and any such determination shall be final unless the Trustees vote otherwise. . . . Any of the foregoing rules may be modified, or waived during the session, by vote of the Trustees.[60]

8. The evidence. The unusual fact that an academic controversy has developed into an adversary hearing requires at least these general warnings:

First, even if the institution is very large, the quarrel is a kind of family affair; and most of those participating will have to live with each other in the near and distant future. For this reason one may at times discover a tendency to substitute for academic due process a way of handling matters which might be called "domestic due process"—a kinder or a harsher system, but of doubtful appropriateness.

Second, the infrequency of cases at most institutions means that when a dismissal question arises there will come into play seldom-used machinery which may creak noticeably. The innumerable safeguards which the law daily applies to the handling of evidence in courts are hardly matched by academic due process which is "occasional" in application and infinitely less comprehensive in detail. Nevertheless, "the law protects," and since a dismissal proceeding is likely to call for all the protection available, some borrowing from the law's way of doing things is both likely and desirable.

Parenthetically, one may note that there is a transcendent prin-

[60] *Id.*, 45:561 (1959).

ciple which can solve many procedural problems, even for the inexperienced. The principle is that of fairness. Under that aegis, difficult questions of procedural management may disappear or at least assume determinable form.

(a) *Presence.* All the policy statements imply, and several state, that the person involved shall be at the hearing during the presentation of evidence. (It appears to be common practice for the parties to withdraw when the hearing committee goes into executive session for purposes of deliberation and judgment.) There have not been many cases raising the issue of the right to be present at one's own trial, but there is at least one extraordinary example. In the 1958 South Dakota State College-Worzella case the governing board considered the report of an administrator who, in resigning, attacked a number of persons, including Professor Worzella; the teacher was not asked to comment on the report, and did not know that it would be considered as a basis for a determination regarding his dismissal. He was not present and was not heard, nor was the president of the institution; there was, of course, no opportunity to cross-examine or to submit testimony.[61]

(b) *Confrontation.* "The principle embodied in the legal concept of confrontation should govern academic due process. The teacher should be informed of all the charges and all the evidence against him; he should have full opportunity to deny, to refute, and to rebut."[62] The AAUP statements display a puzzling oscillation: that of 1915 does not mention confrontation, although the spirit of the principle is present; 1925 holds that the teacher has the right to "face his accusers"; 1940 says nothing on this point; and 1958 reads: "The faculty member should have the opportunity to be confronted by all witnesses adverse to him."[63] The issue arises at times in specific instances. The Catawba College cases disclose the teachers appearing for their hearing before the board and confronting for the first time a report by a self-constituted alumni committee which was hostile to them; the faculty members were in a seriously handicapped position because they had no way of challeng-

[61] *Id.*, 47:253 (1961).

[62] *Academic Due Process*, 4.

[63] *Statement on Procedural Standards*, 273.

ing their accusers.[64] In the Lowell Technological Institute cases, one part of the over-all denial of due process was the ruling made at the outset that neither the president nor any member of the faculty would be available for questioning.[65]

(c) *Witnesses for the defense.* The 1915, 1925, and 1940 AAUP statements do not specifically state the right of the faculty member generally to present witnesses in support of his position; but they do state his right to do so in a designated way on the particular issue of competence—and there is no indication that this right in a limited area is not part of a harmonious whole. The statements are deficient in letter but not in spirit. The ACLU 1954 *Academic Due Process* says: "Both the teacher and the administration should have the right to present and examine witnesses and to cross-examine witnesses. The administration should make available to the teacher such authority as it may possess to require the presence of witnesses." The 1958 *Statement on Procedural Standards* says nothing about the larger problem of presenting witnesses, but proceeds to the next step—subpoena power—which permits our assuming existence of the main right.[66]

The Reed College-Moore case reveals a member of the faculty being examined in a dismissal proceeding, who was denied the aid of the college when he sought to have appear as witnesses the president and a former college official in order that he might question them about their knowledge of him at the time he was appointed, and later. The AAUP investigating committee regarded this denial as vital to the determination of facts and a violation of academic due process, but also came to the conclusion that the evidence which would have been obtained would have been merely cumulative and that the denial did not therefore fatally affect the proceedings.[67] This view can be challenged. It is one thing to hold that a particular element of evidence which has been submitted is in fact cumulative; but there is an element of unauthorized prophecy in a conclusion that what would have been heard would have been of such and such a character or weight.

[64] *AAUP Bulletin*, 43:220 (1957).

[65] *Id.*, 45:563 (1959).

[66] *Academic Due Process*, 6; *Statement on Procedural Standards*, 273.

[67] *AAUP Bulletin*, 44:123–24 (1958).

(d) *Expert witnesses.* In 1915 the writers of the *Declaration of Principles* must have assumed that charges of incompetence would be the issue from time to time. They wrote:

> . . . if the charge is one of professional incompetency, a formal report upon his work should be first made in writing by the teachers of his own department and of cognate departments in the university, and, if the teacher concerned so desires, by a committee of his fellow-specialists from other institutions, appointed by some competent authority.[68]

As a matter of fact, the issue of competence has seldom been in dispute in reported cases, although it may be suspected to have existed in a number of situations which were resolved one way or another without public notice. In the very recent Grove City College-Gara case, the administration alleged incompetence; but since nothing remotely resembling a trial of the issue ever took place, the AAUP investigating committee felt obliged to report on this matter in a statement supplementary to their main report on the denial of academic due process.[69]

(e) *Cross-examination.* The earliest AAUP statement, in 1915, refers to a "fair trial"; this may carry with it the idea of cross-examination. The 1925 *Conference Statement* states that the teacher "should always have the opportunity to face his accusers." 1940 is weaker and requires that cross-examination be read into the phrase "heard in his own defense," if it is to be found at all. 1958 reads: "The faculty member or his counsel and the representative designated by the president should have the right, within reasonable limits, to question all witnesses who testify orally."[70] *Academic Due Process* plainly sets forth, for both parties, the right to "present," to "examine," and to "cross-examine."

The cases which raise a question of the right to cross-examine are not numerous, but the importance of the issue may be seen in those at North Dakota Agricultural College where cross-examination revealed the nature of much unsatisfactory evidence; evidence

[68] 1915 *Declaration of Principles,* 111.

[69] *AAUP Bulletin,* 49:21–23 (1963).

[70] *Statement on Procedural Standards,* 273.

so poor in quality that the AAUP investigating committee characterized it as "in large measure hearsay, rumor, opinion, innuendo, and irrelevancies, most of which would not have been admitted over objection in a properly conducted court of law."[71]

It would be interesting to determine, if any standards existed for an opinion, whether the placing of witnesses under oath could be regarded as a kind of protection, akin to the right of cross-examination. The case record on this point is thin, but one can probably assume that sworn testimony will occur more frequently where public boards are concerned.[72]

(f) *The hearing committee acting on its own authority.* The 1958 *Statement on Procedural Standards* explicitly states what may have been understood for a long time but is here first set down—the power of the committee to control the proceedings in the interest of justice: "The committee should determine the order of proof, should normally conduct the questioning of witnesses, and, if necessary, should secure the presentation of evidence important to the case."[73] This injunction is new to the scene, but has great potentiality for strengthening the administration of justice in academic proceedings. A courageous, intelligent hearing committee could, in many situations, seek out and hear useful evidence which has not been offered by the parties. In short, here lies the opportunity for the faculty authority to offer constructive leadership. For instance, there is always the question whether a fault has been viewed in the light of all the teacher has been and done, for good or bad. The investigating committee of the AAUP in the Reed College-Moore case observed:

> At a minimum, academic due process seems to us to require that a faculty member with tenure is entitled to consideration of factors which might conceivably offset his possible misconduct of non-cooperation. These factors should include (1) his record of performance in service in the College, and (2) his motives or reasons for the act of non-cooperation.[74]

[71] *AAUP Bulletin,* 42:146–47 (1956).

[72] *Id.,* 42:552 (1956).

[73] *Statement on Procedural Standards,* 273.

[74] *AAUP Bulletin,* 44:127 (1958).

The failure of a committee to control its hearing is unhappily a matter of record in two very recent cases. In the Arkansas State College-Higgins case, an administrator answered for a committee of all the full professors, stating that the function of the group was "to endorse or not to endorse the decision of the Board of Trustees." In the George Washington University-Reichard case, the informal hearing committee appears to have done nothing to correct the failure of "university authorities . . . to follow the natural and reasonable course of attempting to find supporting evidence for their position, and . . . [to rely] instead merely upon speculation about motives."[75]

(g) *Evidence exempt from cross-examination.* The 1958 *Statement on Procedural Standards* at one point states that cross-examination is a right "within reasonable limits"; and, even more fundamentally, confrontation may be denied the faculty member by the committee. "Where unusual and urgent reasons move the hearing committee to withhold this right, or where the witness cannot appear, the identity of the witness, as well as his statements, should nevertheless be disclosed to the faculty member."[76] In sharp contrast the ACLU *Academic Due Process* states that "The principle of confrontation should apply throughout the hearing."[77] In the opinion of the present writer, it is a serious error to permit the exceptions to the principle of confrontation which are set forth in the *Statement on Procedural Standards*. If the history of cases involving academic due process recounted only the occasional lapses of great institutions, and lapses of small degree, the issue might be hypothetical. But this is simply not the historical fact. Denials of academic due process constitute a record of unjust treatment of the worst sort by institutions who know or care nothing about the principles involved, or, at best, are the story of serious lapses from grace of institutions which ordinarily behave well. The analogy is irresistible; one should consider the restrictions placed upon confrontation by the security agencies of the national defense

[75] *Id.*, 48:246 (1962).
[76] *Statement on Procedural Standards*, 273.
[77] *Academic Due Process*, 6.

apparatus.[78] The only conceivable ground which can safely be yielded here would be with respect to depositions of distant witnesses under oath, introduced under strict and exact rules as to weight, openness to challenge, and every other safeguard needed to protect the teacher.

9. Burden of proof. Academic Due Process states that "it is a fundamental principle of fairness that charges against a person are to be made the basis of action only when proven, and that the burden of proof rests upon those who bring them."[79] There cannot be much question about the operation of this principle in practice under the several AAUP statements, but for some reason, not apparent, it has never been written into this series of documents. It is only in the 1956 *Academic Freedom and Tenure in the Quest for National Security,* the report of a special committee, that one can read: "The burden of proof should rest upon the administrative officer bringing the charge, and should not be placed upon the faculty member. . . ."[80] The authors of *Tenure in American Higher Education* state that the appropriate ". . . administrative official should have the burden of proving the charges by a preponderance of the evidence."[81]

The cases which present a question of burden of proof are numerous and serious. At the University of Nevada, in the Richardson case, the administration ordered the faculty member to "show cause" why he should be continued in his post.[82] At New York University, in the Burgum case, the teacher was suspended and then allowed to appeal to a board of review the adverse action taken against him;[83] this unjust procedure has fortunately been completely eliminated in a recent revision of the New York University regulations. The Board of Trustees of Lowell Technologi-

[78] Joughin, "Scrutiny of Professors: Impact and Modification of Section 6-i (old 7-e) of the Industrial Security Manual," *AAUP Bulletin,* 44:199 (1958).

[79] *Academic Due Process,* 4.

[80] *AAUP Bulletin,* 42:60 (1956).

[81] Byse and Joughin, *Tenure in American Higher Education,* 149.

[82] *AAUP Bulletin,* 42:554 (1956).

[83] *Id.,* 44:50 (1958).

cal Institute informed the teachers that the hearing to be given them was for "the purpose of reviewing the provisional appointment . . . [and whether they] should be dismissed."[84] The President of the Board of Regents of the Texas State Teachers Colleges in a recent so-called hearing said to the counsel for a teacher: "Our Board is concerned with what you as a representative might say and what [the teacher's] . . . reasons are for this Board to employ him."[85]

One difficult problem with respect to burden of proof, which has not been really solved, is that of the teacher in probationary status —that is, not yet having achieved tenure—who claims that his notice of non-renewal of appointment involves an academic freedom issue. The AAUP offers as policy a statement that "during the probationary period a teacher should have the academic freedom that all other members of the faculty have."[86] The principle, of course, is obvious and good, but further guidance may be needed. In fact, it is only fair to the teacher in probationary status that he be told the burden of proof is upon him in most instances. The ACLU statement offers the following approach:

> American educational practice permits great fluidity in the testing of teachers as to their permanent usefulness in a particular institution. This experimental phase of a teacher's career is wisely characterized by a minimum of formal judgment; teachers come and go without recorded praise or blame. Furthermore, non-tenure appointments often fall within the marginal area of an institution's educational and financial program; the dropping of a teacher may have no bearing whatsoever upon his professional capacity. But, although non-retention does not necessarily raise an academic freedom issue, such an issue may be present in non-retention. For example, improper consideration may have been given to non-academic matters, such as a teacher's race, or his religious or political beliefs and associations. Such improper consideration is a violation of academic freedom and the non-tenure teacher is

[84] *Id.*, 45:561 (1959).

[85] *Id.*, 49:46 (1963). Note also *supra* p. 291, where the function of a faculty hearing committee was described as an endorsement or non-endorsement of the governing board decision.

[86] 1940 *Statement of Principles*, 109.

> entitled to all the protections of academic due process. . . .
>
> Action in non-tenure academic freedom cases should take this general form:
>
> 1. If the non-tenure teacher believes that improper considerations have unmistakably affected the decision not to retain him, he should, with appropriate advice, determine whether he can assemble adequate proof in support of his contention.
> 2. The teacher should decide whether he is willing to hazard the possible disclosure of professional weaknesses he may have displayed at an early point in his career.
> 3. If his decisions under "1" and "2" are positive, he should request an opportunity for informal conciliation as set forth . . . above.
> 4. If such informal conciliation is denied, or unsuccessful, he should then request a formal hearing, and submit a written waiver of the traditional right of non-tenure teachers to non-disclosure of the grounds upon which they have been released.
> 5. The administration should then grant to the teacher the entire procedure for adjudication [available to tenure teachers.][87]

The advantage of this approach is that, in addition to being offered procedural guidance, the teacher is himself given the responsibility of making his case and abiding by the results. This would seem to be the only kind of a rule which, in the last analysis, can offer full opportunity for adjudication.

10. Findings and conclusions. For unexplored reasons, the 1915, 1925, and 1940 AAUP statements say nothing about the findings and conclusions which the hearing committee should offer. The 1954 ACLU statement says that "the full text of the findings and conclusions of the hearing committee should be made available in identical form and at the same time to the administration and the teacher."[88] A much stronger rule is that of the 1958 *Statement on Procedural Standards* which asks that the hearing committee "make explicit findings with respect to each of the grounds of removal presented, and a reasoned opinion may be desirable."[89]

[87] *Academic Due Process,* 7–8.
[88] *Id.,* 6.
[89] *Statement on Procedural Standards,* 274.

Here, it seems the American Association of University Professors is moving toward a norm much like that established by the practice of the courts to render a decision on the facts and a statement on the law when present and future justice will be served thereby. The need for the norm is understandable when one considers the cases.

In one of the University of Michigan cases, where communism was the issue, the AAUP investigating committee noted that "no finding of Communist Party membership, innocent or otherwise, or of illegal or immoral activities, was supported by substantial evidence in the record."[90] In the South Dakota State College-Worzella case, the 1958 judgment of the governing board included a statement that the teacher had been found to be "the main controversial issue" in events of 1948 to 1951, and "prior thereto"; these findings were on issues of great complexity, long past, in which the teacher would by some students of the matter be thought to have been vindicated, and in any event the issues had long since been disposed of officially as closed.[91] The governing board of Dickinson College, with twelve items of complaint before it, did not indicate which of these it regarded as proved.[92] The faculty committee at New York University in the Burgum case submitted several memoranda to the trustees; on one main charge, a committee member said the teacher had lied, a second member said that the teacher's connection with the Communist Party was proved, and the third member said the teacher was guilty of academic turpitude.[93] Professor Novikoff, in his vicissitudes at the University of Vermont, confronted three charges; in the decision by the Board of Trustees the first charge was dismissed, the second charge was disregarded, and nothing was said about the third charge.[94] In the North Dakota Agricultural College cases, the Advisory Committee sent no written report to the governing board, and consequently a decision was made only upon a decision.[95] And one of the teachers involved in the Lowell Technological cases has complained that the adverse

[90] *AAUP Bulletin,* 44:82 (1958).
[91] *Id.,* 47:250 (1961).
[92] *Id.,* 44:142 (1958).
[93] *Id.,* 44:47 (1958).
[94] *Id.,* 44:12 (1958).
[95] *Id.,* 42:147 (1956),

verdict of the governing board, embodying no judgment on the evidence and a dismissal without stated reason, has been harmful to him in his efforts to continue in the profession.[96]

The speed with which a hearing committee should act should certainly be as great as possible, and it should render judgment as quickly as possible.[97] But surely neither expedition nor delay are in themselves issues of justice; the answer must always be that the best speed is that which serves justice best in each case.

11. The record. Until 1940 the AAUP statements said nothing about the record; then the injunction is given that a "full stenographic record of the hearing [should be made available] to the parties concerned."[98] The 1958 statement, which, of course, carries with it all of the 1940 statement, adds that "all of the evidence should be duly recorded" and the president and the faculty member should be "given a copy of the record of the hearing."[99] The ACLU *Academic Due Process* notes: "A full record should be taken at the hearing; it should be made available in identical form and at the same time to the hearing group, the administration, and the teacher. The cost should be met by the institution."[100] Here the requirement of simultaneous presentation would seem to rule out the 1958 AAUP provision for a judgment in advance of the completion of the record if such speed is fair.

12. Two special questions: time to prepare, and waiver of rights. For all practical purposes none of the policy statements offer any detailed rules or guidance with respect to the time that should be allowed for preparation, for study of the record, and for other chronological questions which might arise; this would seem to be a wise silence in the light of the great variety of academic situations which occur in very different kinds of institutions. But

[96] *Id.*, 45:553, 564 (1959).

[97] *Academic Due Process*, 6, reads: "The hearing committee should promptly and forth-rightly adjudicate the issues." *Statement on Procedural Standards*, 274, reads: "The committee may proceed to decision promptly, without having a record of the hearing transcribed, if its decision would be aided thereby."

[98] 1940 *Statement of Principles*, 109.

[99] *Statement on Procedural Standards*, 273–74.

[100] *Academic Due Process*, 6.

some notorious cases exhibit the need at least for the rule of fairness. Not the worst but perhaps the most conspicuous cases were those at the University of Michigan where the findings and conclusions of a kind of hearing committee were not placed before the faculty members involved until immediately before the next and conclusive hearing.[101]

Waiver is said to present difficult problems even for a fully developed legal system. The few instances which have occurred in academic controversy have generally led to the view that a teacher cannot waive rights which have been published as accruing to the whole profession. An individual may not waive a right for himself when by so doing he affects the rights of other members of the profession. In the Long Island University-Post College-Sittler case, where there was prior agreement to resign, the judgment of the AAUP was that "unless the administration removes the compulsion which is a necessary consequence of an agreement to resign upon request, failure to seek a hearing is not the result of an informed and uncoerced decision to waive the protections of academic due process."[102]

13. Appellate procedure. It should be understood at the outset that in almost every academic institution the final authority lies in the hands of the governing board, either under a charter issued by the state to a private college or university, or by statutory or constitutional authorization and delegation of power to a public institution. No statistical count exists to indicate the frequency of appeal by a dissatisfied teacher or a dissatisfied administration; but it is known that one or the other party, when ruled against by the hearing committee, rather frequently concludes the matter without appeal.

The 1915, 1925, and 1940 statements by the AAUP indicate with increasing clarity the obvious fact that the ultimate authority in a college or university can be involved on appeal, and, perhaps, by original jurisdiction. *Academic Due Process* indicates that the findings of the faculty hearing committee should be final on matters of professional competence and integrity.[103]

[101] *AAUP Bulletin,* 44:46 (1958).
[102] *Id.,* 48:9 (1962).
[103] *Academic Due Process,* 7.

The 1958 *Statement on Procedural Standards* at this point makes a major contribution to the principles which govern academic due process. It states that:

> If the governing body chooses to review the case, its review should be based on the record of the previous hearing, accompanied by opportunity for argument, oral or written or both, by the principals at the hearing or their representatives. The decision of the hearing committee should either be sustained or the proceeding be returned to the committee with objections specified. In such a case the committee should reconsider, taking account of the stated objections and receiving new evidence if necessary. It should frame its decision and communicate it in the same manner as before. Only after study of the committee's reconsideration should the governing body make a final decision overruling the committee.[104]

If this rule were to be applied in full force and faith to the adjudication of an academic controversy such as dismissal action, one might almost be warranted in regarding academic due process as in effect genuinely established. One would hope seldom to meet a hearing committee judgment which was a poor or careless job, since the members of the group would know that, in addition to possible rejection, it might be referred back with the detailed judgment of a responsible governing board; conversely, it is difficult to conceive of a governing board indulging in peremptory or arbitrary decision when it knew that its adverse view would be subjected to the detailed study and comment of an articulate faculty committee. Two powerful voices responsible to each other's judgment for both a first and second time would offer a strong likelihood of justice in most academic cases.

The cases which involve appellate problems are not numerous if one looks only to the procedure involved, although there are numerous instances of arbitrary over-riding of faculty judgment. At the University of Michigan a superior committee gave a hearing to

[104] *Statement on Procedural Standards,* 274. At the beginning of this study it was noted that the 1925, 1940, and 1958 statements were jointly promulgated by the AAUP and the Association of American Colleges. Here, near the end of the systematic analysis, it is well to remember that in these three instances there were partners in the enterprise.

a teacher involved, but "it based its hearing and its conclusions very largely upon the record of the hearing held by [an inferior committee] . . . which record had not been made available to the two teachers."[105] And, as noted above,[106] the teacher did not have adequate time to study the record of the first hearing. Even less happy is the recent University of Illinois-Koch case where the governing board unanimously overruled the recommendation regarding penalty offered by unanimous vote of the faculty hearing committee.[107]

III. Overall denial of academic due process

The reports which describe a general denial of academic due process to some unfortunate teacher are dramatic and even lurid, but it must be confessed that they may contribute less to the understanding of academic due process than to the annals of social pathology. In most cases the broad denial of procedural rights to a faculty member usually turns out to be a matter of ignorance or fear, or some amalgam of these two saddening aspects of institutional compulsiveness.

"Although the dismissal . . . was for stated cause, neither evidence nor argument was presented in a hearing before any faculty committee, or any Board committee, or the Board as a whole within the framework of any recognizable form of due process, academic or general."[108] The opinion of the investigating committee which examined the Grove City College situation for the American Association of University Professors led to the further conclusion that "the absence of due process in this case raises in the minds of the Investigating Committee grave doubts regarding the academic security of any persons who may hold appointment at Grove City College under existing administrative practice."[109]

[105] *AAUP Bulletin,* 44:61 (1958).
[106] *Supra,* p. 298.
[107] *AAUP Bulletin,* 49:29–31 (1963).
[108] *Id.,* 49:16 (1963).
[109] *Ibid.*

There have, of course, been other instances of blank denial.[110] The usual picture is a large composition which may include a denial of charges or the exploration of charges so general as to be irrefutable by ordinary means, absence of counsel, failure to make a record, no hearing before a faculty committee, no hearing before anyone, or plain dismissal as of the moment of notification.

Sometimes the denial of due process is mitigated by elements of confusion; in the University of Vermont-Novikoff case nobody was familiar with and called upon procedural safeguards which actually existed in the Articles of Organization of the University.[111] Or, as in the George Washington University-Reichard case, the denial seems to have come about from a mixture of dubious legalism, ill-defined function of the examining group, and short-sighted failure to seek out information which was needed and could be had.[112]

Since institutions are no more exempt from fear than individual men, it is not surprising to find colleges and universities attempting to dispose of irritants by summary action, usually involving denial of established principles of academic due process. Thus, Benedict College first offered "normal academic procedures" to a faculty member with tenure, and then denied him a hearing.[113] At Alabama Polytechnic Institute (now Auburn University), long after the president's office had assumed a minor matter to have died down, the governing board met in executive session and denied reappointment to a teacher without even a semblance of a hearing.[114] In the same commonwealth, the president of the Alabama State College wrote to a professor, saying, "Just a few minutes ago I had the telephone message through the State Superintendent of Education that the State Board of Education has directed this afternoon that your services be discontinued as of this afternoon."[115] And, most recently, the Board of Regents of the

[110] Eastern Washington College, *AAUP Bulletin,* 43:235 (1957); Fisk University, *id.,* 45:36–37 (1959); Alcorn Agricultural and Mechanical College, *id.,* 48:251 (1962).

[111] *Id.,* 44:13 (1959).

[112] *Id.,* 48:240 (1962).

[113] *Id.,* 46:101 (1960).

[114] *Id.,* 44:158 *et seq.* (1958).

[115] *Id.,* 47:306 (1961).

Texas State Teachers Colleges gave a faculty member notice of a hearing only at 2:00 P.M. of the preceding day, and also indicated that he would have his hearing only if he signed a waiver of a bill of particulars; the "hearing" took place and the teacher found himself conclusively dismissed.[116]

The annals of the Visigoths of American education soon pall, and, in any event, are not very instructive for any positive purpose. Consequently, this brief review of instances of virtually total denial of academic due process may conclude with one last example: a case which presents a few elements of academic due process but introduces other procedural distortions of a most extraordinary nature. The hearing took place before the Board of Trustees of the Lowell Technological Institute, an institution situated in Massachusetts about thirty miles distant from Harvard University and the Massachusetts Institute of Technology.

In the Lowell Technological Institute-Snitzer and Fine cases, there were no charges; unsworn evidence was introduced into a record where other evidence was under oath; there were no findings or judgments on the evidence. Counsel for the teachers was present; and carefully introduced at the beginning, and recapitulated at the end, the elements of academic due process. But the Board had its mind on another way of doing things. The Assistant Attorney General of the state of Massachusetts in charge of criminal investigations was asked by the Board to conduct the hearing; he acted as prosecutor and also ruled as judge on the admissibility of objections. To complete the picture, the Assistant Attorney General then apparently went into executive session with the Board as a person in the jury room. The American Association of University Professors was denied the right to have an observer present; a lieutenant of the Massachusetts state police was in attendance throughout the hearing. And yet the Assistant Attorney General stipulated that no issue of criminal behavior had been raised; nor was any ever raised. In short, the whole record of the event over which the Board of Trustees presided probably constitutes the further limit to which any governing body has gone in outright disregard of the

[116] *Id.*, 49:46 (1963).

established principles and practices by which determinations of justice are made on the academic scene.[117]

IV. The future of academic due process

The American college or university, like any living organism, is constantly changing, as current values and passions tangle with old traditions and inertias. And, in any particular institution, academic due process is likely to be particularly shaped by the interplay of the campus pattern for handling controversial matters and public opinion regarding the "sensitive question" of the moment. So fluid a scene, so delicate and mobile a balance, obviously means that academic due process will experience a good deal of change as life moves on. The prospects for such change merit brief notice.

First, there will be change in academic due process resulting from ordinary self-scrutiny. Procedures which have proved useful will receive a blessing as intelligent custom and become stronger; failures and archaisms will drop out. There will be fillings-in to take care of the obvious gaps revealed by logic or pain.

It may be possible to rely less upon analogy and more upon critical comparison with other kinds of systems for being fair. Useful exploration may suggest differences in the problems arising in public and private institutions. Academic due process for these two types of college or university may, of course, have to wait upon the discovery of the actual distinctions which exist between private and public college or university. In the private institution the supposed base is in the contract. But is an institution really private which receives tax exemption for itself, establishes tax deduction for its donors, and has ninety per cent of its operations in some of its chief departments paid for by government funds?

As for the unquestionably public institution, nonlawyers are unable to escape hearing of a few uncertainties. They know about the large body of administrative law which concerns itself with the delegated authority and responsibility of public agencies, constitutional or statutory in origin, and seek to discover how much of that law is relevant to an agency which is an institution of higher education. There is a suspicion abroad that the silences on this

[117] *Id.*, 45:550–67 (1959).

point are vast, and that the voices heard are sometimes not in harmony.[118]

Second, academic due process will develop as it confronts the threats always made against anything which is in any way connected with freedom. Chafee's great first chapter of *Free Speech in the United States* remains one of the wisest, and one of the saddest, commentaries ever written on human nature. He tells us that freedom rises and falls almost in exact relationship to our fears and insecurity. And there is no reason to believe that the particular kind of freedom which exists in the academy has any magic which will exempt it from the generic fate.

Third, academic due process will need to keep its integrity when it observes the seductive success of other kinds of systems which have proved effective in apparently like affairs. For instance, the civil service system offers some very attractive safeguards. But civil service is mainly intended to protect large groups of persons who are willing to accept a large measure of routinization in the personnel decisions which affect their lives. They are willing to move forward at a generally even pace, treated with generally even fairness, and—in time of trouble—to be judged by broadly applicable standards and procedures. There is no implication in this observation that civil service is a poorer kind of thing than academic due process. It is simply different, and not particularly suited to the judgments which may attend the adventurous journey of a professor who begins as a servant in the hall of Poison Bluff College and concludes his career ruling over a ducal seigniory at a major university.

Fourth, it seems likely that the future of academic due process will in the main be dependent upon its close identification, as a necessary instrumentality, with the fundamental principle of intellectual freedom. It is intellectual freedom, in the college or university called academic freedom, which is the object of value. It is the principle that must be protected at all costs. This will sometimes

[118] State *ex rel.* Richardson v. Board of Regents, 70 Nev. 144, 261 P.2d 515 (1953), 70 Nev. 347, 269 P.2d 265 (1954). Posin v. State Board of Higher Education, 86 N.W. 2d 31 (N.D. 1957). Worzella v. Board of Regents, 77 S.D. 447, 93 N.W. 2d 411 (1958).

require especially sensitive, peculiarly complicated, procedures for handling the problems of the men who work under the principle of freedom. Obviously, tried and good ideas should not be abandoned without thorough scrutiny and the widest possible experience; it is not likely that the idea of confrontation will depart from academic due process. On the other hand, the instrument must be flexible and subject to needed modification. In every instance, the process which best assists in the wise and just handling of people using free minds will be the best academic due process.

Appendix G

IN DEFENSE OF ACADEMIC TENURE[1]

By Fritz Machlup

Let me begin with a quotation:

> The exact meaning and intent of this so-called tenure policy eludes us. Its vaporous objectives, purposes, and procedures are lost in a fog of nebulous verbiage.

Thus spoke the Supreme Court of South Dakota in 1958 in a case in which a professor contested his dismissal from the State College.[2] One might think that judges of a State court who do not have permanent tenure would surely know about federal judges, who do have life tenure under the U.S. Constitution, and would know about the objectives and purposes of this protective provision. If, nevertheless, some learned judges have given no thought to the principles of judicial and academic tenure, we must not condescendingly smile nor angrily frown. For, alas, we can find a similar lack of understanding among academic people, including some (exceptional, I hope) presidents of colleges or universities. Not long ago, a very able university president publicly predicted "an end to the tenure principle" and, as a result of its abolition, "better teaching and better learning."[3] If some presidents express opposition to the tenure principle, let us welcome their arguments as a challenge to reexamine our position. By no means must we be

[1] Presidential address given at the Fiftieth Annual Meeting of the American Association of University Professors in St. Louis, April 10, 1964. First printed in *AAUP Bulletin,* 50:112–24 (Summer, 1964).

Fritz Machlup is Walker Professor of Economics and International Finance at Princeton University.

[2] Worzella v. Board of Regents, Sup. Ct. of South Dakota, 77 S.D. 447, 93 N.W. 2d 411 (1958).

[3] Francis H. Horn, "Forces Shaping the College of Arts and Sciences." Address at a meeting of the Division of Arts and Sciences, Association of State Universities and Land-Grant Colleges, November 12, 1963.

unduly critical of administrators who fail to appreciate the purposes of tenure rules, for we must admit that many professors are even less well informed on the subject. In many chapter meetings at various places, I have found that large numbers of our members neither know the rules of academic tenure nor understand the objective they are designed to serve. A good many hardly know anything at all about the 1940 *Statement of Principles,* formulated jointly by the Association of American Colleges and the American Association of University Professors.[4]

I am reminded of the experiments in which men in the street were polled about the desirability of particular provisions of the U.S. Bill of Rights. An overwhelming majority of those polled rejected these provisions of our Constitution; some mistook them for Communist propaganda, endangering the survival of our republic, other merely found them "going too far." Likewise, when the 1940 rules, limiting the length of the probationary period for academic teachers, are recited, professors, hearing them for the first time or again after having forgotten them, find them unduly strict, "going too far."

The critics of strict tenure rules rely chiefly on three arguments: first, that the rules have disadvantages for many institutions of

[4] There was first the 1915 *Declaration of Principles,* formulated by a committee of the AAUP. This was superseded by the 1925 *Conference Statement,* approved by both the AAC and the AAUP. Subsequently, after prolonged discussions over a period of six years begun in 1934, the two organizations agreed on the 1940 *Statement of Principles,* which is still "on the books" and has been endorsed by 24 [42 in 1967] professional and learned societies. The principles enunciated in the 1940 *Statement* have the status of "norms," not merely guidelines—although, of course, they are not norms that could be enforced against those who do not observe them, but merely norms by which the profession can judge academic practices which have become the subject of complaints. The important distinction between norm and guide was made in the *Statement on Procedural Standards in Faculty Dismissal Proceedings,* approved in 1958 by the AAC and the AAUP. The Preamble states that the standards recommended for dismissal proceedings "are not intended to establish a *norm in the same manner as the 1940 Statement of Principles on Academic Freedom and Tenure,* but are presented rather as a *guide* to be used according to the nature and traditions of particular institutions . . ." (italics are mine). This shows that the tenure principles were recognized by presidents as well as professors as applicable to all institutions of higher education without special reservations regarding differences in the "nature and traditions of particular institutions."

higher education; second, that they have disadvantages for many young academic teachers and scholars; and third, that they have disadvantages even for the academic profession as a whole.

I shall argue that all these contentions are correct—but that strict tenure rules are desirable nonetheless. The point is that the tenure rules are not designed to be advantageous to most institutions, to most individual scholars, or to the entire profession. Their purpose is altogether different.

For the benefit of those who have forgotten them, I shall first recall just what the "strict" tenure rules provide. Then I shall present the reasons why I admit their having the harmful effects to which their opponents point. Only in the end shall I attempt to show why we need them in spite of all.

The "strict" tenure rules

Instead of quoting the provisions on "Academic Tenure" from the 1940 *Statement of Principles,* I shall use my own language, designed to point up why they are widely regarded as excessively "strict." Perhaps I interpret them more strictly than do some of the AAUP experts on "tenure and notice."

1. Permanent tenure can be acquired automatically, without any particular act by the institution, simply by length of service of the teacher.

2. Permanent tenure is not confined to holders of any particular academic rank or title; nor is it confined to those who have served for a stated period in any particular rank; an instructor, assistant professor, lecturer, etc., holding a full-time appointment, acquires permanent tenure after the same probationary period as an associate professor or professor.

3. The probationary period should in general not exceed seven years, beginning with the first appointment to rank of full-time instructor, including within this period full-time service in all institutions of higher education. Hence, in the absence of a written agreement to the contrary, a teacher who has held full-time positions in other institutions acquires permanent tenure in a new academic position at once if he has served elsewhere seven years, or after one year if he has served elsewhere six years, etc.

4. The probationary period of seven years, including all pre-

vious service in institutions of higher education, can be extended only under the following conditions: If the teacher, after probationary service of more than three years in one or more places, is called to another institution, it may be agreed in writing that his new appointment is for a new probationary period of not more than four years. Since a full year's notice is required, the teacher in effect is assured of permanent tenure in his new position if no notice of nonrenewal of his appointment is received by him before the end of his third year of service.

A number of colleges and universities have adopted regulations which are at variance with these provisions. For example, contrary to the first two rules, the regulations at many institutions provide that continuous tenure is not acquired automatically but conferred only through promotion to the rank of full professor or, in stated circumstances, through promotion to the rank of associate professor.

This need not imply, and indeed should not imply, a deviation from the 1940 principles; for, if the promotions to tenure positions occur within a time interval not exceeding the maximum probationary period, all is well and the practice conforms to the principle. An institution with a definite "up-or-out" practice, under which after a stated number of years of service a decision of either promotion or separation must be made, satisfies both principles at the same time: tenure is conferred only by special action and the probationary period is strictly limited. Where, however, tenure depends on special action but the decision is postponed, until finally reappointment is denied to a teacher with a record of eight, nine, or ten years of service, the failure to retain him violates the 1940 principles.

The third and fourth of the agreed rules are disregarded by institutions which refuse to recognize a faculty member's previous service at other colleges or universities and do not, through a written agreement with the appointee, make sure that a new probationary period of four years is commenced with his new appointment. Again, the mere deviation of such regulations from the 1940 principles does not constitute a conflict. A conflict arises only when an appointment is not continued after the appointee should have acquired continuous tenure under the rule counting previous academic service elsewhere.

Four kinds of tenure

The possibility that the tenure rules under the 1940 principles and the tenure regulations in particular institutions may differ, and that the actual tenure practices of the same institutions may be at variance with both, makes us realize how confusing things are and how ambiguous may be a statement to the effect that a professor "has" tenure. How can it be possible that he has tenure under one set of rules, has no tenure under a conflicting set of regulations, and may *de facto* be safe in his position or actually be separated from it under policies that conform with neither rules nor regulations? To clear this up, we must engage in a bit of semantics, an attempt at a definition, and an exercise in taxonomy.

The phrase "life tenure" obviously refers to an office-holder's right to keep his office until he dies. Such rights exist, with some reservations, for federal judges in this country and for the dons in some of the English colleges. No self-explanatory adjective, however, is available to abbreviate the phrase "tenure until retirement or removal for adequate cause," which is the meaning of academic tenure in the United States. The adjectives actually used are "permanent," "continuous," or "indefinite." The first two of these can at least be made intelligible by interpreting "permanence" and "continuity" not as never-ending but as ending at a stipulated time or occasion. The word "indefinite" in this context sounds too indefinite to me, as if it were intended to avoid firm commitments and yet to give the impression of genuine promises.[5] In some institutions the phrase "indefinite tenure" is meant to denote a middle position between a definite-term appointment and a permanent-tenure appointment. Many administrators, however, use indefinite, continuous, and permanent as synonyms. This is also the intended meaning of "indefinite tenure" in the bylaws of numerous institutions.

Let us then define academic tenure as the "title" to this (qualified) permanence of the position or as the ground on which the teacher or investigator may confidently expect to hold his posi-

[5] This is especially likely where the bylaws of the institution assure the professors of "indefinite" tenure—"at the pleasure of the Board of Trustees."

tion until he is retired for age or permanent disability or separated for adequate cause under due process or because of financial exigencies of the institution.[6] We may distinguish four grounds of such expectations, or four types of tenure:

1. Tenure by law.
2. Tenure by contract.
3. Tenure by moral commitment under a widely accepted academic code.
4. Tenure by courtesy, kindness, timidity, or inertia.

Tenure by law exists for certain state institutions. Tenure by contract exists in a good many institutions where the bylaws contain provisions about the continuity of appointments and where these bylaws are made an integral part of the contracts with the faculty members. Tenure by moral commitment, or moral code, rests on what the profession has come to regard as "acceptable academic practice," as it is, for example, spelled out in the 1940 *Statement of Principles.* Tenure by courtesy, kindness, timidity, or inertia is merely a *de facto* status without legal, contractual, or moral commitment.

[6] "Adequate cause" for separation under due process may be incompetence, neglect of duty, and gross personal misconduct which makes the faculty member unfit for association with young students (often called "moral turpitude"). For a statement on due process, see Louis Joughin, "Academic Due Process," *AAUP Bulletin,* 50:19–35 (Spring, 1964), [reprinted in this volume, pp. 264–305]. My definition makes "tenure" and "job security" equivalent terms in all those institutions which provide, for cases of nonrenewal of contract with a person with job security, the same or similar procedures as for cases of dismissal of a person on permanent tenure. Senior faculty members are sometimes jealous of the word "tenure" and would not permit its use where they have not voted the grant of tenure to those judged deserving of this honor: but they do not mind if other teachers or researchers are given virtually the same assurance against loss of employment under the less honorific name "security of employment." Where the protection against nonretention is practically the same, and only the designation is different, the term "tenure" as used in the rest of this paper is meant to include "security of employment." Perhaps I may add that institutions which grant "security of employment" ought to be quite precise in their descriptions of the procedures for cases of nonrenewal and, particularly, make sure that both groups enjoy all the procedural safeguards needed to protect their academic freedom.

Tenure by law and tenure by contract can be enforced by the courts.[7] Tenure by moral code can be enforced only by the pressure of moral forces, particularly the threat of public condemnation or censure by organizations enjoying the respect of a large part of the profession and therefore expressing "professional opinion." Tenure without commitment cannot be enforced, though it is the actual state of affairs at a good many places. It may be only a tenuous tenure, but it is nevertheless real and practical: many members of the academic profession can expect to hold their positions indefinitely because the administrative officers are nice, kind, timid, or lazy. After all, it is rather unpleasant to send someone on the staff packing, and quite a bother to look for a replacement.

Tenure by courtesy has all the disadvantages which are associated with tenure of any sort without having the one advantage acceptable as a sound justification of tenure commitments. But before I can show this, I must discuss the various disadvantages. I begin with the disadvantages to the institutions.

Disadvantages to academic institutions

Of the disadvantages which strict tenure rules may inflict upon colleges or universities, the following four deserve special consideration:

1. The institution cannot get rid of deadwood and, hence, cannot within a reasonable period accomplish a desired upgrading of its faculty.

2. The institution cannot judge the qualifications of new junior faculty members in the "too short" probationary period and, hence, it either loses some "late bloomers" by letting them out before they acquire tenure, or it gets stuck with some "never bloomers" by keeping them too long.

[7] Legal tenure can be enforced by a court ordering reinstatement, whereas contractual tenure is more likely to be enforced by a court awarding only money damages to the wrongfully dismissed professor. See Clark Byse and Louis Joughin, *Tenure in American Higher Education* (Ithaca, N.Y.: Cornell University Press, 1959), pp. 71–76. The book by Byse and Joughin is a rich source of information and illumination on the subject of academic tenure.

3. The institution finds its faculty deteriorating because some professors on tenure may get lazy, stale, and dull.

4. The institution which needs a large junior faculty for elementary courses with large undergraduate enrollment, but cannot possibly grant tenure to all or most of these teachers, must terminate these junior faculty members just when they have enough experience to do a good job of teaching; the quick turnover, therefore, lowers the quality of teaching and, moreover, imposes a heavy burden of recruiting many more young teachers every year than would be necessary if they could be kept on longer.

Let us look at the four arguments in turn.

1. The problem of deadwood. This argument is only partly valid. There is no doubt that strict tenure rules make it imperative for an institution to be more careful in selecting its faculty and more courageous in sending away those who do not meet its standards. Without such care and courage, to be sure, strict tenure rules would lead to an accumulation of substandard teachers on the permanent faculty. I submit, however, that the observance of strict tenure rules will actually increase both the care and the courage of administration and senior faculty responsible for appointments and promotions, so much so that the quality of the faculty will be better under strict rules than under lax rules.

Without strict tenure rules, without severe up-or-out practice, senior faculty and administration can easily become careless and their selections for appointment may be less than satisfactory—after all, "if he does not turn out well, we can always get rid of him." Then they become dilatory—"let us try him for another year," and still "another year." And finally they find that they "cannot decently let him out," even without tenure having been granted and without giving him anything but *de facto* continuance of appointment. Personal friendships will have been formed within the academic community, and nonprofessional considerations and attachments of various sorts make it practically impossible to terminate the appointment although, from a purely professional point of view, deadwood has accumulated. Tenure by courtesy, or the absence of tenure by commitment, is responsible for this.

With strict tenure rules, implemented through a firm up-or-out practice, the risks of appointing and retaining persons not meeting the standards of the institution are too great. Consequently, administrators and senior faculty will be more alert and conscious of constant "quality control" in appointments, promotion, and retention. If in a particular institution, however, judgment and courage have been lacking, so that inadequate teacher-scholars have been kept beyond the stated probationary period, one cannot reasonably blame the accumulation of deadwood in its faculty upon its strict tenure rules. By and large, the deadwood problem seems to be more characteristic of institutions not enforcing strict limits to probationary periods than of institutions where these limits are strictly observed. I have not tested this proposition, but I believe that corroborative evidence could easily be assembled.

This does not, however, dispose of the argument. Indeed, in at least one aspect, its validity cannot be denied. I refer to the case of an institution that wants to raise its standards and improve its faculty quickly. Assume a new president takes office and finds a large part of the faculty in the category of deadwood by the higher standard of excellence. To remove the deadwood quickly would be difficult or, at least, very expensive. Some faculty members may be willing to accept premature retirement, others, large separation payments (say, three years' salary), still others, assignment to nonteaching positions at the institution. Such a program, however, may be too expensive for the institution, and without such a program the unsatisfactory professors must be retained until they retire on schedule. This involves waiting for several years, and the president, however impatient, may have to settle for a very slow improvement of the faculty. Instead of doing it in three or four years, it may take him ten years.[8]

The case of a single department in need of improvement is more frequent than the case of an entire college or university raising its

[8] This slow process may be further retarded where the president cannot rely on the judgment and advice of his faculty. A mediocre faculty tends to perpetuate its mediocrity by bringing in equally mediocre persons to fill vacancies. The ambitious president will have to resort to outside committees to advise on new appointments and promotions. (Of course, if he understands his job, he will carefully avoid the suspicion that he judges and selects his faculty himself. Otherwise he may not be able to attract many good scholars, for, as a rule, such persons dislike administrators who exercise faculty prerogatives.)

academic standards. It happens in the best of institutions: a department may be "run down" and enjoy relatively poor standing; it ought to be strengthened in the interest of the students in the particular field and the professors in other disciplines, indeed for the good of the entire institution. The existence of tenure, however, makes it difficult to replace the mediocre scholars by outstanding ones, and the only alternatives are to enlarge the department by making some good additional appointments, which is expensive, or to wait until the present senior professors retire, which takes time.

In any event, strict tenure rules are a serious handicap in upgrading the faculty, and this may be a definite disadvantage to many institutions.

2. *The judging of qualifications.* The argument that the probationary period stipulated in the 1940 *Statement* by the AAC and the AAUP is too short to allow a proper evaluation of the qualifications of a young teacher-scholar does not apply to undergraduate colleges that look chiefly for good teaching and are less concerned with productivity in research. The argument is made for universities mainly interested in published research as an evidence of originality and scholarship. Even there a distinction is usually made between fields in which the research capacity of a young man can be judged relatively quickly (as in the experimental sciences, mathematics, and economics) and other fields, in which it may take many years to complete a scholarly study (as in some of the humanities, especially English literature, classics, languages, and the descriptive social sciences).

The point, then, is that six years may not be enough to judge the capabilities of a scholar in most of the humanities and in some of the social sciences. He may have started full-time teaching two or three years before he completed his doctoral work; by the time he has recovered from his dissertation, selected a new project, and embarked on new research, another three or four years may have passed and he still has nothing published to prove his scholarly productivity. Under the strict tenure rules his university must make the decision—to let him go or to give him permanent tenure—before his eligibility for a tenure position can be appraised. If he is sent away and later develops into an outstanding scholar, the university will have lost a valuable asset. If he is kept and turns out to be a dud the university will be saddled with an embarrassing liability. Hence, is it not perfectly reasonable for universities to oppose rules which would force them to make decisions without sufficient information? Is it not clear that strict tenure rules, requiring such decisions after six years of service, are contrary to the interests of the institution?

Even if this is granted, the situation is not quite so grave as it may sound. A university which errs on the side of caution and loses the still unproven talent, can try to bring him back as soon as he has demonstrated his scholarly productivity. To be sure, this will cost more money than if he had been kept on in the first place, but it will hardly be an excessive burden on the budget in the long run. Perhaps, though, the scholar resents not having had his promise recognized earlier, and now refuses to return to the university which let him go. The loss will then be permanent; yet, the loss to that institution will be a gain for another; even if the scholar forsakes a university career for one in government or industry, he is not lost to the nation or to mankind—and this, surely, is what matters most.

As far as the institution is concerned, however, the disadvantage which it suffers cannot be denied.

3. The growth of mediocrity. The contention that permanent tenure promotes mediocrity in the faculty must, to avoid confusion, be divided into two parts: (a) mediocrity grows if an increasing number of mediocre persons are appointed or promoted to tenure positions, and (b) mediocrity grows if able men, assured of permanent tenure, lose interest in hard work and change into mediocre persons. The two issues are different and must not be confused.

The first version of the contention is supported by a good many educators, professors as well as administrators. In the words of one professor, "Tenure provides the conditions under which bad or mediocre teaching may be perpetuated, and "Tenure . . . gives . . . the mediocre the right to continue to be mediocre."[9] This is merely

[9] Charles Gordon Post, "On Relinquishing Tenure," *Vassar Alumnæ Magazine,* March, 1959.

another form of the deadwood argument, previously examined. There the tenure rules were said to prevent upgrading a faculty; now they are said to perpetuate its poor quality and, if more mediocre teacher-scholars are added, to reduce its quality still further. This is not a tenable argument. It puts the blame on the rule book instead of on bad policies, on the rules against dismissal instead of on the practice of poor selection and evaluation of faculty. The real responsibility for accumulating mediocrity in the tenure faculty lies in poor judgment and inertia on the part of those in charge of appointments and promotions.

The second version of the mediocrity argument, on the other hand, presents a problem that cannot be blamed on poor judgment or bad policies. The problem is that some professors, secure in their position under strict tenure rules, deteriorate over the years. Perhaps they were good teachers and promising scholars at the time they were given tenure, but gradually, feeling secure in their jobs no matter how well they perform, they grow lazy, stale, and dull. They stop producing as scholars, they do not prepare new course material, they do not inspire, indeed they bore their students.

Is it really tenure, however, is it really security of continuous employment that has such sad effects on the performance of potentially good teachers and scholars? May there not be something lacking in the academic atmosphere in which they work, in the leadership of the institution which should make academic performance continuously interesting, rewarding, exciting? Is it really believable that many faculty members, once alert, ambitious, inspiring, and productive, but now lazy and dull, would still be live wires, full of spark, and constantly recharged with new learning, if only they had no assured tenure, if only they had to live in constant fear for their jobs? And what about the contrary argument that some people, especially scholars, work much better when they have no worries, no fears?

One may ask whether the doubts which I have expressed in these questions cannot be resolved by some empirical evidence. One might line up institutions with strict tenure commitments against institutions with no tenure (or only tenure by courtesy) and compare the relative number of cases of "deteriorated professors."

My guess is one would find less deterioration in the institutions with the strict tenure provisions—but such comparisons would not be legitimate, because several other important variables could hide the relationship between tenure and deterioration. One might propose to confine the comparison to institutions equal in all respects except tenure commitments—if this were possible. It is not. The quality of the faculty is probably different from the outset, since institutions granting and those not granting permanent tenure are likely to attract different types of academic people. In other words, it may be impossible to devise empirical techniques which allow to isolate the long-run effects of tenure upon performance. This difficulty of empirical testing is not exceptional, but is encountered in many or most problems in the social sciences.

My doubts about the frequency and importance of cases of faculty deterioration due to tenure must not be mistaken for a denial of their existence. Some of us know of cases of this sort. We know of professors who once were promising but have not fulfilled the promise: they have not kept up with the progress in their fields, have not done any decent research in years, do not prepare their lectures, do not carry their share of the burden in the department, are not accessible to students; but who, possibly, would still perform satisfactorily if they were not secure in their jobs, that is, if their contracts were subject to termination or renewal depending on performance. Hence, with due reservations regarding the frequency and importance of actual cases in point, it must be granted that the tenure system may contribute to some deterioration in the performance of some professors and, consequently, may harm the institutions which are stuck with the retrograde members of the faculty.

4. The rate of turnover. The fourth argument is both valid and important. It concerns institutions which require a large teaching staff in junior ranks to conduct elementary courses. The shorter the probationary period, the faster will be the turnover of teaching personnel; hence, under strict tenure rules, the percentage of less experienced teachers will be greater and the quality of teaching will be poorer.

If illustrations are needed, consider Freshman English, Elementary French, American History 101, and other courses with enrollments too large to make it possible for the institution to use mainly senior faculty to teach them. For these courses large colleges and universities tend to employ fledgling instructors, often still studying towards M.A. and Ph.D. degrees, and older ones whose wings have not grown strong enough to lift them into higher ranks. The institutions do not want to grant permanent tenure to these not sufficiently scholarly but often quite effective teachers; nor do they want to send them away too quickly, because they hate to lose the most experienced of this junior faculty and to have to go to the trouble every year of recruiting replacements and administering on-the-job training to these novice teachers.

Several administrators have been concerned with this problem. It has been suggested that teachers of elementary courses in disciplines that require drill and routine work rather than a constant search for new truths would not need, and should not be granted, permanent tenure. For example, the teaching of irregular verbs in Elementary French or of remedial English composition is not so sensitive that it would require protection from interference; and hence, it is argued, it should be permissible to employ in such subjects teachers for ten, twelve, or more years without granting them permanent tenure. The same argument, however, does not apply to the teaching of literature or history, and it would surely be difficult to draw a line that would reasonably distinguish between teachers who ought to be given tenure and those who can safely do without it.

No solution has been found for this problem and we are left with the conclusion that the observance of strict tenure rules, with the agreed limits to the probationary period, increases the cost and lowers the quality of elementary instruction in certain colleges and universities.

Having evaluated the four main disadvantages which strict tenure rules impose upon institutions of higher education, I should not leave this part of our discourse without making two reservations. First, there may be still other disadvantages; and secondly, there are certainly some offsetting advantages. These advantages, however, to the extent that they are not merely part of the competition among institutions to attract and hold the best scholars, are closely connected with the one reason that outweighs all other arguments, and which I shall state and discuss after I have done full justice to the various disadvantages.

Disadvantages to individual scholars

I turn to the second of the main contentions, that tenure holds disadvantages for many individual scholars. Again, this does not mean that tenure does not also have advantages for many. The question is which are greater, the advantages or the disadvantages. Let us try to consider both.

Different types of academic persons will be impressed with different advantages and different disadvantages; the balance of advantages and disadvantages, therefore, will depend on the composition of the academic population. One may expect that the security of income which tenure affords will be appreciated less by younger men without dependents than by men in their forties, or older, with families; less by the enterprising and courageous than by the spiritless and timid; less by the self-confident than by the self-conscious; less by the professors in safe and noncontroversial subjects than by those in politically sensitive subjects; less by those satisfied with the *status quo* than by those who want to challenge tradition. Thus, in order to estimate the relative numbers of those who may personally and individually benefit from strict rules of academic tenure, one would have to estimate the sizes of the various categories enumerated. This I cannot undertake, except for one of the divisions, where the distribution is obvious without any empirical check. I refer to the fact that the teacher-scholars in safe subjects are an overwhelming majority and those in politically sensitive fields a small minority.

Apart from these general observations, I submit that for two special categories of academic teachers strict tenure rules entail distinct disadvantages. There are, first, the younger teachers in the most prestigious universities who cannot obtain promotion to tenure rank within the stipulated probationary period and thus must be "let out" under a merciless up-or-out practice. The probationary period is just a little too short for them: either they are unable to complete and publish the research that would prove their scholarly qualifications or there is at the moment no vacancy with tenure rank. In a couple of years, perhaps, a young teacher in this category might obtain his promotion, either because his eligibility as a scholar would then be established or because a tenure position at his university would then become vacant. Now, under the cruel, inflexible rules he must go.

The second category is that of the teacher who starts in a top-rank university and, unable to prove his scholarly qualifications, must be given notice at the end of his sixth year. He secures a position at another university where, still unable to meet the standards, he will be told after three years that he must leave at the end of his fourth year. (I assume the institution was careful enough to agree in writing on a new probationary period.) From now on he may have to pack and move every four years until he finds at last a position in an institution where he is able to meet standards.

The first category consists of good scholars who must move elsewhere in spite of fine qualifications; the second, of less able scholars who must move from place to place because of only-average qualifications. In both cases, the individuals concerned will resent the cost and inconvenience; indeed, sometimes the dislocation involves real hardships for them and their families.

Both types of teachers may blame the strict tenure rules for their tough luck. The top-rate scholar might have earned his permanent tenure at his first university, had he been allowed to stay for just another two years. The so-so scholar might have secured tenure by courtesy in his first or second post, what with his nice personality, sociability, and ability to make friends; only those "inhuman" rules forced him out and onto his arduous peregrination to less and less desirable academic institutions.

The disadvantages to both types of teachers are undeniable. From the point of view of academic excellence, however, one cannot complain of an avoidable social cost or waste in these instances. In the second case, certainly, the hardships which the strict system inflicts upon the individuals are more than offset by the advantages to the institution that is saved from loading up with nice persons who do not really meet the high academic standards to which it aspires. In the first case, the hardships to the individuals might be avoided if their first university recognized their scholarly qualifications earlier, or if it created new tenure positions where none is vacant, or if it extended the probationary period beyond that provided under the strict rules. The last expedient, I submit, is the least desirable from the point of view of the entire academic community, not only because it sets a bad precedent which can undermine the system, but even from the point of view of the class of "young, promising scholars." This assertion calls for an explanation.

My category of good teacher-scholars forced out of their first position by an inflexible up-or-out practice is a class of people whose membership can be determined only *ex post*. At the time when, under the strict rule, the decision of promotion or separation must be made, it may not yet be certain that the individuals concerned really belong in this class. Can one say that individual scholars whose eligibility for a tenure position at their first university is not yet established would be better off if the decision were postponed? This is so only for those who in fact later prove their eligibility, but not for those who do not succeed. For the entire group of young scholars it is much fairer, much less embarrassing, and much more opportune if they are "let out" at the end of a fixed, short probationary period than after one extended by special consideration. If a scholar is dropped at the end of a short period, one may honestly say that "one cannot yet be sure" of his productivity; but if he is dropped after an extended period, for example, after eight or nine years, the clear implication is that "now one knows he is not good enough." This may ruin his career, for he may have to go several steps down, as far as quality and prestige of institution are concerned, to find a place for himself.

This reasonable argument will probably not convince the young scholars who are confident that, given time, they will make the grade and will be able to stay on at the institution and in the community where they have made friends. To these individuals the strict tenure rules appear disadvantageous, and we cannot prove that they are not.

Disadvantages to the profession

From the individual members, or groups of members, of the academic profession we turn now to the profession as a whole. Some of the disadvantages which strict tenure rules hold for particular institutions or for individual teachers may, of course, be also disadvantages for the profession as a whole. For example, if tenure tends to corrupt, and permanent tenure corrupts permanently, this disadvantage to the institution suffering from deteriorated faculty members is surely an injury to the entire profession. Our present task, however, is to find out whether the profession may suffer disadvantages besides those so far discussed.

Two arguments to this effect can be found, one socio-psychological, the other economic. The former is based on the generalization that a tenure system is likely to attract security-minded rather than enterprising, timid rather than adventurous characters, and that the academic profession would be better if it attracted fewer milksops and more fire-eaters. I am not competent to pass judgment on this hypothesis. I cannot see, however, why originality and intellectual daring should be associated with civil courage and social intrepidity; as a matter of fact, I suspect that many of the best scholars are rather timid and prefer to stay out of a hard fight. None the less, I shall not attempt to argue either for or against this thesis, and I proceed to the economic discourse, where I feel at home.

What I have to say on the economic effects of tenure rules is old hat to economists but may startle educators in other subjects. The point is that the existence of the tenure privilege tends to keep professorial salaries lower than they would be otherwise. Some non economists have recognized this tendency but have advanced inadequate explanations. One critic of the tenure system, for example, argued as follows:

> If I had to keep a man on for 15, 20 or 25 years—not knowing whether in the long run he would be worth it—but having to pay him month in and month out as long as he was doing a passable job, and couldn't dismiss him, my tendency would be to pay him as little as possible.[10]

[10] Charles Gordon Post, *op. cit.* Post's explanation gets support from the analysis by a very competent economist, who stated that "the beginning [salary] rate under tenure will be lower than under non-tenure as a result of the risks of long-term contracts." Armen A. Alchian, "Private Property and the Relative Cost of Tenure," in Philip D. Bradley, ed., *The Public Stake in Union Power* (Charlottesville: University of Virginia Press, 1959), pp. 360–61.

To translate this hypothesis—of a tendency to pay "as little as possible"—into economic terms, one may hold that the risk of institutions getting stuck with mediocre teachers on permanent tenure reduces the demand for academic personnel.[11] This may be so, though it is not very likely under the conditions of financing our academic institutions; but what is really relevant is that the supply of teachers is increased if job security is added to pecuniary rewards offered. Even with a given demand, an increase in supply will tend to reduce the money salary on the average.[12]

The assumption that the offer of job security increases the supply of teachers is sometimes rejected on the ground that many, perhaps even most, people do not really care for tenure, and therefore would enter the academic profession regardless of tenure. This fact is beyond dispute, but of no relevance to the point. Even if the overwhelming majority of the potential supply of academic teachers did not give two hoots about tenure, it is the "margin" that counts in the determination of price. In other words, if only ten per cent of all teachers were attracted by the combination of salary and security, it would be this ten per cent that counts. Withdraw the security provision from the package, and these people withdraw from the academic market to other occupations, where they find higher pecuniary rewards, higher fringe benefits, more security, more prestige, or more fun.

[11] Where the risks are greater, the quantity demanded at any given price or the price offered for any given quantity will often be smaller. The economist, therefore, says that the demand will be smaller the greater the risk involved.

[12] Some people hold that, at any one time, the amount of funds which institutions of higher education can raise for salary payments is fixed, and average money payments to teachers will then be determined by the number of teachers attracted. (Economists call this a "wages fund" theory.) The greater the number of teachers who are attracted by a package of "salary plus job security," the greater will be the number of those who compete for a share in the available funds, and the smaller will be the salary per head. This hypothesis of a fixed fund, available to the institutions for teachers' salaries, may be helpful as a first step in explaining the effect of an increased supply; but it is by no means essential. Even if the "demand curve" for teachers is "very elastic," an increase in supply will still reduce the average salary.

We possess no statistical evidence to verify these relationships. Some institutions that have the best tenure practice also pay the highest salaries—so that there is no inverse correlation between pecuniary rewards and security. This is because there are still other variables involved, for example, different qualities of faculty, and good institutions compete for top-rank professors with both salary and tenure terms. But the general thesis, that tenure provisions, if they attract some people to the academic profession, tend to keep academic salaries lower, is not questioned by economists.

At least one economist has criticized tenure as a most inefficient system. Since the professors must pay for the security they purchase by accepting lower salaries, tenure, he said, "benefits the older, less able people at the expense of the younger, more able . . . individuals."[13] If teachers had a choice, the security-minded would go to institutions that offered tenure and lower salaries, while the confident would go to institutions offering higher salaries without tenure. If, however, tenure is more or less generally (though not quite voluntarily) provided by all institutions of higher education, the academic teachers have no choice and even those who do not care for tenure must buy it and pay for it by accepting lower salaries. Whether society has a right to restrict the professors' freedom of choice and to force them to buy the security of permanent tenure even if they are not interested in it—this is a question which I shall have to answer presently. At this point, I must concede that the academic profession suffers an economic, or at least pecuniary, disadvantage as a result of the existence of tenure rules.

One may look at this also from a different point of view. If it is an increase in the supply of academic teachers that tends to keep their salaries lower than they would be without tenure provisions, this same increase in supply may be credited with securing to society a larger number of teachers for a given amount of money. Assuming that the funds which society can scrape together for purposes of higher education are limited, the promise of tenure, attractive to some, makes these funds go farther and procures more teachers for the educational establishment. A greater number in the academic profession is perhaps an advantage to society; but if

[13] Alchian, *op. cit.*, p. 361.

it means smaller material compensation per teacher one can hardly call it an advantage for the profession.[14]

The benefit to society

As I suggested at the beginning of this discourse, all the disadvantages of a strict tenure system, whether they are borne by the institutions, by the individual teachers, or by the entire academic profession, are outweighed by one important advantage, accruing chiefly to society at large. This one advantage—really the only justification for the system of academic tenure—lies in the social products of academic freedom, a freedom which in many situations (more about this later) can be guaranteed only by the instrument of tenure. The various disadvantages, serious as they may be, are parts of the cost which society must incur in order to secure the great benefit of academic freedom and of the fruits it bears.

These fruits, it should be noted, accrue only in negligible part to the individual professors, their institutions, or the academic profession as a whole. That the "products" of freedom accrue chiefly to society at large explains why the academic profession would not willingly pay the cost of tenure. If individual teachers had a chance to "opt out" or "contract out" of the tenure system, too many of them would do so, would choose higher salaries without tenure. Here is an instance of what economists usually call "external benefits" or "third-party benefits." The largest part of the benefits derived from the scholars' exercise of their freedom to inquire, speak, teach, and publish accrues not to them, but to millions of their contemporaries and millions again in posterity. Only the

[14] That tenure may allow society to buy more teachers with a given appropriation of funds was evidently recognized as a benefit to society by the representatives of the AAC and AAUP. For they wrote into the 1940 *Statement of Principles* that one of the objectives of academic tenure was to provide "a sufficient degree of economic security to make the profession attractive to men and women of ability." If the writers of this statement meant to say that at a *given* salary level, the offer of economic security would attract more persons, including those of high ability, to the teaching profession, they were right, but they failed to realize that the increased attractiveness would *reduce* the money-salary level. If they meant to say that economic security is more attractive to abler persons than to less able ones, no support could be adduced for such a hypothesis.

most idealistic of the scholars would be willing to buy and pay for the tenure rights securing their unchallengeable freedom (a freedom, incidentally, which most of them find no occasion to exercise). Society, therefore, in a sort of social contract between trustees, regents, administrators, scholars and teachers, ordains a system of strict rule of academic tenure for the entire profession.

My language here may have been somewhat fancy, using some of the economic theorist's technical jargon. This was deliberate, in order to convince some of my fellow-economists that the free competitive market for higher learning would not guarantee all the academic freedom which society ought to provide in the interest of progress; without the "interference" through the universal tenure system the degree of academic freedom would be only that which professors would be willing to pay for, and this would be much less than what is socially desirable.

Noneconomists, it seems, can assimilate these ideas, without the use of technical language. The drafters of the 1940 *Statement* were quite explicit on the conflict of interests between the individual teachers and the institutions, on the one hand, and society, on the other. This is how they expressed it:

> Institutions of higher education are conducted for the common good and not to further the interest of either the individual teacher or the institution as a whole. The common good depends upon the free search for truth and its free exposition.

For a variation of this theme, with a very appropriate emphasis on the essential components of the search for truth, we are indebted to the authors of the best treatise on tenure:

> Academic freedom and tenure do not exist because of a peculiar solicitude for the human beings who staff our academic institutions. They exist, instead, in order that society may have the benefit of honest judgment and independent criticism which otherwise might be withheld because of fear of offending a dominant social group or transient social attitude.[15]

[15] Byse and Joughin, *op. cit.*, p. 4.

The benefits of academic freedom may be either material or intangible. Materialists are chiefly impressed with technological innovations based on scientific discoveries, and it is quite proper to point out to them how scientific research is most effectively carried on in an environment of full academic freedom. Others, however, who appreciate intellectual, moral, and aesthetic values, who esteem political and social progress, and who recognize cultural advances as an important achievement of academic scholarship and higher education, will understand that the social benefits of academic freedom are of a scope much wider than that indicated by the output of goods and services entering the statistic of our gross national product.

The exercise of academic freedom has many facets; it goes far beyond the scientist's much heralded search for scientific truth. The less sublime aspects of academic freedom are not sufficiently noted and this makes it appropriate for me to attempt a catalogue.

Aspects of academic freedom

My catalogue contains six items. Five of them are so easily comprehended that one simple sentence with five brief clauses will suffice to describe them: only the sixth will call for elaboration. All have in common that they imply absence of institutional sanctions for unpopular pronouncements and, consequently, a conviction on the part of teachers and scholars that they have little to fear if their words or actions are offensive to many.

We want the teacher and scholar to be uninhibited in criticizing, and in advocating changes of,

(1) accepted theories,

(2) widely held beliefs,

(3) existing social, political, and economic institutions,

(4) the policies and programs of the educational institution at which he serves, and

(5) the administration and governing board of the institution at which he serves.

(6) In addition, we want him to be uninhibited in coming to the aid of any of his colleagues whose academic freedom is in jeopardy.

The last point may need a supporting argument. All infringements of academic freedom begin with the charge that a teacher or scholar has, by his words or actions, abused his freedom. As I once wrote, "so-called abuses are the only proofs that the freedom really exists."[16] Since the temptation to go after the "abuser" of freedom may be irresistible to the powers that be, the protection of freedom may depend on the strength of the defense. Hence we need and want teachers and scholars who would unhesitatingly come to the defense of the "odd ball," the heretic, the dissenter, the troublemaker, whose freedom to speak and to write is under some threat from colleagues, administrators, governing board, government, or pressure groups. The impulse to take up the cudgels for the "odd ball" is all too easily suppressed if unpleasant consequences must be feared by those who defend him.

It happens that some of the greatest agents of progress in human affairs and scientific knowledge about nature or society have been "troublemakers." One of the most important tasks of true, freedom-and-progress-loving scholars is to come to the aid of a troublemaker under attack, even if they disagree with what he professes and dislike him for his personal traits, manners or practices.

Tenure as an instrument of freedom

I have heard it argued that permanent tenure is not an indispensable instrument for the guarantee of academic freedom; that freedom can be safeguarded without tenure rules.

This argument is valid under two conditions: First, that all governing boards and administrators of institutions of higher education believe so strongly in academic freedom that every charge of abuse, and every suspicion of abuse, would inspire them with such a zeal to protect the offender that they would rather see the institution which they govern or administer impoverished or destroyed than allow the offender to be removed from his post. Second, that it is always possible to distinguish offenses that come under the heading of abuse of freedom from all other reasons for dispensing with the services of a teacher or scholar.

Neither of the two conditions is satisfied. The difficulty of distinguishing between different reasons for "noncontinuance" is well

[16] Fritz Machlup, "On Some Misconceptions Concerning Academic Freedom." [See above, pp. 177–209.]

attested to by the experience with nonrenewals of contracts of non-tenured teachers. It is rarely possible to prove that the decision not to renew a contract was influenced, let alone determined, by some offensive or embarrassing publications or utterances of the teacher concerned. As a matter of fact, the persons who make the decision may themselves not know what motivates them: do they judge him to be a poor teacher, do they dislike him as a person, or do they dislike what he wrote or said? It is probably unavoidable that ineffectiveness in teaching and lack of scholarly publications are so readily noticed in a faculty member who has taken liberties and thereby embarrassed his institution; the same defects may go unnoticed in a pleasant chap who conforms and gets along well with everybody.

To say that the first condition is not "realistic" would be the biggest understatement of the year. Without strict tenure rules, the governing boards and administrative officers of the majority of colleges and universities could not succeed in protecting a faculty member accused of having abused his freedom. Many of us can, without long deliberation, recite a list of names of well-known scholars whose survival on the faculty of their institution has been possible only thanks to the rules of tenure. The president of the institution can say to those clamoring for the dismissal of the presumed public enemy: "I am sorry, much as I should like to get rid of Professor X, we cannot do it, for he has permanent tenure."

Full efficacy of tenure as a protection of freedom requires that tenure be regarded as a genuine commitment. Tenure by courtesy, mere *de facto* tenure, is likely to break down just when it would be needed most as a protection against outside pressures. If tenure is not based on legal constraints or contractual obligations, it may be difficult for administrators or governing boards to resist a strong and vociferous public campaign for the removal of a controversial educator accused of attempts to subvert tradition or corrupt the young. Tenure based only on the recognition of a widely accepted academic code may be helpful as long as the leaders of the campaign can be convinced that violations of these moral principles would have injurious consequences for the institution. Herein lies the importance of the ACC–AAUP *Statement* for institutions that have failed to incorporate these principles into their own bylaws.[17]

I cannot understand, although I have tried hard, why some experienced administrators prefer informal, *de facto* tenure to formal, binding tenure regulations. Nonenforceable tenure has, as I see it, all the disadvantages but few of the advantages of binding tenure commitments. It reduces the attractiveness of the institution to faculty and makes it harder to compete for the most desirable scholars; it contributes to mediocrity in the faculty by reducing caution and courage in policies for appointment and retention, while creating the same obstacles to removing deadwood that exist under formal tenure commitments; and it does not achieve the really important objectives of tenure, namely, to protect against outside pressures for the removal of the expositors of unpopular ideas and to create a feeling of complete security in the minds of sensitive scholars dealing with sensitive issues.

The feeling of some faculty members on the question of tenure is well characterized by a professor's comment on his president's opposition to tenure rules: "If our president says that only without tenure will the faculty be kept on its toes, his anatomical metaphor is slightly off; he wants us less on our toes than on our knees."

Once it is understood that academic freedom serves the purposes of society, not of individual teachers or institutions, it will also be understood that academic tenure, the safeguard of freedom, should not depend on the preferences and idiosyncrasies of particular institutions. It has been proposed that the rules of tenure be adjusted to the character of each institution. Admittedly, such flexibility might alleviate some of the disadvantages which strict tenure rules hold for individual institutions. More important, however, is the danger that institutional self-determination of rules of tenure might weaken the respect for and observance of the basic principle. It would be too easy for those who want to go after some supposed "abuses" of freedom to argue that the special nature of "their" in-

[17] There are, to be sure, a few exceptional universities where freedom might be safe without formal tenure. These are universities with long tradition, great prestige, large endowments, independence from public funds, and with trustees steeped in the absolute values of "academe."

stitution demanded the denial of tenure to many members of the faculty. This danger makes it imperative that we insist on national standards.

The proportion of the faculty with tenure

If tenure is to serve freedom, it is not enough to make tenure rules inviolable or enforceable, but it is also essential to make them cover as large a proportion of the faculty as is possible without jeopardizing other equally important objectives.

How large a part of the faculty of our institutions of higher education is now in tenure positions? How many years does it take until new entrants into the academic career acquire tenure? At what age and after how many years at their institutions do they obtain tenure, and what is the age distribution of the nontenure faculty?

These are some of the questions that must be answered if we want to get a picture of the tenure status of the academic profession. Partial answers to the first question have been obtained by various students of the subject. For example, we have for 1955 a tabulation of 80 colleges and universities in California, Illinois, and Pennsylvania, with the numbers, wherever available, for (a) total faculty members, (b) full-time faculty members, and (c) tenured faculty members (where the tenure status is defined by the individual institution).[18] For 1961–62 we have information of a similar nature for 31 major universities.[19]

The findings of these studies are rather disappointing. I examined the data for the 1955 tenure situation at 80 institutions in three states, both individually and in various aggregations. The table below presents the figures, for 68 of these institutions for which complete information was given, broken down according to the size of

[18] Byse and Joughin, *op. cit.*, pp. 162–65.

[19] Paul L. Dressel, "A Review of the Tenure Policies of Thirty-One Major Universities," *The Educational Record* (July 1963), 248–53.

Numbers and Percentages of Faculty Members, Total, Full-Time, and Tenured, in 68 Institutions of Higher Education in California, Illinois, and Pennsylvania, 1955

	Numbers			Percentages		
	Total (1)	Full-time (2)	Tenure (3)	(2) of (1)	(3) of (2)	(3) of (1)
52 institutions with less than 120 faculty members	2,949	2,342	1,240	79	53	42
6 institutions with between 120 and 200 faculty members	966	781	505	81	65	52
10 institutions with more than 200 faculty members	15,621	8,327	4,305	53	52	28
68 institutions	19,536	11,450	6,050	59	53	31

Source: Byse and Joughin, *op. cit.* [Constructed from data on pp. 162–65, *passim.*]

the faculty. (A geographic breakdown looked too arbitrary because some important institutions were omitted on account of incomplete information.) For the entire sample we find that only 31 per cent of the total faculty had tenure (by the definitions of the individual institutions). The even lower figure for the largest institutions, 28 per cent of the total faculty, was clearly due to the large number of part-time teachers in the large universities. But the percentages of full-time teachers with tenure—53 per cent for all 68 institutions, and between 52 and 65 per cent for the various size brackets—are still rather low.

The 1961–62 data for 31 major universities are not very different. Four of the universities had less than 50 per cent of their total faculty on tenure, and 17 of the 31 universities had less than 60 per cent of their total faculty on tenure.[20]

An examination of the 1955 data for individual institutions is even more depressing. In only a handful of the institutions studied did a large percentage of the faculty have tenure status. Rare are

[20] *Ibid.*, p. 251.

institutions in which more than one-half of the faculty have tenure. In several places less than one-fifth of the faculty are on tenure.

The distinction between "total" and "full-time" faculty is, of course, significant, since one cannot expect tenure status to be conferred on part-time teachers. Yet, it would be a mistake to confine the statistical account to full-time faculty. For one might easily misjudge the situation if one encountered a university with a record of close to 100 per cent of the full-time faculty enjoying permanent tenure, and failed to realize that the total faculty of this institution might be several times as large as its full-time contingent.

The other questions which I have found relevant for an analysis, the questions concerning age distribution and length of service of full-time faculty without tenure, can be answered only on the basis of a questionnaire study which would impose a good deal on the administrative officers of the institutions willing to cooperate. I devised forms for such a study and obtained the cooperation of kindly officers at two universities for a trial run. The returns from both institutions contained some peculiar results. For example, among the faculty without tenure there were associate professors over 40 years old, and in one institution some over 50 years old.

The returns concerning length of service at the institutions and in the profession (that is, at the institution plus previous full-time teaching experience elsewhere) also had some surprising items. There were, among the full-time faculty without tenure, several assistant professors with more than seven years at the particular institution and up to thirteen years in the profession; there was an instructor with twelve years of service at the reporting university, an associate professor with thirteen years, and a full professor with more than twenty years in the profession—all these, I repeat, without tenure.

A hypothesis to the effect that probationary periods of extraordinary length would occur chiefly in the humanities was tested, but disconfirmed by one of the two returns. Faculty members with many years of full-time teaching experience but no tenure status were reported in the columns of the division of natural sciences no less frequently than in other columns. Needless to say, information for only two institutions need not show any typical relationships.

I hope that the cooperation of several more institutions can be obtained for an analysis of the tenure and nontenure faculty in a significant sample of colleges and universities.

Without anticipating the findings of such a study, we may expect them to shed light on the approximate strength of protection of academic freedom. For, since enforceable tenure status is, by and large, the most reliable safeguard of academic freedom, and since such freedom ought to be secured to the largest possible proportion of the faculties, a quantitative indication of this guarantee of academic freedom can be found in

(a) the percentage of the total number of faculty members whose tenure status is recognized by their institutions;

(b) the percentage of the number of full-time faculty members whose tenure status is recognized by their institutions;

(c) the numbers of full-time faculty members in various age groups, especially those over 35 years of age, who have not obtained tenure status;

(d) the numbers of full-time faculty members with various lengths of full-time teaching experience, especially those with seven years or more, who have not obtained tenure status; and

(e) the numbers of full-time faculty members with various lengths of full-time teaching experience, especially those with ten years or more, who have not obtained tenure status.

Such a study with aggregate figures broken down by different types of institutions and perhaps also by major divisions (such as [A] Natural Sciences, Mathematics, and Psychology, [B] Social Sciences, History, and Business, [C] Humanities, and [D] Engineering and other Professional Schools) would afford us many insights which we lack today. In addition, if institutions were willing to permit publication of the individual data with identification of each reporting institution, we would obtain indices of faculty protection at each college and university. Institutions with particularly high indices of faculty protection would probably be glad to have such information become public knowledge; institutions with less impressive indices might either explain the circumstances which prevent higher measures of protection or state the reasons which induce them to keep them purposely low.

The years without tenure

One may wonder why I place so much emphasis on the "years without tenure," particularly on the fact that faculty members with ten or more years of teaching experience may not yet have obtained tenure status.

That unusually long probationary periods may be embarrassing for the individuals concerned, would not be a sufficient reason for this emphasis. My grounds are (a) that society, by withholding tenure from younger faculty members, may lose some of the most vigorous criticism and most provocative thought, because the "Young Turks" may prefer to restrain themselves and play safe; and (b) that society, by conditioning younger faculty members to attitudes of restraint, may lose some of their potential deviationist ideas even when they are older and protected by tenure.

I am not saying that all teachers and scholars are cowards; but I am saying that many are "realistic" and will hesitate to jeopardize their careers when they can be safe and comfortable by holding back and deferring their criticism of traditional theories, convictions, and conventions. And I am saying, furthermore, that many persons who for ten years of their professional careers have learned to sit back, to avoid irritating their senior colleagues, and to wait for more appropriate occasions to state opinions that may be offensive to others, may acquire habits of excessive judiciousness that will reduce their effectiveness for the rest of their careers.

I now expect a chorus of objections to my views, led by some harassed deans and department heads, exclaiming that far too many junior faculty members show far too little restraint, and that too many senior faculty members have never lost their proclivities to rise and dissent vigorously from virtually every proposal, program, or policy. True, there are usually some vociferous dissenters in practically every faculty, there are obstreperous extroverts among those without tenure, and immature rebels among the senior professors with tenure. But I did not contend that *every* young teacher will be inhibited by the absence of tenure status or that *every* young scholar will acquire habits of undue restraint. I submitted only the thesis that *some* will be inhibited in the years without tenure and may remain inhibited for the rest of their careers.

If we consider that an academic career in active service may, on the average, be something like 35 years, we cannot help noting that probationary periods of as much as one-fourth of the entire career are excessive. If we consider, furthermore, that some highly productive ideas about nature and society have come from men in their twenties, it must give us pause when we realize how many academic teachers in their upper thirties and in their forties are still without the protection which tenure is supposed to provide for their intramural and extramural utterances.

Conclusion

I shall probably be accused of having overstated my case, of having exaggerated, in particular, the dangers to which lack of tenure would expose the academic teacher or the fears and inhibitions which he would suffer, or both. If so, I may plead that exaggeration in these matters can hardly do as much harm as could underestimation. The case for tenure does not rest on the probability that a large proportion of all academic teachers and scholars would suppress some of their thoughts or sentiments in the absence of the security which tenure provides; nor does it rest on the probability that some of the suppressed thoughts or sentiments would be of extraordinary significance. It is not necessary to assume that there are several Galileos in every generation or several men who have similarly subversive ideas of similar importance to communicate. The case for tenure would be sufficiently supported by showing that a few men once in a while might feel insecure and suppress or postpone the communication of views which, true or false, wise or foolish, could inspire or provoke others to embark on or continue along lines of reasoning which may eventually lead to new insights, new judgments, or new appraisals regarding nature or society.

One incident during my term of office has, more than anything else, reinforced my belief in the importance of tenure. It had to do with a young medical researcher in the last year of his probationary period, who had discovered toxic qualities of a drug distributed by a company which was supporting his university with generous research grants. Should he publish the report on his findings? Would he risk nonrenewals of his appointment if his publication angered the donor and the chairman of his department? As it was, or as I was told, the young man decided to publish and he lost his post. I discouraged him from filing a complaint with the AAUP, because it would be impossible to prove that his chairman's decision not to renew the contract was influenced by his decision to publish the embarrassing findings of his research. Just think how easy it would have been for this scientist to postpone publication by just one year; and what consequences for the health, perhaps the lives, of many could be entailed by postponement of such publications by as little as a month.

I am also impressed with the importance of uninhibited expression of academic opinion on public policy. Let me single out, as of paramount importance to the nation, the open discussion of sensitive questions of foreign policy, such as those involving relations with Soviet Russia, Red China, Yugoslavia, Cuba, etc. In some instances, changes of government policies toward foreign countries presuppose adequate preparation of public opinion—exposure of the "myths" recently referred to by Senator Fulbright—through candid discussion of the controversial issues, including free-spirited attacks on taboos fanatically expressed and enforced by convention or strong pressure groups. To get such candid discussions by all who can contribute to them, it is necessary that the unpopular, allegedly unpatriotic "rabble-rousers" be protected through strict and comprehensive tenure rules.

The cost of tenure to particular institutions of higher education, to many individuals, and to the academic profession as a whole, may be high. I have not tried to deny or to minimize the various disadvantages of tenure, so often emphasized by its opponents. But the high cost of tenure must not deter us, since its benefits to society are so much greater. On balance, society gains much more from academic tenure than it loses, and this is what counts.

SUPPLEMENT TO THE 1969 EDITION

Supplement

Constitution of the Association[1]

Here are set forth those Articles and sections of the Constitution which relate directly to the area of academic freedom and tenure, and to academic due process.

Article I—Purpose

The name of this Association shall be the American Association of University Professors. Its purpose shall be to facilitate a more effective cooperation among teachers and research scholars in universities and colleges, and in professional schools of similar grade, for the promotion of the interests of higher education and research, and in general to increase the usefulness and advance the standards, ideals, and welfare of the profession.

Article VI—Meetings of the Association

1. The Association shall meet annually except when prevented by war or other national emergency. The General Secretary shall give notice to the membership of a meeting at least 30 days in advance. A quorum shall be a majority of the delegates registered for a meeting. A meeting of the Association shall have authority (a) to amend the Constitution in the manner herein provided; (b) to express its views on professional matters; (c) to act on recommendations presented to it by the Council; (d) to require the Council to report to the ensuing meeting on subjects within the province of the Association; (e) to propose action which, upon concurrence by the Council, shall become the action of the Association; and (f) in the event of disagreement between the Council and a meeting of the Association, to take final action as provided in the following section.

[1] Last amended at the Fifty-Third Annual Meeting of the Association, at Cleveland, Ohio, April 28–29, 1967.

2. If the Council declines to concur in a proposal of a meeting of the Association, it shall report its reasons to the ensuing meeting. If that meeting concurs in the action of the previous meeting, the action shall become that of the Association. An action of the Association reached (a) by concurrence of the Council in an action of a meeting of the Association or (b) in two successive meetings shall not be changed except by the joint action of the Council and a meeting of the Association or by two successive meetings of the Association.

1968 Standards for Committee T Investigations in the Area of College and University Government

Academic freedom and tenure questions are often closely related to questions of corporate and individual faculty status, to questions of faculty participation in institutional government, and to other concerns of Committee T on College and University Government. That Committee's current standards for investigation are set forth below.

1. *Area of concern.* In considering the necessity or desirability of investigation and report on institutional situations involving college or university government, the Association looks to the condition of faculty status and of faculty-administration relations. Investigation will be considered in situations where it appears likely that corporate or individual functions of the faculty have been seriously impaired or threatened.

2. *Exploration of local remedies.* Investigation will ordinarily be undertaken only after normal avenues for local correction have been explored without substantial success. This condition, recognizably, may not operate in situations where local remedies are inadequate or where their use would worsen the situation or expose individual faculty members to harm.

3. *Decision to investigate.* The General Secretary, after such consultation as appears to be appropriate, will determine whether to authorize an investigation. His decision may result from a request for investigation from any responsible group of faculty members or may be based upon evidence otherwise available to the Association. A request for a Committee T investigation submitted to the General Secretary should present: (a) a general description of the situation, (b) specific information regarding the past or contemplated use of local remedies, and (c) an indication of the nature and extent of supporting documentary evidence. It should describe the available resources in the faculty for study of the situation and for local action looking toward improvement.

In reaching a determination, the General Secretary will give weight to the magnitude of the problem both for the faculty concerned and for the Association as a whole in its capacity as a representative organization for teachers in higher education. If an investigation is to take place, the General Secretary will appoint one or more persons to serve as an *ad hoc* committee.

4. *The report.* The report of the *ad hoc* committee will be submitted to Committee T, and that body will determine whether the report should be published in the *AAUP Bulletin.* Committee T may also wish to advise the General Secretary as to the dissemination of the report, which will ordinarily be sent to the administration of an institution, to its trustees, to the concerned accrediting body, and to other appropriate agencies and groups, together with the recommendations of Committee T.

5. Committee T will determine whether to propose further action to the Council of the Association, either concurrently with the dissemination of the report, or on a subsequent finding by Committee T that its recommendations have not been satisfactorily effected.

1968 Statement on the Role of the Faculty in the Accrediting of Colleges and Universities

The Winter, 1966, *Bulletin,* with the approval of the Council, presented a draft statement, prepared by Committee D, on The Role of the Faculty in the Accrediting of Colleges and Universities, with an invitation for comments from members and other interested persons.

In May, 1967, after examining comments received, Committee D produced a revised draft which was circulated among leaders in accreditation with a request for further comments. With a few additional changes which Committee D made as a result of these subsequent comments, the revised draft was submitted in October, 1967, to the Council, which approved its publication in the Winter, 1967, *Bulletin,* accompanied by a further invitation for comment.

Meeting in March, 1968, Committee D considered all comments which had been submitted. The Committee presented the following Statement to the Council and it was approved by that body in April, 1968, and endorsed by the Fifty-Fourth Annual Meeting as Association policy.

The members of Committee D who prepared the Statement which follows are: Joseph M. Conant (Classics, Emory University), *Chairman,* Harold T. Christensen (Sociology, Purdue University), Jordan E. Kurland (History and Russian, Washington Office), Mildred E. Mathias (Botany, University of California at Los Angeles), Carl M. Stevens (Economics, Reed College), Marx W. Wartofsky (Philosophy, Boston University), and Robert K. Webb (History, Columbia University).

Institutional evaluation is a joint enterprise between institutions of higher education and the accrediting commissions of regional associations. For their most effective work the accrediting commissions require the cooperative effort of qualified faculty members and administrators, who should be encouraged by their colleges and universities to participate in the work of the commissions. Within a college or university, the nature of the accrediting process requires common enterprise among the faculty, the administration, and to some extent the governing board. The appraisal of the academic program should be largely the responsibility of faculty members. They should play a major role in the evaluation of the curriculum, the library, teaching loads and conditions, research, professional activities, laboratories and other academic facilities, and faculty welfare and compensation, all in relation to the institution's objectives and in the light of its financial resources. To higher education generally, faculty members may exercise a special responsibility as the segment of the educational community which is in the best position to recognize and appraise circumstances affecting academic freedom, faculty tenure, faculty role in institutional government, and faculty status and morale. This statement presents standards for the expression of faculty interest and responsibility in the accreditation process.

Recommended standards for institutions of higher education

1. Primary responsibility for the preparation of the academic aspects of the self-evaluation should rest with a committee composed largely of faculty members and responsible to the faculty as a whole. Additions or deletions should be made only after consultation with the authors of the sections of the report which are affected.

2. The self-evaluation should include a description of:

a. Conditions of academic freedom and tenure (including provisions for due process);

b. Conditions of faculty participation in institutional government (including provisions for the orderly handling of grievances and disputes);

c. Faculty status and morale (including working conditions and total compensation).

Significant differences of opinion in these and other areas should be reflected in the self-evaluation.

3. The completed self-evaluation should be made available to the entire faculty prior to its submission to the accrediting commission and should be subject to amendment in the light of faculty suggestions.

4. Representative faculty, including members of appropriate faculty committees, should be available to meet with the visiting committee to discuss questions of faculty concern.

5. The report of the visiting committee should be made available to the entire faculty.

6. The faculty should be fully informed of the accrediting commission's action after an evaluation and should be kept abreast of all significant developments and issues arising between the accrediting commission and the institution. It should participate, as in the self-evaluation, in any subsequent activities regarding the institution's accreditation.

Recommended standards for the regional accrediting commissions

1. Regular visiting committees should include full-time teaching or research faculty members.

2. A formally adopted institutional policy on academic freedom and tenure, consistent with the major provisions of the 1940 *Statement of Principles on Academic Freedom and Tenure,* should be a condition for accreditation.

3. Reports by regular visiting committees should take explicit account of:

a. Conditions of academic freedom and tenure (including provisions for due process);

b. Conditions of faculty participation in institutional government (including provisions for the orderly handling of grievances and disputes);

c. Faculty status and morale (including working conditions and total compensation).

The reports should describe any significant shortcomings in these areas.

4. When significant shortcomings in the areas listed above have been found, the commissions should deal with these as with similar shortcomings in other areas, endeavoring to secure improvement and applying appropriate sanctions in the absence of improvement within a reasonable time.

5. A gross violation of academic freedom, tenure, or due process should, unless promptly corrected, lead to action looking towards withdrawal of accreditation.

1968 Statement of Policy on Representation of Economic Interests

Approved by Committee T on January 13, 1968, and by the Council on April 25, 1968. On April 27, 1968, the Fifty-Fourth Annual Meeting passed a motion stating: "It is the sense of this Meeting that it concurs in the Statement of Policy on Representation of Economic Interests."

The statement constitutes present Association policy, and will be further reviewed by the Council in time for consideration by a later Annual Meeting.

INTRODUCTION

The American Association of University Professors has long maintained that faculty members should have an effective voice in making and carrying out decisions affecting the educational and scholarly life of the institution. The 1966 *Statement on Government of Colleges and Universities* is the latest reaffirmation of this position. It declares that the faculty has a major role to play in determining the educational and research policies of the institution, and should also have an effective voice in appointments, promotions, actions resulting in tenure, and dismissals or nonreappointments. The faculty should play a part in the selection of principal academic officers and the heads or chairmen of departments; it should have a voice in budgetary decisions relating to teaching and research activities. The Association believes that the nature of the academic enterprise is such that the faculty properly shares in responsibilities which in nonacademic institutions might be entirely those of ownership or management.

The Association has further maintained that the goals of higher education include effective meeting of such economic and professional interests of the faculty as appropriate salary scales, fringe benefits, teaching loads and other conditions of teaching and research. The Committee on the Economic Status of the Profession in making its first salary grading report in 1959 declared: "The objective of the Association's program is to accelerate the adjustment of salary levels. . . . The basic idea of the program is to create additional incentives for governing boards and other friends of institutions of higher education to make the needed salary adjustments and to provide the funds required. . . ."

The outstanding colleges and universities of the United States characteristically afford to their faculty a genuine voice in all matters of educational policy and academic concern, and likewise provide adequately for the economic interests of their teaching and research personnel. Unfortunately, many institutions, for a variety of reasons, fail to meet these two essential and related needs, an effective voice and proper compensation. Such failures demand correction. Two main kinds of approach have been developed: (1) collective bargaining by an exclusive bargaining agent, patterned after union procedures in industry, and (2) professional self-representation by an internal faculty agency, based upon faculty authority of the kind which the Association supports for the handling of all kinds of faculty interests.

The Association recommends that faculty members, in decisions relating to the protection of their economic interests, should participate through structures of self-government within the institution, with the faculty participating either directly or through faculty-elected councils or senates. As integral parts of the institution, such councils or senates can effectively represent the faculty without taking on the adversary and sometimes arbitrary attitudes of an outside representative.

Faculties in publicly supported institutions, after achieving what they can by themselves, will increasingly need to join hands with their colleagues on other campuses in order to deal with governing and coordinating boards that have broad jurisdiction, with executive agencies, with the legislatures, and with the national government. For these negotiating and educational functions, strong professional organizations are needed. This Association, through its national Council and state and regional conferences, must equip itself for these functions, and then proceed to discharge its duties to the academic profession with vigor and wisdom.

Whatever means may be developed for representation, the faculty must have a truly effective voice both in decisions affecting its economic interests and in the wider issues of educational policy that confront higher education.

POLICY STATEMENT

I. Policy on legislation

A. Legislatures in several states have enacted statutes that promote collective bargaining by public employees. Other such statutes will probably come into being. The protections and remedies that they offer are doubtless advantageous for employees who have little or no voice in setting the terms and conditions of their employment. But statutory models of general application may be ill-suited to the situation of the faculty member in higher education. As stated above, he has, or should have, access to avenues of self-government and of shared authority and responsibility. Because of the importance of these special characteristics of the academic community, professors should be especially concerned to avoid dependence on external representative agencies that diminish the opportunities of the faculty for self-government.

B. The Association will therefore oppose legislation imposing upon faculty members in higher education the principle of exclusive representation derived from models of industrial collective bargaining. When legislation of this character exists or is proposed, the Association will rather support measures that will encourage institutions of higher education to establish adequate internal structures of faculty participation in the government of the institution.

C. To implement this policy, chapters and conferences should be alert to see that either proposed or existing laws avoid rigid prescriptions of exclusive representation.

1. Any statute authorizing collective bargaining for public employees should permit, for faculty members of colleges and universities, some system of joint representation. In such a system, collective bargaining might be conducted by a committee composed of delegates from each of the organizations which represented a substantial number of faculty members and which were willing to take part in the system of joint representation.

2. Any such legislation should make it clear that, in higher education, a faculty-elected council or senate is eligible to represent the faculty, since such an internal representative can have the requisite autonomy and independence of the administration to carry out its functions.

D. Great importance is attached, in the next few years, to having the views of the Association made known to legislators and incorporated in new or existing statutes bearing on collective bargaining by public employees. Specific guidance to these ends will be offered by the Washington Office, through memoranda on statutory drafting problems, and advice in particular circumstances.

II. Policy on the role of a chapter or other Association agency in deciding whether to seek representative status

A. If conditions of effective faculty voice and adequate protection and promotion of faculty economic interests are not met, and a faculty is considering representation through an outside organization, the Association believes itself, by virtue of its principles, programs, experience and broad membership, to be well qualified to act as representative of the faculty in institutions of higher education.

B. The initial decision to consider representative status, whether through a chapter or other agency of the Association (including a university-wide council of chapters in a multi-campus institution, or a conference in the case of a state-wide system), should be made in consultation with the General Secretary, and should be the result of judgment about the following considerations:

1. Is the internal organization of the faculty, and its share in the government of the institution, such that, with timely and achievable adjustments, a faculty senate or like body could adequately undertake the role of representation? If so, then the chapter or other Association agency should strive to see that the necessary improvements are made, should support the internal agency of representation, and should not offer itself as a representative.

2. But the pressure of events and of other claims for representation may make it unfeasible to accomplish necessary improvements before choices must be made. In such circumstances, the chapter or other Association agency may decide, as an interim measure, to offer itself as the faculty's representative.

3. Is the institution itself so new, or its practice of faculty participation so undeveloped, that a period of some years may be necessary before an effective internal faculty voice is attainable? If this is the judgment, then the chapter or other Association agency may decide to offer itself as the faculty's representative.

4. If the judgment is made that the existing structure and practice of institutional government seriously impairs the ability of the faculty to fulfill the purposes of the *Statement on Government of*

Colleges and Universities and it appears that there is little prospect of remedying this situation under existing procedures, then a conclusion may also be reached that a chapter ought to offer itself as the faculty's representative.

C. A practical judgment that must always be made, also in consultation with the General Secretary, goes beyond the evaluation of institutional government. It relates to the capacity of the chapter or other Association agency to undertake the task of representation, considering the extent of support from its members, their readiness to accept a substantial increase in dues to finance services that may be required, and whether the leadership is ready and equipped to devote the necessary time and energy.

D. A chapter or other Association agency, before it makes a final decision to seek representative status, should again consult with the General Secretary and consider his appraisal of the situation. If the final decision is to proceed, it will then take the necessary formal steps to permit it to be voted or designated as having representative status.

III. Policy for a chapter or other Association agency which achieves representative status

A. When a chapter or other agency of the Association attains the status of representative of the faculty, whether exclusive or otherwise, it will, when acting as representative, and in negotiations with the administration and the governing board, pursue the following objectives:

1. To protect and promote the economic and other interests of the faculty as a whole in accordance with the established principles of the Association.
2. To establish within the institution democratic structures which provide full participation by all faculty members in accordance with the *Statement on Government of Colleges and Universities.*
3. To obtain explicit guarantees of academic freedom and tenure in accordance with the 1940 *Statement of Principles on Academic Freedom and Tenure,* the 1958 *Statement on Procedural Standards in Faculty Dismissal Proceedings,* and other policy statements of the Association.

4. To create an orderly and clearly defined procedure within the faculty governmental structure for prompt consideration of problems and grievances of faculty members, to which procedure any individual or group shall have full access.

B. No person shall be required to become a member of or make any financial contribution to the Association as a condition of his enjoying the benefits of representation.

C. It is the policy of the Association (with which chapters should comply whether or not they are acting in a representative capacity) not to call or support a faculty strike or other work stoppage, except in the extraordinary circumstances suggested in the provisional Statement on Faculty Participation in Strikes.

Advisory Letters

LETTER NO. 18. SAFEGUARDING THE ACCURACY AND INTEGRITY OF THE ASSOCIATION'S REPORTS ON ACADEMIC FREEDOM AND TENURE

[*AAUP Bulletin,* 52:357–58 (Autumn, 1966)]

Complaints are usually brought to the Association's Washington Office directly by faculty members who consider that they have grievances against their institutions. A faculty member on tenure status, for example, may complain that he has been dismissed without an opportunity to defend himself in an appropriate hearing, as prescribed in the enclosed 1940 *Statement of Principles,* our basic working document in the area of academic freedom and tenure. Before we write to the chief administrator of the institution about the complaint, we secure from the faculty member all the relevant information and documentation that we can—for example, information on his rank and length of service at that institution and others, copies of his original and most recent letters or contracts of appointment, of the letter of dismissal, and of the institution's regulations—and we base our preliminary judgment on the facts as he has given them to us viewed in the light of the 1940 *Statement of Principles* and the institution's regulations. When we conclude that he may have a justifiable grievance and have his authorization to do so, we write to the chief administrator presenting the facts as we have them, normally advancing a recommendation, but assuring the administrator that the recommendation is subject to revision pending receipt of whatever additional pertinent information he can supply; and of course we invite him to provide as full information as possible. If, after studying this additional information, we conclude that a justifiable complaint still exists, we exert our influence to effect some appropriate resolution of the case, very often by means of a personal visit to the president's office by Association representatives.

If our correspondence and personal representations are unsuccessful in effecting a satisfactory resolution of the case and the violation of academic freedom and tenure appears sufficiently serious, we then appoint a special committee to visit the campus to make a personal inquiry into the case with a view to preparing a report for possible publication in the *AAUP Bulletin.* The committee usually consists of two or three Association members, selected primarily because of their good judgment and experience in academic freedom and tenure. Each member of the committee is provided a file containing the significant documents and correspondence relating to the case; and a member of the Association's staff prepares for the special committee a brief which outlines the basic facts of the case, points out the central issues to be investigated, suggests certain procedures to be followed, and provides the committee with names of the persons to be interviewed. The committee calls first at the office of the president, and then proceeds to interview administrative officers, the professor who has complained, and faculty members suggested by the president, the complaining faculty member, and the Association's staff. A visit by an investigating committee normally lasts two or three days.

The investigating committee, which is instructed to reach its own conclusions on the basis of the facts of the case, the 1940 *Statement,* and the institution's regulations, then prepares a report for submission to the Association's Committee A on Academic Freedom and Tenure. The finished report is first reviewed by one or more members of the Association's staff, who may make suggestions for revision before the report goes to Committee A. When the investigating committee has agreed to any changes, the report is sent to each member of Committee A with a reply form on which he may make comments upon the report and indicate approval or disapproval of publication in the *AAUP Bulletin.* On the basis of the comments received from the members of Committee A, the Association's staff then further revises the report in consultation with the investigating committee.

After this revision has been agreed upon, the report is sent to the president of the college or university concerned, to the complaining faculty member, to the president of the Association's chapter at that institution, and to other persons who may have figured prominently in the report. (The report is stamped "Confidential and Not for Publication," and those receiving the report are specifically requested to observe the confidentiality.) Each of these persons is invited to call attention to any errors in the report of which he may be aware and to provide his general comments upon the report. These comments usually lead to further revision of the report before its publication.

If the report is published in the *AAUP Bulletin,* Committee A on Academic Freedom and Tenure, at its April meeting, will then consider whether the report documents a sufficiently serious violation of academic freedom and tenure to recommend a vote of censure by the Association's Annual Meeting. Such votes of censure are visited only upon the administration of the institution and remain in effect until Committee A is satisfied that the conditions which led to the recommendation of censure have been corrected and a subsequent Annual Meeting has accepted Committee A's recommendation for removal. The list of "Censured Administrations" is published in each quarterly issue of the *AAUP Bulletin.* I should add, however, that all reports do not lead to an action of censure by the Annual Meeting. The violation of principles recorded in the published report may not be sufficiently serious to justify a vote of censure, or the conditions which led to the investigation may have been corrected between the time of publication and the Annual Meeting. An investigating committee may conclude that no violation of academic freedom and tenure principles has occurred.

This process, particularly if it culminates in publication of a report, is a lengthy one. The minimum time lapse between the receipt of a complaint and the publication of a report has been about one year. If the Association's purpose were merely to publicize an institutional or administrative action it thought improper, it could doubtless shorten this time; its purpose, however, has been to apprise the academic profession of a problem of general professional interest and of conditions of academic freedom and tenure on a particular campus which do not meet those standards set by this Association and others in the 1940 *Statement of Principles.* It attempts to do this with such precision and accuracy that the validity of the investigating committee's conclusions will be readily apparent to the academic profession. Many of the cases with which the Association has dealt have been of great complexity, involving problems requiring careful examination and interpretation. The Association, through Committee A, the staff, and the investigating committee, makes every attempt to verify and document the facts which provide the basis of the report and to interpret them fairly in the light of the 1940 *Statement of Principles* and the institution's regulations.

To assure the accuracy and integrity of its reports, the Association thus employs a number of safeguards. The investigating committee is provided with all the essential documentation that is available. It has before it the regulations of the institution at which its investigation is being conducted. It is assisted in reaching its conclusions by the 1940 *Statement of Principles,* which is a standard prepared for the profession by our own Association and the Association of American Colleges and endorsed by 67 additional educational or professional associations. Reports are reviewed before publication by staff members, including the staff counsel, and by Committee A on Academic Freedom and Tenure; and they are submitted to interested and informed persons who are invited to call attention to factual errors or to interpretations or conclusions which they think unfounded.

LETTER NO. 19. REVIEW BY THE WASHINGTON OFFICE OF THE RECORD OF DISMISSAL HEARINGS

[*AAUP Bulletin,* 52:451 (Winter, 1966)]

Thank you for your letter of . . . and your helpful account of the proceedings at Professor———'s dismissal hearing.

Please be assured that my request for a statement of the charges which were upheld as cause for the dismissal and a copy of the record was not intended as a criticism or judgment of the hearing. In fact, the report from our observer substantiates much of what you said in your letter.

Our interests are reflected in our commitments as a professional association to the establishment and maintenance of effective national standards. From our very beginning more than half a century ago, a primary concern of AAUP has been the protection of academic freedom in all institutions of higher education so that they can make the contribution to society which is expected of them. We believe that academic freedom requires a strong tenure system, and, consequently, that the dismissal of a tenured faculty member is a very grave action. This is not a self-serving attitude held by professors alone, but is a view espoused by at least those more-than-40 scholarly and professional organizations which have endorsed the 1940 *Statement of Principles on Academic Freedom and Tenure,* and by college administrators as represented by the Association of American Colleges, which, with this Association, jointly composed that Statement as a standard for American higher education.

In recognition of the gravity of such a dismissal hearing, certain practices have come to be widely accepted:

(1) Academic due process must be observed. This would include a written statement of specific charges, the right to counsel, a hearing by one's peers (if possible), the right to appeal, and the right to receive a copy of the record of the hearing on which such an appeal might be based.

(2) Only the most serious charges, if sustained, can be considered adequate cause for dismissal of a tenured faculty member. The granting of tenure assumes that a probationary period has been served, that an evaluation of the candidate has been made by his colleagues and by his administration, and that one who has met the standards of his judges during this period will no longer be subject to dismissal on relatively minor charges. If this were not so, then tenure would be meaningless and every faculty member would retain his position at the whim of his administration. Under those conditions he could not be expected to make the kind of contribution that justifies the existence and support of colleges and universities.

(3) Except in very unusual circumstances, a tenured faculty member who is dismissed is entitled to receive his salary for at least a year from the date of notification of dismissal. This is partly in recognition of services of the quality which earned him tenure in the first place, partly in compensation for the revocation of what is tantamount to a lifetime appointment, and partly to enable him—under a terrible onus—to try to find an appropriate appointment elsewhere, often at a time of the academic year when this is most

difficult to do, but especially so when he has not anticipated the necessity.

These are standards that this Association has supported and attempted to enforce for many years, and the success that we have had has been based in part on the necessary rejection of some local institutional or regional standards which fall short. I am sure you can see that this must be done, or no progress could be made toward the establishment of national minimums.

To return to my request, it was based not on any prejudgment of the propriety of the hearing procedures or the adequacy of the charges, but as part of the normal routine of this Association in every dismissal hearing involving academic freedom or a tenured faculty member. We must have the requested material in order to evaluate it; and we must evaluate it in order to protect sound professional standards.

I recognize that your Board may not be familiar with this procedure, but I hope they will agree to its value and necessity and will approve the granting of our request. If any further clarification would help, please feel free to write me.

LETTER NO. 20. ORAL AGREEMENTS AT THE TIME OF APPOINTMENT

[*AAUP Bulletin,* 53:349 (Autumn, 1967)]

Alleged oral agreements offer one of the most difficult problems the Association has to face in attempting to assist faculties and administrations in the solution of differences. After a time, there are often different recollections or interpretations of what was agreed upon. Both parties often have reason to believe that they are acting in good faith in defending their recollections of the agreement. The Association urges appointing officers to follow up oral understandings with a letter of confirmation which sets forth every particular of the agreement. If this is not done promptly, the faculty member should feel free to send a letter to the appointing officer which contains his understanding of the particulars, with a request for correction of erroneous impressions or inclusions of omitted portions of the agreement.

All of us recognize that in a teachers' market there must be prompt action to obtain a valuable scholar, and at times the oral approach must be used. However, if time permits, the initial offer should be put in writing, with full particulars, and the candidate should be asked to accept or reject in writing. Included with a letter of appointment should be copies of the institution's faculty handbook and all regulations which affect faculty performance and rights.

If a difference arises over an oral agreement, and there was no third-party witness or written confirmation of terms, a faculty committee (composed of individuals without a departmental or personal interest in the alleged agreement) might be asked to hear both parties and make a recommendation. Some institutions have standing Grievance Committees established to consider such matters.

LETTER NO. 22. APPOINTMENT PROCEDURES

[*AAUP Bulletin,* 53:437–38 (Winter, 1967)]

This is in reply to your request for information on the Association's position regarding appointment procedures. The recently formulated *Statement on Government of Colleges and Universities* defines, in general terms, the faculty's role in this area. I suspect that the reason the Association has not recommended a specific set of procedures in appointment matters is that different approaches have individual merits, and the faculty and administration of a given institution or division of it should determine the procedure which best fits its needs.

Perhaps a few general observations from my own experience in the Washington Office will be useful to you. Quite large universities leave appointment matters in the hands of individual departments and their deans; seldom does a president or a board reject a firm departmental recommendation which has the approval of both the dean and the group of tenured professors in the discipline. At small colleges and universities, the president plays a more prominent role in faculty appointments, but at all of the better administered institutions, the participation of the teaching faculty is encouraged and welcomed.

If an offer depends upon certain conditions (such as presidential or board approval) they should be stated in the letter of appointment. Ideally, the large department should be given authority, after consultation with and approval of the dean, to make firm, binding offers. Where several disciplines are components of a single department, a representative committee usually handles the screening of candidates and makes recommendations to the department head and the dean at large institutions, and to the dean and president at the smaller ones. The letter of appointment sometimes goes out over the signature of the department head, sometimes over that of the dean or president.

This brings me to one of the most sensitive aspects in the appointment procedure: the limits of the authority of the department head and the divisional dean in determining whether a given letter of appointment should go out following receipt of the departmental recommendation. Under optimum circumstances, the appointing officer's degree of authority depends upon practices which the faculty has permitted to exist, which in turn depend upon the confidence which the faculty has placed in its appointing officers. But, as we well know, optimum circumstances come and go, even in our best administered large institutions. In this as in most academic matters, the faculty can resort to the old gambit: to have departmental or divisional faculty committees study recent appointment practices and use their influence to have procedures adopted which the given faculty considers proper.

After appropriate screening of candidates has taken place—in all instances with meaningful participation by the tenured faculty—personal interviews with likely candidates are extremely important. It would be advisable to have full-time departmental faculty members at all ranks participate, in some degree, in the interviewing process.

When a consensus is reached to make an offer to an individual, the crucial consideration is that the candidate be given an unequivocal letter of appointment, complete in all the respects which are listed below. If the following matters have not been stated and agreed upon in the preliminary correspondence prior to the issuance of an offer, each should be clearly stated in the letter of appointment or the contract: (1) a commitment as to whether the offer at hand is official or tentative; (2) if tentative, the nature of further consideration is explained, as well as the approximate date when a binding offer can be expected; (3) the initial rank; (4) the length of the appointment; (5) the amount of credit toward the probationary period for prior service, and the total length of the probationary period (credit for prior service plus the probationary period at the appointing institution); (6) the amount of the annual salary and collateral benefits; (7) the length of annual service expected for the stated salary and benefits (e.g., 2 semesters, 3 quarters, 2 trimesters, etc.); (8) the prospect, or lack of it, for teaching in the summer session, and the approximate salary terms for summer teaching; (9) the teaching load in credit or contact hours, and some indication of the courses to be taught; (10) the date when the appointee is expected to report and the approximate date of his final annual duties under the appointment; and (11) detailed references to the provisions in the institution's by-laws and regulations which have a bearing upon the appointment.

Specific information on the numbered items set forth above is of value both to the faculty candidate and to the appointing institution. Many later misunderstandings can be avoided by inclusion of all terms of the appointments. Regardless of who signs the letter of appointment, information on these terms should be given to the appointee.

Some institutional charters or statutes of the state require that governing boards approve all appointments. Trustees would be well advised to delegate full authority to the administration and faculty in selecting faculty members. In some rare instances where the trustees believe that they have sound professional reasons for questioning a faculty and administrative recommendation, there should be ample opportunity for consultation between the trustees and the faculty and administration. A clear understanding should be reached among all components of the institution that appointments will not be questioned for reasons related to political beliefs or associations, race, religious affiliation or lack of it, and national origin of the candidate.

Index

This Index is an aid for readers who have a practical need to work with Association policy statements and with related literature in the areas of academic freedom, tenure, and academic due process. The scope and depth of the reference system, however, is modest and offers only introductory guidance. Those seeking mastery of all the ramifications and linkings of the subjects here covered will remember that in a *Handbook* the text itself is the index.

AAC. *See* Association of American Colleges

AAUP. *See* American Association of University Professors

Academic authority: basis of, 158–61

Academic calling: nature of, 161

Academic due process: defined, 6, 264; minimal safeguards listed, 6; for students, 71–74; rationale of, 269–71; future of, 303–5; mentioned, 44, 53–54. *See also* 1915 *Declaration of Principles;* Joughin, Louis; 1958 *Statement on Procedural Standards in Faculty Dismissal Proceedings*

Academic Due Process (ACLU publication): analyzed, 264–305

Academic Due Process (Joughin), 264–305

Academic freedom: violations of, related to denial of proper faculty role, 7, 343–44; defined, analyzed, 34–36, 158, 178, 231–33, 242; in probationary appointment, 38, 75; justification of, 47–49; Princeton University Chapter statement on, 49; and freedom of expression, 64–65, 132–34, 179–80, 193–94; of students, 66–74 *passim;* of probationary appointees, 75; obligation to promote understanding of, 89; defense of, by governing board, 97; range of threats to, 184–86; scope of, in U.S., 243–46; European backgrounds of, 246–50; formulation of, in U.S., 250–56; and the courts, 256–62; relation to academic responsibility, 342; and *Constitution* of AAUP, 342; faculty members to evaluate, 346; condition of accreditation, 347. *See also* 1956 *Academic Freedom and Tenure . . .* ; Capen, Samuel P.; Carlson, A. J.; Carmichael, Oliver C.; Citizens' rights; 1925 *Conference Statement . . .* ; 1915 *Declaration of Principles;* Dewey, John; Eliot, Charles William; Fuchs, Ralph F.; Jones, Howard Mumford; *Lehrfreiheit; Lernfreiheit;* Lovejoy, A. O.; Machlup, Fritz; MacIver, Robert M.; National Science Foundation; 1940 *Statement of Principles on Academic Freedom . . .* ; Tenure; Wriston, Henry; Wyzanski, Charles E., Jr.

Academic Freedom . . . , Statement of Principles on. See 1940

Statement of Principles on Academic Freedom and Tenure
Academic Freedom and Civil Liberties of Students, 91*n*
1956 *Academic Freedom and Tenure in the Quest for National Security:* text, 47–56; origin of, 47; 1958 *Supplement,* 47, 56–63; quoted, 293
Academic institution: need for joint effort in government of, 92–95; external relations of, 95; basis of authority in U.S., 158–61; function of, 163–74; differences between U.S. and European, 224–28. *See also* Faculty; Governing board; President
Academic proceedings. *See* Academic due process
Academic responsibility: violations of, 133; relation to academic freedom, 186–89; and tenure, 215. *See also* 1966 *Statement on Professional Ethics*
Accreditation: faculty role in, 345–46; recommended standards, 346–47
Accrediting of Colleges and Universities, 1968 *Statement on the Role of the Faculty in the,* 345–47
ACLU. *See* American Civil Liberties Union
Ad hoc investigating committee: guided by 1940 *Statement of Principles,* 5; decision to appoint, 15; selection of members, 16; list of interviewees furnished to, 16; briefing of, 16–18; available off campus, 17; avoids publicity and social relations, 17; expenses met by AAUP, 17; function of, 17; interview procedures, 18
—reports: number published, 4; implementation of AAUP policy, not statement thereof, 5; resulting in censure, list of, 143–47; not resulting in censure, list of, 148–49; Advisory Letter on safeguarding accuracy and integrity of, 354–57. *See also* Report by *ad hoc* committee
Adler v. *Board of Education* case, 259
Administrative personnel: AAUP does not normally handle complaints relating to, 7; academic freedom of, 75; selection of, 94–95
Adviser. *See* Counsel
Advisory Letters, 121–41, 354–62
Alabama State College-Reddick case, 301
Allen University cases, 277
American Association of University Professors (AAUP): founded in 1915, 3; sponsorship of joint statements, 3; stated purpose, 3, 9, 341; development of, 253–54
American Civil Liberties Union (ACLU), 91*n,* 264–305 *passim*
American Council on Education: joint statements with AAUP, 3, 90–91; mentioned, 4, 82
Annual Meeting of AAUP: guided by 1940 *Statement of Principles,* 5; sole authority to impose or withdraw censure, 22; resolutions of, 105–19; scope of, defined, 341
Appellate procedures, 298–300
Appointment: offer of, at censured institution, 24; irregular or special, 36*n7;* need for written agreement, 37; conditions for probationary period, 37, 308–9; academic due process required in cases of termination before expiration, 38; academic freedom during probationary period, 38, 75; duty to honor, 81; latest acceptable date for offer of, 81; Advisory Letter on ques-

tions put to a candidate for, 129–31; Advisory Letter on procedures and standards for, 360–62. *See also* Dismissal proceedings; Non-reappointment; Tenure

Arkansas State Teachers College-Higgins case, 284–85, 292

Association of American Colleges (AAC): joint statements with AAUP, 3; mentioned, 4, 253, 254, 265, 267

Association of Governing Boards of Universities and Colleges: joint formulation of 1966 *Statement on Government . . .*, 90–91

Barenblatt v. *United States* case, 261*n65*

Benedict College cases, 301

Boycott: not established by censure of an institution, 24

Budgeting: area of joint effort, 94

Burden of proof: in Fifth Amendment cases, 54; before hearing committee, 293–95; in case of non-tenure complainant, 294–95

Byse, Clark, and Louis Joughin, on tenure: plans for, 212–13, 220–21; and legislation, 213–15; obligations of tenured faculty members, 215–16; in institutions conducted by religious groups, 216; should not be a condition of rank, 217; after probationary period, 217–18; standards for acquisition of tenure desirable, 218; faculty role in matters of, 218; grounds for dismissal, 219–23

Candor. *See* Disclosure

Capen, Samuel P., Chancellor of University of Buffalo: on academic freedom, 183–84

Carlson, A. J.: on prescribed oaths, 206

Carmichael, Oliver C., President, Carnegie Foundation for the Advancement of Teaching: on folly of stifling academic freedom, 117

Carr, Robert K., President of Oberlin College: on academic due process, 270

Case reports. *See Ad hoc* investigating committee reports; Report by *ad hoc* committee

Cases (in alphabetical order): *Adler* v. *Board of Education,* 259; *Alabama State College-Reddick,* 301; *Allen University,* 277; *Arkansas State Teachers College-Higgins,* 284–85, 292; *Barenblatt* v. *United States,* 261*n65; Benedict College,* 301; *Catawba College,* 276, 281, 285, 288; *Dickinson College-La Vallee,* 57, 274, 296; *Dixon* v. *Alabama State Board of Education,* 91*n; Fisk University-Lorch,* 277, 284; *George Washington University-Reichard,* 273, 286, 292, 301; *Grove City College-Gara,* 290, 300; *Kansas State Agricultural College,* 234; *Konigsberg* v. *State Bar of California,* 57*n; Long Island University, Post College-Sittler,* 298; *Lowell Institute of Technology,* 287, 289, 293–94, 296–97, 302; *New York University-Bradley,* 58, 285; *New York University-Burgum,* 57–58, 274, 282, 293; *North Dakota Agricultural College,* 281, 290–91, 296; *Princeton Theological Seminary-Theron,* 277; *Reed College-Moore,* 57, 289, 291; *Rutgers University,* 284; *Sam Houston State Teachers College-Koeninger,* 294, 301–2; *Slochower* v. *Board of Higher Education,* 57*n; South Dakota State College-Worzella,* 288, 296, 306, 306*n2; Sweezy* v.

New Hampshire, 57*n,* 260; *University of Illinois-Koch,* 274, 300; *University of Kansas City-Horace B. Davis,* 57, 281; *University of Michigan,* 58, 285, 296, 298, 299–300; *University of Michigan-H. Chandler Davis,* 57, 285; *University of Michigan-Nickerson,* 58, 295; *University of Nevada-Richardson,* 273, 284, 293; *University of Southern California-Deinum,* 58, 284; *University of Vermont-Novikoff,* 57, 58, 279, 296, 301; *Watkins* v. *United States,* 57*n*

Case status: basis of, 11, 14–15; yearly number of complaints reaching, 11

Catawba College cases, 276, 281, 285, 288

Censorship: of student publications, 70–71; of textbooks, resolution on, 105. *See also* Academic freedom, Citizens' rights

Censure: imposition of, 4; number of censured administrations, 4; withdrawal of, 4–5, 23; only on administration, 22, 24; guidance toward achieving withdrawal of, 24; consequences of, 24; list of censured administrations, 143–47

Chairmen of departments: selection of, 99

Challenges. *See* Hearing committee

Chapter of AAUP: communication with, regarding complaints, 13; as faculty representative, 353

—and case status situations: general position in, 24–28; guidance preceding, 25–26; disengagement during, 26–27; continuing responsibility during, 28; position during institutional censure status, 28

Charges: to be in writing, 38; importance of, 283–86

Citizens' rights: general, 36, 39, 172; freedom of speech, 36, 65, 95, 134; freedom of association, 51–52; student freedom to learn, 66–67; student press, 70–71; and academic freedom, 175–78. *See also* 1964 *Committee A Statement on Extramural Utterances;* Extramural utterances

Civil penalties: relation to student status, 71–72

Collective bargaining. *See* Economic interests

Committee A on Academic Freedom and Tenure: guided by 1940 *Statement of Principles,* 5; determination of jurisdiction, 12; function in cases, 17, 26–27; recommendations to Annual Meeting, 22; Council endorsement of recommendations, 22; mentioned, 4

1964 *Committee A Statement on Extramural Utterances,* 64–65

Committee B on Professional Ethics: relation to Committee A work, 6–7

Committee T on College and University Government: relation to Committee A work, 7; standards for investigations by, 343–44

Communist party membership: relation to academic status, 52; candor regarding, 128–31; and academic freedom, 204–6, 251

Competence: testimony on, 38; right to witnesses on issue of, 38; an issue seldom raised, 290

Complainants: warning regarding risk, 13

Complaints: most do not receive public notice, 4; increasing frequency of formal mediation, 4; number received during first fifty years, 4; some not handled by AAUP, 7, 7*n5;* receipt of, by Gen-

eral Secretary, 11; annual number of, 11; formulation of, 11–12; possible mediation of, 11–14; risk involved in making, 13
Conant, James B., President of Harvard University: on academic freedom and tenure, 219
Conciliation, informal: a preliminary proceeding, 42, 272–74
Conclusions (in a hearing), 295–97
Conference (state or regional) of AAUP: action in censure situations, 29
1925 *Conference Statement on Academic Freedom and Tenure:* origin of, 4, 33, 266–67; and academic due process, 264–305 *passim;* mentioned, 39, 157
Conflicts of Interest . . . , 1964 *Statement on Preventing,* 82–86
Confrontation: right of, 44, 288–89, 292–93
Constitution of AAUP: relevant provisions, 341–42
Contract renewal. *See* Nonreappointment
Council of AAUP: may endorse Committee A recommendations, 22
Counsel: at formal proceedings, 38, 43–44, 278–79
Court proceedings: effect on AAUP action, 8
Cross-examination: right to, 44, 290–91, 292–93

1915 *Declaration of Principles:* text, 155–76; origin of, 4, 155–57; general declaration of principles, 157–75; basis of authority in academic institutions, 158–61; nature of the academic calling, 161–63; function of the academic institution, 163–74; practical proposals of, 174–76; and academic due process, 264–305 *passim;* mentioned, 33
Dewey, John, first president of AAUP: on academic freedom, 156; mentioned, 235
Dickinson College-La Vallee case, 57, 274, 296
Disclaimer oaths: AAUP opposes, 50–51, 113–18; inconsistent with academic freedom, 206–9, 256–57
Disclosure: faculty member's obligation of, 55; instances of, discussed, 57–58; a qualified obligation, 62; Advisory Letter on, 129–31
Dismissal proceedings: preliminary steps, 42, 53; 274–79; formal stages, 42–43; basis for, 88; Advisory Letter on record of, 357–59. *See also* Academic due process; Faculty; Hearing committee
Dismissal Proceedings, Statement on . . . . See 1958 *Statement on Procedural Standards in Faculty Dismissal Proceedings*
Dixon v. *Alabama State Board of Education,* 91*n*
Due process, 6. *See also* Academic due process

Economic interests: security of, and tenure, 35; faculty senate as representative of, 349; AAUP policy toward collective bargaining, 349–51; exclusive representation opposed, 350; role of chapter in representation of, 351–52. *See also* Faculty; Salary
Economic Interests, 1968 *Statement of Policy on Representation of,* 348–53
Eliot, Charles William, President of Harvard University: violation of academic freedom by governing boards, 160–61

Ethics: relation to academic freedom and tenure investigations, 6–7; and dismissal proceedings, 88
Ethics, 1966 *Statement on Professional,* 87–89
Evidence: in academic proceedings, 287–88
Extramural utterances: disclaimer as institutional spokesman where necessary, 64, 70; Advisory Letter on, 132–34. *See also* Citizens' rights
Extramural Utterances, 1964 *Committee A Statement on,* 64–65

Faculty: status related to lack of academic freedom, 7; definition of, 40–41; status a faculty concern and responsibility, 40–41, 95, 99; effect of mobility of, 79–80, 211–12; must participate in dismissal proceedings, 188–89, 222–23, 255–56; role in granting of tenure, 218; role in accrediting of a college or university, 345–47; role of faculty senate in representation of economic interests of, 348–49. *See also* Appointment; Hearing committee; 1968 *Standards for Committee T Investigations*
Faculty participation in institutional government: relation to academic freedom and tenure, 7, 343
Fifth Amendment: a constitutional privilege, 52; public silence and private disclosure, 61–62. *See also* Citizens' rights; Disclaimer oaths
Financial exigency. *See* Termination
Fisk University-Lorch case, 277, 284
Foreign scholars: resolution on oppression of, 106–7
Freedom of association. *See* Citizens' rights
Freedom of press: and student publications, 70–71. *See also* Citizens' rights
Freedom of speech. *See* Academic freedom; Citizens' rights
Fuchs, Ralph F.: on violation of academic responsibility, 133
—on academic freedom: defined, 242; scope, 243–46; development of, 246–52; formulation of and support for the principles of, in U.S., 250–56; legal impairment and protection of, 256–62; and loyalty oaths, 257
Fulbright scholars: resolution on selection standards, 107

Gabriel, Ralph H., 237
Gellhorn, Walter: on academic due process, 271
George Washington University-Reichard case, 273, 286, 292, 301
Governing board: appellate procedures before, 45; role in institutional government, 96–97; comment on violation of academic freedom by, 160–61; limits of authority, 173; and academic freedom, 182–84; historical development of, in U.S., 239–40
Government of Colleges and Universities, 1966 *Statement on,* 90–101; origin of, 90; undeveloped areas noted, 91
Grove City College-Gara case, 290, 300

Hearing committee: proceedings of, 38, 43–44, 277–303 *passim;* constitution and creation of, 43, 280–83; findings and conclusions of, 44, 295–97; constitution of, in cases of student discipline, 93–94; challenges to members of, 124–25, 282–83; presence of teacher

at, axiomatic, 286; can act on own authority, 291–92
—, record of: necessity for, 38, 297; cost of, 297; Advisory Letter on AAUP review of, 357–59. *See also* Academic due process

Incompetence. *See* Competence
In loco parentis: a force in U.S. higher education, 226
Insurance Programs, 1958 *Statement of Principles on . . . ,* 76–78
"Interpretations": added to 1940 *Statement of Principles,* 38–39
Interviews: by *ad hoc* investigating committee, 18
Investigations, special and emergency, 16. *See also* Cases

Jefferson, Thomas: 1801 Inaugural Address quoted, 197
1967 *Joint Statement on Rights and Freedoms of Students:* text, 66–74; origin of, 66
Jones, Howard Mumford, on academic freedom: breadth of responsibility of U.S. institutions, 225; in U.S. mainly enjoyed in higher education, 229; tenure defined, 231; academic freedom defined, 231–33; U.S. higher education embodies an aristocracy of intelligence, 234–37; U.S. colleges and universities mainly government-created, 239–40
Joughin, Louis, on academic due process: defined, 264; rationale, 269; informal conciliation, 272–74; preliminary proceedings, 274; the psychological bridge to adversary status, 277–78; legal counsel, 278–79; constitution and creation of hearing committee, 280; the charges, 283–87; the evidence, 287–88; burden of proof, 293–95; findings and conclusions, 295–97; the record, 297; time to prepare, 297; waiver of rights, 297; appellate procedure, 298–300; overall denial of, 300; future of, 303–5. *See also* Byse and Joughin

Kansas State Agricultural College case, 234
Kirkland, E. C., former president of AAUP: on academic due process, 269
Konigsberg v. *State Bar of California* case, 57*n*

Late notice. *See* Notice
Late resignation. *See* Resignation
Law: relation of, to academic proceedings, 8; and academic freedom, 256–62
Leave of absence: and tenure, 127–28
Legal proceedings. *See* Litigation
Legislation, economic: AAUP policy on, 349–51. *See also* Economic interests
Legislative committee investigations: resolution on, 108
Lehrfreiheit, 157, 225, 228, 229–31, 244*n6,* 263*n*
Lernfreiheit, 157, 225–29, 244*n6*
Letters of advice from Washington Office of AAUP: serve as a gloss on policy, 121
Lincoln, Abraham: 1861 Inaugural Address quoted, 198
Litigation: effect on AAUP action, 8
Long Island University, Post College-Sittler case, 298
Lovejoy, A. O.: on prescribed oaths, 206
Lowell Institute of Technology cases, 287, 289, 293–94, 296–97, 302
Loyalty: to institution, Advisory Letter on, 128–29. *See also* Disclaimer oaths

Loyalty oaths. *See* Disclaimer oaths

McGuire, John M.: on academic due process, 270

Machlup, Fritz, on academic freedom: defined, 178; not merely freedom of speech, 179–80; relation to special group interests, 181–82; who threatens, who protects?, 182–84; range of threats to, 184–86; relation to academic responsibility, 186–89; for dissenters, 189–91; for those who abuse it, 191–92; and extramural utterances, 193–94; extends beyond the scholar's specific competence, 193–96; freedom to teach subversive ideas, 196–99; not only for loyal citizens, 199–202; independence of thought not testable within concept of, 202–3; for enemies of freedom, 203–6; and prescribed oaths, 206–9

—, on academic tenure: disadvantages of, 307–8, 312–26; "strict" tenure rules described, 308–9; defined, 310–12; types of, 310–12; disadvantages to institutions, 312–20; disadvantages to individual scholars, 320–22; disadvantages to the profession, 322–26; benefits to society in general, 326–28; benefits in terms of academic freedom, 328–32; proportion of faculty with, 332–35

MacIver, Robert M.: on need for public appreciation of universities, 241

Mediation: basis for, 13; manner of, 13–14

Merger, institutional: relation to tenure, 118

Military security. *See* Security, military

Moral turpitude, 37*n8,* 38

National Defense Education Act: objections to disclaimer affidavit, 117–18

National Science Foundation: investigation of grantees objected to, 114–15

New York University-Bradley case, 58, 285

New York University-Burgum case, 57–58, 274, 282, 293

Nonreappointment: limitation on AAUP involvement, 7, 7*n;* standards for notice of, 46; Advisory Letter on stating reasons for, 136–37. *See also* Appointment; Dismissal proceedings; Notice

Nonreappointment, 1964 *Statement on the Standards for Notice of,* 46

Nonrenewal of contract. *See* Nonreappointment

North Dakota Agricultural College cases, 281, 290–91, 296

Notice: procedural safeguards, 75; Advisory letter on institution's obligation to provide year's notice, 121–23; list of late notice case reports, 150

Oaths, teachers'. *See* Disclaimer oaths

Observers at hearings: attendance should be permitted, 54

Oral arguments: teacher's right to make, at hearing, 44

Passports for scholars: resolution on, 109

Paulsen, Friedrich: description of academic freedom, 249–50

Physical resources: area for joint effort, 94

Plagiarism: Advisory Letter on, 138–39

Post, Charles Gordon: observation on tenure, 316
Preliminary inquiry. *See* Dismissal proceedings
Prescribed oaths. *See* Dismissal oaths
President of an institution: his selection an area of joint effort, 94; role in institutional government, 97–98
Princeton Theological Seminary-Theron case, 277
Princeton University Chapter of AAUP: statement on academic freedom, 49
Probationary appointees: academic freedom of, 75
Probationary appointment. *See* Appointment
Probationary period: defined, 37; academic freedom during, 38
Procedural Standards . . . , Statement on. See 1958 *Statement on Procedural Standards in Faculty Dismissal Proceedings*
Procedures: minimal safeguards, 6; variety of, 286; deficiencies noted, 286–87. *See also* Academic due process
Professional Ethics, 1966 *Statement on,* 87–89
Professional responsibility, 155–76. *See also* 1966 *Statement on Professional Ethics*
Promotion: an area of faculty judgment, 7; limitations on AAUP involvement, 7
Publicity: mediation precludes, 14; avoidance of, 17, 19, 45; publication of Annual Meeting action, 23
Published reports. *See Ad hoc* investigating committee reports

Race: an improper admission standard, 67; resolutions concerning, 109–12
1957 *Recommended Institutional Regulations on Academic Freedom and Tenure:* positions not covered elsewhere, 75
Record of the hearing. *See* Hearing committee, record of
Recruitment . . . , 1961 *Statement on,* 79–81; mentioned, 5
Redress: and withdrawal of censure, 23
Reed College-Moore case, 57, 289, 291
Regents. *See* Governing board
Religious institutions: aims need written definition, 36; and student admissions, 67; Advisory Letter on limitations imposed by, 139–41
Report by *ad hoc* committee: action thereon, 19–22; Committee A votes on publication of, 20–21; confidentiality of, before publication, 21; publication in *Bulletin,* 21; submission to the parties, 21; lists of published reports, 143–52. *See also Ad hoc* investigating committee
Research: payment for, 35; standards of conduct where Government is sponsor, 82–86
Resignation: responsibility of teacher, 79*n;* latest date acceptable, 80–81; Advisory Letter on late resignations, 134–36
Resignation . . . , 1961 *Statement on . . . ,* 79–81; mentioned, 5
Resolutions of the Annual Meetings of AAUP, 105–19
Retirement: age of, 76; safeguards against involuntary, 76–77; system of annuities, 77
Retirement . . . , 1958 *Statement of Principles on Academic,* 76–78; mentioned, 5

Rutgers University cases, 284

Salary: limitations on AAUP involvement, 7; area of faculty participation, 7, 99; in cases of terminal appointment, 38. *See also* Economic interests
Sam Houston State Teachers College-Koeninger case, 294, 301–2
Security, military: and academic freedom, 49. *See also* Disclaimer oaths
Security, national. *See* 1956 *Academic Freedom and Tenure in the Quest for National Security*
Self-evaluation: faculty role in accreditation, 345–46; faculty access to draft of report, 346
Slochower v. *Board of Higher Education* case, 57*n*
Soper, Morris A.: view of academic freedom disputed by Machlup, 190
South Dakota State College-Worzella case, 288, 296, 306, 306*n2*
Speakers on campuses: invitation of, by students, 69; resolution on, 112–13
Speech, freedom of. *See* Academic freedom; Citizens' rights
1968 *Standards for Committee T Investigations in the Area of College and University Government:* text, 343–44; area of concern, 343; local remedies, 343; decision to investigate, 343; report, 344
1968 *Statement of Policy on Representation of Economic Interests:* text, 348–53; origin of, 348
1940 *Statement of Principles on Academic Freedom and Tenure:* text, 33–39; origin of, 4, 33–34; guides *ad hoc* investigating committees, 5; guides Annual Meeting, 5; guides Committee A, 5; related statements listed, 5; purpose, 34; endorsers of, 34–35; interpretations, 38–39; not retroactive, 39, 39*n;* and academic due process, 264–305 *passim;* mentioned, 9, 44, 51, 53, 64, 347
1958 *Statement of Principles on Academic Retirement and Insurance Programs,* 76–78
Statement on Extramural Utterances, 1964 *Committee A,* 64–65
1966 *Statement on Government of Colleges and Universities:* text, 90–101; origin of, 90; undeveloped areas, 91
1964 *Statement on Preventing Conflicts of Interest in Government-Sponsored Research at Universities:* text, 82–86; conflict situations, 82–84; university responsibility, 84–86
1958 *Statement on Procedural Standards in Faculty Dismissal Proceedings:* text, 40–45; origin of, 40; guide, not a norm, 40, 41; and academic due process, 264–305 *passim;* mentioned, 38*n*
1966 *Statement on Professional Ethics:* text, 87–89; origin of, 87; related statements, 87
1961 *Statement on Recruitment and Resignation of Faculty Members:* text, 79–81; origin of, 79; mentioned, 5
1968 *Statement on the Role of the Faculty in the Accrediting of Colleges and Universities:* text, 345–47; origin of, 345
1964 *Statement on the Standards for Notice of Nonreappointment:* text, 46; mentioned, 5
Students: freedom in learning, 34; academic freedom of, 66, 243–44; bases for admission of, 67; freedom of expression, 67; protection

against improper evaluation, 67; confidentiality of associations and beliefs, 68; freedom of association, 68; affiliation with outside organizations, 68; campus advisers for, 68; records of, confidential, 68; invitation of speakers, 69–70; participation in institutional government, 70, 91, 100–101; publications, 70–71; civil liberties of, 71; and civil penalties, 71; off-campus freedoms, 71–72; disciplinary proceedings, 71–74; standards of conduct, 72; search of premises occupied by, 73; hearing procedures, 73–74; professor's obligation to, 88

Students, 1967 *Joint Statement on Rights and Freedoms of,* 66–74

Subversion of educational process, 50

Subversive ideas: freedom to teach, 196–99. *See also* Communist party membership

Suspension: grounds for, 43; pay during, 43; limited justification for, 55–56, 274

Sweezy v. *New Hampshire* case, 57*n*, 260

Teacher: special position of, imposes obligations, 36

Tenure: minimal safeguards, 5–6; and national emergency, resolution on, 118–19; and change of status, Advisory Letter on, 125–27; and leave of absence, Advisory Letter on, 127–28; defined, described, 210–12, 231, 308–12; plans for, and the courts, 214; status legally enforceable and recognizable, 214–15; and academic responsibility, 215; in religious group management institutions, 216; not a condition of rank, 217; inadequate appeal procedures in denial of, 218; faculty participation in decisions, 218–20; grounds for termination, 220; disadvantages of, 312–26; benefits of, 326–35; and academic freedom, 328–32; proportion of faculty with, 332–35. *See also* Byse, Clark, and Louis Joughin; Conant, James B.; 1925 *Conference Statement* . . . ; 1915 *Declaration of Principles;* Jones, Howard Mumford; Machlup, Fritz; Post, Charles Gordon; 1957 *Recommended Institutional Regulations* . . . ; 1940 *Statement of Principles on Academic Freedom and Tenure*

Tenure, Statement of Principles on . . . . *See* 1940 *Statement of Principles on Academic Freedom and Tenure*

Termination: adequate cause for, 37, 37*n8*, 41; for financial reasons, 38, 75; salary in cases of, 38

Testimony: weight to be given to refusal to testify, 52–55, 60–62; specific cases, 57–58. *See also* Witnesses

Texas State Teachers Colleges. *See Sam Houston State Teachers College-Koeninger* case

Transcript: of dismissal hearing, 44; of student record, 68

Trustees. *See* Governing board

Unaccredited institutions: complaints at, limitation on action, 8*n*

United States National Student Association, 91*n*

University of Illinois-Koch case, 274, 300

University of Kansas City-Horace B. Davis case, 57, 281

University of Michigan cases, 58, 285, 296, 298, 299–300

University of Michigan-H. Chandler Davis case, 57, 285
University of Michigan-Nickerson case, 58, 295
University of Nevada-Richardson case, 273, 284, 293
University of Southern California-Deinum case, 58, 284
University of Vermont-Novikoff case, 57, 58, 279, 296, 301
Waiver: barrier to waiving rights, 298
Watkins v. *United States* case, 57*n*
Withdrawal of censure: grounds for, 4–5; number since beginning, 4
Witnesses: right to present, 289–90; subpoena power, 289. *See also* Testimony
Wriston, Henry, president of Brown University, 187
Written agreement, need for. *See* Appointment
Wyzanski, Charles E., Jr., 220